A CULTURAL HISTORY OF SEXUALITY

VOLUME 4

A Cultural History of Sexuality
General Editor: Julie Peakman

Volume 1
A Cultural History of Sexuality in the Classical World
Edited by Mark Golden and Peter Toohey

Volume 2
A Cultural History of Sexuality in the Middle Ages
Edited by Ruth Evans

Volume 3
A Cultural History of Sexuality in the Renaissance
Edited by Bette Talvacchia

Volume 4
A Cultural History of Sexuality in the Enlightenment
Edited by Julie Peakman

Volume 5
A Cultural History of Sexuality in the Age of Empire
Edited by Chiara Beccalossi and Ivan Crozier

Volume 6
A Cultural History of Sexuality in the Modern Age
Edited by Gert Hekma

A CULTURAL HISTORY OF SEXUALITY

IN THE ENLIGHTENMENT

Edited by Julie Peakman

Bloomsbury Academic
An imprint of Bloomsbury Publishing Plc

BLOOMSBURY
LONDON · OXFORD · NEW YORK · NEW DELHI · SYDNEY

Bloomsbury Academic
An imprint of Bloomsbury Publishing Plc

50 Bedford Square	1385 Broadway
London	New York
WC1B 3DP	NY 10018
UK	USA

www.bloomsbury.com

BLOOMSBURY and the Diana logo are trademarks of Bloomsbury Publishing Plc

Hardback edition first published in 2011 by Berg Publishers, an imprint of Bloomsbury Academic

Paperback edition first published by Bloomsbury Academic 2014
Reprinted 2015

© Julie Peakman 2011, 2014

Julie Peakman has asserted her right under the Copyright, Designs and Patents Act, 1988, to be identified as Editor of this work.

All rights reserved. No part of this publication may be reproduced or transmitted in any form or by any means, electronic or mechanical, including photocopying, recording, or any information storage or retrieval system, without prior permission in writing from the publishers.

No responsibility for loss caused to any individual or organization acting on or refraining from action as a result of the material in this publication can be accepted by Bloomsbury or the author.

British Library Cataloguing-in-Publication Data
A catalogue record for this book is available from the British Library.

ISBN: HB: 978-1-84788-803-7
PB: 978-1-4725-5476-5
HB Set: 978-1-84520-702-1
PB Set: 978-1-4725-5480-2

Library of Congress Cataloging-in-Publication Data
A catalog record for this book is available from the Library of Congress.

Series: The Cultural Histories Series

Typeset by Apex CoVantage, LLC, Madison, WI, USA

CONTENTS

	SERIES PREFACE	vii
	SERIES ACKNOWLEDGMENTS	ix
	ACKNOWLEDGMENTS	xi
	LIST OF ILLUSTRATIONS	xiii
1	Introduction *Julie Peakman*	1
2	Heterosexuality: Europe and North America *Anna Clark*	33
3	Homosexuality *Rictor Norton*	57
4	Sexual Variations *Marianna Muravyeva*	85
5	Sex, Religion and the Law *Merril D. Smith*	107
6	Sex, Medicine and Disease *George Rousseau*	133
7	Sex, Popular Beliefs and Culture *Heike Bauer*	159

8	Prostitution *Randolph Trumbach*	183
9	Erotica: Representing Sex in the Eighteenth Century *Katherine Crawford*	203
	NOTES	223
	BIBLIOGRAPHY	267
	CONTRIBUTORS	295
	INDEX	299

PREFACE

A Cultural History of Sexuality is a six-volume series reviewing changes in sexual attitudes and behavior throughout history. Each volume follows the same basic structure and begins with an outline account of sexuality in the period under consideration. Academic experts examine major aspects of sex and sexuality under seven key headings: heterosexuality, homosexuality, sexual variations, religion and the law, medicine and disease, popular beliefs and culture, prostitution, and erotica. Readers can choose a synchronic or a diachronic approach to the material—a single volume can be read to obtain a thorough knowledge of the body in a given period, or one of the seven themes can be followed through time by reading the relevant chapters of all six volumes, providing a thematic understanding of changes and developments over the long term. The six volumes divide the history of sexuality as follows:

Volume 1: A Cultural History of Sexuality in the Classical World (800 B.C.E. to 350 C.E.)

Volume 2: A Cultural History of Sexuality in the Middle Ages (350 C.E. to 1450)

Volume 3: A Cultural History of Sexuality in the Renaissance (1450 to 1650)

Volume 4: A Cultural History of Sexuality in the Enlightenment (1650 to 1820)

Volume 5: A Cultural History of Sexuality in the Age of Empire (1820 to 1920)

Volume 6: A Cultural History of Sexuality in the Modern Age (1920 to 2000)

Julie Peakman, General Editor

SERIES ACKNOWLEDGMENTS

This series has been a long time in the making, mainly because it is not an easy task to bring together fifty-four international scholars, even when we were all willing and eager. Every one of us had other commitments—to our universities, other books, and/or to our families. I therefore appreciate those who came together to create this special project. I want to thank the editors of all the volumes; Peter Toohey and Mark Golden, Ruth Evans, Bette Talvacchia, Ivan Crozier and Chiara Beccalossi, and Gert Hekma for their sterling efforts in the face of my continual demands, and for helping to keep their contributors on track, especially when the occasional one dropped out with little warning. Huge thanks also go to all the contributors who freely committed their time and efforts. I also want to thank Tristan Palmer at Berg for all his support and Catherine Draycott from the Wellcome Trust Picture Library for making available the Wellcome images.

Julie Peakman, General Editor

ACKNOWLEDGMENTS

I am grateful to all the contributors in this volume—Anna Clark, Rictor Norton, Marianna Muravyeva, Merril Smith, George Rousseau, Heike Bauer, Randy Trumbach, and Katherine Crawford—who have made it sparkle. I appreciated continued support from colleagues at Birkbeck College, University of London, Catherine Edwards, Joanna Bourke, and Sean Brady; I want to give extra special thanks to my friends Jess Mookerjee, Philippa O'Neill, Diana Peschier, and Philip Timmins for all their support through the difficult times when I was laid up with a broken leg. They visited constantly bearing gifts and entertained me when I could not move. I do not know what I would have done without them. Lastly and most importantly, I could never have survived the ordeal (the leg or the project) without the continued love and support of my ever-patient (well, mostly) partner, Jad Adams. Like some of the couples in this book, my kisses and desire still chase after him after 28 years together.

ILLUSTRATIONS

CHAPTER 1

Figure 1.1: While her chaperone sleeps, a young girl keeps watch on her as her lover, on bended knee, kisses her hand.	3
Figure 1.2: A merry crowd that includes a fiddler playing a tune celebrates a marriage as the groom kisses the bride.	5
Figure 1.3: A young woman of Otaheite, dancing.	7
Figure 1.4: A Nautch (dancing) girl.	8
Figure 1.5: "Son corps est couvert de pustules."	14
Figure 1.6: "Les Charmes de la Masturbation."	16
Figure 1.7: Two young girls with bound feet lie together on a mattress.	17
Figure 1.8: Illustration of a Dutch printing of the Marquis de Sade's *Juliette* (c. 1800).	19
Figure 1.9: Detail showing the microscope in use in Anthony Van Leeuwenhoek, *Arcana Naturae Detecta* (1695).	21
Figure 1.10: Spermatozoa of a rabbit from "Observationes de natis e semine genitali animalculis."	22

Figure 1.11: A young woman dressing her hair with feathers. 24

Figure 1.12: A Japanese couple making love. 31

CHAPTER 2

Figure 2.1: An outdoor marriage ceremony is performed by a priest; the young couple is surrounded by family. 34

Figure 2.2: *Le Baiser Pris de Force* (a stolen kiss). 35

Figure 2.3: The Roman Catholic sacraments: baptism. 36

Figure 2.4: European men examining slaves at the slave market of Rio de Janeiro. 37

Figure 2.5: John Wesley preaching to American Indians. 38

Figure 2.6: A Protestant couple stands before a clergyman in a pulpit as they take their marriage vows. 39

Figure 2.7: *The Dance of Death: The Courtship*. 40

Figure 2.8: The Foundling Hospital, Holborn, London. 44

Figure 2.9: A crowd gathers (with some onlookers throwing confetti) to cheer on a couple whose horse-drawn carriage waits to take them to the church for their wedding. 50

Figure 2.10: A young couple waits as a contract of marriage is drawn up. 54

CHAPTER 3

Figure 3.1: "The Women-Hater's Lamentation," a broadside ballad printed in 1707, following the arrest of about forty mollies. 63

Figure 3.2: "This is not the Thing, or Molly Exalted," a broadside ballad printed in 1762. 66

Figure 3.3: "Tydelyke Straffe, Voorgesteld ten Afschrik aller Goddeloze en Doemwaardige Zondaren" ("Temporal

Punishments Depicted as a Warning to Godless and Damnable Sinners"), a broadside.	68
Figure 3.4: From the Dutch edition of Sade's *La Nouvelle Justine, ou Les Malheurs de la Vertue* (1797).	75
Figure 3.5: Phoebe initiates Fanny Hill in the brothel.	76
Figure 3.6: Mary Hamilton is whipped for posing as a man and marrying a woman in 1746.	78
Figure 3.7: Sarah Ponsonby and Lady Eleanor Butler, known as the Ladies of Llangollen, seated in their library.	80
Figure 3.8: *Love-á-la-Mode, or Two Dear Friends*.	81

CHAPTER 4

Figure 4.1: A man copulating with a goat or deer.	90
Figure 4.2: A Persian woman copulating with an animal.	91
Figure 4.3: "Mlle Ch., agée de 16 ans" (young female, aged 16, after the effects of masturbation).	95
Figure 4.4: Portrait of Tissot.	97
Figure 4.5: Jean-Honoré Fragonard, *The Swing* (1767).	104

CHAPTER 5

Figure 5.1: A (woman) skeleton warns of the dangers of fornication.	113
Figure 5.2: A courtroom scene with a judge, a pregnant woman, a guilty-looking man, and an angry wife.	115
Figure 5.3: As a young man kisses a young lady's hand, a second woman shuts the door against another man attempting to enter the room.	116
Figure 5.4: A secret marriage behind curtains, which is being watched by some men and women from outside.	120

Figure 5.5: The drafting and signing of a marriage contract. 121

Figure 5.6: A marriage ceremony is conducted in a church. 122

Figure 5.7: Camp scene with American Indians. 124

Figure 5.8: Etching illustrating the uncleanliness of the mother after giving birth, according to Jewish law. 129

CHAPTER 6

Figure 6.1: Forepart of the human penis, prepared with mercury, by James Drake. 134

Figure 6.2: Diagram of female internal organs, including kidneys and vagina. 135

Figure 6.3: A hermaphrodite, front and back views, wearing a loose costume. 137

Figure 6.4: Folding plate of hermaphroditic genitalia. 138

Figure 6.5: Spermatozoon and homunculus. 140

Figure 6.6: Mesmer's Tub. 143

Figure 6.7: Title page from M.T.D. de Bienville, *Nymphomania, or A Dissertation Concerning the Furor Uterinus* (London, 1775). 144

Figure 6.8: Title page from François Mauriceau, *The Diseases of Women with Child* (1736). 148

Figure 6.9: Title page to the 1794 edition of Ebenezer Sibly, *The Medical Mirror.* 154

Figure 6.10: A panel of three images from Ebenezer Sibly, *The Medical Mirror.* 155

Figure 6.11: A panel of three images from Ebenezer Sibly, *The Medical Mirror.* 156

Figure 6.12: A panel of three images from Ebenezer Sibly, *The Medical Mirror.* 157

ILLUSTRATIONS xvii

CHAPTER 7

Figure 7.1: Types of "primitive" man, as imagined by seventeenth-century anthropologists. 160

Figure 7.2: Portrait of Lady Mary Wortley Montague. 166

Figure 7.3: Young Werther sits at his writing desk, as a young boy brings him his pistol (which he will use to kill himself), while a young woman tries to prevent the boy from delivering the weapon. 167

Figure 7.4: Southwark Fair, a renowned place of amusement. 171

Figure 7.5: Portrait of Mary Frith (Moll Cutpurse). 173

Figure 7.6: Hannah Snell, a woman who passed as a soldier. 174

Figure 7.7: Le Chevalier d'Éon, a man who passed as a woman. 176

Figure 7.8: A young woman from the island of Otaheite (Tahiti) wearing a large skirt. 178

CHAPTER 8

Figure 8.1: Upstairs at a brothel. 186

Figure 8.2: A man has sex with a boy prostitute, as a woman looks through a window. 186

Figure 8.3: A man has sex with an adult-male transvestite prostitute. 187

Figure 8.4: William Hogarth, *A Rake's Progress*. 195

Figure 8.5: A repentant young woman prays on her knees before a table, upon which is placed the *Book of Common Prayer*. 198

Figure 8.6: William Hogarth, *Harlot's Progress*. 200

Figure 8.7: William Hogarth, *Harlot's Progress*. 201

CHAPTER 9

Figure 9.1: Nicolas Venette, *De la Génération de l'Homme*. 206

Figure 9.2: Title page of *Onania* depicting the effects of masturbation on the health of the individual. 207

Figure 9.3: A physician examining a bare-breasted female patient. 209

Figure 9.4: An affluent man, staring intently out a window, receives electrotherapy from a French pseudo-doctor. 210

Figure 9.5: Frontispiece to the Marquis de Sade's *Justine*. 211

Figure 9.6: Women dancing to music in Cairo, Egypt. 218

CHAPTER ONE

Introduction

JULIE PEAKMAN

For many years, academia deemed the history of sexuality too vulgar or too frivolous a subject for academics to explore. Only recently has it come into the realms of serious study. One of the professed fathers of the investigation of the history of sexuality was French philosopher Michel Foucault, who has since been criticized for his theories and for omissions in his work—not least because of the lack of consideration of gender within his study of sexuality.[1] However, the seeds of the study of the history of sexuality were planted in Britain and the U.S. during the late 1960s and early 1970s and started with the examination of female sexuality. Feminists such as Juliet Mitchell and Sheila Rowbottom retrieved women "hidden in history," which resulted in the flourishing of "women's history" as a distinct individual discipline. Such early feminists were responsible for putting sexuality on the map, followed by gay rights activists in the United States and Britain. The early feminist framework transmuted into "gender history" during the 1990s in order to incorporate the investigation of male sexuality, by which time investigations had already begun into the origins of homosexuality, still a hotly contested issue. Lesbian history emerged slightly later, its exploration taking longer to get started. As yet, it is still not as well examined as male homosexuality in history, though it is quickly catching up.

The early study of the history of sexuality for a long time concentrated disproportionately on heterosexuality and on Western civilization, with a few notable exceptions.² Examination of the topic for the rest of the world has since begun to catch up with some detailed research on the Middle and Far East coming out in recent years.³ Even now, there are still huge gaps in our knowledge about eighteenth-century sexuality in places such as Africa and the Middle East although investigations are expanding. One of the problematic areas is the subjugation of both women and homosexual men (as well as other so-called marginals, such as transvestites, transsexuals, and bisexuals) throughout history, as well as the entrenched position of a "normative" sexual standard by which we are all assumed to operate. Gay and lesbian historians explored increasingly diverse aspects of men's and women's sexuality, concluding that there were many male "sexualities," or masculinities, and many female "sexualities," or femininities—and that one person could carry different aspects of both groups. Queer and psychoanalytical studies further diffused and complicated the debates, adding different dimensions to the overall picture. Increasingly, studies are exploring exactly how diverse a subject sex and sexuality was—and is—and historians are suggesting new ways to incorporate new frameworks for its examination that allow for inclusion of all types of sexuality.

HETEROSEXUALITY

Single men and women in courtships, wives and husbands in marriages, unfaithful spouses in adulterous affairs, widows and widowers bereft of loved ones—overridingly, heterosexuality has been seen as the norm in sexual behavior. The word *heterosexuality* did not exist before the nineteenth century, though it now not only defines a "normative" type of sex, but also automatically acts as a delineation between "acceptable" and "unacceptable" types of sexual acts. Although recently historians have perhaps become too bogged down arguing about semantics,⁴ it needs to be recognized that cultural attitudes and behaviors were different in the past and should be viewed through a different lens. The term *heterosexuality* is therefore not always useful in determining sex or sexuality in the Enlightenment, a period when the laws of nature were seen as essential guidance in what was "normal" or "natural."

The most sweeping generalization that can be made about the world history of sex during the Enlightenment is that it differed dramatically for men and women. Men in most countries—whether in the East or the West—could have sex with whomever they wished, so long as they married and had children. In other words, society expected men to conform to an outward appearance of heterosexuality within marriage, even if their predilections lay elsewhere. In many countries, it was permissible for men to marry more than one woman, and to take mistresses or concubines with impunity. Women's sexual conduct was more closely guarded by their men: they were to remain virgins until they married, and were expected to remain faithful to one husband. With very few exceptions, chastity was regarded as a prized possession in women throughout the world: without her virginity intact, a woman would have difficulty finding a husband. In a few small tribes and other instances, women had equal access to men, but this was relatively rare.

A person's life cycle, their particular status, and their gender affected their sexual parameters. A community—and, often, its authorities—established different boundaries for young, single girls and boys than for married couples, widows, and widowers. The amount of sex a young unmarried couple might have was likely to vary according to class. For the aristocrats (as well as those in the higher economic tiers also concerned about containing property and wealth within the family), women's sexual behavior was more closely monitored and marriages were frequently arranged in both Protestant and

FIGURE 1.1: While her chaperone sleeps a young girl keeps watch on her as her lover, on bended knee, kisses her hand. Engraving by H. C. Shenton after F. P. Stephanoff. Wellcome Library, London.

Catholic countries. Aristocrats expected their women to be virgins when they married because the purity of the bloodline was extremely important: families needed to ensure that their heirs were of known "stock" and marriage served to amalgamate family fortunes. In Catholic countries in Europe—and in the Americas, where that culture had been imported—women were constantly chaperoned by a family member, and their courtships were closely controlled. In most countries, parents and guardians expected their charges to have escorts when entertaining young men—although this strategy did not always successfully keep lovers apart (fig. 1.1). Safeguarding a young woman's virtue was felt to be particularly important among the higher classes, but this ideal was not generally expected—or even possible—among the laboring poor. In Italy, Spain, Portugal, and in the parts of America with Catholic immigrants, respectable Catholic women mixed only with male relatives. When they were permitted access to other men, family members monitored them.

Men in some countries such as China and Japan might take numerous wives, while men in Muslim countries in the Middle East were restricted to four. Even then, men might take as many concubines or lovers as they could afford. In the West, men tended to take only one wife, but frequented brothels for extramarital pleasure. While elite families demanded that their daughters or sons marry into similarly wealthy or aristocratic backgrounds, girls from the gentry and middling sort were increasingly having more say as "companionate marriage" became popular in England (fig. 1.2). Meanwhile, a pretty working-class girl might manage to attract a richer husband, but if not, she typically settled for a man with a good, plebian living. Overwhelmingly, women had more say in marriage the lower down the social scale they were. In England, at least for lower- and middle-class courting couples, easier access to each other was granted by parents if the couple was betrothed. Bundling, which was commonplace, involved a young couple sleeping together partially clothed, or with a wooden plank between them that prevented them from attempting full penetrative sex. For the working classes, fairs and markets were an easy method of meeting the opposite sex. Seductions frequently took place in the open air. In some cases, after too much ale, unwanted pregnancies resulted from harvest drinking parties.[5] Mothers might catch their daughters in the hayloft with their male hired hands, and young apprentices were often a source of anxiety for employers. But a single poor working girl, particularly in a city, ran a greater risk of being seduced or even raped at the hands of her employers. Without the family and community networks of rural places, girls were often left without anyone to protect them, leaving them at the mercy of their employers, or their employers' sons. As a result, domestic work, which was what most women did

FIGURE 1.2: A merry crowd that includes a fiddler playing a tune celebrates a marriage as the groom kisses the bride. Etching. Wellcome Library, London.

for employment during this period, raised concerns for moralists. Elsewhere in the world also, orphans and single girls without protection were in the greatest danger from sexual predators.

In the West, traditional notions about sexuality stemmed from the Christian ethic that women were inferior to men. Sex, if it was to occur at all, should be perfunctory—for the purpose of procreation, and then only in the missionary position, with the man on top. Celibacy was the ideal status, which devout men and women chose in order to attain closeness to God. After the Lutheran reformation, however, this gave way to the notion that the path to salvation might be found in marriage, and that the ideal relationship between a man and a woman was that of husband and wife. The church authorities deemed only sex between married couples as licit, and any couplings outside of this realm were seen as fornication. Both the Catholic and Protestant churches within Europe had strict rules about transgressive activities, and had no difficulty in asserting their religious doctrines. Women were frequently seen as sexually wild, uncontrollable, and in need of a man's direction. Because of this notion, church authorities often believed that women initiated, or enticed, men into fornication and were therefore to blame for encouraging men to commit sexual acts. Men were also punished, but the stigma attached to premarital sex rarely brought with it the same consequences for men as it did for women.

In South America, the invading Spanish and Portuguese conquistadors saw native women as part of their plunder—and rape as part of the general subjugation of the natives en masse. This aggression inevitably led to clashes with local men as they fought to defend their women. In North America, sexual intermingling was initially ignored by the prevailing authorities as the first settlers set up base. Men who traveled to the New World looked to Indian women for sex and companionship, taking them as wives or mistresses. At the outset, the authorities felt such action was acceptable. But, as more white women crossed the sea and settled in America, adjusting the gender balance for settlers, the authorities clamped down, deciding that men must marry within their own race. By the eighteenth century, new laws were being introduced to prevent racially mixed marriages. Because the first Puritan settlers tended to come in family units, there was less of a gender disparity in their communities. Ministers and missionaries made attempts to convert Indians and bring their perceived sexual excesses under control. The Pilgrim Fathers attempted to keep a tight rein on sexual behavior, using sexual slander and gossip as a method to control it within the white community—a reality in England as well.[6] The church authorities set great store by licit couplings, and penalized those who transgressed the rules. They did not hesitate to sentence a woman if she was found pregnant—even when she was already married—if the birth occurred sooner than nine months into the marriage.[7]

Despite the attempts to regulate their flock, Puritan authorities sometimes had no control over others living in or near their communities. Traders married Indians, finding in them good companions who helped them not only form close connections with their kin but also provide valuable assistance in the trade. As slavery increased, and African men and women were imported, settlers such as plantation owners took up with their own slaves for sex, either forcibly or with rewards. The nakedness of both Indian and African women merely reinforced the white man's view of their sexual rapaciousness. Some women managed to save enough to buy themselves out of slavery; others developed close relationships with their masters and had children by them. (Often, these children were taken into the house as domestics.) However, such relationships were never equal: there was always an element of enforcement, with the woman having little ability to deny her owner sex if it was demanded of her.

Many men abandoned any pretense of keeping to a sexual moral code once they had left their home country. In the New World, sexual exchange with the indigenous population was part and parcel of bargaining and trading. With Captain Cook's revolutionary explorations of the South Seas during the 1770s, published shipmates' journals promoted the idea of a new sexual idyll in that region (fig 1.3). Sex-starved sailors welcomed the sexual forthrightness of the islanders, and many of them took native women as their temporary "wives." When the time came for the ships to depart, few among the crew wanted to leave their women behind. Reports of these encounters were popular in the eighteenth century, and the theme provided the basis for much contemporary erotica.

The racial element of sex proved problematic for all countries, whether they were the ones colonizing or being colonized. Laws sprang up to protect the homogeneity of colonizing races—to prevent them from "going native" (that is, from falling into the natives' ways). This is evident not only in America between the settlers and Indians, but also between peoples in other countries that implemented similar laws in their colonies, for example, in India and Africa.

FIGURE 1.3: A young woman of Otaheite, dancing. Engraving by J. Webber del.; J. K. Sherwin sc. c. 1780–85. Wellcome Library, London.

Meanwhile, authorities in China and Japan attempted to shut out foreigners altogether in order to contain their own traditions. In the East, a tradition emerged whereby women were sequestered in the home, segregated from men and rarely seen out alone. Because of this, there were differences in how courtship, marriage, and adultery were viewed. In such countries as India, Japan, and China, if a woman escaped being sold into prostitution and remained under the protection of her family, she was likely to have her behavior closely watched and her marriage arranged. In all these countries, premarital female virginity was considered of prime importance. If a woman lost her virginity prior to marriage, she was invariably cast out of her community, and would have to resort to prostitution. There was a strict divergence, inherited from earlier days, between sex for procreation and sex for pleasure. A wife was expected to bear children; prostitutes were used for entertainment and leisure. In China, prostitutes with smaller feet had a better chance of making more money, while any woman with unbound feet had difficulty finding a husband at all.[8]

FIGURE 1.4: A Nautch (dancing) girl. Gouache drawing. Wellcome Library.

India saw the rise of the Moghul Empire, and a change from its traditional way of life to one that incorporated Muslim rules about sexual behavior. Nautch girls, or dancing girls, were popular at court, as well as at weddings and festivals. In eighteenth-century India (fig. 1.4), these girls initially had held a high status at court—but, with the arrival of the British soldiers, they were pushed into prostitution and their status declined. Tales of their allure and ability to bewitch filled the journals of British memsahibs anxious about the Nautch girls' overt sexuality and their ability to seduce British men. Within respectable Indian families, however, marriages tended to be arranged, with bride and groom often not meeting until their wedding day.

European male travelers wrote their opinions about Japanese women in their diaries, most often portraying them in a positive light. The few male foreigners who visited Japan thought the women delightful, mainly because of their submissive demeanor—though not all of them approved of these women's enforced subservience. Such men often married Japanese women, or took them as temporary wives. They, as well as Japanese men, often resorted to prostitution, and the profession was prominent. Poor or orphaned children were particularly easy prey for brothel-mongers and were frequently bought in order to be trained for a life in the business. However, unlike in the West, the trade carried no obvious stigma, and a woman might easily marry once her time had come to leave the business.

In most societies, as women grew older, the sexual aspect of their personalities was assumed to disappear, and they were no longer seen as sexual beings at all. Yet, a sex life might have been easier for a woman at this stage than at any other because she was free from the burden of pregnancy. Once sexual activity began for a younger woman, her life was a continual round of childbearing. Contraception methods were still basic and undependable, and women relied heavily on herbal potions, magic amulets, or coitus interruptus.[9]

HOMOSEXUALITY

Over the last few decades, historians of homosexuality have been arguing as to whether such a person as the homosexual existed, and whether the word *homosexuality* can be applied to same-sex activities during the Enlightenment when the term was not even developed until the end of the nineteenth century by sexologists.[10] Studies of same-sex behavior have explored various categories: love stories between cowboys; mock marriages between mollies (effeminate men); female "friendships" among middling women; lesbian-like behavior; sodomy, in all its variants (at sea, in the barracks, in fields), sodomy between nuns using dildoes; and fraudulent marriages between cross-dressers.[11]

Although in the eighteenth century the word *homosexual* was not yet invented, certain behaviors between the same sexes were similar to those we recognize now, despite being viewed somewhat differently by their own respective societies. The term *sodomy* was used to describe buggery between two men, but it also included anal sex between a man and a woman, and between a person and an animal. These three categories of sodomy, seen as "crimes against nature" and against God, were deemed sinful and illegal. During the Enlightenment in England, the Buggery Act of 1533 still commanded law over sodomitical acts, under which evidence of both penetration and ejaculation was necessary if a conviction was to take place. It was not until 1828 that a new act was passed, making it easier for conviction of sodomitical acts. In Europe, sex between women generally came under the same sodomy law as men, though few such cases were prosecuted—and, when they were, they mainly involved prosecution of women who usurped male roles (using dildos and pretending to be men).

Attitudes toward sex between men varied throughout the world. In the West, opposition was based on Christian ethics. The biblical platitudes against homosexuality and other deviant behavior originally fell under the jurisdiction of the ecclesiastical courts. By the eighteenth century, however, such cases were prosecuted under secular courts: that a man sodomized another was first a transgression of religious law—a crime against nature—but it was also an infraction of secular law. In most countries, this was a capital crime—but, in England, men tended to be sentenced for "attempted sodomy," which evoked a lesser sentence of at least two years in prison. Elsewhere, sodomy most often resulted in a death sentence. The Spanish inquisition was particularly vigilant in its examination of the cases of sodomy that came to its attention [12] Concern in France ran so deep that authorities there established secret agents called *mouches* (flies), who circulated in known cruising grounds in order to entrap sodomites.[13] Similarly, in London, the Society for the Reformation of Manners contributed to a crackdown on molly houses (male brothels) that brought various cases before the courts in the 1720s.[14] One of the best-known molly houses was Mother Clap's Molly house; the owner of which was brought to trial in the 1720s. Many of the men who took part in the activities were married—and some had children—so their lives did not necessarily exclude women.

Detractors of sodomitical activities believed boarding schools and certain universities to be harborers of such vices. In France, the Abbé Dumay expressed his dismay and concern about the dangers lurking in nearby boarding schools and tennis courts.[15] A boarding school in Oxford came under scrutiny after a college warden was accused of seduction by a young male student. Young men looking for sexual relationships with other men often found it safer to seek illicit love abroad. Byron, for example, scoured Italy and Greece for his youthful companions rather than continue to risk being exposed at home.

Homosexuality was accepted in certain parts of the world. Tribal people lacked the guilt ethic of the Christian West about same-sex behavior and made accommodations within their societies for those who did not fit the overriding gender divisions of male or female. In India, *hijras* were traditionally accepted by the community, as were the *berdache* found in some Native American tribes. Both *hijras* and *berdache* were men who played female roles, dressing in women's clothing and performing traditionally feminine roles; both of these tribal peoples assimilated people with different sexualities, and appear to have had a much more open attitude toward them than the West. *Hijras* were invited to weddings and celebrations to dance and entertain, and were thought to bring good luck. Native Americans took the *berdache* as second wives as they had a reputation for excelling in the domestic sphere, maintaining the household chores.

Eastern countries were similarly free from guilt over same-sex activities, and had no concept of sin. In both Japan and China, male performers traditionally took female roles, and male audience members felt free to seduce the performers after the show. In Japan, it was not unusual for daimyo and samurai to take up with young boys. For men, sex was a guilt-free act, unfaithfulness was not an issue, and sex with other men did not stir the distaste commonly seen among Europeans. Rather, *nanshoku* was viewed as a natural relationship between an older man and a youth—be it a samurai, priest, or actor. Similarly, in China, the "cut sleeve" tradition (a phrase used in connection with homosexuality) developed, although it was curtailed abruptly in the moral clampdown by authorities during the Qing dynasty.

Generally, lesbian acts in most countries created less of a reaction than sex between two males as women were considered to be less important. The exception was Holland, where persecution of lesbians was more commonplace than it was in England and the rest of Europe.[16] Although some lesbians cross-dressed, other women donned men's apparel in order to find work masquerading as men. In Britain and America, jolly tales of cross-dressing women were part of the ballad tradition which was repeated in popular printed pamphlets for the public's amusement. Cross-dressing in the theater, where women took the "breeches role," was a popular form of entertainment. Rather than criticizing these women, authors of biographies and ballads fêted them for their bravado in tales about cross-dressers. Russian soldier Hannah Schnell, British seafarers Mary Read and Anne Bonny, and actress Charlotte Charke were among those championed. Meanwhile, writers of erotica routinely described female boarding schools and convents as places of debauchery, enclosed spaces that facilitated lesbian-like activity. In reality, lesbians within the community, such as Anne Lister, despite dressing in a masculine fashion and wooing local young women, were less at risk of persecution than were men who pursued other men, although Lister did suffer some name-calling and threats. In Italy, lesbians such as Catherine Vizzani caused offense and attracted attention mainly by dressing as a man and running off with a rich man's daughter: their elopement ultimately resulted in Vizzani's death.

Although lesbian activities could be kept hidden, the women who indulged in them were brought to court if they attempted fraud (through marriage) or deception. Furthermore, women were more likely to be sentenced for sodomitical acts when a dildo had been used or a partner had been penetrated. In Prussia, the case of Catherina Link is evidence of a woman persecuted for using a dildo. Lesbianism was rarely mentioned in the East, although cross-dressing of both male actors and female courtesans was popular in both China and Japan.

SEXUAL VARIATIONS

Deviations or variation from sexual acts perceived as "normal" were commonly regarded as perversion. Throughout history, societies have tended to polarize sex into so-called normal and abnormal activities: heterosexuality and homosexuality, adherence to common social mores and deviance from them. Sexual acts have been categorized into what people considered perverted and not perverted at different times in history. It is therefore necessary to focus on what contemporaries thought about certain sexual acts outside their normal codes of reference and on what was commonly seen as socially acceptable.

Sex was generally regulated by a country's religion, its strictures laying down the basis for which behaviors were permissible and which were not. Many societies have taken their codes from their religious writings: for example, the Christian use of the Bible, the Muslim use of the Koran, the Jewish use of the Torah. Usually, unacceptable sex acts were the ones deemed sinful by religious authorities, and these beliefs spread among the general populace. From at least the early modern period, through the eighteenth century and beyond (in many countries, even today), sex acts outside heterosexual intercourse within marriage were considered sinful. The church authorities had originally meted out punishments for deviant behavior in the West, which were later incorporated into state laws. In Christianity, all kinds of sodomy—with animals, with other men, anally penetrating a woman—were punishable by ecclesiastical and, later, canon law. In other religions, these acts were also generally seen as sinful. Where there was no concept of sin, such as in the East, bestiality was considered taboo, although not necessarily transgressing any religious beliefs.

In the Far East, the standard proscriptions for sex were handed down from philosophies such as Confucianism and Taoism, which meant a different understanding from the West's of what was permissible. Although certain sexual behaviors were considered taboo, they were not necessarily the same as the ones considered illicit (or prohibited) in the West. In China and Japan for instance, sex and marriage were considered to be separate spheres—marriage was for procreation and duty, prostitutes for pleasure and leisure. This was also applicable to certain classes in the West, where marriages of convenience among the aristocracy meant that extramarital affairs were commonplace—at least, for men. Though some aristocratic women might carry out such liaisons, they were obliged to maintain an appearance of modesty and discretion. Generally speaking, throughout the world, sex outside of marriage was more acceptable for men than for women.

Morality was, in general, influenced by the rights and wrongs instilled by regulatory bodies. Michel Foucault has asserted that it was the result of power and control that different behaviors came to be labeled as perverse. This power is described in the abstract, but it is usually taken to mean the domain of the most dominant group or groups: those who ruled on what was acceptable and what was not. This came to be understood as the constructionist approach, wherein the dominant power is seen to create (or "construct") and enforce the rules on norms and their opposites (or perversions). Yet, in practice, this abstract power does not fit with reality, since some laws affect the most powerful people. If the most powerful section of society were managing the law, then why did they not give themselves license to do as they wished in their sex lives?[17] This notion also ignores independent agency, as well as spontaneous action. A more incorporative approach is needed to understand the process of creating categories of deviance. Laws tend to come from a hegemonic response from society, taking into account community reaction. Thus, we can see that religion, state, and community came together in policing sexual behavior. Some "abnormal," or deviant, behaviors were dealt with leniently by both authorities and communities, while others were dealt with most harshly, depending on how great the "crime," or "sin," was thought to be by the broader community.

In addition to the religious framework of sexual perversity or deviance, a medical one emerged. Physicians contributed to the ideas of what was harmful or dangerous, making some sexual practices more problematic and, therefore, more inaccessible. Certain sexual practices were medicalized and categorized, falling into either an acceptable (if they were effective and beneficial) or unacceptable (if they were harmful or dangerous) category. Within such arguments and promulgations, the baseline for this division on acceptability was often related to how useful an act was in assisting procreation. Examples can be seen in how flagellation and masturbation were regarded. Flagellation was seen in a positive light—as aiding erection and, therefore, profitable in procreation. As far back as the sixteenth century, Johan Heinrich Meibom (1590–1655)

FIGURE 1.5: "Son corps est couvert de pustules," in S.A.D. Tissot, *L'onanisme; ou dissertation physique sur les maladies produites par la masturbation* (Paris, 1836). Wellcome Library, London.

explored flogging as a cure for impotency in his *De Flagrorum Usu in re Veneria* (1639). The notorious publisher Edmund Curll translated and reprinted the book in 1718 as erotica, under the title *A Treatise of the Use of Flogging in Venereal Affairs*. Because flagellation had its uses in facilitating heterosexual intercourse through promoting an erection, physicians and theologians regarded it as acceptable, if a bit odd—writers of erotica and bawdy poems made jokes about the practice, with devotees of the birch frequently the butt of satirical poems. On the other hand, masturbation was seen as sinful as far back as the medieval period, although at that time, it was not considered to be particularly harmful. It was only during the eighteenth century that masturbation seems to have been considered a dangerous vice (fig. 1.5). For much of the seventeenth century, the act had been viewed as less than threatening. Diarist Samuel Pepys casually mentioned how he had masturbated while reading French pornography, and another diarist, John Cannon, mentioned how he had masturbated among his youthful friends without any guilty feelings.[18] By the eighteenth century, lecherous rakes such as James Boswell were happily fornicating with women but were increasingly anxious about their constant masturbation.

A change in the concept and thinking around masturbation took place in the eighteenth century, to some extent caused as a result of a panic induced by the 1716 publication of a book by "a clergyman," *Onania, or The Heinous Sin of Self-pollution, and All Its Frightful Consequences in Both Sexes Considered with Spiritual and Physical Advice to Those Who Have already Injured Themselves by This Abominable Practice and Seasonable Admonition to the Youth of the Nation of Both Sexes*.[19] Significantly, the book targeted young men *and* young women, recording all sorts of frightening side-effects from masturbation in both genders, including epilepsy, pustulant sores, and various other ailments. Women might grow elongated clitorises, men became weak through excessive loss of sperm. Regardless of the guilt that masturbation allegedly instilled, young men and women continued to indulge in it.

By the second half of the eighteenth century, physicians had entered the fray. The Swiss Calvinist physician Samuel Auguste David Tissot (1728–1797), in his 1760 treatise, *L'Onanisme, ou Dissertation Physique sur les Maladies Produites par la Masturbation,* outlined case studies of terrible physical disorders that had resulted from masturbation. Tissot gave examples of various patients he had treated, and the horrifying symptoms they suffered as a result of habitual masturbation. The case of LD described a clock-maker who, at seventeen, had taken to masturbating three times a day: "The slightest irritation immediately cured an imperfect erection, which was instantly followed by an evacuation of this liquor, which daily augmented his weakness."[20] He became more and more feeble, until he drifted away altogether and died. Translated into English in 1766 as *Onanism, or a Treatise upon the Disorders Produced by Masturbation,* the work had an impact on medical opinion. Tissot believed that all sexual activity was potentially dangerous, with the rush of blood to the head posing a potential threat to one's sanity.[21]

Meanwhile, M.D.T. Bienville brought together masturbation and the nervous system in his 1771 treatise, *Nymphomanie, ou Traité de la Fueuer Uterine,* which was translated into English by Edward Sloane Wilmot in 1775. Bienville believed women to be innately lascivious (a perception shared by the broader population), unable to control either their emotions or their bodies. He saw female onanists as potential nymphomaniacs, and their habit as leading to mental derangement—the imagination now became the seat of torrid thoughts and terrible physical illnesses. If women masturbated it was particularly dangerous because their minds would then unravel into long stretches of fantasy and wild imaginings. Furthermore, a woman's habitual masturbation could lead to an elongated clitoris, nymphomania, or lesbianism.[22] He wrote,

FIGURE 1.6: "Les Charmes de la Masturbation." Erotic vignette from *Invocation a l'amour. Chant philosophique* (London, c. 1825). Wellcome Library, London.

"The real sensation of pleasures, added to the different ideas of which are incessantly filling their imaginations, in a short time renders these wretched sufferers furious, and ungovernable." Epileptic fits, blindness, and strangulation were all symptoms the onanist might experience. Europe was now experiencing a panic about the potential side effects of masturbation. Despite these warnings, the pleasures of masturbation as erotic foreplay continued to sell in pornographic books (fig. 1.6).

In Europe, bestiality was less well-known than either flagellation or masturbation, and what we do know about it tends to come from trial reports. Bestiality fitted in with how sodomy was understood. As such, critics viewed it as one of the worst sins. Few court cases occurred in England—and, when they did, men were more likely to be caught with cattle or horses, whereas women were more likely to be arrested for fornicating with dogs. In both Sweden and Britain—especially in the earlier parts of the Enlightenment—bestiality was still connected to witchcraft.[23]

Although not yet labeled foot fetishism, obsession with (or, at least, the attraction to or admiration of) a lady's feet seems to have been normal in

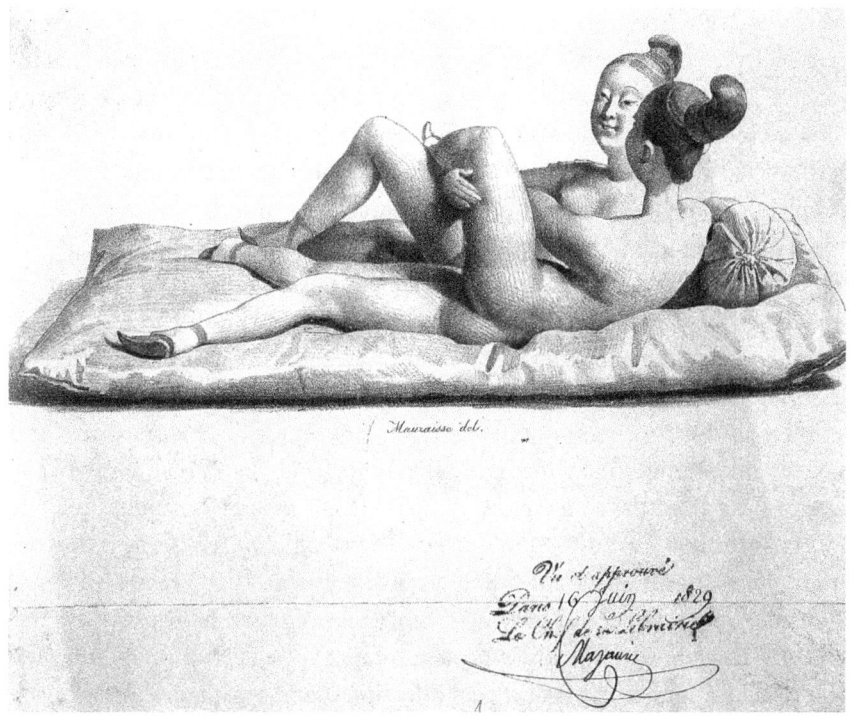

FIGURE 1.7: Two young girls with bound feet lie together on a mattress. Lithograph by Mauzaisse (1784–1844). Wellcome Library, London.

eighteenth-century England. Both men and woman admired the pretty feet of other women, and even shoes and stockings were a source of fascination for some men. One Dublin lady of the town mentions her beau, who delighted in washing and licking her feet; another describes how her lover toured town in hopes of finding fashionable stockings she would like.[24] Although the former seems to be evidence of a genuine foot fetishist, the latter's fascination with particular items of clothing is not dissimilar to the obsession of present-day fashionistas with fashionable stockings or designer shoes—it was an appreciation that was public and out in the open. Obsession with feet in other parts of the world reached its height in China, where the art of foot-binding had been practiced for centuries. Although the Chinese obsession with making feet small was not necessarily a mass sexual fetishism, it was part of the overall attractiveness of women (fig. 1.7). No self-respecting man during this period considered taking a wife with unbound feet. The Japanese also found the gait of a woman with heavily clogged feet attractive. Other obsessions with clothing—such as leather or furs—have not yet been chronicled by historians of this period, and such cases, if there were any, remain hidden.

Another sexual practice that can be classed as a sexual variation is auto-asphyxiation. So far, however, few historians have explored its history, probably because relevant documentation is so difficult to find. One case has been uncovered in Britain,[25] but the practice does seem to have been a rarity there. In 1791, Czech composer Frantisek Kotzwara hit the news when he accidentally hanged while visiting prostitute Susannah Hill in Vine Street in Westminster. Pamphlets about the incident published at the time considered the episode comedic—noosing up for sex appears not to have been taken too seriously. In France, however, it had become more commonplace in the Marquis de Sade's pornographic literature depicting orgies (fig. 1.8). He explored sadistic sex both in his writings and in his personal life—the term *sadism* comes from his name. Sadistic treatment of children had long been commonplace, and terrible tales emerged of cruel and barbaric "keepers" inflicting terrible punishments on young people in their employ. The worse cases came to court and were publicly denigrated in British publications. There does not seem to have been the same moral panic that has emerged in the twenty-first century, with its fears of the molestation of young children. Indeed, the term *pedophilia* is anachronistic for the eighteenth century. It had yet to be invented. At a time when men could pick up twelve-year-old girls as prostitutes, there was little thought given to their protection. The age between ten and twelve for girls was a murky issue, and generally, intercourse with girls under twelve tended to be treated only as a misdemeanor.[26] Although the rape of girls of

FIGURE 1.8: Illustration of a Dutch printing of Marquis de Sade's *Juliette* (c. 1800).

ten and younger was taken seriously in law and brought with it the possibility of capital punishment, in reality, it was difficult to prove and was thought improbable to achieve because of the child's underdeveloped anatomy. If the child was male, the attack would fall under the sodomy laws in England, with the child sometimes deemed just as guilty as the perpetrator. The rape of a dead body was certainly viewed with concern, but few cases came to court in England. Cases of necrophilia have always been difficult to find. However, concerns were increasingly voiced about the practice of dissection in medical schools. The strangest of sexual perversions are inevitably hard for historians to detect as, because of society's negative perceptions about them, they were kept hidden.

REGULATION, LAWS, AND TABOO

Regulation of sexual deviancy came in various forms from both the church and the law. For centuries, the main control over sexual behavior had fallen to religion, and this was no less true during the Enlightenment. For most of the time, these religions saw men as superior and women as secondary creatures intended to follow male authority figures be it their husband, fathers, or sons. Female sexuality itself was tightly reined-in by most religions because women were considered irrational, highly sexual beings. Men were deemed cultured and rational—therefore, the ideal people to keep women in check.

Most of the warnings about female sexuality came from holy books, which were enthusiastic about creating taboos around the body. Women were seen as unclean and polluted—in the Christian, Hindu, Jewish, and Muslim religions-they were to bathe after sexual intercourse, stay away from the preparation of food during menstruation, avoid places of worship during menstruation or pregnancy, and also eschew sex while carrying a child. In Europe, women who had recently given birth were not allowed back into religious services until they had been "churched," a ceremony performed to purify mothers after giving birth.

Sexual regulation in Europe also came through community gossip, and pressure was brought to bear on couples who were not conforming. If a young man and woman were betrothed but had sexual relations before their wedding, he was expected to marry the woman if she became pregnant. Premarital sex was not always necessarily condemned, so long as marriage ensued.

Eastern countries tended to be more strict with their children. Respectable Indian, Chinese, and Japanese parents usually arranged marriages for their children, either through matchmakers or together with the family of a potential spouse. There was often little room for courtship. Historian Matthew Sommer argues that, in late imperial China, regulation of sexuality shifted to come under the strictures of the state as a result of social and demographic changes. Rather than having differentiated attitudes among different family classes, "all people were expected to conform to gender roles defined in terms of marriage." An increase in the young male population was seen to threaten chaste wives and daughters of respectable households, and new laws were introduced to control them.[27]

MEDICINE AND DISEASE

Various scientific experiments led to a rapid increase in medical knowledge and a growing understanding of the workings of the body. William Harvey (1578–1657) had already contributed to the understanding of the body with his experiments on the circulation of the blood, but he also wrote about procreation in his *De Generatione,* describing the basic process of the formation

FIGURE 1.9: Detail showing the microscope in use in Anthony Van Leeuwenhoek, *Arcana Naturae Detecta* (1695). Wellcome Library, London.

of life, and recognizing that eggs were common to all animals. As a result of the invention of the microscope, Leeuwenhoek discovered spermatozoa (figs. 1.9 and 1.10). Because of these developments in science, a new medical understanding emerged that changed attitudes toward the body.

In the past, ancient medics described men and women as opposites—women were seen as natural, men as cultural. In *Making Sex*, Thomas Laqueur has argued that a one-sex-theory laid the foundation for thoughts about the body—that women were inside-out men. This conception of male and female bodies was shifting by the eighteenth century to become a two-sex model, with a separately defined understanding of both the male and female bodies.[28] However, Hippocrates' humoral theory of the body continued to circulate. Many still thought the body's major constituents were air, water, fire, and earth, with each element reflecting the humors of the body. Maintaining a balance of these fluids was essential for one's health: a blockage of sperm, blood, or sweat could cause problems. In women, a major concern was retention of the menses, and such methods as letting blood and administering herbs were used to bring it on.

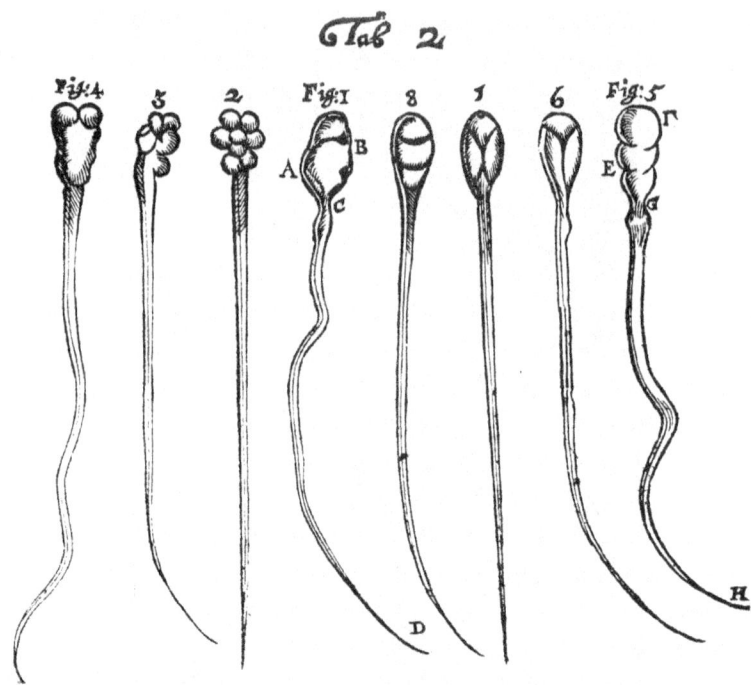

FIGURE 1.10: Spermatozoa of a rabbit from "Observationes de natis e semine genitali animalculis," *Philosophical Transactions* (1677). Wellcome Library, London.

Amenorrhea (the cessation of periods) was known as "greensickness" and was thought to especially affect virgins and widows because in theory, they did not have recourse to sex.[29] For men, the problem lay in their sperm. Overejaculation or too much sex (thus expressing too much sperm) could cause weakness in mind and body. In 1708, the Dutch physician Herman Boerhaave worriedly announced that "the *Semen* discharged too lavishly, occasions a Weariness, Weakness, Indisposition to Motion, Convulsions, Leanness, Driness, Heats and Pains in the Membranes of the Brain, with a Dulness of the Senses; more especially of the Sight, a *Tabes Dorsalis,* Foolishness, and Disorders of the like kind."[30] The answer for both men and women, if they were to avoid these illnesses, was regular—but not excessive—sex.

Medical manuals offered an amalgamation of ancient Greek texts, seventeenth-century French texts, and emerging ideas. Material in Giovanni Sinibaldi's *Geneanthropeiae* (1642) took its message from various early Greek and Roman physicians and philosophers.[31] This, in turn, was integrated into

Rare Verities, the Cabinet of Venus Unlocked and Her Secrets Laid Open (1657–1658) and Nicolas Venette's *Tableau de l'Amour Conjugal* (1686), with an English version appearing in 1703 as *Mysteries of Conjugal Love Reveal'd*.[32] Most of the literature amounted to advice on how to make babies. Female midwives, such as Jane Sharp in her 1671 *The Midwives Book* tended to address the patient directly, giving advice couched in agricultural metaphors based around fertility and crops. The popular best-seller of its day was *Aristotle's Master-Piece* (first published in 1684), which went through various editions throughout the eighteenth century.

By the eighteenth century, the regulation of sex was becoming increasingly medicalized. Physicians and medical manuals not only proffered advice on procreation and the means to sexual good health, but also described the woes and ailments that might beset any person falling foul of the correct path. Certain acts that had been condemned in the past as undesirable because they were sinful, were now categorized as medical ailments and potentially harmful to the health: masturbation was a case in point. Some so-called deviant behavior was controlled via scare tactics rather than through the church or the law.

Venereal disease was rampant worldwide. Anyone with an active sex life was likely to have one of the many diseases in circulation. The distinction between syphilis and gonorrhea was not understood by physicians or the general public: syphilis was thought be a more severe instance, or advanced stage, of gonorrhea. European countries blamed one other for its spread. The British called it the French disease, the French called it the Italian disease—understandably, no nation would lay claim to it. However, venereal disease had been evident in the East for more than 4,000 years.[33] Increased travel had the side effect of transmitting diseases, with whole tribes of indigenous people wiped out in the Americas and the South Seas as a result. Lock hospitals opened in various European cities in attempts to alleviate venereal diseases. Some countries began to regulate prostitution as a way of preventing its spread. The main remedy introduced to cope with the diseases was mercury, used to induce a process of salivation in patients. Doctors believed that salivation expelled toxins, but neither mercury nor other quack treatments provided effective cures.

POPULAR CULTURE

Sex permeated most areas of eighteenth-century life in the Western capitals, whether one strolled through the streets or went to the theater. Art, literature, folklore, science—all contributed to popular beliefs and culture surrounding

FIGURE 1.11: A young woman dressing her hair with feathers (London 1776). Wellcome Library, London.

sex. London was an epicenter of entertainment, where parks, coffeehouses, taverns, and theaters flourished. Pleasure gardens became the rage with people flocking to the operas and watching fireworks at Vauxhall and Ranelagh Gardens. Promenades allowed those from the demi-monde to show off their fashions, often featuring hairstyles that incorporated model ships, vegetable matter, or feathers (fig. 1.11). Coffeehouses served as meeting places for men to discuss recent conquests and share pornographic books. They flocked to taverns to pick up prostitutes for an evening of pleasure with side rooms kept in some establishments for such purposes. A group of friends might hire a room and spend the evening together, drinking and cavorting, then awaken hungover and broke, their pockets picked by their hired paramours. Vulgarity was not so much frowned upon as *de rigueur*.

The theater was a notorious outlet for sex: plays were riddled with sexual innuendo, to the delight of rowdy audiences. Spoofs on seductions, mixed-up meetings, and marriage were popular plot themes. In France, Molière's *School for Husbands* (1661), a comedic farce about marriage and jealous husbands, played to packed audiences. This was quickly followed by his *School for Wives*, which was first performed at the Théâtre du Palais-Royal in December 1662. Critics immediately condemned it for its bad taste and immorality. Fops were lambasted in English Restoration plays such as Etherage's *Man of the Mode, or Sir Fopling Flutter* (1676). These works eventually made way for such newer plays such as Gay's *Three Hours after Marriage* (1717), which, despite playing seven successful nights at the Drury Lane theater, was withdrawn for obscenity. In Gay's more popular *Beggar's Opera*, robbers and "women of the town" roles were played for all they were worth. Its success allowed John Rich, Drury Lane's manager, to build the Theatre Royal. Where new theaters came, whores followed. In Nantes and Marseilles, after new opera houses were built, whores soon clogged the surrounding streets. Actresses were often seen by society as no better than whores, their frequent scandals reinforcing the negative regard.

As well as offering vicarious fictionalized sex, theaters served as pickup places for well-known rakes and courtesans. In most European cities, the theater was considered an acceptable place for courtesans to show themselves off, to entertain their protectors, or to pick up new beaux. The more up-market courtesans hired boxes so they could display themselves and accept courtships from prospective lovers; lower-class prostitutes hung around outside to attract potential clients as they left the theaters. In the East, Japanese male brothels were associated with the Kabuki theater. Young male actors worked as prostitutes, supplying the all-male brothels that often operated next to the theaters. Teahouses were also known hangouts for male prostitution; by the mid-eighteenth century, at least fourteen wards in Edo city had male-sex teahouses.[34]

The theater was also a place where traditional notions of gender might be challenged. In Japan and China, men played the female roles. In China, age-old female impersonation became suspect in the overly prudent Qing dynasty. The Chinese theater came under attack from the authorities for its immorality and association with prostitution. Female impersonators (*dan*) were deemed immoral and subsequently banned from performing in public. Teenage boys, picked for their good looks and feminine features, were trained to play female roles. The lovely, coquettish role was considered particularly threatening because of its sex appeal. Min Tian writes, "The prevalent custom of *xiadan* (dallying with *dan*) suggests the improper intimate relationship between the female impersonators and their admirers from the literati and officialdom."[35]

A new explosion in print culture hit the streets as cheap newspapers and pamphlets. People could now pick up information for a few pence. This spread of newspapers and journals meant sex was being discussed in public on an unprecedented scale. The novel formed the basis for new discussions of a wide variety of subjects such as rape, prostitution, virginity, and seduction found in Daniel Defoe's *The Fortunes and Misfortunes of the Famous Moll Flanders* (1722) and in his *Roxana* (1724). Female authors such as Charlotte Lennox described the dilemma of a young woman in *The Female Quixote,* while Samuel Richardson depicted a young girl's attempts to evade seduction in his epistolary novel, *Pamela, or Virtue Rewarded* (1740). His *Clarissa* (1748) was a much more serious novel about rape, though the scene itself was never mentioned throughout its whole seven volumes. In France, Laclos' *Les Liaisons Dangereuses* (1782) was a more savage erotic novel about the seduction of an innocent. Much of the literary convention in print in both East and West was made up of sexual jokes and innuendoes, or discussed the lives of courtesans. Sexual prescriptive literature was also on offer to young men and women giving advice on how to behave.

PROSTITUTION

Prostitution remained remarkably persistent throughout the world. In the West, girls often fell into prostitution as a result of poverty or early seduction—sometimes as a result of rape. In the East, young girls were often sold into brothels, then educated by the owners on how to entertain future customers. Male prostitution was also prevalent in the East, but in the West it was sodomy itself, rather than the exchange of money for sex, that was the main cause for concern. In certain parts of the Eastern world, both male and female prostitution were an acceptable part of life—though this was to change during the Qing dynasty, as new laws were introduced for its control.

In eighteenth-century London, authorities became increasingly concerned about the many women loitering on street corners and accosting men. Diarist James Boswell insisted that a man could not cross London without being accosted by one whore or another. Assessing the number of prostitutes in any one place was problematic, as many of the women went uncounted, or operated on a part-time or periodic basis, falling into prostitution only when other work was unavailable. Visitor Baron von Uffenbach touring England in 1710 believed there to be 25,000 prostitutes in London.[36] Though this might have been an exaggeration, prostitution was evidently rife in many prominent towns and ports throughout the world.

Prostitutes existed on many levels—from the elite courtesans who were the mistresses of titled men, down to the streetwalkers. Typically, women rose and fell up and down the financial ladder, depending on their age and popularity.

Particular jobs were associated with prostitution including that of mantua-makers, fruit-sellers, and domestic service. The latter were especially vulnerable to the preying hands of their employers, while young apprentices often came directly from the bosom of their families to their first job in a big city. At the Bon Pasteur asylum in Montpellier, 40 percent of the prostitutes had worked in domestic service.[37] This trend was repeated throughout Europe. Many of the authorities saw, the profession as a necessary evil and were unwilling to stamp it out due to fear that men might turn to adulterous affairs with married women.

Legal bodies, physicians, and the general public invariably blamed prostitutes for the spread of venereal disease. In response, authorities typically attempted to combat such disease by regulating prostitution. Many cities introduced the compulsory medical inspection of women suspected of prostitution, although for others this would not happen until the nineteenth century. In Hapsburg, during the second half of the eighteenth century, Maria Theresa (1717–1780) attempted to eradicate prostitution by introducing new laws. Under her imperial law of 1768, any prostitute who robbed her client or infected a client with syphilis might be subjected to having her head shaved and tarred, then be whipped in front of the church. Under the queen's rule, prostitutes were imprisoned, incarcerated in lunatic asylums, or deported to the Ottoman Empire.[38]

In Italy, the first prostitution laws were undertaken only after that country's unification in around 1861. Prior to that, prostitution had been prohibited on the grounds that the Pope deemed it a sin. The women were the focus of the crime, not their clients, and they were persecuted on the basis of fornication. Some Italian cities had attempted to enforce regulation along the Napoleonic lines while still under French rule, but the process was sporadic, with regional variations in punishments and enforcement. In 1823, for example, Palermo issued "licenses of toleration" for brothels in an attempt to maintain some sort of public order. By 1841, an edict from Naples insisted that Palermo made medical examinations of all suspected prostitutes.[39]

Contemporary commentators continued to explore methods by which prostitution could be either regulated or eradicated altogether. In Britain, Bernard Mandeville suggested in his *Modest Defence of Public Stews* (1724) that publicly run brothels were essential if society was to keep ordinary women from moral harm. In contrast, thirty-four years later, Saunders Welch proposed methods to rid the streets of whores in *A Proposal to Render Effectual a Plan to Remove the Nuisance of Common Prostitutes from the Street of This Metropolis* (1758). From the 1740s, Welch had served as High Constable under Magistrate Henry Fielding and had assisted him in suppressing riots in which three brothels were burned down by an angry mob. Welch favored setting up hospitals or orphanages for children as a way of educating them and saving them from a life of crime. He estimated the number of London prostitutes at 3,000, with many of them in the profession as a result of vanity and pride: "How often is the lady's maid seen flaunting in her mistress's left-off clothes, and ridiculously affecting the airs of a woman of quality ... the giddy girl becomes much fitter to be a mistress of a man of quality than a wife in her own station."[40]

These types of suggestions were commonplace throughout the West. In 1770, Restif de Bretonne argued to regulate Parisian brothels in much the same vein. In France, laws were effected from 1684 onward which increasingly regulated prostitution giving police complete authority to place prostitutes in specialized hospitals. As in Italy, actual law enforcement varied among French towns, with prostitutes generally regulated by their own communities. In the port town of Marseilles, *souteneurs* functioned as pimp go-betweens for the waterfront bordellos and the officers of visiting ships. Police left them alone to carry on with their business.[41] In 1792, authorities in Berlin insisted that brothels acquire police approval, then officially register, before they could operate.

There were traditions in China and Japan of state regulation and supervision of prostitution, but changes in the profession took place during this period. The Chinese authorities had divided prostitution into the permissible (in which a debased class of woman facilitated prostitution overseen by the state) and the impermissible (sex sold by commoners). After 1723, new laws were introduced that prohibited prostitution altogether.[42] Japan had established walled state-run compounds that contained prostitution as early as 1617, such as Yoshiwara in Edo (today's Tokyo). These were supported by privately run brothels elsewhere. Different types of sex services emerged: geishas flourished in the eighteenth century, but other types of lower-class prostitutes were increasingly on offer. Establishments such as teahouses opened, offering sex along with other services.

In England, changes in attitudes toward prostitutes began to occur during the second half of the century. In the earlier part of that century, they had been regarded as brazen whores, insatiable women who had turned to prostitution because of their own lust. This image then shifted into one of the seduced young woman—a woman fallen through no fault of her own. Throughout the period, there was a softening of attitudes about prostitution—and it was now thought preferable to save prostitutes, rather than merely to condemn them. Philanthropists established various institutions not only to aid prostitutes and their offspring, but also to regulate them. Thomas Coram established London's Foundling Hospital, Jonas Hanaway set up Magdalene Houses to reform prostitutes, and the Lock hospitals were founded to assist diseased wives of sailors. The side effects of irregular sex were now being institutionalized rather than left to monasteries or society at large.

In some countries, more lenient attitudes toward prostitution had come about much earlier. This can be seen in philanthropic moves to "rescue" prostitutes, and in the establishment of Magdalene Houses around Europe. The intent of these institutions was to re-establish the prostitute in the community. France had an earlier history of this than Britain. In America, the reform movement occurred slightly later, the result of campaigns against prostitution by Christian groups and temperance movements. How successful these reforms were is debatable, since the number of women returning to prostitution was not recorded. Many attempts at reform failed—often because there were so few employment opportunities for women, and so few alternative places for them to go. Regulations on the dress of prostitutes made it easier to identify them, but any attempts at quashing the profession were half-hearted. Despite the importance of marriage as an institution, most contemporaries still considered prostitution a necessary evil. As a result, the eradication of prostitution was never very seriously pursued in any part of the world.

EROTICA AND THE DEVELOPMENT OF PORNOGRAPHY

The emergence of "modern" pornography in the West took place from the sixteenth to the eighteenth centuries. Italy was at the forefront of this development, providing images and supporting text in printed form.[43] The most popular publication included Guilo Romano's illustrations, as engraved by Marcantonio Raimondi. They were found in *Sonette Lussurioso* (1534), with the accompanying text by Pietro Aretino (1492–1556). During the next couple of centuries, the images and the text were reproduced and translated, reaching England in the eighteenth century as *Aretin's Postures*. The images consisted of mythical couplings of the likes of Daphne and Apollo, Dido, Aeneas and Hercules and Deianira. Other sixteenth-century Italian books were translated and plagiarized into English, with the subject of whores proving to be one of the most common forms of erotica. Aretino's second production *Ragionamenti* (1536) became *The Crafty Whore* (1658); *Retorica delle Puttane* (1642) became *The Accomplished Whore*; and *La Puttana Errante* (1660)[44] became *The Whore's Rhetorick* (1683).[45]

By the mid-seventeenth century, Italy's production line was overshadowed by France's—the latter nation forging a path in the creation of pornographic texts, usually in the form of dialogues between two women. The three topsellers were *L'Éscole des Filles* (1655), *L'Académie des Dames* (1680), and *Vénus dans le Cloître* (1683). Meanwhile, in London, Edmund Curll was kept quite busy publishing reprints and translations of these books. Besides marketing rehashed French material, Curll proved to be one of the most prolific publishers of the new British erotica. His actions were momentarily quashed in 1725, when he was prosecuted for "publishing foul, lewd and obscene books tending to corrupt the morals of his Majesty's subjects" with his translation of *Vénus dans le Cloître*.[46] Despite this temporary hiatus, he continued unabated throughout the first half of the eighteenth century, until his death in 1747.[47]

Pornography was slower to take off in England than it had been in France. At the beginning of the eighteenth century, English sex literature came mainly in the form of bawdy erotica, often written by underpaid hacks. These writers took on the scientific outpourings of the Royal Society, satirizing the findings reported in its journal, *Philosophical Transactions*. Readers did not believe the incredible claims made by the society's eminent members, and writers of erotica were keen to ridicule the philosophers by way of sexual innuendo. For example, the new science of botany saw Carl Linnaeus producing a taxonomy for plants that involved sexualized terms for their parts and for fertilization. Related suggestive poems soon followed. In *Arbor Vitae, or The Natural History of the Tree of Life* (1732) and *The Natural History of the Frutex Vulvaria, or Flowering Shrub* (1732), the subject matter—genitalia—was couched in botanical terminology. In the 1770s, electricity was discovered and, once more, whimsies filled with double entendres emerged. *The Electrical Eel* (1777) and *The Torpedo* (1777) based innuendos on fish, genitalia, electricity, and magnetic sexual attraction. Little was available in England in the way of a pornographic novels until John Cleland's *Fanny Hill, or The Memoirs of a Woman of Pleasure* (1749),[48] which is now recognized as one of the first major works within its genre. From Fanny's first passionate introduction to sex by fellow whore Phoebe to her decline into flagellation with Mr. Barville to the final scene of sodomy between two men, Cleland introduced topics in turn, the order depending on their level of debauchery. From the lowest laboring poor to the highest elite, various forms of mass perception on sex emerged through England's print culture.

While the British were experimenting with erotic poems and prose in the eighteenth century, the French took their pornographic writings to new levels, developing full-blown novelistic pornography. The religious settings of the monastery and the convent provided a rich vein of imagery, with various scenarios of the seduction of nuns by monks and of young penitents by priests making use of the confessional. At the core of these writings were satires of Catholics priests, as seen in *Histoire de Dom B ..., Portiers des Chartreux* (1741), and *Thérèse Philosophe* (1748). In terms of both literary genre and the portrayal of gradations of sex scenes, French material surpassed all previous limits with Sade's exploration of depravity (e.g., *Justine, Juliette,* and *120 Days of Sodom*). Attacks on the church targeted taboos, a key ingredient in pornography. The state, royalty, and politicians also became targets of erotic writers, with pseudo-memoirs written about Marie Antoinette, Madame du Barry, and Madame de Pompadour.

Erotica has a checkered history in the East. In China, books such as *The Carnal Prayer Mat* (ca. 1634) described all sorts of sexual activity. Despite crackdowns during the Qing dynasty on sexual immorality, a few new works of erotica managed to emerge: for instance, *Pleasant Spring and Fragrant Character,* which celebrated homosexuality, was written sometime between 1796 and 1843. Lesbianism (*dui shii*) was not as frequently written about, though it was explored in Ming dynasty literature. *Stories to Awaken Men, Loving the Fragrant Companion,* and, later, *Dream of a Red Bedchamber* (1792) depicted

FIGURE 1.12: A Japanese couple making love. Colored reproduction of a woodcut by Moronobu, Edo [Tokyo], c. 1680s. Wellcome Library, London.

sex between servants and concubines, between female prostitutes, and between nuns and novices. The erotic print flourished in Japan (fig. 1.2), reaching its artistic peak during the Edo period (1600–1868), when depictions of brothel quarters and Kabuki performances became the dominant subjects.

CONCLUSION

Throughout the world, the Enlightenment period saw suppressions, and the rebellions against them, in full force. Though the prevailing authorities attempted to control sexuality and its associated behaviors and attitudes, most societies were infused with sex—whether on the streets or in the home. Overall, this was a period when procreation and fertility were considered important in virtually every country in the world. Prostitution was thought a necessary vice, its regulation attempted sporadically—but little was done to curtail it altogether. Men sought out both male and female prostitutes in order to satisfy their desires. Authorities throughout the world made more serious attempts to curb sodomy—in all its forms—and their punishments were more strict for men than for women. Little serious effort was made to curtail lesbian activities, and in many places, it went ignored. Unruly female behavior was considered a threat, and when it was noted by the community in the form of premarital sex, adultery, sexual flagrancy, or playing male roles, the authorities moved to clamp down. By the end of the eighteenth century, an increase in politeness and a rise in middle-class manners combined to inspire attitudes supportive of a more contained sexual expression within certain sections of society. Nevertheless, other sections (such as the upper classes and the laboring poor) continued to exhibit sexual licentiousness throughout the following century.

CHAPTER TWO

Heterosexuality: Europe and North America

ANNA CLARK

In eighteenth century Europe, historians have claimed, people started to have more procreative, penetrative, heterosexual sex. The evidence can be seen in the dramatic rise in the number of births inside and outside of marriage.[1] Romantic love, it is widely agreed, also became a more pervasive ideal linked to marriage (fig. 2.1). But historians have long debated why this happened, and its significance. Whatever the answer, it is clearly related to changing attitudes toward heterosexuality itself, although of course the word itself was not used until the late nineteenth century.

Today, heterosexuality is defined as the opposite of homosexuality, also a late-nineteenth-century word, but in the early modern world, heterosexuality—in terms of an identity defined by a sexual relationship with the opposite sex—is better seen in opposition to celibacy or singleness.[2] In the traditional southern European marriage pattern, men married late, and women married young. If they could not marry, many would become priests, monks, or nuns. In northern Europe, 10 to 20 percent of the population never had the opportunity to marry and form their own households, often working instead as servants or laborers for others.[3]

Northern and southern Europe shared certain assumptions about male and female sexual desires and gender roles. Medical texts advised that female

FIGURE 2.1: An outdoor marriage ceremony is performed by a priest; the young couple is surrounded by family. Engraving by P. Lightfoot after Alex Johnston (n.d.). Wellcome Library, London.

sexual pleasure was necessary for procreation, and advised husbands to please their wives. But it was still feared that women would become lusty and out of control, for their sexual desires were seen as insatiable and perhaps stronger than those of men. At the same time, as Laura Gowing writes, sex was seen as something men did to women, and women were assumed to be passive. They were supposed to control these desires and to be pure and chaste.[4] Men were supposed to be respectable, controlled patriarchs who defended the honor of their families, but it was assumed that young men—apprentices, journeymen, the unmarried—had dangerous desires that might lead them to drink, riot, rape, or seduce respectable daughters (fig 2.2).[5] In Italy, authorities might have feared that these young men would have sex with other males, but in the German states, sex between men was rarely spoken of and if men engaged in it they might regard it as a "twilight moment"—a secret shame, hard to articulate or understand.[6]

By 1650, both Protestant and Catholic authorities had been trying to emphasize the importance of monogamous marital love and to exert stricter controls over sexual morality. Protestant theologians emphasized the importance of the sexual bond between husband and wife more than did their Catholic

FIGURE 2.2: *Le Baiser Pris de Force* (a stolen kiss). Eighteenth-century engraving by Pelligrino Da Colle. Wellcome Library, London.

counterparts, yet this was still a system of strict control of sexuality. According to historian Ruth Bloch, the Puritans celebrated marital sex, but they did not necessarily see romantic love as a proper motive for marriage or as an end in itself; marital love was to be a conduit to the superior spiritual love of God. The human passions of love and lust were inferior to spiritual love.[7] The Catholic Church also emphasized mutual love within marriage; some Jesuits had tried to soften its traditional hostility toward marital sexual pleasure as an end in itself, not just for procreation (fig. 2.3), but the fear of sexual pleasure as sinful persisted. The Church also cracked on down on fornication, sodomy, and prostitution.[8]

In Spain and colonial Latin America, Catholicism coexisted with an honor culture, in which a woman's sexual chastity determined her family's honor. Church and state cooperated to exert control over marriage to preserve purity of blood. They wanted to ensure that elite political and military positions would only go to those men who descended from "old Christians," rather than converted Muslims or Jews. However, some tension existed between secular

FIGURE 2.3: The Roman Catholic sacraments: baptism. Etching published by H. Overton and J. Hoole, London (n.d.). Wellcome Library, London.

and clerical attitudes toward sexuality. The Church warned men to maintain self-control, holding up the chaste St. Joseph as an exemplar of male behavior.[9] However, aristocratic Spanish men often kept mistresses and flaunted a rather flamboyant style of masculinity. In Spanish Golden Age literature and culture, plays often depicted men as quick to kill their wives' or daughters' lovers in order to protect their family's honor, but as Abigail Dyer and Ann Twinam have shown, this culture was actually more flexible than it appeared. First, public reputation mattered more than private behavior. Among elite families, if a daughter had been seduced, Catholic priests might privately pressure her lover to marry her. An illegitimate child could also be whisked away and brought up secretly, although the seduced woman was expected to repent and to lead a blameless, pious, secluded life from then on.[10] Second, plebeian people had long held the view that fornication outside of marriage was not necessarily a sin. The Inquisition had repressed this attitude vigorously, but some remnants remained. For instance, artisanal, merchant, and laboring families might bring an action for seduction, claiming that a man had seduced one of their daughters with the promise of marriage. If the woman could show that she had lived a quiet life and had only interacted with the father of her child, the authorities were likely to force her lover to pay damages, or even to marry her. Her honor was damaged, but her public reputation could be restored by this action.[11]

In colonial Latin America, the honor culture was complicated still further by the racial hierarchy. In colonial Mexico, illegitimacy rates were quite high among urban Spanish people, Mestizos (mixed-race people), Indians, and blacks, although they were low for some rural Spanish and Indian people.[12] Rural Indians were exempted from marriage fees imposed by the state, which made it easier for them to marry. Mestizos and blacks had to obtain official permission to marry and pay high fees, which served as a deterrent, but marriage was not necessarily part of their culture. African slaves often came from polygamous societies, and masters did not encourage them to marry, as it was more profitable to break families up and sell individuals as slaves (fig 2.4).[13] As historian Susan M. Deeds observes, "Persuading Spanish men that Indian and mixed-race women were lacking in morality and worthiness was crucial to maintaining a race-based hierarchy (fig 2.5)."[14] Colonial Spanish men often engaged in short- and long-term

FIGURE 2.4: European men examining slaves at the slave market of Rio de Janeiro, by Augustus Earle after Edward Francis Finden and Maria Callcott. Published by J. Murray, London, April 5, 1824. Wellcome Library, London.

FIGURE 2.5: John Wesley preaching to American Indians. Engraving (n.d.). Wellcome Library, London.

relationships with women of Indian or African descent. These affairs were always seen as "twilight moments," hidden from the light of day, as open secrets that did not damage elite men's reputations, nor did they create a permanent lineage.[15]

As in Spain, the church had forced men to marry women they impregnated to uphold the honor of the white Spaniards. However, historian Patricia Seed has found that, from the 1670s on in Mexico, the church became less likely to enforce such marriages and more likely to enforce strict standards of chastity without the slightest hint of leeway. The church was now more interested in preventing unsuitable marriages, especially those that might bring racial or social mixing.[16] In 1776, Charles III of Spain warned young people not to get married out of love's passion, and he strengthened parental control over marriage.[17]

In northern Europe, both Protestant and Catholic authorities were trying to exert more control over marriages. Although most couples married in church with great festivity, technically, a man was considered to have married a woman if he betrothed her, that is, if he promised to marry her and had sex with her. By the mid-seventeenth century, authorities tried to restrict the validity of marriages solemnized by betrothals rather than by weddings. The French state and the Catholic Church cooperated to prevent marriages without

FIGURE 2.6: A Protestant couple stands before a clergyman in a pulpit as they take their marriage vows. Engraving (n.d.). Wellcome Library, London.

parental consent, to prevent marriages across class lines, and to enable parents to take advantage of unions from the point of view of alliances and property. Beginning in the sixteenth century, a man who married a woman without the permission of her parents could be prosecuted for *rapt de séduction:* carrying away a woman from her family without their consent, whether or not violence was used. Couples could also be pursued with a lettre de cachet from their families.[18] In England and in German-speaking areas, seventeenth century authorities became concerned that the poor would marry without being able to support themselves. In seventeenth-century Bavaria, local authorities reinforced the earlier policy of restricting marriages by license to those who could support themselves, since they did not want servants or the idle marrying and producing beggars.[19] Several rural English parishes banned marriages of laborers without permission.[20] In England, these controls over marriage were often ineffectual, because couples could still marry by license, without public bans being read, and many married in the vicinity of the Fleet in London, which had its own rules allowing for clandestine marriages.

In northern Europe, young people customarily waited until their late twenties to marry (fig. 2.6). Men did not inherit farms or businesses until their parents died, and they spent long years as apprentices, learning a trade and

FIGURE 2.7: *The Dance of Death: The Courtship*. Colored aquatint by T. Rowlandson, 1816. Wellcome Library, London.

saving enough to establish themselves. Women, too, left their families to work as servants, squirreling away their meager pay for a dowry and acquiring the skills to run a household and business. The idea of romantic love certainly existed in popular culture in ballads and broadsides, which are full of tales of courtship (fig. 2.7). Yet these popular sources also admonished young people to take practical considerations into account when choosing a spouse—was a woman frugal, a good worker, a wise companion? Or a flibbertigibbet and flighty? Was a man a spendthrift or unfaithful, did he drink too much? Or did he have a good trade and a steady temperament? Autobiographies and diaries of working people reveal that some of them certainly made impulsive matches with women or men who had no resources, but they usually consulted their "friends" (the wider group of kin, employers, and neighbors who helped and advised them) about the suitability of a match.[21] The youth, especially male youths, and their parents may have had conflicts over who controlled courting, and young men closely observed nearby girls as a way of ensuring they would marry locally, chasing off boys from other villages.[22]

Young men and women flirted with each other at church, fairs, and dances, and they also engaged in kissing and fondling without penetrative intercourse.[23] It is unclear if this was a new phenomenon or an ancient one. For instance, clerics described such practices among French peasants in the Vendée as *maraichinage vendéan*, an "ancient custom." Although Church leaders preached against such indulgences, they were not regarded as a terrible sin, but merely as something people were not supposed to do but did anyhow. These activities might have incurred shame and anxiety, but would not result in social disgrace.[24]

Young people could engage in such sexual practices during ritualized night courting. In parts of Germany, young men would sneak into the spinning rooms, where young women would meet at night to spin and share candlelight. But local authorities tried to ensure that matrons would be present and that they kept track of the boys and girls who attended.[25] In Norway, parents allowed their daughters' beaux to visit at night, cuddling and courting in a dark corner, or even staying the night, keeping their clothes on—or at least their undergarments; the girl would stay under the covers and the boy would lie on top of the covers; or a board could be put between the two in bed. By permitting this, parents at least knew who was courting their daughter, and they could supervise.[26] Even for colonial American Puritans, night courting allowed couples to get to know each other, since affection, companionship, and even sexual pleasure were thought to be the basis for a strong marriage.[27]

Clerical and secular authorities kept down the number of out-of-wedlock pregnancies, issuing harsh punishments for both the women and men involved. In England during the mid-seventeenth-century, the Puritan church courts scrutinized the sexual behavior of villagers, and prenuptial pregnancy and illegitimacy remained very low and even declined.[28] Along with local authorities, masters and mistresses of servants closely monitored female servants in northern England, watching for signs of pregnancy, because they feared they might be left with the burden of raising a fatherless child.[29] In Scotland, unmarried couples were scolded by Kirk courts and had to stand in sackcloth and ashes in front of the church door.[30] In seventeenth-century Virginia, "whippings, fines, and public confession were the punishments for fornication."[31] In New England, courts even prosecuted couples who gave birth to children less than nine months after marriage.[32] In Sweden, churches punished and shunned unmarried mothers. They could not take part in church activities and had to face official humiliation in front of the congregation. As a result, few of them subsequently married.[33] In France, authorities required that every pregnancy be registered, and midwives harshly questioned women when they were in labor in order to discover the father of their child so that he might be forced to pay child support. Women also closely monitored their neighbors for sexual misbehavior, such as illicit pregnancy, selling sex, or adultery; if a woman was reported, she could be incarcerated in the Hôpital des Refuges in Marseilles, or the Pitié-Salpêtrière hospital in Paris.[34]

Illegitimacy, however, started to grow, and by the middle of the eighteenth century, it was skyrocketing. Prenuptial pregnancy was rising at the same time.

The rate of illegitimacy followed the rate of legitimate births; people were having more heterosexual sex within and without marriage and having more offspring. During the eighteenth century, whatever factors had inhibited young people from full penetrative intercourse during customs such as night courting seem to have been eroded. In New England, the word *bundling* began to be used for night courting in the eighteenth century, describing a custom by which young men and women would lie together in bed, fully clothed. Richard Godbeer suggests that bundling became institutionalized in response to the decline of Puritan influence and the rise of premarital pregnancies.[35] In German states, for instance, almost one-third of births were conceived before marriage by 1839, which represented a significant rise since 1700, according to historian John Knodel.[36] In the Netherlands, bridal pregnancies rose to 20 to 30 percent after 1750 and remained high, but except in times of hardship, illegitimacy was also low. With the custom of night courtship, parents knew who their daughters were courting.[37] In rural Kent villages in England, pregnancy rates could be as high as 40 to 46 percent in the early nineteenth century, suggesting that sex between betrothed couples was widely accepted.[38] In nineteenth-century Swedish villages, about 30 percent of prides were pregnant.[39] As historian Richard Adair points out, high rates of prenuptial pregnancy were not necessarily accompanied by high rates of illegitimacy.[40]

Some historians suggest that proto-industrialization caused premarital sex, illegitimacy, and population growth. As new opportunities for waged work emerged, young people did not have to wait to save enough to start a business or to inherit a farm in order to marry. Young men, and even young women, were at the peak of their earning power in their early twenties. And indeed, the age of marriage dropped in many places, especially in England. A segment of the population responded to the availability of waged labor by marrying at younger ages and therefore having more children. Some may have had sex intending to get married, but other factors foiled their plans, and illegitimate births resulted.[41] But the age of marriage also dropped in areas with no proto-industrialization, possibly because declining wages for women made them more inclined to marry earlier.[42] In contrast, in southern Europe the age of marriage rose in many areas, most notably for women, and fewer women married during the eighteenth century, which may have been due to economic decline. In southern Germany, the age of marriage rose, but illegitimacy and premarital sex increased.[43] In general, the rise of illegitimacy preceded industrialization. In some countries, such as many of the German and Austrian states and Scotland, illegitimacy was higher in rural areas. In France, illegitimacy rose in cities prior to industrialization.[44]

Although economic changes, such as the growth in the number of landless laborers) were important, cultural factors probably played a greater role in determining the changes in the age of marriage, prenuptial pregnancy, and illegitimacy. For instance, in parts of Germany and Italy, the rates of these behaviors were similar in contiguous urban and rural districts where people would migrate back and forth.[45] The rise in illegitimacy therefore seems to have been caused by the persistence of the custom of sex after a promise of marriage, combined with economic upheaval and migration, which prevented men from fulfilling these promises, and a decline in the ability and willingness of authorities to prevent and punish sex outside of marriage. This was coupled with the fact that traditional religious authorities were losing influence, and their ability to punish illegitimate pregnancies diminished. In the early nineteenth century in the Netherlands, churches became less democratic and less enmeshed in their communities as they become more hierarchical, and therefore they lost their influence over the sexual customs of young people.[46] In Sweden, from 1741 on, unmarried mothers no longer had to go through a public purification ceremony to cleanse their shame, but instead they faced the minister in private. The authorities were increasingly worried that such intense public shame had increased infanticide and deprived the country of the population it needed for military and economic growth.[47] In 1765, Frederick the Great declared that unmarried mothers would no longer have to submit to shaming punishments, because he saw them as victims of seduction and abandonment.[48] Similarly, in England, church courts no longer prosecuted fornication, although in Scotland, Kirk sessions still charged unwed mothers—as well as fathers—with that offense. In France, courts were more concerned with forcing men to marry or provide for their illegitimate offspring than with punishing unwed mothers.[49] In New England, young people, especially in urban areas, were no longer so interested in the old Puritan ideals. In two counties in eighteenth-century Virginia, the number of couples summoned by parish authorities for premarital sex, fornication, or bastardy declined greatly.[50]

Secular authorities started to become concerned with the health and numbers of their inhabitants, so they tried to prevent infanticide by opening foundling hospitals and softening the laws on illegitimacy. Instead of punishing unmarried mothers, the benefactors of the Foundling Hospital in London (fig. 2.8) wanted to provide the opportunity for them to restore their reputations.[51] In Italy, parish priests actually encouraged young, pregnant, unwed women to abandon their newborn babies at the foundling hospital, so that they could conceal their shame. This would also prevent them from causing trouble for the men who impregnated them.[52] In eighteenth-century France, it was very

FIGURE 2.8: The Foundling Hospital, Holborn, London: a perspective view looking northeast at the main building, with penitent mothers arriving beside a statue of fortune. Engraving by Samuel Wale after Charles Grignion, Pierre-Charles Canot, Theodore Jacobsen, John Russell, and Margrett Granville. London, 1749. Wellcome Library, London.

common for married women to put babies out to nurse, so unmarried mothers could easily send their babies to nurse and go back to life as a "respectable" woman. However, these nurslings often died, and mortality rates in the foundling hospitals were extremely high.[53]

Another major reason for the rise in illegitimacy was that working women continued to follow the tradition of sex after a man promised marriage, but changing social and economic conditions meant that some men were no longer willing or able to fulfill these promises. Women who courted soldiers or sailors were particularly unlucky, for the many wars of the century could tear the fathers of their children away from them. In Lille in the second half of the eighteenth century, the textile industry declined and the price of bread rose, making it more difficult for couples to marry, and increasing the number of illegitimate births.[54] In the early-nineteenth-century Netherlands, an economic depression significantly increased the rate of illegitimacy, as couples who might have previously married upon pregnancy could no longer do so.[55] In one rural

Swedish town in the early nineteenth century, the timber industry began to buy up farms, making it difficult for a young man to afford to buy a new farm when he married. As a result, they continued to engage in premarital sex with their sweethearts but delayed marrying them until they had given birth to several children.[56]

In northern Burgundy, a woman could be abandoned if her boyfriend's parents refused to allow him to marry her.[57] Female orphans were particularly vulnerable because they had no fathers to pressure the men who impregnated them; in Lille, 70 percent of unmarried mothers had lost one parent, most often the father.[58] Servants were especially at risk because they were likely to have left their homes in search of work. As a result, they were lonely and isolated, and they were eager for male attention. The stereotype of popular literature, as seen in Samuel Richardson's *Pamela,* was that these women were raped or seduced by their masters, but far more often, the fathers of their children were men of their own class. They met men as they did the shopping in the market, cleaned the front doorstep, and did other errands. Usually, they were courted by men they worked with—the butlers, grooms, and other male servants who worked in the house, or apprentices and journeymen.[59] But if a servant became pregnant, her parents were far away and could not pressure a man to marry her.

Some women became pregnant as a result of rape. In Lille, a few of the women examined by midwives declared they had been raped on the roads as they traveled in search of work, or when they had encountered a band of soldiers.[60] But most women were raped by men they knew, and once again, servants were the most vulnerable. In 1772, London publican George Carter apparently raped his new sixteen-year-old servant; his wife told her, "he always served all his servants so the night they came into the house," inferring that it was common practice for her husband to force all his female employees to have sex with him. But servants were much more likely to be raped by fellow servants, whom they encountered while cleaning the silver together, or alone in a back parlor. Yet authorities were reluctant to convict men for rape; in England, juries convicted only 7 to 13 percent of men accused of raping adult women. However, conviction rates for attempted rape were higher, about twenty five percent. Part of this is due to the fact that juries were reluctant to sentence men to death for rape, even though they were willing to convict men to death for minor property offenses. Furthermore, a woman who had been raped was regarded as having lost her chastity. If she took her rapist to court, she had to testify about the sexual act of violence, and by speaking about sex, her reputation was further damaged. In colonial America, most men who were punished for rape were of African descent, while white men were usually not convicted for the same offense.[61]

Furthermore, rape and seduction tended to be confused by the culture of the time. In either case, a woman had lost her honor, and her consent was not terribly relevant—except to her. In Foundling Hospital cases, women sometimes said they had been "seduced by force" or "seduced without her consent," usually by men they knew, such as fellow servants or even fiancés. Between 1815 and 1824, 9.5 percent of petitioners to the Foundling Hospital in London used such language; it does not seem that officials at that time asked them if they had been forced, and evidence of force made little difference in whether they were admitted.[62]

Not all women were seduced—or forced—into sex. Women could also be tempted by their own desires: before the 1790s, only 18 percent of petitioners to the London Foundling Hospital excused their pregnancy by saying the father promised marriage.[63] In rural areas, women may have been carried away at times of special events such as hiring fairs, harvest festivals, or dances. Women may have expected a romantic relationship, not necessarily marriage, but perhaps cohabitation. Female servants in urban areas could be tempted into sex by the promise of a pastry or a trip to the theater.

In some areas of Scotland, southern Germany, Austria, and Sweden, illegitimacy was often the outcome of independent customs in which it was common to have sex before, or instead of, marriage. In these areas, owners of large farms would hire servants who would sleep in haylofts, barns, and what in Scotland were called "bothies." Landless farm laborers were quite mobile, so the fathers of these illegitimate children could easily disappear, although they would not have been able to afford to support children in any case. The stigma attached to illegitimate children diminished, and the need for labor was so great that employers would willingly accept these illegitimate children to use as farmhands. The young women who worked in the fields were involved in reaping, harvesting, and tending the fields while their parents helped to bring up their offspring.[64]

Changes in the definition of marriage meant that some couples may have considered themselves married when authorities did not, and therefore their children would appear in the statistics of illegitimacy. In northern Burgundy a persistent popular belief that marriage was defined by a solemn promise and cohabitation continued although the church opposed this belief and insisted on a proper ceremony.[65] In England, Hardwicke's Marriage Act of 1753, which was introduced to prevent clandestine marriage, may have contributed to the rise in illegitimacy. Previously, a woman could claim she had been married if she had consented to sex after betrothal, but these unions were no longer valid.

Historian Jona Schellekens asserts that Hardwicke's Act could explain one-third of the rise in illegitimacy; the rest she attributes to the decline in real wages, and the rise in the number of people expecting to marry whose plans were thwarted.[66] However, Rebecca Probert has argued that the idea that a solemn contract and sexual intercourse formed a marriage had faded in English society long before Hardwick's Act, and that most couples solemnized their marriages in church. While many couples did cohabit after Hardwicke's Act, evidence for popular alternative marriage ceremonies, such as jumping the broomstick, is largely mythical.[67] Furthermore, illegitimacy rates rose before the passing of the Marriage Act, rising also in other parts of Europe where regulations about marriage did not change. However, in Scotland, irregular marriage remained both illegal and accepted. The Kirk sessions would impose a fine on couples who had forgone the marriage ceremony, but if the marriage was based on the consent of the parties and they paid the fine, the marriage acquired legal standing. Furthermore, one-third of marriages were irregular because they took place in non-Church of Scotland Kirks.[68]

In urban areas, some people may have cohabited rather than married, although it is unclear how much this was an alternative form of morality or just the result of the difficulty of marrying. In Paris in the early nineteenth century, the illegitimacy rate was 30 percent, which suggests that many of the parents of these children were actually cohabiting. One reason for this was that couples had to travel to their hometowns to gain expensive letters from local authorities in order to marry, which many could not afford to do. Needleworkers and artisans were among those most likely to cohabit, although historian Rachel Fuchs suggests that many of these women would probably have preferred the security of marriage.[69] In the German states, the policy of restricting marriage was intensified in the early nineteenth century, causing a rise in births outside of marriage, many of which may have been from cohabiting couples.[70] However, in London many people who cohabited did not openly affirm their unmarried status as an alternative morality; rather, they often passed as married. Neighbors, however, might spread rumors that women were not actually married.

In all classes, female adultery was anathema. Traditionally, villagers shamed men whose wives cuckolded them by putting horns on their doors, and by putting bushes in front of the houses of unchaste women. "Rough music"—banging pots and pans—could also be inflicted on women who accused men of rape.[71] But plebeians also recognized that marriages could break down, and divorce was not available at all to them. Only the very rich could afford the act of parliament required to divorce and remarry. So some English plebeians developed a custom of "wife sales," in which a husband who wanted to get rid of his wife would bring her along to a market, put a halter around her, and sell her to the highest bidder. In London, this usually took place at Smithfield meatmarket, but it was also practiced in rural areas. This custom, however, may have been characteristic of the more misogynist sentiment of English plebeian society and certainly was not universally accepted. Furthermore, the "sale" was often prearranged with the wife's lover, because it was seen as giving a contractual legitimacy to the breakup of one marriage and the formation of another, even though it was not legal in the eyes of higher authorities.[72]

While men could visit prostitutes, keep mistresses, and father bastard children, only prostitutes, gamblers, and actresses could have affairs with men without ruining their livelihoods—their reputations were already compromised. For instance, Mme de Saint-Amarand managed to land on her feet after her husband ran through both their fortunes; she began liaisons with the Prince de Conti and other well-connected noblemen in the world of late-eighteenth-century high finance. These connections enabled her to open up a salon that featured gambling, allowing her a lucrative pursuit. But families of such women could often limit their activities with a lettre de cachet from the government ordering them to be imprisoned.[73] Mary Robinson was an actress who became the mistress of the Prince of Wales, and she acquired a generous financial settlement when he moved on. She eventually became the lover for many years of the rakish politician Banastre Tarleton. However, he eventually left her for a younger woman, whereupon she wrote a feminist tract complaining that men would rather enjoy the mindless pleasures of young beauty than the mature companionship of an intellectual women.[74] Even women in radical philosophical circles felt it best to remain discreet when conducting love affairs. Julie de Lespinasse, for instance, knew well of the torments of love in her own life. The illegitimate daughter of a married noblewoman and her lover, she was not recognized by her family and was left without a fortune. However, she was able to become an influential *salonierre,* forming a close platonic friendship with the mathematician d'Alembert, living in adjoining apartments, although d'Alembert was unaware that Julie was wracked with a fatal passion for a young libertine man. She apparently died of heartbreak after he married.[75]

One characteristic of this era was increasing class differences in terms of sexual morality. In the earlier period, the commitment to religious ideals of chastity was probably universally shared. However, differences between the classes started to widen in the mid-eighteenth century, as premarital pregnancy, and to an even greater extent, illegitimacy, became much higher among plebeians. In early-nineteenth-century Kent, the only families with no illegitimate births were gentry, clergy, large farmers, and craftsmen. In the German states, prenuptial births were highest among proletarians, lowest among farmers, but prenuptial pregnancy was high among all groups except businessmen.[76] However, class differences in morality could still be quite blurred, especially among those on the borderline of classes, such as some English artisans, tradesmen, and shopkeepers, who might keep up a facade of respectability but still engage in premarital sex and cohabitation. For the higher ranks of the middle class merchants, bankers, farmers and professionals, a reputation for chastity was much more important. They depended on obtaining credit from a network of kin and fellow professionals or merchants, and a respectable reputation was essential for these transactions. Of course, they did not always live up to this ideal in practice, and middle-class families particularly worried about sons sowing wild oats.[77]

Religion often created fault lines around sexual respectability, cutting across families and neighborhoods. The Jansenists in France, the Pietists in Germany, and the Methodists and Evangelicals in Britain followed very strict sexual practices. However, these standards were not imposed from without by authorities; instead, believers internalized the pious practice of chastity, controlling themselves through self-discipline and prayer, as well as through the scrutiny of chapel meetings, where those who indulged in the pleasures of popular culture, such as dancing and masquerades, were expelled.

The ideal of romantic love—and the view that it led to marriage and continued within it—became prevalent in the late eighteenth century. While affection was not unknown in earlier centuries, husbands and wives tended to write to each other in more formal terms. But historians of northern Europe have found increasing evidence that husbands and wives wrote more affectionately and romantically to each other in the eighteenth century. This was also found in Spain and the New World. Husbands began writing to their wives, pining during their absence, describing themselves as their "slaves," and using such endearments as "esteemed mistress of my heart" and "beloved."[78] Beginning in the late seventeenth century, sex manuals such as *Aristotle's Masterpiece* (published in many editions from the seventeenth through the nineteenth centuries) and Nicholas de Venette's *Conjugal Love* (first published in 1691, with many subsequent editions) gave detailed instructions of how husbands should give their wives orgasms which no doubt aided marital romance (see Chapter 6). Historians have debated whether it was the aristocracy or the middle class and gentry that initiated the transition in which romantic love came to be seen as a prerequisite for marriage. Among the middle class, young people could choose their own partners—if they came from the right family and had the right property or profession. Among the aristocracy, marriages had traditionally been arranged for reasons of dynastic connection and property, although parents would allow marriage for love if the potential partner was an advantageous match for the family. Men kept mistresses and could even keep a *maîtresse en titre,* such as Louis XV's Madame de Pompadour. Aristocratic women did take lovers after producing an heir, yet they needed to be extremely discreet, for they faced the danger of being imprisoned in a convent (in France) or divorced and disgraced (from the 1690s on in England). Randolph Trumbach has argued that, by the mid-eighteenth century, the ideal of romantic love emerged in the aristocracy, linked with ideas of egalitarianism, more permissive child-rearing, and the challenge to patriarchal control over sons.[79] But romantic love was not the same as egalitarianism.[80] Once married, a wife needed to carefully cultivate her husband's affections and subordinate her interests to his. Romantic love made the subordination of a wife to her husband seem glamorous and sentimental, not just a grim duty.

The punishment of adultery among the elite could paradoxically be seen as an outcome of the emphasis on romantic love. With the expansion of the press,

FIGURE 2.9: A crowd gathers (with some onlookers throwing confetti) to cheer on a couple whose horse-drawn carriage waits to take them to the church for their wedding. Engraving (n.d.). Wellcome Library, London.

especially by the 1770s in England, elite adultery came under public scrutiny. In 1770, the Duke of Cumberland (the king's son) was charged by the Earl of Grosvenor with seducing his wife and forced to pay a huge sum in damages (what would amount to around $2,000,000 today), which was widely seen as discrediting the reputation of the monarchy. Although many moralists, as was traditional, blamed women for adultery, increasingly the seducer was seen as at fault. Both moralists and press commentators blamed men for seeing the seduction of married women as a form of entertaining "gallantry." Some commentators argued that marital fidelity was characteristic of the middle class, as opposed to aristocratic decadence. Furthermore, as Donna Andrew has found, they blamed adultery on the perceived aristocratic practice of arranging marriages (fig. 2.9), rather than allowing romantic love to blossom between two young people. By the early nineteenth century, the campaign against aristocratic adultery was so vigorous that far fewer cases were publicized in the newspapers. It is not known if the incidence diminished, but perhaps lovers became more discreet.[81]

This issue demonstrates the tension between two ideals of sexual conduct: libertinism and romantic love. They were at odds with each other in eighteenth-century culture, providing grist for the mill of novelists and philosophers alike. Among oppositional Enlightenment thinkers, known as *philosophes,* both libertinism and romantic love were seen as ways of struggling against the dictates of church and state, which had conspired to ensure that marriages were based on parental wishes and property concerns. These thinkers celebrated heterosexual desire, against older religious assumptions that sexual desire was polluting. The philosophes attacked the Catholic church for celebrating chastity and irrationally suppressing a natural sexual desire that did not hurt anyone. Chastity, or its close relative, continence, Diderot argued, brought no benefits to the celibate individual, or to society as a whole. In fact, he proclaimed, "there is nothing so puerile, ridiculous, absurd, harmful, contemptible and bad as these two rare qualities." For Diderot, pleasure was the "principle of life and energy" that drove human beings to action.[82] Desire for sex, like ambition and pleasure-seeking, impelled humans toward each other; it spurred not only love, but sociability, commerce, and society itself.[83]

Libertinism stemmed from two sources, the philosophical and the social. The eighteenth-century libertine descended from the seventeenth-century rake, a familiar character in literature and life. The classic male libertine pursued and seduced the most unavailable women.[84] The most notorious of all rakes was Lord Rochester, Earl of Wilmot, who led a merry band of men who "frolicked" near London, drank to excess, ran through parks naked, seduced (and even assaulted) women, and in general caused scandal.[85] But Rochester also had a philosophical basis for his actions. Libertinism was originally associated with freethinkers, those who questioned religion.[86]

Many of these philosophers were part of what is known as the Radical Enlightenment. They rejected the idea that conventional religious morality came from God and they were accused of criticizing the idea of original sin and divine retribution in order to justify their own debauchery. As Jonathan Israel has noted, "why live in dread of divine retribution for profligacy, adultery, and debauchery if one can live entirely free of remorse and dread of the Day of Judgment?" But many libertines actually had a serious philosophical basis for their beliefs, as historian Israel observes. The basis of human knowledge should not be ancient authorities, but direct observation and physical experience—as in the experience of sex.[87] As they learned of other cultures where sexual customs were very different, they began to realize the relativity of morality, and focus on "Nature," rather than the institution of the church, as the origin of right and wrong. Some philosophes admired the Canadian Indians, whom the writer Lahontan described as deist, worshiping nature and leaving "their daughters free, outside marriage, to enjoy the use of men for sex just as they pleased."[88]

For most, although not all libertines, sexual pleasure was intended to be strictly heterosexual (although they did not yet use that word), between men and women. John Wilkes, for instance, was a classic late-eighteenth-century libertine. His notorious clandestine publication, *The Essay on Woman,* romped through ridiculously erudite puns celebrating the joys of sex between men and women (and denigrating sex between men). Above all, it proclaimed, "Fucking's the End and cause of human State, / And man must fuck, or God will not create." But the *Essay* also satirized political and religious targets with a more serious intent.[89] Wilkes felt it was his duty to use obscenity against the king and clerical authority, because, according to one theory, European monarchs became theocratic despots when they regarded any criticisms of themselves as blasphemy. In other works, he declared that "at least he sinned naturally," implying that his enemies committed sodomy.[90] Because sodomites were increasingly thought to be sexually interested only in men, a man accused of sodomy could assert his adventures with prostitutes, for instance, to demonstrate his innocence.[91] French Enlightenment philosophers for the most part defined sodomites as *anti-physiques*—that is, those who rejected the natural imperative to love women and procreate.[92] More radical philosophers (especially in the pornographic genre) challenged the link between procreation and pleasure, arguing specifically that nonprocreative forms of pleasure, such as masturbation, were acceptable; some even entertained, although they did not endorse, the notion that sex between men was not necessarily unnatural.[93] But for the most part, those philosophes were underground and beyond the pale of respectability.

Libertinage, not surprisingly, was much more problematic for women. The radical philosophical pornographers portrayed women as endlessly curious about sex, eager to entertain any adventures with any combination of men and women; but these authors invented these characters out of their own fantasies. But the eponymous Thérèse Philosophe, the heroine of the pornographic novel of the same name, hesitates to engage in heterosexual penetrative sex because she fears pregnancy. Her lover then teaches her means of avoiding that fate, practicing withdrawal.[94] It is possible that such information contributed to the decline in the French birth rate in the eighteenth century.[95] However, especially by the later eighteenth century libertine philosophers presented sex in a rather cold way, as the indulgence of physical appetites—man as a machine—rather than as a relationship between two people; women were a means to an end, to be manipulated and discarded.[96] Late-eighteenth-century libertines feared and denigrated romantic love, because this emotion would leave them enthralled to women and unable to continue experiencing new sensations.[97]

Choderlos de Laclos' novel, *Les Liaisons Dangereuses,* demonstrated the tensions between libertinism and romantic love. The main character, the Marquise de Merteuil, takes many lovers, but she follows a policy of utmost discretion, never writing letters to her lovers, and admitting them to her apartments only at night through a back entrance. In public, she presents herself as a prude. The marquise and her former lover, Valmont, regard love as a game of conquest. The marquise therefore sets Valmont a challenge: to seduce the virtuous, pious Madame de Tourvel—and obtain love letters from her as proof. However, Valmont falls desperately in love with Madame de Tourvel. The marquise is furious, because she is really still in love with Valmont. Romantic love proved more powerful than libertinism, although in some ways Laclos was satirizing both tendencies.[98]

The philosophe Denis Diderot served as a link between libertinism and romantic love. In his earlier published writings and later unpublished writings, he playfully explored libertine adventures, though he linked nature, romantic love, sexual passion, and procreation in his published writings. Unlike the Catholic Church, he did not see procreation as the only justification for sexual desire; instead, he posited that nature implanted sexual desires and pleasure in humans to draw men and women together for the purposes of procreation. But it was specifically relations between men and women that he saw as natural. As Diderot wrote in the *Encyclopédie,* "When an individual presents himself to another of the same species and a different sex, the feeling for all other needs is suspended; the heart palpitates; the limbs quiver; voluptuous images roam the brain; the torrents of the spirit flow into the nerves, irritate them and then move to the core of a new sense, which manifests itself and torments in turn. Vision is blurred, delirium is born; reason, a slave to instinct, contents itself with serving it, and Nature is satisfied."[99] Of course, Diderot also differentiated between lust, which was just the desire for the body, and true love, which could restrain these impetuous passions. Marriage should be founded on the excitement of *jouissance* (enjoyment, often sexual), but tempered over the years with friendship, companionship, and trust.[100]

In the eighteenth century, novelists began to explore romantic love not just as a tremendous passion that overcame lovers, but as an internal emotion that demonstrates their acute sensibility, especially the sensibility of women. Rousseau's exploration of romantic love in the novel *Julie, or la Nouvelle Heloise,* appealed to women because he focused on the emotions, the imagination, and the moral dilemmas faced by women as they struggled between arranged

FIGURE 2.10: A young couple waits as a contract of marriage is drawn up and the servant waits to take the stop out of the barrel. Etching and engraving by Jean-Charles Boquoy after Jan Steen (n.d.). Wellcome Library, London.

marriages and romantic love (fig. 2.10). Julie is madly and mutually in love with her tutor, St. Preux, and they indulge in sexual passion. But they cannot marry, because Julie's father has arranged a match with his friend, an older man. Julie dutifully accepts the match, but she eventually drowns, perhaps unable to reconcile her romantic passion with her marriage. Rousseau upheld the value of conventional marriage but made romantic love seem attractive. For Rousseau and other French philosophers, marriage should not be based on property, but on genuine and natural love between men and women.[101]

Moralists feared that women would be adversely influenced by reading novels and would be lead into romantic delusions; they might even run off with unsuitable men. But romantic love could also be seen as an emanation of women's superior refinement and sensibility, motivated not by crude lust but by genuine emotion. The romantic love of a good woman, some novels hinted, could reform a rake.[102] Whereas earlier moralists had drawn on religion to warn that women must restrain their natural sexual voraciousness to preserve their sexual honor, late-eighteenth-century British moralists began to assume that women did not have strong sexual feelings, and that their inner sense of honor would enable them to withstand the temptations of illicit romance.[103] According to Ruth Bloch, the emotions of romantic love came to be valued in part because of the evangelical revival, which stressed intense personal conversion experiences.[104] Protestant moralists in Germany, for instance, celebrated the custom of allowing young men and women to socialize in parlors, balls, and churches, so that they could learn to interact with each other while controlling their emotions, and so girls could learn to judge men's characters.[105] For instance, one English novel argued that "girls should not be brought up as mere passive machines, or encourage a weak pliancy of temper that may render them liable to imposition."[106] Women were seen as more modest and virtuous than men, as Dr. Gregory of the famous advice books noted, women's "superior delicacy, your modesty, and the usual severity of your education, preserve you ... from any temptation to those vices to which [men] are most subjected."[107] But this also placed on women the responsibility to control men's passions.

Romantic love was also linked to changes in masculinity. Commentators recognized the rake's continuing appeal—his dangerous pleasure-seeking—but the new image of the sentimental man challenged him, at least in fiction. The ideal man in both middle-class and aristocratic circles was self-controlled above all, polished, polite, and refined. The man of sensibility could feel intense romantic love, but he could control his sexual desires until marriage.[108]

Eighteenth-century philosophers also used romantic love as a way of thinking about the stages of civilization. As Bloch writes, romantic love was now seen as "civilizing and stabilizing rather than individualistic and anarchic." By learning to love their wives and children, men learned to love their neighbors and society as a whole. By loving in a refined and delicate way, they also advanced civilization.[109] Some more optimistic Enlightenment philosophers believed that rational men could control their own sexual energies as part of the democratic process, for men must also learn to govern their own desires in order to govern themselves in a democratic system. As Thomas Laqueur notes, Kant differentiated between sexual desire as an animalistic appetite, and the love for others, which was the foundation of the family. Civil society could manage these passions, as men became "self-determining" citizens "whose actions would be governed by reason."[110] As Isabel Hull explores, heterosexual desire was an important theme for the eighteenth-century cameralists, the German theorists about government in states such as Bavaria. They believed that desire was a form of energy that, if channeled into marriage, would become a source of genius, innovation, and industry. By pursuing their own interests, à la Adam Smith, they would benefit the stability of society.[111] Thomas Malthus also recognized sexual desire as the drive that impelled men to form attachments, motivating them to labor for their families. However, Malthus thought that this drive toward procreation would inevitably cause overpopulation, leading to famine and death. He therefore exposed the dangers even in the seemingly benign vision of the procreative heterosexual family.[112]

By the first decades of the nineteenth century, Malthusian theorists sought to deter working-class people from marrying, so they would not breed paupers. Nonetheless, demographic changes and romantic love meant that heterosexuality (as opposed to celibacy) was becoming a more universal ideal, at least in northern Europe. More people were having procreative sex, whether in or outside of marriage. Significant changes occurred in notions about feminine sexuality—instead of being seen as insatiable, women were now seen as more delicate and refined. They were now thought better able to control their passions and to have weaker sexual feelings than men. Romantic love was now seen as the glue that held society together via marriage—but sexual passion outside of marriage was still feared for its destructive power to dissolve these bonds.

CHAPTER THREE

Homosexuality

RICTOR NORTON

The period between 1650 and 1820 witnessed several significant new developments in the history of homosexuality. In mainland Europe, laws against homosexuality were significantly reformed or abolished, and even in Britain they were subjected to critical rational scrutiny and sometimes judged to be unjust or at least too severe. From the late seventeenth century onward, the religious discourse of sodomy became increasingly superseded by a secular conception of the homosexual as a type of person, having a clearly recognized sexual orientation, characterized mainly in terms of gender inversion. Despite pleas by philosophers and legal thinkers for greater tolerance, homosexual behavior was more actively prosecuted and regulated during this period than in preceding centuries, with the result that abundant evidence about ordinary homosexual lives has become available (especially in trial records) for the modern historian to study. And perhaps most significantly, a well-organized male homosexual subculture became highly visible—to contemporary society as well as to modern historians—with its own social networks, clubs, cruising grounds, and subcultural practices including homosexual marriages. This primarily working-class subculture seemed to have much in common with modern homosexual subcultures, in contrast to the elite court circles that had previously been the focus of scholarly study. These developments apply mainly to male homosexuality, but lesbians also attracted greater public attention during this period and became more visible in the historical record as well. Taken together, these new developments suggest the emergence of a "modern" understanding of homosexuality.

HISTORY AND THEORY

There has, however, been much debate among historians and theorists about precisely when—or even *if*, and if so, why—there arose a genuinely "modern homosexual" who could be distinguished from a "premodern homosexual" (or sodomite). Most of the argument concerning this subject has arisen from social constructionist theories, expressed notably by Mary McIntosh, Michel Foucault, Jeffrey Weeks, Robert Padgug, Kenneth Plummer, Alan Bray, and David Halperin[1]—and, subsequently, by a new generation addressing the subject of queer theory (notably, Judith Butler, Eve Kosofsky Sedgwick, Thomas Laqueur,[2] and a few French theorists such as Jacques Lacan, Jacques Derrida, Gilles Deleuze, and Félix Guattari). Some of the key constructionist claims are that the sodomite has been construed (constructed) by society with such a wide variety of meanings that he cannot be pinned down to a fixed category with an unchanging meaning, or essence; that the very idea of sexual orientation is a modern invention established in the late nineteenth century, mainly through medical discourse, which constructed a strict heterosexual/homosexual dichotomy (or binarism) to facilitate the needs of bourgeois capitalism (thus Halperin states, "'sexuality' seems indeed to be a uniquely modern, Western, even bourgeois production"[3]); that, prior to what we consider modern times, homosexuality was characterized not by a sense of identity, but by sexual acts, which were usually aligned along so-called active/passive roles (or "structures of power"); that sexuality is a "discursive" construct constituted, for example, by labels, hence "homosexuals" did not exist until the term (and its contextual "discourse") was invented in 1869 (thus Foucault states, "Homosexuality appeared as one of the forms of sexuality when it was transposed from the practice of sodomy onto a kind of superior androgyny, a hermaphroditism of the soul. The sodomite had been a temporary aberration; the homosexual was now a species"[4]). Although these theoretical claims have focused mainly on the contrasts between ancient and medieval history on the one hand, and nineteenth- and twentieth-century history on the other, they have informed many histories of the Enlightenment period between these two extremes.

In contrast, many traditional historians, who have been branded as "essentialists" because they take a "commonsense" view of reality, have been rather bemused by all this theorizing, which seems to fly in the face of empirical evidence. The claim that no modern conceptualization of homosexuality existed prior to 1870 is, in my view,[5] the weakest part of the constructionist theory, because the evidence to the contrary is so abundant before that date. For instance, even as early as 1734, Dutch sodomites were described by contemporaries as "hermaphrodites in their minds"[6]—an exact match for Foucault's "hermaphroditism of the soul." Although the modern concept of homosexual orientation seems to be easily matched by premodern discourse that regularly used similar directional metaphors such as "unnatural inclination," and although some essentialists have pointed to abundant evidence documenting a premodern perception that a certain minority of men and women had a so-called deviant form of desire that was integral to their personality, the constructionist approach attained hegemonic dominance by the mid-1990s. But increasing recognition of the inadequacy of the Foucauldian model has been gathering apace. For example, Amy Richlin has demonstrated that, in ancient Rome, passive homosexual men "lived with a social identity and a social burden much like the one that Foucault defined for the modern term 'homosexual.'"[7] Thomas Hubbard has similarly concluded that many ancient writers considered sexual preference to be an inborn and distinguishing characteristic of individuals,[8] while David Robinson has demonstrated, "against the overwhelming consensus in the History of Sexuality, Lesbian and Gay Studies, and queer theory, that there are important continuities in the history of male and female same-sex love and lust, spanning the periods before, during, and after the modern 'invention' of homosexuality," specifically by demonstrating the existence of a type of coded communication in late-sixteenth- through mid-eighteenth-century British and French literature that would have been impossible without the existence of self-aware homosexual mentalities.[9] For medieval northern Europe, Bernd-Ulrich Hergemöller acknowledges the striking analogies and parallels between early forms of everyday homosexual life and more modern homosexual subcultures, commenting that, "with each finding of a new source, the basis of 'essentialist' facts expands."[10] For Renaissance England, Michael Young argues that a distinctively modern view of homosexuality was already well established by the early seventeenth century[11]—and that, contrary to the claims of Alan Bray,[12] the Jacobean discourse about King James I's love for other men employed concepts familiar today, rather than the medieval "sodomitical discourse." (Young further finds no evidence to support the claim that bisexuality was the norm before the eighteenth century, or that a binary construct between heterosexual and homosexual did not exist until modern times.) Borris and Rousseau have established that scientific explanations for "same-sexual affinities rooted in singular natures ... are not a modern invention, but have long been characteristic of European thought ... from the late medieval scientific revival to the early Enlightenment."[13] David Halperin (widely regarded as the leader of the constructionist school), in response to criticism of claims put forward in his essay "How to Do the History of Male Homosexuality," has, in effect, withdrawn them. "In short," he states, "I'm happy to admit that the hypotheses in that article of mine are wrong: in fact, they're so general, and so historically ungrounded, that they're bound to be wrong, or at least misleading and imprecise, within the context of many different historical periods and geographic locations."[14]

Randolph Trumbach, who for the past thirty years has been the major contributor to empirical findings about homosexuality in eighteenth-century England, continues to claim that, "in the first decade of the eighteenth century ... a profound transformation had occurred in the nature of sexual attraction in the societies of western Europe."[15] Before this time, he claims, the model was that of the bisexual libertine whose relationships were age-structured; afterward, it was that of the effeminate "molly," who was exclusively homosexual, and whose relationships were mostly with similar-age adult partners. But Trumbach remains unconvinced by the theories—whether of the economic, psychological, or postmodern varieties—put forward to account for this change, concluding that "no one at the present moment has any satisfactory explanation as to why this transformation occurred."[16] At the present time, many issues that the more doctrinaire theorists claimed to have resolved a dozen years ago are being subjected to more nuanced reconsideration and revision.

RESTORATION DRAMA AND THE LIBERTINE

Although there are numerous references to homosexuality in seventeenth-century drama, they almost uniformly condemn predatory sodomites and their catamites.[17] Such characters probably indicate the playwrights' chase after fashion rather than anything of deeper import.[18] Sodomitical scenes and allusions tended to be set in foreign courts or exotic lands; the stage was peopled by womanizing fops and masculine sodomites. By the turn of the century, the settings and characters had changed, with the first appearance of effeminate men who loved men, notably Coupler, a kind of male-bawd in Vanbrugh's *The Relapse* (1696), who is perhaps the first "queen" whom a modern homosexual man might recognize, and Mr. Maiden in Thomas Baker's *Tunbridge-Walks, or the Yeoman of Kent* (1703).

Despite these exceptions, the archetypal "libertine" in life and literature was a womanizer, and his dissolute sexuality was almost exclusively heterosexual. The Restoration rake debauched women, not youths. Other than John Wilmot, Earl of Rochester (1647–1680), there are only three or four examples of the bisexual libertine in England. As Michael Young points out, "anyone who reads widely in the history of homosexuality finds these few examples repeated incestuously from one work to another."[19] Wilmot's obscene poetry asserts an indiscriminate bisexuality: "This dart of love, .../ Stiffly resolved,'twould carelessly invade/Woman or man, nor ought its fury stayed/Where'er it pierced, a cunt it found or made." But anecdotes about Wilmot's personal life are overwhelmingly about his mistresses, and only one tale mentions his occasional taste for sex with a pageboy. Wilmot's work is not genuinely homoerotic; it is simply designed to shock: "There's a sweet, soft page of mine/Does the trick worth forty wenches." The notorious play *Sodom; or, the Quintessence of Debauchery* has been attributed to Wilmot on slim evidence. It was published anonymously in England in 1684, but there was an earlier French translation, and it probably circulated in manuscript in the mid-1670s. In 1688, the printer and publisher were prosecuted under the Licensing Act for selling an "obscene and lascivious" book.[20] One character, Bolloxinion (the king of Sodom), proclaims "that bugg'ry may be us'd/Through all the land, so cunt be not abus'd/That's the proviso,"—but the play's eroticism is thoroughly heterosexual.[21]

However publicly homosexuality was flaunted on the stage, sodomy was very rarely prosecuted during the sixteenth or seventeenth centuries. The statute known as the Buggery Act of 1533 declared "the detestable and abominable Vice of Buggery committed with mankind or beast" to be a felony punishable by hanging. The word *buggery* meant anal intercourse, and technically buggery and sodomy also included bestiality, though relations with animals were very rarely prosecuted. The statute was reenacted several times under Henry VIII and repealed under Edward VI but reenacted in 1548 and repealed on Mary's succession in 1553. Revived in 1563 by Elizabeth I, its status subsequently remained basically unchanged until the mid-nineteenth century. In the important precedent trial in 1631 of Mervyn Touchet, Earl of Castlehaven (for sodomy with two menservants, and for assisting in the rape of his wife), a special commission of the House of Lords decided that Castlehaven was guilty on all counts—although he had only ejaculated between the thighs of his male partners, and although the evidence came solely from his partners, rather than third-party witnesses—and he was beheaded, while two of his servants were hanged for sodomy. By the end of the century, the legal authorities had determined that capital conviction (i.e., a felony punishable by death) could only be obtained by proof of penetration and ejaculation inside the anus. This remained the standard throughout the eighteenth century. However, although the felony was "full" sodomy, many other homosexual relations were regularly prosecuted as "an assault with attempt to commit sodomy"—a misdemeanor punishable typically by public humiliation in the pillory, a fine, and imprisonment for up to two years. Such "assaults" regularly included two men who consented to have sex together, and the "attempt to commit sodomy" could range from anal intercourse but with withdrawal before emission, to oral intercourse, to groping the genitals of another man through his clothing, to kissing and embracing with genital arousal, to sexual solicitation. Convictions for the felony of sodomy were relatively few, usually obtained solely on the confession of the so-called passive partner; men who were acquitted on the charge of sodomy were regularly retried on the charge of "an attempt to commit sodomy," since a conviction for this misdemeanor was much easier to obtain. There was no age of consent for homosexual relations, which were illegal regardless of the age of the partners or their consent. Boys under the age of fourteen could not be prosecuted, but over that age they could be capitally convicted if they had given consent. Consent was never allowed by the court as a defense in felony cases, although, in misdemeanor cases, it sometimes mitigated the severity of the sentence. Also, since this was a crime that "cried aloud to God," the court deemed that it could never be said to take place "in private," but was always classed as a public outrage. This is the legal background for the sudden explosion of prosecutions that began at the very end of the seventeenth century, organized primarily by a moral reform movement.

Societies for the Reformation of Manners had been formed in Tower Hamlets, East London, in 1690, among young Christian men, mainly artisans and tradesmen, who felt that their devotion to the religious life was being seriously disturbed by constantly hearing profanity in the public streets, by the open solicitations of prostitutes, and by a rise in street crime. By 1698, a network of about twenty of these societies were actively informing on keepers of bawdy houses, as well as on Sabbath-breakers, and they successfully persuaded magistrates and grand juries to suppress lewd and disorderly behavior. In 1698 "reforming" justices of the peace suppressed dancing and masquerades and closed all taverns on Sundays. The societies' concern over female prostitution led directly to a well-organized attempt to suppress sodomitical debauchery, and their efforts were behind most of the prosecutions for homosexual offenses over the next thirty years.

LONDON'S MOLLY HOUSES

From about 1700, a well-organized homosexual subculture became evident in the city of London. It was patronized by men who used specialized slang (for instance, "picking up trade"), frequented homosexual cruising areas, and engaged in effeminate behavior among themselves. They socialized in coffeehouses and taverns called molly houses, where they sang and danced together, behaved in a disorderly fashion, and sometimes got "married." In Britain, molly houses seem to have been established only in London—though there were networks of homosexuals in cities such as Warrington[22] and Bristol.[23]

The cruising grounds of London—which were called molly markets—could be found in public parks and on the streets outside theaters during evening hours, as well as around bridges and similar areas. These were places where large numbers of people congregated, thereby providing homosexuals an excuse to loiter. London Bridge was such a place: as early as the first decade of the eighteenth century, a dozen men were arrested (fig. 3.1) there for homosexual

FIGURE 3.1: "The Women-Hater's Lamentation," a broadside ballad printed in 1707, following the arrest of about forty mollies. Two sodomites kissing one another (center), one cutting his own throat and one hanging himself (left), and one being cut down (right). Courtesy Guildhall Library, City of London.

solicitation by agents who, working for the Society for the Reformation of Manners, acted as "trepanners" (entrappers).

Other popular areas for making homosexual contact included the covered arcades of the Royal Exchange and Covent Garden, the entertainment district around Drury Lane, and open fields. Moorfields, just north of the city walls, was especially notorious. It was crossed by a walled path known as the Sodomites' Walk, where men stood, pretending to urinate, as they waited to be picked up. St James's Park was frequented by guardsmen acting as male prostitutes, or as blackmailers of the men who approached them for sex. Blackmail and male prostitution went hand in hand, just as pick-pocketing and female prostitution did. A hustler named John Mitchell, who bragged that his penis was nine inches long, admitted, "When I wanted Money, I took a Walk in the Park, and got 4 or 5 Guineas a-Night from Gentlemen, because they would not be expos'd." Similarly, the soldier James Brown and his brother Thomas confessed they had picked up and then blackmailed a total of five hundred men in Bird Cage Alley at St James's Park, in the early 1760s. The walk along Bird Cage Alley was commonly used by homosexual men to pick each other up—as well as to pick up nonhomosexual soldiers. They used a system of signals, or coded gestures (such as sitting on a bench and patting the backs of their hands), to indicate their availability. If they wanted someone to follow them, they poked a white handkerchief through the tails of their frock coat, waving it to and fro, before heading toward some bushes off the path.

Public latrines with multiple cubicles were built in London, starting in the late seventeenth century, and quickly became popular places for somewhat private sexual encounters between men. The Savoy precinct "bog house" (slang for a privy or outhouse) was regularly used for sex, as was the Temple precinct bog house, where a hole was deliberately cut in the partition wall between two stalls.[24] Trials record that men were regularly caught having sex in the Lincoln's Inn bog house, on the east side of New Square, Lincoln's Inn Fields. In most cases, the men involved had already agreed to have sex before they entered the latrine.

Molly houses were frequented by men who probably possessed a collective sociocultural identity, as well as a sexual one. Court records document investigations into about thirty of these "disorderly houses for the entertainment of sodomites" during the course of the eighteenth century. At one end of the scale, eight or ten mollies might meet in a private room at the back of a small gin shop to pick one another up, or a man might host a small drag party at his private lodgings. At the other end of the scale were alehouses that were well-known locally for catering exclusively to mollies.

Although most of the molly houses were public alehouses, some were coffeehouses. One molly ran two molly coffeehouses near Moorfields. Another molly kept a molly lodging house. The Royal Oak, a well-known alehouse on a corner of St George's Square, Pall Mall, had a front room for the regular customers and a back room for the mollies. It also had a small room called the Chapel, where men could "marry." While several molly houses were kept by married men and women, most of them were run by homosexual men who were characterized as queens. Their striking use of "maiden names" for one another is a telling instance of group identity: in a mock baptism, they were given a female nickname as a glass of gin was thrown in their face. Thomas Mugg (nicknamed Judith) kept a molly house in Windmill Street, Piccadilly; John Torleton (nicknamed Mary Magdalen) ran one in Christopher Alley, off Moorfields. Another one was kept by Samuel Roper (nicknamed Plump Nelly), a married man who, charged with sodomy, eventually died in prison. Some molly houses were run by a male couple who were "married"; Robert Whale and his partner, York Horner, known to their friends as Peggy and Pru, kept a molly pub in King Street, Westminster. They had been living together for at least three years before their pub was raided.

Strictly speaking, the molly houses were not brothels, and there is no evidence that money ever changed hands for sex. Men were not enticed into molly houses by hustlers the way heterosexual men were approached by female streetwalkers and then taken to a bawdy house. Mock weddings took place in order to cement long-term relationships. In 1728, a molly wedding was celebrated between a butcher named Thomas Coleman and John Hyons, a French immigrant nicknamed Queen Irons; they had previously been pilloried together and imprisoned for three months. The bridesmaids were James Oviat (known as Miss Kitten), a street robber who blackmailed men after offering to have sex with them, and John Cooper (known as Princess Seraphina), who was an unemployed gentleman's valet and cross-dresser who earned money by prostitution at the Vauxhall Gardens masquerades. Cooper was liked by the women in his neighborhood, who called him by his nickname, also referring to him as "her" and "she."

London's most popular molly house was a coffeehouse located in Field Lane in Holborn—a notorious criminal slum and no-go area for police. It was owned by John Clap and run by his wife, Margaret, known as Mother Clap. Every night of the week, about thirty men would gather at her establishment, which was in business for at least ten years. The main party night was Sunday, when forty or fifty gay men would gather at her premises, sometimes coming from thirty or forty miles away. In 1726, Mother Clap's molly house

FIGURE 3.2: "This is not the Thing: or, Molly Exalted," a broadside ballad printed in 1762. The master of a china shop, Mr. Shann, is put in the pillory on Cheapside, London, for a homosexual offense. One woman in the mob shouts "Cut it off." Courtesy City of London, London Metropolitan Archives.

was raided, after more than a year of police surveillance and infiltration by agents of the Society for the Reformation of Manners. Forty men were arrested, while Margaret Clap was convicted for keeping a disorderly house. The public onlookers treated her so severely in the pillory, she went into convulsions and most likely died before serving her prison sentence. Half a dozen of her customers were also pilloried, fined, and imprisoned for up to two years; three more were hanged for sodomy (fig. 3.2).

The Society for the Reformation of Manners had persuaded the government to pay for these prosecutions; previously, the societies themselves had paid for such undertakings. A crackdown on molly houses ensued, and a police patrol was established to clean up St James's Park. The crusade appears to have been successful, as by the 1740s, the organized molly subculture disappeared from view. When it began to reappear in the 1770s, we hear less about private parties and social gatherings—and more about organized male prostitution. One of the earliest male brothels was the White Swan public house on Vere Street, near Clare Market, which was set up in 1810 by a married heterosexual man. The men who provided the services were mainly very masculine types, though some of them (along with their customers) used effeminate nicknames. Black-Eyed Leonora, for instance, was a drummer of the guards; Pretty Harriet was a butcher. The focus narrowed to the provision of sexual services, with the exchange of money in prostitute—client relationships coming to dominate all facets of the homosexual subculture.

Almost all of the men who participated in the subculture of molly houses were small-time tradesmen and artisans: brewers, candle-makers, cabinetmakers, grocers, publicans, tailors, wig-makers, upholsterers, drapers, coachmen, and servants of various sorts. A large majority of men who were prosecuted for having sex in a public place exhibited ordinary masculine demeanors and had masculine-type occupations (such as butchers or coal merchants). Most of these men were part of the respectable working class who had found their social and sexual center in the molly house. However, once inside these establishments' relative privacy, they dropped their social facades and adopted camp or effeminate mannerisms, mimicking the voices of women and having mock "bitch" fights.

Effeminacy has always been a feature of satire against sodomites, and some effete courtiers have been notoriously effeminate. John, the second Lord Hervey (1696–1743) was a well-known bisexual who was satirized by Alexander Pope in the character of Sporus: "Now high, now low, now Master up, now Miss,/ And he himself one vile Antithesis." However, most eighteenth-century homosexuals were called sodomites, buggerers, and indorsers (a variant of endorser) rather than mollies. The evidence arising from criminal prosecutions document effeminacy only within the confines of the molly houses, suggesting it was especially characteristic of the men who were active in the organized subculture rather than broadly characteristic of homosexual men in general. While a few men, such as Princess Seraphina, appear to have enacted a female gender identity, many more men seem to have adopted effeminate nicknames and a set of subcultural markers as a way of identifying themselves specifically as homosexuals, rather than as women.

HOMOSEXUAL SUBCULTURES IN THE REST OF EUROPE AND ITS COLONIES

Homosexual subcultures similar to those in England are evident in several cities across Europe. Relationships ranged from transient encounters to long-term marriage contracts sealed with blood, a clear indication that homosexual love lay at the heart of some men's identity. In the Netherlands, prosecutions for homosexuality had been rare before the eighteenth century; the first traces of a subculture come with the discovery in 1689 of a gang of blackmailers in Amsterdam. Men made contact with each other by using certain signs: in The Hague in 1702, the court learned that men would raise a white handkerchief to signal their leanings to one another. The town hall was used as a center for homosexual cruising, and shady lanes near the city forest served as meeting places for male prostitutes, who sometimes dressed in women's clothes. By the 1720s, extensive networks of sodomites were also to be found in Rotterdam, Haarlem, and Utrecht. Some men had long-term relationships and addressed one another as *nicht* (female cousin).[25] Transvestism was not usual among Dutch homosexuals, though they commonly called each other by their female nicknames.[26] In June and July 1730, at least sixty men were sentenced to death for sodomy,[27] a purge that was widely reported in British newspapers and some of the Dutch sodomites fled to England to escape prosecution (fig. 3.3).[28] Waves of persecution in 1730, 1764, and 1776 resulted in hundreds of trials, providing abundant evidence of sodomitical subcultures.[29] In Frisia and Groningen, as well as in other towns, homosexuals used female nicknames or love names. In Amsterdam, special meeting places included the arcades of the town hall, dark parts of churches and theaters, public urinals, and parks. By mid-century, there were *lolhuysen*—special houses or taverns patronized by homosexual men.

FIGURE 3.3: "Tydelyke Straffe, voorgesteld ten afschrik aller goddeloze en doemwaardige Zondaren" ("Temporal Punishments Depicted as a Warning to Godless and Damnable Sinners"), a broadside by G. Tysens, 1730, illustrating the Dutch persecutions: (1) two men in a homosexual meeting place; (2) two men flee their homes as an allegory of Despair looks on; *(continued)*

FIGURE 3.3 *(continued)*: (3) suspects are arrested, as Fear looks on; (4) two sodomites in prison awaiting their fate; (5) and (6) sodomites are burned and hanged in Amsterdam, while a skeleton holds a banner showing others being drowned in the sea and a figure holds the flaming sword of divine wrath. Courtesy Rijksprentenkabinet, Rijksmuseum, Amsterdam, The Netherlands.

The death penalty was imposed in about 10 percent of cases (as in Britain, capital conviction required proof of ejaculation inside the anus); most sentences involved corporal punishment, long prison terms, banishment, and confiscation of property. The last death penalty was imposed in 1803. From 1600 to 1690, about a dozen women who dressed as men and were "married" to other women were punished with banishment. Prosecutions for lesbianism, or "tribadism" (from the Greek root for "rub"), were very rare: three women were charged in Leiden in the seventeenth century, and thirteen more in Amsterdam between 1792 and 1798.[30]

Though prosecutions of men focused on sodomitical acts, much testimony concerned homosexual temperaments, if not identities. The publicity given to the 1730 persecutions altered public perception of the sodomite as not simply a man who occasionally committed a certain act—but a type of person. One pamphlet speaks of "a feminine mind in a man's body,"[31] while another says that sodomites are a "race" that can be recognized in the absence of any incriminating circumstances solely because of their "changed voice and behavior, just like the female sex."[32] Dutch sodomites discussed among themselves why they seemed to be constituted like females, though most men who were prosecuted claimed that an early seduction caused them to be the way they were.[33]

There is also evidence of a homosexual subculture in Lisbon and elsewhere in Portugal during the mid-seventeenth century.[34] Effeminate homosexuals (*fanchons*) met together in rooming houses, danced together *en travesti* (wearing women's clothing) in the streets, and used female nicknames or men's names modified by feminine diminutives. Love letters between the sacristan of the cathedral of Silves and a guitarist nicknamed Francisquinha in 1664 tell a vivid story of love and desire, incidentally revealing that coitus between the thighs was practiced specifically to avoid the sin of sodomy. In the more organized subculture of Lisbon, sodomites patronized certain inns and met one another in private homes, also using a widespread street culture of male prostitution. Detailed cases from the records of the Portuguese Inquisition suggest that most sexual relations between males followed the adult–adolescent pattern, not only in brief client–hustler encounters, but in long-term relationships perceived as being similar to men cohabiting with concubines.[35] Many of the sodomites were married, but nevertheless recognized themselves as part of a group sharing homosexual tastes. Many were also exclusively male-oriented. The Portuguese Inquisition burned about thirty-five sodomites between 1660 and 1700, whipping, imprisoning, and exiling many more.[36] In 1698, Father Machado was tried for having thirteen teenage partners over a period of nearly nine years, including a tailor, soldiers, students, a surgeon, a silversmith, and a bookshop employee.

In early-eighteenth-century Paris, homosexuals looked for pickups on the Pont Neuf and then would go to a tavern where they hired a private room. Groups of fifteen to thirty homosexual men would meet in a tavern, its shutters closed, where they ate, danced, sang, performed sexual initiation rituals, mimicked women, and used female nicknames and rituals (eight such taverns from 1748 have been recorded[37]). As early as 1706, sodomites met at certain taverns in the St-Antoine district, in groups that had a "grand master" and a "mother in charge of novices."[38] Cruising grounds that were popular in the 1710s, when they were first discovered by police agents, were still popular in the 1780s.[39] Police records reveal men who had long-term homosexual relationships, recognizing in themselves a lifelong inclination that made them different from most other men.⁴⁰ There was an extensive network of homosexual aristocrats in the courts of Savoy, Lorraine, and Orléans during the mid- to late seventeenth century, in the court of Louis XIV at the beginning of the eighteenth century,⁴¹ and in the court of Louis XVI in the late eighteenth century,⁴² but the vice once associated only with noblemen became most visible in the lower social classes (or "lowlifes"). Of the 244 men arrested for sodomy in 1749, only 28 were noblemen and bourgeois, while 129 were small merchants and artisans, and 58 were domestic servants.⁴³ Police commissioners estimated there to be 20,000 sodomites in Paris in 1725, and as many as 40,000 in 1780. Numerous sodomites were arrested in Paris, especially between 1723 and 1747, by *mouches* (flies, or entrappers hired by the police), and, later, by so-called pederasty patrols. Men cruised the quays, especially on Sundays, and young male prostitutes regularly blackmailed their older partners. In a few notorious cases, sodomites were burned at the stake, but, in general, there were few capital convictions, and sodomy came to be regarded as a secular vice rather than as a religious sin. Beginning in 1738, the word *sodomite* was replaced in the police records by the nonreligious word *pederast*, a term incidentally, not linked to a specific act.⁴⁴ In Paris, the homosexual subculture was closely tied to male prostitution from an earlier period than that of London.

Until the end of the eighteenth century, there is less evidence of a homosexual subculture in the German states. In Hamburg, two dozen sodomites were arrested in a tavern in 1790, which suggests some social organization between men sharing the same taste. The homosexual subculture of Berlin was first exposed in an account published in 1782, describing how "warm brothers" gathered in *Knabentabagie* or boy bordellos.⁴⁵ (*Schwül,* meaning "hot," or "humid," dates from 1648 and is still the main slang for German gay men.) German homosexuality is most visible in the elite circles centered around Frederick the Great, Alexander von Humboldt, Johann Wolfgang von Goethe, Johann Winckelmann, Friedrich Schlegel, and Heinrich von Kleist.⁴⁶ The medicalization of the homosexual associated with mid- to late-nineteenth-century German sexology and jurisprudence was predated by German legal and forensic discourses on same-sex eroticism in the late eighteenth and early nineteenth centuries.⁴⁷ Many enlightened forensic practitioners concluded that masturbation and pederasty, or *Knabenschand* (boy defilement), were the result of a fragile nervous system thrown into disorder by predisposition, disease, education, example, or seduction, which might be cured with medication. The habitual active sodomite was diagnosed as suffering the physiological deterioration of the body deemed typical of habitual masturbators (e.g., dull eyes sunk into their sockets) due to the nonprocreative loss of semen.

In Denmark and the other Scandinavian countries, sporadic prosecutions of sodomites during the Enlightenment period mostly concerned individual incidents rather than social networks. The main pattern of sexual relations there was the adult–adolescent encounter, with not much evidence of effeminacy or male prostitution. Homosexual subcultures in the Western world were not visible outside the areas mentioned above. One would assume that the sodomitical subcultures documented in fifteenth- and sixteenth-century Italian cities continued into the eighteenth century, but this has not been established.

The rich body of data has prompted some historians to speak of "the birth of the queen"[48] and the emergence of the homosexual subculture during the Enlightenment as if they were new phenomena. However, strictly speaking, it may be only their *visibility* that is new. It is possible that they existed previously, but were only now discovered by new regimes of surveillance, specifically, through the use of undercover agents acting for the Society for the Reformation of Manners.[49] In England, nearly everything we know about the early molly subculture is directly linked to the prosecutions organized by the Society for the Reformation of Manners: our knowledge begins when the society was founded in 1690, and it ceases when it was disbanded in 1738. Nearly all the pamphlets satirizing the mollies, as well as the newspaper reports, were directly triggered by a raid, an arrest, a trial, or a pillorying: hence, public conceptions also grew out of the prosecutions instigated by the Societies. Had the Societies not been active, modern historians would not know that the molly subculture existed before the mid- to late eighteenth century. Our knowledge about the pederast subculture of Paris similarly parallels the use of the *mouche* by the police, starting in around 1720. In the Dutch Republic, around 1725, legal authorities acquired an independent role in tracing and investigating crimes (it had previously been left to civilians to prosecute charges). It is mostly from this date, as agents began gathering information, that the sodomitical subculture there came to light. Of course, it is likely that highly organized subcultures arose in part because homosexuals were exploiting the new opportunities offered by urbanization and an increase in leisure and pleasure-seeking. But the factors contributing to the *production of knowledge* about effeminate homosexuals and the homosexual subculture enjoin some caution about concluding that, in around 1700, there was a sudden shift in the alleged "roles" played by homosexuals—or that there was a dramatic change at that time in sexual or gender relations. But whether or not such a transformation occurred around

1700, the most striking point about the history of the homosexual subculture is the continuity between the past and the present. The eighteenth-century sodomitical records reveal men who saw themselves as members of a homosexual community and, though they lacked political awareness, they possessed many features characteristic of modern gay identities.

Homosexual activities and identities in the European colonies are more difficult to uncover. In colonial America, there may have been some homosexual networks in Philadelphia[50]—but evidence for overt homosexuality throughout the rest of the country amounts to fewer than half a dozen legal cases. Most early American homosexual history consists of speculation about situational homosexuality that *might* have arisen: for example, in frontier societies, where men formed intense romantic friendships in the absence of women.[51]

Though Brazil and other South American countries had a long indigenous tradition of gender-variant men, classed as *berdache* by the early European explorers, there may have been a homosexual subculture in the Portuguese bases of Bahia and Rio de Janeiro.[52] In 1686, a widowed grocer picked up a sixteen-year-old boy playing the part of a woman at the theater. The two lived together as husband and wife for almost three years, until the Inquisition responded to the scandalized public and brought them to trial. Both men were exiled, but the grocer formed more homosexual liaisons later in life. Similar long-term domestic relationships, some of them interracial, were regularly documented. In Rio, certain shopkeepers permitted sodomites to use their premises as meeting places. Part of the Passeio Público, which was built in the late eighteenth century, was used for homosexual cruising, and the track left by the demolition of an old aqueduct became a path for *travesti* prostitution.

The major difference between the Enlightenment era and modern sexual activity is that there are only half a dozen references to oral sex between men in the eighteenth-century English trials. Nevertheless, it was recognized that venereal disease could be transmitted by oral sex between men, and that some men enjoyed this practice.[53] In the Dutch Republic this was also rare, and it was considered a special treat. In 1730, a wealthy patrician was prosecuted for sucking his servants; one of the things he liked to do was to spit their semen into a glass of wine and drink it.[54] But in all other respects, the sex that took place between men in the eighteenth century is not much different from the sex that takes place between men today. It was predominantly reciprocal, even when anal intercourse was the main point. As in England, the Dutch trials reveal many individuals who "committed the crime both actively and passively," rather than taking just one role or the other.[55] The claim that sex between men during the eighteenth century aligned itself along lines of so-called "active" and "passive" "role playing" is countered by ample evidence in the English trial records that men charged with sodomy practiced a wide range of activities, including kissing, cuddling, love talk, fondling, sexual display, mutual masturbation, oral intercourse, and reciprocal anal intercourse—sometimes indulging in all these activities during the course of a single encounter.[56] A reductive "discourse of penetration" is inadequate in analyzing such relations—even though, in many encounters, the older man clearly held greater power over the younger man. Nevertheless, the older man regularly expressed a desire for sexual contact characterized by mutuality and equality. The model suggesting that older ("active") men dominated younger ("passive") youths fails to account for the innumerable cases in which, after a man picked up and sodomized an errand boy, he then asked the youth to do the same to him. A more accurate model for such situations would classify the older partner as simply a man with a homosexual orientation—and the younger partner as simply a nonhomosexual male exploiting a situation, or experimenting out of curiosity. That is, a model using concepts of sexual orientation and desire has greater explanatory purchase than a model using concepts of binary roles.[57]

PORNOGRAPHY

European erotica generally excludes or excoriates homosexuality. When it is depicted, it occurs primarily as a humorous digression in bawdy books about female prostitution, or in scurrilous political satire. Sodomy was perceived as being as "unnatural" as incest, bestiality, or necrophilia. Even in libertine France, only rarely was homosexual desire allowed to be one of the innocent instincts of nature. An exception is *Les Plaisirs du Cloître* (1773), a three-act comedy with obscene lesbian scenes.[58] In Denis Diderot's anticlerical novel, *La Religieuse* (written in 1760 and published in 1796), the mother superior's lesbian seduction of a novice mirrors the theme that hypocrisy and the suppression of natural instincts give rise to uncontrolled and unnatural sexuality. Extreme anticlericalism characterizes the Marquis de Sade's pornographic novels *Justine* (1787) (fig. 3.4) and *120 Days of Sodom* (1785), both of which have the leading male and female characters practicing homosexuality as a way to rise above the procreative grip of Nature (which, in any case, according to Sade, is utterly devoid of moral

FIGURE 3.4: From the Dutch edition of Sade's *La nouvelle Justine; ou, Les malheurs de la vertue* (1797).

intent). In Sade's argument, the "New Woman" could liberate herself only by rejecting the view that reproduction was essential to her nature. Even Sade's most violent lesbian sadism, found in *Philosophy in the Bedroom*, has been seen as feminist rather than misogynist.[59] Much earlier, in Italy, Antonio Rocco's *L'Alcibiade Fanciullo a Scola* (*Alcibiades As a Schoolboy*) was first published in 1662 (though it was probably written before then) and gained widespread notoriety for its defense of sodomy and pederasty within the libertine ideology of "natural" freedom.

In England, erotic literature that featured homosexuality was sporadic and idiosyncratic rather than part of a coherent tradition.[60] In 1749, Thomas Cannon, son of the deceased Dean of Lincoln, published *Ancient and Modern Pederasty Investigated and Exemplified,* an astonishing defense of homosexuality.[61] This contained not only pornographic celebrations of the pleasure of buggery, but also discussions of gender ambiguity, an anthology of homosexual passages from the classical writers, and a rational, Enlightenment defense of same-sex love: "Unnatural Desire is a Contradiction in Terms; downright Nonsense. Desire is an amatory Impulse of the inmost human Parts: Are not they, however constructed, and consequently impelling, Nature?" John Cleland's *Memoirs of a Woman of Pleasure,* also published in 1749, contained a notorious passage describing sodomy between a man and a youth—the first extended and realistic homosexual scene to appear in erotica. Cleland was immediately arrested for obscenity, and the homosexual passage was removed when his novel was reprinted as *Fanny Hill* in 1750. (Cannon and Cleland had once worked together; Cleland libeled Canon as a sodomite, but also gained the reputation of being one himself.) Cleland's novel also contained pseudo-lesbian scenes, in which the heroine is initiated by a woman preparatory to the pleasures of heterosexual sex (fig. 3.5). This common pornographic framework of one woman "instructing" another is used in *The Sappho-an* (1749), a rare example of bawdy describing lesbian relations, as well as many

FIGURE 3.5: Phoebe initiates Fanny Hill in the brothel, from John Cleland, *Memoirs of a Woman of Pleasure*, with engravings ascribed to Gravelot (1766 edition). By permission of the British Library.

other sexual tastes.⁶² Many political diatribes, taking their lead from French pornography, portrayed Marie Antoinette as a lesbian.⁶³

LESBIANISM

Sex between women has rarely been deemed illegal in Europe, though there were some rare prosecutions of female same-sex fornication.⁶⁴ In Saxony, in 1721, two women were prosecuted for lesbian relations: Catharina Linck pretended to be a man and used a false penis constructed of stuffed leather; she was convicted of sodomy and beheaded. Her partner, Catharina Mühlhahn, whom she married in church, was imprisoned and then banished.⁶⁵ At the beginning of the century in Britain, it was widely believed that Queen Anne had a lesbian relationship with her servant Abigail Masham. In 1708, Sarah Churchill said that Queen Anne had "noe inclination for any but one's own sex," and scurrilous pamphlets described the affair.⁶⁶

By the mid-eighteenth century, lesbian sexuality was identified as a deviant sexual orientation through the employment of generic terms such as *kind* and *species*; by abstract phrases such as "feminine congression" and "accompanying with other women"; and by abundant euphemisms such as "irregular," "unnatural," "uncommon and preternatural lust," "unnatural appetites," and "deviation from the natural inclinations."⁶⁷ People regularly speculated about the etiology of lesbianism, as well as about male homosexuality. In a study of the case of Catherine Vizzani, her father felt that his daughter's love for women was an inborn "constitution" that could not be "repressed." The Italian surgeon who published the study in 1744 anatomized her body in search for a physiological cause; the translator of the 1751 English edition (who was probably John Cleland) thought it was due to early seduction by a woman.⁶⁸ Women with this inclination were called lesbians, starting at least in 1732, though the terms most frequently applied to them were *tribades, tommies,* and *sapphists*. Sex between women was called "the game of flats" (a term that dates to 1663, and whose precise meaning is now obscure).

Lesbians are virtually absent from the English legal record, but many women were prosecuted for fraud, for wearing men's clothes. Many cases involved women dressing as soldiers or sailors, often to join their husbands in the army or navy, or as laborers, in order to earn a better living for themselves. Such cases are strictly part of gender, rather than lesbian, history.⁶⁹ In England, there were some interesting cases of women marrying women. For example, in 1777, Ann Marrow was convicted for impersonating a man and marrying three different women for their money. She was put in the pillory and, pelted mercilessly by the crowd, was blinded in both eyes. In 1760, Sarah Paul was arrested for pretending to be a man, and for being married to a woman for several years. Following a lovers' quarrel, her "wife" brought a charge of fraud against her. But the two women made up, and the partner subsequently refused to testify against her "husband." The presiding magistrate had no choice but to discharge her, ordering only that her male clothes be burned in his presence.

Such women were dubbed "female husbands." A famous example was Mary East. In 1731, she donned masculine clothing and took a small public house in Epping with her "wife." There, and, later, at another public house in Poplar, the two women lived together as man and wife for eighteen years. They became relatively wealthy, but kept no servants, presumably, to keep the husband's real sex a secret. For many years, East was blackmailed by someone who knew her real sex. In 1765, East's "wife" died after thirty-nine years of matrimony. In a bold move, East then revealed her true sex, and prosecuted her blackmailer in court. He was convicted and sentenced to four years'

FIGURE 3.6: Mary Hamilton is whipped for posing as a man and marrying a woman in 1746. Illustration by George Cruikshank for *The Surprising Adventures of a Female Husband* (1813). Courtesy Harry Elkins Widener Collection, Houghton Library, Harvard University.

imprisonment, but her public disclosure made it necessary for East to go into retirement. Henry Fielding's twenty-four-page pamphlet, *The Female Husband* (1746), exploited public interest in the conviction of Mary Hamilton, alias Dr. Charles Hamilton, who fraudently posed as a man and married a woman in Somersetshire (fig. 3.6). Fielding colorfully embellished the historical facts, which he culled from newspapers and, possibly, insider information from his cousin Henry Gould, a legal counselor who advised the court on the case.[70]

"Romantic friendship" was held to be especially typical of women who loved women, and historians have argued about the degree to which the most intensely passionate affairs were overtly sexual.[71] The "paradigmatic narrative of intimate female friendship"[72] was the relationship of the so-called Ladies of Llangollen, Lady Eleanor Butler and Sarah Ponsonby, who, in 1778, eloped and set up home together in Wales (fig. 3.7). There, they became famous and were visited by the celebrities of the Romantic age. Most historians concur with Mavor's insistence that Butler and Ponsonby were not lesbians.[73] However, Hester Thrale Piozzi, whose daughter once visited them, described the two women as "damned Sapphists" in her diary, and claimed that female visitors were reluctant to stay the night with them unless accompanied by men.[74] During his journeys in America between 1793 and 1798, Saint Méry observed many romantic women friends, stating, "they are not at all strangers to being willing to seek unnatural pleasures with persons of their own sex."[75]

Whereas most male homosexual couples followed older/younger pairings rather than male/female role-playing, lesbian relationships usually had one of the pair regularly taking on the masculine role, sometimes actually pretending to be a man. For example, the actress Charlotte Charke (1710–1760), famous for playing breeches parts on the stage, often pretended to be a man in her private life, living as a man with a younger woman as Mr. and Mrs. Brown. Lesbians and women passionately committed to one another developed private domestic arrangements rather than a subculture of social networks (fig. 3.8). Wider lesbian networks may have arisen later in the century. For example, many satirical jibes were aimed at the sculptor Anne Seymour Damer, who apparently had an affair with the actress Kitty Clive, among others. *A Sapphick Epistle* (1778) refers to this small circle of well-bred lesbians as the Twickenham set.[76] A female whipping club that allegedly existed in London in 1792 was probably imaginary, as were the all-female cabals mentioned by Baron K. von Reizenstein in his *Trip to Vienna* (1795). However, numerous references to a lesbian club called the Order of Anandrynes, which was supposed to have flourished in Paris in the 1780s, may have been based on a genuine network

FIGURE 3.7: Sarah Ponsonby (left) and Lady Eleanor Butler, known as the Ladies of Llangollen, seated in their library. Lithograph by R. J. Lane, ca. 1832, after Mary Parker (later Lady Leighton), 1828. Courtesy Wellcome Library, London.

of lesbians. The notorious actress Mlle. Raucourt, who organized orgies in the 1770s, was, believed to be among its numbers.[77]

The clear chronological development of distinct lesbian typologies—from the tribade (with her supposedly enlarged clitoris), to the often bisexual and licentious sapphist, to roles ranging from the female husband and the romantic "friend", to the self-aware, modern lesbian—as perceived by Trumbach[78] is disputed by others,[79] who instead see overlapping types in all periods. Nevertheless, many recognize the first "modern lesbian" in the Yorkshire landowner Anne Lister (1791–1840), who recorded her active sex life with other women in coded diaries.[80] Lister had several long-term lovers whom she married in special ceremonies that included exchanging lockets containing cuttings of the couple's pubic hair. She seduced many women, often flirting with potential partners by alluding to classical texts such as Juvenal or Suetonius to judge if they were *au fait* with homosexuality and lesbianism. She disguised her love

FIGURE 3.8: *Love-a-la-Mode, or Two Dear Friends* (Clinch, c. 1820): Lady Strachan and Lady Warwick making love in a park, while their husbands look on with disapproval. Wellcome Library, London.

letters by using the language of female friendship to avoid recognition if they were intercepted. Attempting to understand the nature of her sexuality, she consulted works of anatomy, as well as the standard ancient texts. She rejected being labeled a sapphic—to her, that implied the use of a dildo, which was artificial, not "natural," as she felt herself to be. She was masculine in her looks, had erotic fantasies about possessing a penis, and always took the male role in manually masturbating and penetrating her partners with her fingers.

CHANGING ATTITUDES TOWARD HOMOSEXUALITY

When William Brown was arrested in 1726 and was asked why he had taken indecent liberties with another man, he "was not ashamed to answer, 'I did it because I thought I knew him, and I think there is no Crime in making what use I please of my own Body.'" Similarly, in 1718, when a watchman caught two men making love against the railings in front of Covent Garden Church and called them filthy buggerers, one of them replied, "Sirrah! What's that to you, can't I make use of my own Body? I have done nothing but what I will do again."[81] French Revolutionary pamphlets half-seriously defended buggery on the same grounds: "I may dispose of my property ... according to my taste and my fantasies. Thus, my cock and my balls belong to me, and ... whether I put them in a cunt or an asshole is of no business to anyone else."[82]

Ownership and control over one's own body became an integral part of Enlightenment philosophy, which was sometimes reflected in serious discussions of homosexuality. In *A Philosophical Dissertation* (1731), Count Radicati di Passerano advocated the right to engage in homosexual behavior and defended suicide on the grounds that different cultures practiced different customs, concluding that there were therefore no universal mores or morals. French philosophers often viewed homosexuality with a wry sense of humor, deeming it worthy of public, rational discussion (e.g., Voltaire's essay "*Amour Socratique*," in his *Dictionnaire Philosophique*).[83] In *De l'esprit des lois* (1748), Montesquieu observed that only three crimes were punished by fire—witchcraft, heresy, and sodomy—implying that these old religious offenses were dealt with too severely by modern civil law. Cesare Beccaria argued in *On Crimes and Punishments* (1764) that laws severely punishing crimes such as adultery and sodomy were not only useless, but pernicious. In the Netherlands, some pamphlets argued that the separation of church and state ought to entail the abolition of antihomosexual laws originating in ecclesiastical (or divine) law.[84] France's Constituent Assembly decriminalized sodomy in 1791, classing it with such "imaginary crimes" as bestiality, heresy, and witchcraft. This status was unchanged by either the Civil Code of 1804 (the Code Napoléon) or the Penal Code of 1810—hence, most countries conquered by Napoleon stopped prosecuting homosexual offenses (except in cases involving minors or the use of force).

In Britain, the first public debate about homosexuality occurred in 1772, in response to the arrest, conviction, and subsequent royal pardon (on condition that he leave the country) granted to Captain Robert Jones, who had been sentenced to death for sodomy with a thirteen-year-old boy. Scores of Letters to the Editor were sent to the mainstream newspapers, reports appeared in the provincial newspapers, the government was both attacked and defended for allowing the pardon, and satirical pamphlets flew from the press.[85] The legal arguments (especially regarding conviction solely on the basis of evidence from a boy who had consented, and who would himself have been prosecuted had he been a year older) were debated in great detail. The British legal system was contrasted with the legal systems of other countries—from ancient Rome to modern France—whose rules of evidence would not have convicted Jones, and calls were made to reform the penal laws, citing the views of Montesquieu and Beccaria. The debate ranged widely, from advocating Christian intolerance toward homosexuality, to defending the rights of homosexual men deemed to have an inborn propensity. Perhaps as a result of this publicity, the utilitarian philosopher Jeremy Bentham, in extensive manuscript notes on pederasty written between 1774 and 1816, judged that, from the utilitarian—not to mention the commonsense and humane—standpoint, there was "no reason for punishing it at all: much less for punishing it with the degree of severity with which it has been commonly punished."[86] Bentham felt that the persecution of homosexuals encouraged exclusive homosexuality and the formation of the homosexual subculture. Bentham never published his reflections, for fear of being branded a sodomite himself.

However, despite such expressions of greater tolerance in intellectual discourse, prosecutions in Britain steadily increased during the early nineteenth century.[87] Sixty-one men were hanged for sodomy in England between 1800 and 1835, after which death sentences were commuted to life imprisonment. Despite this legal stasis, during the years between 1650 and 1820, it came to be recognized (in part aided by the romantic discourse of "sensibility"),[88] that the homosexual was not a pasteboard monster, but a real person with a psychology.[89] The cultural constructions of the symbolic universe prior to the Enlightenment were being replaced by empirical observations of the real world.

CHAPTER FOUR

Sexual Variations

MARIANNA MURAVYEVA

Sexual variation, or "unnatural lewdness," as such acts were more often called in the eighteenth century, has attracted a lot of attention from contemporary commentators, both from the general public and from specialists. The politically-correct word *variations* has emerged as a new concept of sexual behavior and marks a contemporary attitude of open-mindedness. It covers "sexual desires and behaviors outside what is considered to be the normal range, although what is unusual or atypical varies between cultures and from one period to another."[1] Heterosexual sex during the eighteenth century was viewed as the norm. All deviations from it—such as masturbation and other forms of nonpenetrative sex—were considered excessive and licentious. Penetrative, nonheterosexual sex, such as bestiality and sodomy between men, was also condemned in general. Some of those forms were criminalized in the societies that treated them as dangerous to the state and public order. Others, such as fetishism or flagellation, were merely ridiculed because the public did not see that they harmed anyone but those who indulged in them.

The sexual discourse of the age can be seen in the dichotomy between the natural and the unnatural: all nonprocreative sexuality was seen as unnatural, or perverse, since it was considered against the laws of both nature and God as well as highly offensive to most of society. In laying the groundwork for medicalizing and pathologizing nonprocreative sex, two groups vied for control: the moralists (mostly grouped in the church and educational institutions) and the physicians. By the beginning of the nineteenth century, medicine had triumphed; thus, dominion over "perverse" sexuality moved from the preserves of the prisons to that of the clinics—perversion was now seen as a illness to be treated rather than a crime to be punished.

The eighteenth century witnessed the development of many "unnatural" sexual practices but with it came the traditional practice of community shaming. Unnatural sex was classed into one of two forms: the sort where sexual desire involved penetrative sex with other living humans (such as same-sex relations), and the sort where sexual arousal was derived from certain objects, animals, or corpses. Here, we are concerned with the second type, which includes bestiality, masturbation, fetishism, flagellation, sadism, and necrophilia.

Eighteenth-century Europe has always attracted the attention of social and cultural historians as a "gallant" era—a time of hypersexuality, sexual promiscuity, and extreme tolerance toward the sexual "variations." This was the century of Casanova, Fanny Hill, Catherine the Great, and other notoriously excessive lovers. Blatant pornography, mild erotica, and sentimental and moralistic literature circulated; sex and the body were simultaneously liberated.[2] In her account of eighteenth-century scholarship on sexuality and the body, Karen Harvey states that the historiography of sexuality has become a context for discussion of long-standing questions about the period—particularly those concerning modernity and the ancient regimes. Historians view this century as a time of great change in the ways in which bodies were understood and sexually constructed—and in which sexual activity was carried out.[3] Both absolute and enlightened monarchs such as Augustus of Saxony, Louis XV, and Catherine the Great added to this understanding of permissiveness, promiscuity, and sexual experimentation.

The eighteenth century truly was an era of unruly desires. But evidence points to the situation as not being such a cheerful or positive one: court records show unprecedented suppression of sexual desires, from bestiality to extramarital sex, deemed unnatural; didactic literature condemned masturbation and other sexual practices considered lewd, while physicians cautioned that syphilis and other diseases came from unconventional sex; and politicians and social hygienists lamented the spread of prostitution. Meanwhile, perversions became a filter through which diversity could be expressed.[4]

BESTIALITY RECONSIDERED

In England, the word *bestiality* went into common use after the King James Bible was introduced in 1611. Bestiality could mean possession of bestial qualities as well as "unnatural" connection (sexual intercourse) with an animal. The law used the word *buggery* in a narrower sense, applying it to unnatural connections between a man (or a woman) and an animal—or to anal intercourse between a man and a woman, or between two men. In his *New Law Dictionary* (1729), Giles Jacob defined buggery as being "*carnalis copula contra Naturam, & hoc vel per confusionem Specierum*, sc. a Man or Woman with a brute Beast; *vel Sexuum*, a Man with a Man, or Man with a Woman ... "[5] In other European countries and cultures, the words deriving from the Latin *bestialitas* sometimes marked the action, sometimes the crime (*bestialität* in German; *bestialité* in French). Some cultures were more explicit: Russians had the notion of *skotolozhstvo* (lying with a beast); Swedes used the term *tidelagsbrott*, which had the same meaning. Although the majority of eighteenth-century European lawyers grouped bestiality with other sodomitical crimes—as crimes against nature—language practices underscored the essential differences among the actions.

In legal spheres, bestiality easily made its way from canon law into the state systems of modern criminal law, though the jurisdiction stayed relatively undefined. French tradition, deriving from Charlemagne, meted out burning as a punishment. Daniel Jousse, an eighteenth-century French criminologist, declared that those guilty of bestiality were to be burned alive, and with them the animal on which the crime had been perpetrated.[6] Another eighteenth-century criminologist, P. F. Muyart de Vouglans, attested that the common custom was to punish them with burning.[7] In Tuscan laws of 1786, bestiality committed by any man was "punished in the most ultimate painful way possible with death."[8]

German law followed the Carolina article 116 that ordered burning for sodomy, bestiality, and other "crimes against nature." Thus, the Prussian Law of 1721 stated that un-Christian and unnatural crimes (sodomy and bestiality) should be punished by death through fire.[9] Thirty years later, however, Frederick the Great of Prussia came out against the death penalty for bestiality. Similarly, in America, Thomas Jefferson—in his draft code of Virginia—could find no reason for persecuting bestiality, claiming that "it cannot therefore be injurious to society in any great degree, which is the true measure of criminality in *foro civili* [civil forum], and will ever be properly and severely punished by universal derision."[10] He effectively removed bestiality from the list of capital crimes, returning to the seventeenth-century tradition of colonial law. Thus, the Quaker colonies of West Jersey and Pennsylvania never defined bestiality as a capital crime in the seventeenth century. Pennsylvania allowed whippings for sodomy and bestiality, plus the forfeiture of one-third of the accused person's estate and imprisonment for six months (first offense) or for life (second offense). This changed in 1700, when Pennsylvania toughened its laws. Both offenses then became punishable by life imprisonment, with a whipping every three months for the first year. A married man convicted of sodomy or bestiality would be castrated, whipped every three months for a year, and imprisoned for life. The spouse of someone convicted of either crime could receive a divorce. In 1706, after the English Parliament objected to castration as a punishment, it was removed as a penalty. In Pennsylvania, both crimes finally became capital offenses in 1718, when the state adopted most of the English criminal laws in exchange for concessions to Quakers on judicial oaths.[11]

English law maintained the death penalty for sodomy, from the buggery acts of 1533 and 1548 right up until 1828. Sir Edward Coke treated bestiality as a felony—as an abominable sin "among Christians not to be named," punishable by hanging.[12] William Blackstone, an eighteenth-century jurist, called bestiality "so dark a nature, so easily charged, and the negative so difficult to be proved, that the accusation should be clearly made out; for if false, it deserves a punishment inferior only to that of the crime itself." In other words, as a capital offense, it should be punished by hanging.[13] Scottish law did not have any particular statute on sodomy or bestiality—the reason being, as claimed by Sir George Mackenzie, that they were "crimes Extraordinat and rarely committed in this Kingdom." Mackenzie, however, suggested the "ordinary" punishment of burning, though he recognized hanging as a suitable punishment as well.[14] In contrast, by the end of the eighteenth century, David Hume thought the crime more prevalent, stating that "there have been more frequent instances of prosecution for bestiality as for sodomy in this kingdom." Hume also supported the death penalty.[15]

Sweden and Denmark had high incidents of bestiality. In 1608, Swedish authorities incorporated the Bible and the Ten Commandments into official law—which meant that all types of sinful behavior mentioned therein (including a wide range of sexual practices) became criminalized.[16] A direct connection was made between being lured by the Devil and illicit sexuality. This implied a greater danger to the public of some sex crimes (including incest and bestiality) which sometimes ended in witch-hunts. A firm association was established between bestiality and witchcraft that made the former even more abominable and threatening. In both Sweden and Denmark, bestiality was classed as sodomy, and was prosecuted under military codes. Similarly, Russia criminalized bestiality in the Military Code of 1716, which stated that "he who lies with the beast or other senseless creature should be given harsh corporal punishment."[17]

This was the only law that did not stipulate the death penalty for bestiality. Canon law was also implemented in Russia which prescribed between three and fifteen years of penance.[18] But exactly how widespread was bestiality? Did it happen more often in some countries than in others, due to cultural and legal restrictions? An author from the 1960s claimed that bestiality was still so common in Europe that priests in France, Germany, and Poland continued to ask parishioners, during confession, if they had had intercourse with an animal.[19]

Because bestiality was classed in law as sodomy, it is difficult to form a proper statistical picture. Scattered evidence comes from various European countries. Some, such as Sweden, have left a considerable amount, while others, such as Russia, lack any evidence at all. The German physician Hans Haustein, examining Prussian court records for the years 1700 to 1730, found that nine individuals were executed for bestiality and only three for homosexuality:[20] these figures imply that bestiality was either considered a greater crime, or was more obvious. Polly Morris has found twenty-seven prosecutions for bestiality (compared with fifty-five for sodomy) in Somerset courts between 1740 and 1849.[21] Arend H. Huussen found only two mentions of bestiality in Frisian criminal court records between 1730 and 1811.[22] P. G. Maxwell-Stuart discovered seventy-seven cases of bestiality for the period between 1570 and 1734, with thirty-seven occurring during the years 1654 to 1659.[23] French specialist Gaston Dubois-Desaulle detected forty-seven cases of bestiality in eighteenth-century France.[24] Eighteen cases of bestiality appear in eighteenth-century northwestern Russia, with the majority coming from the Saint Petersburg region. Henry Bamford Parkes counted eight cases of bestiality in colonial America, five of them committed in the seventeenth century.[25]

However, systematic studies show that bestiality occupied quite a visible place in criminal records. Andres Fernandez has found 492 cases in Aragon between 1560 and 1700, which constitute 27 percent of all crimes brought before Aragonese tribunals.[26] In Sweden, there appear to have been focused "bugger-hunts" aimed at those committing bestiality. These reached their peak in the eighteenth century, while very little attention was paid to homosexual acts between men (which are not even mentioned in the new law code of 1734). Most of the homosexual cases involved men in the army using violence, rather than instances of consensual relations.[27] Jonas Liliequist uncovered 1,500 cases of bestiality for the years between 1635 and 1754, so far the biggest database in existence.[28]

Eighteenth-century jurists agreed that bestiality was a crime against nature, so their object was to prevent the infringement of nature through such improper sexual relations. But what form did this concern take? According to Jonas Liliequist, Swedish authorities were most worried about preventing the birth of hybrids or monsters (a nymph was thought to be the result of copulation between a shepherd and a mare). This fear, shared by judges and scientists alike, increased during the first half of the eighteenth century. Analyzing the cases of sexual intercourse between a demon (such as a water nymph or a forest ghost) and a man (women are rarely involved), Liliequist shows that judges tried perpetrators on a count of bestiality rather than on one of witchcraft. This magic-bestiality connection was at the same time reaffirmed by the idea that, when witches copulated with the Devil, he usually assumed animal form—often, that of a dog.[29] Americans believed that sexual relations with animals could have negative reproductive consequences. Fearing that the mating of humans and animals would produce monstrous offspring, they inflicted harsh penalties on those found guilty of such crimes.[30] In New Haven, Connecticut, when Thomas Hogg was accused of bestiality after a sow had given birth to a deformed piglet, which "had a faire and white skinne & head, as Thomas Hogg is," he was imprisoned, put on a harsh diet, and whipped regularly to bridle his lusts.[31]

Although the act of bestiality meant sexual intercourse between a man or a woman and an animal (figs. 4.1 and 4.2), it had implicitly different meaning,

FIGURE 4.1: A man copulating with a goat or deer. Gouache nineteenth century. Wellcome Library, London.

FIGURE 4.2: A Persian woman copulating with an animal. Illuminated manuscript, 1824. Wellcome Library, London.

depending on gender. For men, sexual intercourse meant penetration with emission of the seed; for a woman, it meant an act by which she could conceive.[32] In order to provide evidence of penetration, a surgeon might be called in. In one case, where a man was accused of copulating with a dog, three surgeons were asked if it were possible to do such a thing. They were "of the opinion that it is possible for a man to have carnal knowledge of a large bitch she being proud ... as to its being possible to have carnal knowledge of a dog." However, they thought it not possible "without the dog be either first tied, or held by an assistant and not even then without the parts being lubricated." In 1809, Edward Caldwell, an assistant surgeon, gave testimony that helped convict Samuel Branter, who was being tried for bestiality with a goat: "The parts appeared of a florid colour and more dilated than usual; moisture appeared on the external parts; for fear of any mistakes, I examined another goat. She appeared quite normal." The surgeon also had to testify that there was no male goat about that could have been responsible for the female goat's inflamed condition.[33]

Both men and women were seen as potential offenders. Any animal involved in such acts was also punished. This leads us to the issue of the animal's consent. Daniel Jousse compared bestiality to molesting children with regard to the degrees of abomination and public danger involved.[34] This comparison also prompts us to see animals as equal to children in terms of victim characteristics. According to this comparison, an animal—if treated like an infant—was not able to give any consent, so sexual intercourse was illegal. In other words, the agents of the crime should be capable of understanding the illegal nature of their actions. Yet, the law rarely followed this assumption, and animals were tried alongside the perpetrator. The types of animals used in this act varied. In France, Gaston Dubois-Desaulle gives specific numbers of the types and numbers of animals involved: out of forty-seven cases, there were fourteen mares, ten female donkeys, eleven cows, four female goats, three dogs, three mules, and three sheep. Thus, the majority of animals could be classified as large.[35] In Scotland, mares and cows were the animals of choice, though there were anomalies: in 1718, John Rennie had intercourse with a ewe.[36] Various unconventional methods were used to gain access to animals. In 1703 in South Carolina, John Dixon was seen to have intercourse with a brown bitch; witnesses told how they had heard him instructing his companions how to bugger a cat, and "in particular told them to tye her head in a Bag, and hold up her Taill."[37]

Execution of animals involved in bestiality cases resulted from the need to annihilate all connections to, or evidence of, the crime because it was so abomnible.[38] The perpetrators were made to witness the death of the animal with which they had committed the crime, thus implying a further punishment—that of the perpetrator witnessing the death of their lover. William Hacketts, "found in buggery with a cow, upon a Lord's day," first had to witness the execution of the cow before his own sentence was carried out. In another case, the court ordered identification of the animals with which the accused had had intercourse: the perpetrator identified his sexual partners (five sheep), "willed before his face," all which were then executed.[39] John Murrin, in his study of bestiality in colonial America, noted that "bestiality lowered a man to the level of a beast, but it also left something human in the animal. To eat a defiled animal thus involved the danger of cannibalism."[40] This might have been another reason for executing the animals involved in crimes of bestiality. There was a certain fear of milking a cow that had been sexually abused, as a Russian case shows. In 1779, a cow-owner, who had witnessed and prevented an attempted buggery perpetrated upon her, stated that, since the time he had caught his laborer in the attempt, he had never used milk from the cow in question.[41]

In Sweden, there was the same anxiety about ingesting milk or meat from abused livestock, as it was considered a type of cannibalism to have milk or flesh from a "humanized" animal.[42]

The group of accused perpetrators appears to be diverse, not necessarily confirming the idea of bestiality as an agricultural crime in the eighteenth century. Dubois-Desaulle's analysis gives only eleven peasants and agricultural laborers out of forty-seven. Others include three winegrowers, three weavers, two footmen, two cabmen, five servants, four merchants, a butler, a shepherd, a gardener, a shoemaker, a carpenter, an assistant surgeon, a chemist, a soldier, and a civil servant.[43] Andre Fernandez noted that limiting this sort of practice to peasantry and to country life would be to deny the reality of a behavior that concerned many social classes other than those strictly connected with agriculture.[44] Age, however, was a very significant factor. Maxwell-Stuart noticed the age discrepancy between the accused and the witnesses: the majority of the accused were younger than twenty years old, whereas the majority of witnesses were between forty and fifty years of age.[45] In the Russian cases, only two accused were around forty—everyone else was not yet twenty.

Bestiality was considered a male crime. However, some women could also commit bestial acts, rare though this seems to have been. In England, only a handful of women were convicted: one woman and her dog were hanged at Tyburn in 1679.[46] In the American colonies, only two cases of female bestiality have come to light. A 1702 case in Boston had the grand jury refusing to indict one woman accused of bestiality, while in Monmouth County, New Jersey, Hannah Corkin was indicted in 1757 for buggery—but was only convicted of attempted buggery. Her offense must have been flagrant, however, for she received an exceptionally severe sentence: four whippings, each consisting of twenty lashes, in four different towns, over consecutive weeks.[47]

Sex with birds might have been considered a distinct corpus delicti of bestiality. Russian penitentials always distinguish between bestiality (*skotolozhstvo*) and "birdiality" (*ptitselozhstvo*), as classed by the Holy Fathers and apostolic canons. The mention of using birds for sex comes from trial records, as well as from literature and mythology. For example, Zeus turned himself into a swan in order to have sex with Leda. European art often depicted this scene in famous paintings by Michelangelo, Leonardo, Fragonard, and Boucher, among others. Different species of birds have been involved in sex acts. Sixteen-year-old Thomas Glazer from Plymouth confessed to buggery "with a mare, a cow, two goats, five sheep, two calves, and a turkey."[48] In October 1789, on the island of Dominica, a soldier (appropriately named Sparrow), "the tallest straitest & cleanest Grenadier in the whole Regt.," was seen—in full uniform—buggering a turkey. The witness was a thirteen-year-old girl, but because she was too young to testify under oath, the bloodied turkey became the evidence against Sparrow. "The Turkey was killed her feathers plucked off & body thrown down the precipice. The soldier was dresst in her feathers and drummed out of the Regt. wt. the Rogue's March. ... if the Girl had been of age he would have been hung." Sparrow tried to escape on a ship to America, but when the captain learned who he was, he denied him passage. "Oh says the Capt. I am to carry a Cargo of Turkeys & if you go with me I am afraid that I'll lose the sell of them." Evidently, the offense was so notorious that news of it could have been expected to cross hundreds of miles of ocean—spread enthusiastically, no doubt, by the ship's crew.[49]

Certain Parisian brothels were known to have provided turkeys for their clients. As the men were about to experience orgasm through having intercourse with the turkey, they would break the bird's neck, which caused the bird's cloacal sphincter to constrict and spasm, clamping down on their penises and creating pleasurable sensations.[50] This seems to have been an unusually specialized service—one as yet not uncovered in other metropolitan brothels. Bestiality became even more closely observed in the nineteenth century, when notorious cases spread over the pages of medical and legal journals. Eventually, it was decriminalized, ending up as sexual deviations in the annals of mental health.

SELF-POLLUTION, SEED-SPILLING, AND OTHER DANGERS AND PLEASURES OF MASTURBATION

The idea of masturbation as unacceptable comes from Genesis 38:8–10, in the story of Onan. However, the biblical text reads ambiguously as to whether it intends masturbation or *coitus interruptus* but is generally interpreted to mean spilling seed outside the womb—though this is still a topic of discussion. Medieval theologians came to agree that it was an abominable sin, comparable to sodomy and murder.[51] Masturbation was subject to both church and state punishment, in the form of either canon or criminal laws. Protestant countries included masturbation in the category of criminal sex offenses, and punished it as such. The German criminal code of Charles V, under Carolina article 116, gave the death penalty (burning at the stake, "according to the laws of this land") for bestiality, same-sex relations, and masturbation.[52] Authoritarian German lawyer Benedict Carpzov insisted that masturbation be punished with the same penalty as sodomy: both warranted burning at the stake.[53] Though the German tradition persisted throughout Central Europe, by the end of the eighteenth century, most criminologists agreed that masturbation no longer belonged to the category of sodomy and should instead be punished by banishment, imprisonment, or flogging.[54] American Puritans, concerned about all types of indecency, tended to punish acts such as public masturbation with whipping.[55] John Winthrop discussed legal prosecution for masturbation in the case of William Plane of Guilford, who was hanged for sodomy in 1646. Winthrop said that "he had corrupted a great parte of the youth of Gilford by masturbation, which he had committed & provoked others to the like, above 100 tymes." To cover such incidents, New Haven adopted a special law that declared public masturbation, by "corrupting or tempting others to doe the like, ... tends to the sin of Sodomy, if it be not one kind of it," and, "if the case considered with the aggravating circumstances, shall according to the mind of God revealed in his word require to death, as the court of magistrates shall determine."[56]

FIGURE 4.3: "Mlle Ch., agee de 16 ans" (young female, aged 16, suffering from the effects of masturbation). Engraving from Samuel-Auguste Tissot, *L'onanisme; ou dissertation physique sur les maladies produites par la masturbation* 1836. Wellcome Library, London.

By the eighteenth century, the subject of masturbation had become problematic among contemporaries, provoking much discussion. Historians of sexuality have dated the beginnings of a mass phobia of masturbation to the start of that century. Arguments around the humoral body and emerging sciences converged on the issue of prohibiting masturbation. Current scholars have viewed the discourses of suppression and prohibition as an indication that bourgeois society placed restraints on nonprocreative sex.[57] Because masturbation is a nonprocreative practice, it was considered a needless loss of valuable semen. Also it was blamed for different diseases and generally thought to weaken body and soul (fig. 4.3).

Thomas Laqueur believes the discussion of masturbation started with the "founding text" on the subject, *Onania*. He claims that the work inspired modern ideas about masturbation.[58] Other scholars agree that masturbation was not an issue prior to the eighteenth century.[59] Lawrence Stone pointed out that, in France, propaganda against masturbation peaked between 1810 and 1850. Meanwhile, Isabel Hull has shown that the Germans started to be concerned about masturbation as early as the 1780s.[60] In Russia, there were no campaigns against masturbation, even though Samuel Auguste David Tissot's *L'Onanisme* was translated and published several times. Despite debate about the causes, consequences, methods, and discursive practices of masturbation, there seems to be general agreement among historians on major texts and the timing of a masturbation phobia.

Historians have treated the popularity of *Onania* and *L'Onanisme* in a number of ways. *Onania* has been seen largely in the context of the development of eighteenth-century pornography, while Tissot's emphasis on "spermatic economy" has been associated with mercantilism. The eighteenth-century emphasis on masturbation has also been associated with a redefinition of childhood and the search for new "scientific" explanations for madness during an age of growing rationality.[61]

Onania was the first text to signal the growing concerns over disciplining sexuality within medical and pathological discourses overseeing a secularization of masturbation.[62] Yet, as Patrick Singy points out, *Onania* also represents a theological text, whose goal was "to promote virtue and Christian purity."[63] This early text sees masturbation as a sin, placing all consequences of its practice within the framework of impurity. When the New York Puritan minister Joseph Moody read *Onania* in 1724, he found that it confirmed all his fears.[64] Though *Onania* suggested that masturbation threatened not only the body, but also the soul, it mostly concentrated on the bodily harm wrought by masturbation—thus signaling the dawn of somatic discourse about the topic.[65] On the other hand, historian Peter Wagner has suggested that *Onania* emerged

FIGURE 4.4: Portrait of Tissot. Etching after A. Guanzati. Wellcome Library, London.

among a highly voyeuristic genre intending to produce a sexual response—in particular, because its accounts of the experience of masturbators were meant to arouse the reader.[66] By the mid-eighteenth century, medical writers started providing "scientific" information about masturbation. Tissot's dissertation attempted to provide a scientific account of the problem by way of classical arguments. It became popular, translated into many European languages, including even Russian.[67] Tissot (fig. 4.4) grounded his ideas about masturbation in terms of bodily need and cause of physical disease. It is notable that Tissot's other works did not leave such a mark in the history of medicine, though they were much more consistent and scientifically founded.[68]

Over time, three groups of discourse on masturbation emerged: theological, medical, and pedagogical. Specialists studying different aspects of masturbation suggested various methods for its prevention and treatment. Theologians presented the church's traditional view of masturbation as a vice and a sin; doctors concerned themselves with diagnosis and possible remedies; and teachers focused on eradicating masturbation among the young, with the vice thought to be particularly prevalent in boarding schools.[69]

Though the eighteenth century has been recognized by historians as a pivotal time for the emergence of concerns over masturbation, the practice was in evidence earlier. Literature, diaries, and pornography all suggest masturbation to be a familiar experience for people during that era. Men especially share their intimate secrets in diaries. The seventeenth-century American Puritan minister Michael Wigglesworth, who wrote his diary between 1653 and 1657, recounted his dismay over frequent "unresistable torments of carnal lusts"—seminal emissions—that were provoked when he read, dreamed, or felt "fond affections" for his pupils at Harvard College. Similarly, Cotton Mather prayed and fasted for fear that, as "a Young Man in my Single Estate," he might fall into "lascivious violations of the Seventh Commandment."[70] Joseph Moody, who encoded his diary in Latin, referred to masturbation fifty-five times over a period of four years, two months, and three weeks (August 22, 1720 to November 11, 1724), detailing the time, place, and the circumstances of each act. Though Moody called his acts "self-pollution," he did not consider all forms of sexual release to be equally sinful. He distinguished between masturbation to orgasm and stimulating himself without ejaculation—handling and "playing" with his "member," as he called it. A third form of masturbation involved doing so while half-asleep (nocturnal emissions), which was also considered less sinful: it, too, denoted no loss of self-control,[71] no intentional "spilling the seed." Moody also described the masturbatory experiences of others, writing, for example, about those of the doctor he lodged with.[72] Similarly, in Scotland, William Drummond, a young gentleman, recorded the occasions between the years 1657 and 1659 on which he masturbated—there were sixty-two altogether.[73] In England, John Canon (1684–1743), an excise officer and charity schoolmaster at Glastonbury, learned how to masturbate at the age of twelve from a seventeen-year-old schoolmate and cousin. He reveals in his diary how he would masturbate after reading a midwifery manual. When he was caught by his mother, but this did not seem to have stopped him.[74] Ivan Dolgorukov (1764–1823), a Russian prince, learned "solitary pleasures" at the age of fourteen from his cousin, who was sent away from the house when this was discovered by family.[75] In his *Confessions,* writing in the 1770s, Rousseau called masturbation a "vice" that was "very attractive to those of lively imagination," and confessed to practicing it.[76]

The diarists did not clearly state the reasons for masturbation except that they had a need; we do not find them thinking the experience perverse. Joseph Moody described his motivations as "evil," "impious," and "willful," expressing anxiety about masturbation that was common in colonial New England[77]—but he made no link between masturbation and criminality or illegality.[78] Brian D. Carroll argues that this anxiety came mostly from the lack of self-control since sexual self-mastery was one of the key elements in a man's proper sexual performance.[79]

All of these men writing their memoirs and diaries at an adult age expressed guilt over their adolescent "unbridled lust" and masturbatory experiences: firstly because they considered it sinful (Joseph Moody was most reflective on this issue); and secondly because the practice was thought to be bad for one's health. Dolgorukov has pointed out that only when people began "to reason," did they start to understand that masturbation was bad for their health.[80] Prior to Tissot's *L'Onanisme,* concern about masturbation was connected to loss of virility[81] rather than to the diseases it might cause. Rousseau felt that masturbation saved "young men of my temperament from many disorders, but at the expense of their health, their strength, and sometimes their life itself."[82]

So far, no evidence on masturbation has been found in women's diaries, but that does not mean that women did not masturbate. Female masturbation was constructed through pornography and erotic literature. In certain texts, masturbation becomes a major tool of arousal and marks sexual desire and promiscuity. In the early French pornographic text *L'Escole des Filles,* masturbation is presented as an alternative for women who wish to experience enjoyment without male intervention. Thus, when Fanchon asks what such women can do, Susanne describes different masturbatory methods, concluding that sex is natural and that women can be satisfied, even without men.[83] Another French text, *Histoire de Dom Bourge, Portier de Chartreaux,* written by Gervaise de Latouch (1748), describes many different pleasurable instances of both male and female masturbation.[84] The first thing Fanny Hill learns in the pornographic novel *Memoirs of a Woman of Pleasure* (1749) is how to masturbate. Lyndal Roper, in her article on child-witches, provides evidence of masturbating girls, whose "indecency" was directly connected as being inspired by the Devil. Describing the Poor Children's House, founded in 1723 in Augsburg, she reveals (through examination of the warders' reports) that Juliane Trichtler and Anne Regine Gruber "were committing indecency with each other by means of a sheet." Gruber was thought to be "incorrigible" because she "corrupted" other girls. Finally, it was decided to clap her in irons and put her into solitary confinement. It was even suggested that the children's sleep patterns be changed, putting them to sleep during the day and keeping them awake at night. That way, the Devil could not induce fantasies, and masturbation would be avoided.[85] German theologian and teacher Peter

Villiaume (1746–1825) asserted in 1787 that 50 percent of the middle classes, and 25 percent of the lower ones, had been *bestecht* (corrupted); he compared this to an "interminable rampant epidemic disease."[86]

In literature, negative attitudes toward masturbation prevailed during the eighteenth century, though positive attitudes could also be found. Bernard Mandeville acknowledges the attractions of masturbation as it invoked "Safety, Privacy, Convenience, and Cheapness."[87] As late as the 1760s, Robert Wallace, in his unpublished essay, "Of Venery," described the teenage male's discovery of masturbation as an "agreeable experience."[88]

Nonetheless, masturbation continued to be punished under certain circumstances, most notably, when it was connected with sodomy. Flogging was administered by Dutch colonial authorities in the Cape of Good Hope on sailors who had committed mutual masturbation. When sailor Gerrit Wijntjes was caught committing mutual masturbation with two soldiers in 1749, all three confessed, but declared their innocence on the grounds that they did not know what sodomy was. They were bound to a stake and flogged, and afterward sentenced to hard labor at Cape Town for one year. In 1765, a fourteen-year-old sailor named Francois was sentenced to whipping and banishment from Netherlands to Cape Town for seducing another boy into participating in mutual masturbation back in Delft.[89]

In countries where the church oversaw sexual offenses, masturbators often received penance as punishment. It was easier for the church to discover cases of masturbation, since confession allowed priests to collect the necessary admission. Russia offers a good example of such monitoring. Orthodox religion was especially intolerant about any type of sexuality. One of the first questions a priest would ask was, "And tell me, child, did not you corrupt your virginity with self-pollution; do you still pollute yourself ...?"[90] This question was asked of both men and women. Penance varied, from forty days of fasting to three years of excommunication from communion.[91] French confessionaries were as arbitrary as the Russian ones, imposing the same types of penance.[92] In Paris in 1736, a police inspector named Simonnet arrested a fourteen-year-old worker who had masturbated on the street while watching a woman passing by. He then arrested another boy, who said "that in his native region, there would be twenty boys batting together and screwing each other." Simonnet imprisoned the boys, then condemned their behavior in the presence of their fathers as a way of shaming them.[93]

In general, most contemporaries were preoccupied with male rather than female masturbation, although warnings against the latter were expressed by several authors, including Mary Wollstonecraft. Female masturbation never developed into the great cause for concern that male masturbation did, probably because women were considered to be less important. Franz Eder argues that the discrepancy was due to the focus on the male bourgeois body and its characteristics such as steadfastness, health, controllability, general rationality of purpose, and the procreative potential of the male seed. Masturbation endangered male sexual identity because it led to the appearance of such female traits as fluidity, softness, and loss of mastery over the body—all oppositional to what constituted the autonomous bourgeois man.[94] On the other hand, Randolph Trumbach connects this process with the fear of sodomy and the specter of the effeminate sodomite. The taboos against sodomy and masturbation were mutually reinforced because heterosexuality required that men receive sexual pleasure from women and never from themselves or other males. Masturbation was a part of adolescent male socializing as few men learned to masturbate on their own.[95] Perhaps most significantly, the social implications of masturbation seem to have been more crucial than understanding the anatomical aspects of male and female bodies. Social control over the body, penetrative sex, and procreation became the ultimate goals of anti-masturbation discourses.

JOYFUL DEVIANCIES AND PERVERSIONS

The perception of perversion in the eighteenth century depended on an understanding that the transgressors were crossing recognized acceptable boundaries of behavior. This involved infringing major zones of human habitat: moral laws (rape, murder); religious taboos (on masturbation, sodomy or blasphemy); conventional mores (for example, sex with the very old or the very young); "natural" or socially conditioned reflexes of repulsion (urophilia, coprophilia); gender or species boundaries (transvestism, bestiality, necrophilia). We have discussed bestiality and masturbation, two major issues in eighteenth-century sexuality. Now we turn to other methods of achieving pleasure that were considered perverted or outside the norm.

Necrophilia

Love of the dead and a sexual desire for corpses appear to have fallen somewhere between sodomy, fornication, and bestiality on the scale of unnaturalness. In the early Middle Ages, the Catholic church considered necrophilia as neither whoring (i.e., fornication) nor bestiality, instead terming it as "pollution with a tendency to whoring."[96] Early modern German lawyers suggested beheading for sex with a dead body.[97]

Dead bodies attracted curiosity, and watching an execution was a popular pastime for the learned classes and peasants alike. Hanging, particularly of women, comprised some of the darker fantasies of repressed individuals. This danger was tacitly acknowledged in the peculiar punishments inflicted on female felons. In early modern Europe, most notably in Russia, women were often buried alive to avoid the exposure of being hanged. In England, up until the end of the eighteenth century, female traitors were burned rather than disemboweled. Sir William Blackstone, the distinguished eighteenth-century judge and academic, suggested that this was due to the "decency owing to their sex."[98] Dissection was also thought sordid because of the exposure of dead bodies to public view, but it attracted attention nonetheless. Dated at around 1780, Thomas Rowlandson's sardonic drawing of anatomists ogling and fondling the leg of a dissected and naked female corpse was an early comment on the medical fraternity.[99]

Attraction to death and the dead became a popular topic in literature—particularly in the emerging genre of gothic novels. The central idea involves a continuation of love when one in a pair of lovers—usually, a young, attractive female—dies. In Lois Mercier's *Lettre de Dulis à Son Ami* (1767), Dulis, a young man, falls in love with Junie, but does not tell her of his feelings for two years. When she dies, and he sees her dead body lying veiled on her bed, he is overcome with an unspeakable desire. Dulis commits an act of necrophilia on Junie's body, after which she awakens from death. It is later revealed that she is pregnant (though she was presumed to have been a virgin betrothed to someone.) Dulis confesses his crime and is imprisoned.[100]

Necrophilia was also invoked as a powerful metaphor in political writings of the age—especially those centering upon the French Revolution. In his pamphlet "Cannibal's Progress," William Cobbett draws a connection between the necrophiliac's sexual violence and the excesses of the French Revolutionary Army: "Even the bodies of young women, who had expired under their barbarity, and of women who but a few hours before had been in labour, were made use of to satiate the internal lust of these monsters in human shape ... the corpses of several women were found, who had been violated and abused even unto death ... the monsters satisfied their brutal appetites with corpses, and with some unhappy victims in the agonies of death."[101]

Scant evidence makes it difficult to assess the degree to which these stories were inspired by real events. The Marquis de Sade described a Parisian who paid to have the corpses of young men and women delivered to his house, where he committed "atrocities" on their bodies. De Sade's claims are confirmed by a document, addressed to the superintendent of Paris, reporting indecencies inflicted upon bodies in the common grave.[102] With so few cases uncovered thus far, we must presume that necrophilia was a rarity in practice.

Flagellation

Sade was fond of flogging, as well as other methods of sexual arousal reached through pain or death. A fashion for flagellation developed in the eighteenth century, establishing it as a mainstay of the commercial sex industry. Flagellation achieved sexual arousal through either beating, or being beaten, on the buttocks. In spite of de Sade's frequent use of it in his texts, flagellation was considered to be more of an English specialty (it was especially popular among the English upper classes).[103] The standard explanation of this phenomenon is that the habit was picked up (by men, at least) in public schools such as Westminster. Richard Busby, one headmaster there, was made infamous by his predilection for flogging pupils. Flagellation is first described in *Memoirs of a Woman of Pleasure* (1749), later emerging as fully themed pornographic texts during the 1770s in publications such as *Exhibition of Female Flagellants*.[104]

In London, prostitutes provided flagellation services at various brothels: Theresa Berkley had an establishment at 28 Charlotte Street, Portland Place, in the 1790s, and Mrs. Collett maintained a facility at Tavistock Court, Covent Garden, that was allegedly patronized by George IV. These houses were stocked with rods, birches, and more elaborate equipment to satisfy all clients' desires: "A notorious machine was invented for Mrs Berkley to flog gentlemen upon, in the spring of 1828. It is capable of being opened to a considerable extent, so as to bring the body to any angle that might be desirable."[105] Reports emerged of flagellation taking place in a case involving an early-eighteenth-century group of Norwich libertines. Lawrence Stone gives details of their flagellation orgies, where a group of them—two men and three women—whipped each other. The case came to the attention of the court, which charged the participants with "gross and unnatural" behavior. In the end, the presiding officials decided it would be unwise to deprave the morals of the city further by giving more publicity to such sensational disclosures.[106] Well-known figures were occasionally reported to have indulged in the vice. In 1816, there was a notable scandal when General Eyre Coote was found to be paying fifteen- and sixteen-year-old boys at Christ's Hospital school to let him beat them, and then to beat him. Despite the intercession of several peers, members of Parliament, and other respectable individuals, Coote was stripped of his military rank and honors, as well as his Knighthood of the Bath.[107]

Voyeurism and Exhibitionism

Flagellation was closely connected with other "variations," such as voyeurism and exhibitionism.[108] This is evident from the example of the Norwich libertines, whose voyeurism involved long hours of peering through keyholes and the holes they had drilled to look in the bedrooms of guests.[109] There are examples of similar court cases and witness accounts. At the age of sixteen, John Cannon (1684–1743) drilled holes in a privy wall so he could view the genitals of a female servant living in the house.[110]

The voyeur motif was popular in eighteenth-century French rococo art. The voyeur—almost always male—remains hidden behind curtains, doors, or bushes, while looking at a woman, who is usually depicted so the paintings' viewer shares in the voyeur's excitement. Jean-Honoré Fragonard's *The Swing* (1767) is a typical example (fig. 4.5).[111] Depicted voyeurism extended to showing bodily functions being observed: earthy acts that could be construed as urophilia and coprophilia on the part of the artist. *Le Parfumeur* and *Les Deux Fontaines,* a couple of sixteenth-century engravings ascribed

FIGURE 4.5: Jean-Honoré Fragonard, *The Swing* (1767).

to Bernard Picart, depict a defecating man and a pissing woman: images from nature that could incite sexual arousal. Rembrandt's *Woman Pissing* belongs to the same genre.[112]

The other side to voyeurism was exhibitionism. Displays of nakedness were part of rituals practiced by libertines and notorious rakes. There was a famous 1663 episode in which Sir Charles Sedley revealed his buttocks on a balcony, in public view. He was heavily fined. Samuel Pepys wrote of the incident:

> Mr. Batten telling us of a late triall of Sir Charles Sydly [sic] the other day, before my Lord Chief Justice Foster and the whole bench, for his debauchery a little while since at Oxford Kate's, coming in open day into the Balcone and showed his nakedness, actin all the postures of lust and buggery that coul be imagined.[113]

Throughout the Enlightenment, exhibitionism was a natural way to provoke excitement, via pornography as well as actual experience. In general, unless it created a public nuisance, exhibitionism was not considered a perversion in private circles—even if its public version could lead to arrest.

CONCLUSION

By maintaining systems of norms and rules, European societies were able to place certain limitations on the body and on sexual behaviors. In these systems, moral and legal codes defined what was permissible for individuals to indulge in. Only "abnormal conduct" was condemned, persecuted, or punished—by laws or local communities. The worst abnormal behaviors were classed as crimes, with authorities attempting to place unconventional sexual practices under the jurisdiction of the legal system. Attitudes toward these practices slowly changed, when other disciplinary systems (such as medicine) emerged. Sex and sexuality were beginning to be medicalized and came increasingly under the domain of doctors, psychiatrists, sexologists, and sexopathologists. By the end of the nineteenth century, essentialist attitudes toward the sexes and the many forms of sexuality developed. It was during the eighteenth century, however, that the foundation for contemporary cognitive practices of "sexual variations" was established, and we understand them in our present society by way of those traditions.

CHAPTER FIVE

Sex, Religion and the Law

MERRIL D. SMITH

In 1792, James McMullin of Chester County, Pennsylvania, brought a suit against Robert Wilken and William Hickman. McMullin accused the two men of spreading rumors about him, saying that he had had a venereal disease and that he "bedded with" his nurse, Betsy Hill, "and made use of her ... in a whorish manner." Wilken and Hickman claimed that McMullin mistreated his wife, Rachel, and that his immoral behavior was causing "an uneasiness in the Neighborhood." McMullin asserted that the men were lying, and that their lies were injuring both his reputation and his business. James and Rachel's behavior, and the stories their neighbors told about them, would prove important in subsequent legal actions over the years, including James's attempt to divorce Rachel for adultery in 1804.[1]

The gossip of their neighbors affected the McMullins' reputations and probably influenced the decisions of judges, but it did not lead to prosecutions for James or Rachel's alleged sexual misconduct, as it might have in the previous century. Since fornication was a crime in seventeenth-century Massachusetts, as it was in many places, neighborhood talk and opinion *did* have bearing on the prosecution of Priscilla Willson, a sixteen-year-old orphan, and Samuel Appleton, a married man of twenty-nine, who were tried for fornication in 1683, after Priscilla had become pregnant and named Samuel as the baby's father. Fornication was defined as sexual intercourse between any man, single or married, and a single woman. Adultery was considered a more serious crime, as it involved sexual intercourse between a man and a married woman. Because she was pregnant, it was obvious that Priscilla had had sexual relations, and therefore, in Puritan New England, the young unmarried woman was guilty of a crime, despite testimony from witnesses stating that she had asked Samuel several times to let her go. According to early modern medical beliefs, women, as well as men, had to have an orgasm in order for conception to occur. English legal authorities, therefore, affirmed that women could not become pregnant as a result of rape. Thus, friends and family who had believed in Priscilla's good character saw in her pregnancy proof that she had sinned. However, they did not blame her entirely. In an unusual step, fourteen of her neighbors in Lynn, Massachusetts, signed a statement testifying that they had never known her to be anything but modest and civil, but that they believed "she was overcome by some subtill slights and temptations of one that beguiled her to yeeld to his lust and wee are all perswaded that shee doth not wrongly accuse him whoe she doth lay the charge upon." Samuel Appleton, a gentleman with connections to at least four of the six judges, denied that he was the father of Priscilla's baby. The judges dismissed the charges against Samuel, but they decreed Priscilla guilty of fornication. Nevertheless, they did require Samuel to pay one half of the court costs and one half of Priscilla's childbirth expenses, the midwife's fee, a nurse's fee, and the costs for taking care of the baby, who lived only a brief time, as well as for her burial. With this arrangement, Samuel Appleton maintained his honor, even as the court implied that he was actually the father of Priscilla Willson's baby.[2]

This chapter will focus mainly on North America and Western Europe. The two cases just discussed illustrate the social—and legal—regulation of sexuality in seventeenth- and eighteenth-century Anglo-America. Although medical and theological beliefs had a direct bearing on the enactment and enforcement of laws in the seventeenth century, the regulation of sexuality in both centuries depended greatly upon the observations of family members, neighbors, and people in the community.[3] Unlike seventeenth-century prosecutions, however, eighteenth-century courts were less concerned with sexual conduct and more concerned with its economic consequences. Moreover, in the small, intimate communities of the seventeenth-century American colonies, when people whispered about the loose behavior or scandalous conduct of a man or woman, those whispers generally reached the ears of a magistrate or clergyman who was also a member of the community. Such gossip could then lead to a court summons but ultimately helped to regulate sexuality through the monitoring of behavior within communities.

Seventeenth-century magistrates accepted gossip as valid testimony in court cases, and much of the gossip involved allegations of premarital or extramarital sexual activity.[4] For example, on her voyage to Massachusetts in 1672, Sarah Blacklock indiscreetly confessed to shipboard companions that back in England she had become pregnant by her Dutch lover, but that she had suffered a miscarriage after four months. Unfortunately for Sarah, someone reported her confession to officials in Massachusetts, and she was summoned to court and then sent back to England.[5] Gossip, however, was not limited to the passengers confined for months aboard crowded ships. Most seventeenth-century white Americans lived in small, cramped houses. Often, several people shared a room, and perhaps even a bed at night. It was difficult to keep secrets in these close quarters and in the generally communal work situations of colonial America. In these settings, any unusual behavior, changes in appearance, or ill-chosen words could easily generate talk in the neighborhood.

In Puritan New England, watching one's neighbors became a moral imperative based on religious convictions. Puritan leaders directed members of their congregations to watch one another as a way of preventing them from committing acts of "uncleanness." As the prominent Puritan minister Cotton Mather stated, "If the neighbor of an elected saint sins, then the saint sins also."[6] Puritans believed that only with constant vigilance could they fight sin, which was a necessary struggle if they were to preserve their covenant with God and protect their "city on a hill." Although they believed that sex within marriage was not only desirable but also obligatory, they viewed nonmarital and nonprocreative sex as sinful and potentially disruptive to the community. In fact, they frequently linked sexual deviance with religious heresy.

Puritans, and indeed, many Anglo-Americans, viewed women who spoke in public, challenged religious authorities, or otherwise stepped outside accepted female roles, as troublemakers. In addition, these women were often thought to be sexually promiscuous. "Unruly" women were seen as incapable of being restrained by male household heads, and liable to cause all sorts of destruction—to their homes and families, to their communities, and even to political authority. Under English common law, carried over to the American colonies, a woman lost her legal identity when she married, as she was "covered" by her husband in the legal concept known as coverture. This meant that a husband was responsible for any damages and debts incurred by his wife, even when the debts were a result of defamation suits brought by neighbors she had slandered. Recognizing, however, that husbands could not always control "brabbling women," the colony of Virginia enacted a law in 1662 stating that a husband could choose to have his outspoken wife ducked rather than pay her fines.[7]

Despite the prevalence of gossip, seventeenth-century men and women still had to be careful of what they said about others. Those who engaged in bawdy talk could be brought before the court on charges of "filthy" or "unclean" speech, just as they could be charged with behaving immodestly.[8] Yet, sexual gossip was common in New England—and elsewhere in the colonies—as people then, just as now, enjoyed the titillation derived from discussing a neighbor's scandalous behavior, or boasting about their own sexual prowess. However, a person's reputation was of vast importance in the early modern world, and one way to inflict harm on a neighbor was to ruin his or her good name. Slander suits were quite common in early American courts. Men complained mainly about being called a "knave" or some term alluding to being untrustworthy or dishonorable, but women who were slandered were usually called "whores," "sluts," or other disparaging terms indicating their sexual looseness. Although men could be dishonored by sexual slander, it did not usually affect their reputations as seriously or permanently as it did women's. For a woman, chastity was all-important; it was part of her image as a "proper" young woman, or a good wife. Having a reputation as a promiscuous woman could greatly reduce her chance of finding a spouse, or damage her relationship with her husband if she was already married. It might also make her more vulnerable to sexual attacks by men who knew of her reputation.

In seventeenth-century England, too, gossip could affect reputations. For women, this was particularly true—anyone could injure a woman's standing simply by calling her a whore or its equivalent, while a woman had to make specific claims about a man in order to damage his reputation. Nevertheless, through gossip, women in both England and its colonies asserted some power over others, since they were denied political and legal authority. In England, however, women were also permitted to bring cases before the church courts—something they could not do in the same way in the American colonies. In the mid-seventeenth century, the majority of cases brought before London's main church court were defamation cases brought by women against other women who had slandered them. Elsewhere in Europe, gossip by and about women both regulated behavior and threatened official legal and social structures. In early modern Spain, for example, gossip brought news of scandalous behavior to authorities, leaving the reputations of seduced and abandoned women in tatters. Yet when women assembled together to work, they also had an opportunity to talk about men. Thus, activities such as spinning bees, where women and girls gathered together to spin, might be viewed with suspicion. Such was the case in eighteenth-century Germany, where officials believed spinning bees were dangerous because women could discuss and pass judgment on male authorities.[9]

Gossip also spread rumors of witchcraft and possession, which could lead to the prosecution and possible torture and execution of those alleged to be witches. Witchcraft was seen as a particular threat to the stability of a community. Although some men were charged and prosecuted for witchcraft, women were most often accused of being witches in both Europe and the colonies. In a few regions—Normandy, Russia, Estonia, and Iceland—the percentage of men accused of being witches was greater than the percentage of women, but in most areas of Europe and the American colonies, accusations against women far exceeded those against men.[10] In part this stemmed from the prevalent belief that women were sexually voracious and driven by lust. Both Europeans and colonial Americans viewed women as lust-filled creatures—the "daughters of Eve"—who were incapable of controlling themselves. This image of women did not change until the mid-eighteenth century, when women (or, more precisely, white women) began to be viewed as chaste and passionless. Yet, while educated men believed women to be sexual temptresses, they also considered women to be physically and morally weaker than men, and thus more susceptible to temptation by the Devil. Many accepted as fact that witches had sexual intercourse with the Devil and engaged in orgies with imps and other witches. Indeed, women charged as witches sometimes confessed to sexual relations with both devils and men. Frequently, though not always, women accused of witchcraft were already social outcasts, and some had a past history of sexual misbehavior.[11]

Puritans in England and New England sometimes accused women of being witches if they were also thought to be guilty of such crimes as abortion or infanticide, or even if they gave birth to illegitimate children. Puritans considered these crimes to be sins because they appeared to interfere with God's will in determining who should live and die. Abortion and infanticide were also attempts to cover up the initial sin of fornication. Some Puritan women internalized their guilt about committing these acts, believing they should be punished for their sins, even if they were not witches. For example, Margaret Lakes would not confess that she was a witch, even when she was about to be hanged for being one. Nevertheless, she was reported to have said that God was justified in making her pay for her sin in this way, because "she had when a single woman played the harlot, and being with Child used means to destroy the fruit of her body to conceal her sin and shame."[12]

In both Europe and America, female healers and midwives were occasionally blamed when a sudden illness appeared, or when the death of an infant or its mother could not be readily explained. Although their use of potions and folk magic might be overlooked—or even valued—most of the time, in times of social or political stress, midwives often became scapegoats. Moreover, in early modern Europe, it was also widely believed that witches eagerly sought unbaptized babies for their rituals, thus providing another reason for suspecting midwives, who had access to newborns, of devilish practices. In some areas, these beliefs lingered into the eighteenth century. As late as 1728, a Hungarian midwife was executed after being "charged with baptizing 2,000 children in the Devil's name."[13]

Female witches were seen to invert the "natural order" of society by subverting the power of the household head, keeping couples from consummating their marriages, destroying families by preventing conception or births, and seducing men. They were the antithesis of the "good wife"; instead of being submissive, chaste, and obedient, they were unruly, sexually voracious, and independent. In some instances, they were also linked to Satan and accused of using *maleficium*, or supernatural means, to hurt crops, animals, and people.

Accused witches were believed to be flouting authority, overstepping their boundaries, ignoring or perverting gender roles, and/or overturning the natural order. By so doing, they not only endangered their own souls, but they also brought physical and spiritual harm to their communities. Because of this, they had to be stopped; in the most extreme cases, and if convicted of witchcraft, they were executed. In other cases they were fined, whipped, ducked, or punished in some other fashion. By the eighteenth century, due to Enlightenment thought and an emphasis on science, there was more skepticism about the existence of witches and witchcraft, and witchcraft trials all but ceased in both England and Europe. In addition, the upper classes may have disparaged witchcraft beliefs to distance themselves from the lower classes and the uneducated, who continued to believe in witches well into the eighteenth century.[14]

In England and its colonies, as well as in most of early modern Europe, the only legally permissible sexual activity was that between husband and wife. Premarital sex was illegal, but the degree to which it was actually prosecuted varied from place to place. In some places, sexual relations between a man and woman who were betrothed were overlooked, but most communities had regulations against fornication (fig. 5.1), adultery, and sexual relations between men. In Italy, the church and city governments required single mothers to leave

FIGURE 5.1: A (woman) skeleton warns of the dangers of fornication. Oil painting attributed to a Spanish painter, about 1680. Wellcome Library, London.

their babies in foundling homes. Those who could not pay the required fees had to work as wet nurses in the foundling homes, after giving birth in jail. In 1680, the Synod of Troyes in France went even further in trying to prevent illegitimate births by attempting to eliminate opportunities for men and women to even meet. Men and boys were threatened with excommunication if they ignored the prohibition against meeting "with women and girls in the places where they gather at night to spin and work."[15]

To restrain women and to keep them from seducing men and creating community disturbances, seventeenth-century lawmakers, philosophers, and theologians believed that they needed to live in a household controlled by their fathers, employers, or husbands. The city council of Strasbourg noted in 1665 that, when single women did not live under male-supervised households, it caused "nothing but shame, immodesty, wantonness, and immorality."[16]

In fact, both young, single men and women were expected to live within households where they would be supervised. Prior to marriage, even the sons and daughters of the well-to-do often lived in the households of others to learn various skills, but in these other households they might also be subjected to sexual innuendo, temptation, or advances. Still, English officials and their colonial counterparts often regarded the household and the family to be one and the same, and they considered the family to be the cornerstone of society. Indeed, the family was known as "the little commonwealth," with the husband/father at its head in a position similar to that of the monarch, and his wife, children, and servants all under his rule. Laws were enacted in the American colonies ensuring that single people lived within households, and that parents or masters would provide them with the skills and education necessary for their futures.

Despite law, custom, and attempts at keeping young men and women closely supervised, unmarried couples did engage in sexual relations, with and without intending to marry. In seventeenth-century England, fornication and bastardy were crimes, but the rate of actual prosecution varied throughout the century. In most areas, however, poor women were more likely to be prosecuted than women who had the family and resources to support a child. Similarly, couples who married before officials made a bastardy charge against them were usually given only mild punishments, as were couples whose babies arrived within seven and a half months of marriage. Daughters of the gentry, and those with substantial dowries, were less likely to have premarital sexual encounters.[17]

In contrast, authorities in Puritan New England punished both women and men for fornication, and couples whose babies were born too soon after the wedding date were still prosecuted for fornication (fig. 5.2). Although they did not condone illicit sexuality, officials in the Chesapeake settlements were more concerned with the economic costs of bastardy than with the moral lapses of those who produced the illegitimate children. Tobacco, the labor-intensive crop on which the fortunes of Chesapeake planters were based, demanded a supply of workers. Chesapeake planters were therefore more concerned with the loss of a female servant's ability to work due to pregnancy and childbirth than with whether she had sinned. Men greatly outnumbered women in the Chesapeake. Servants were not permitted to marry, but once their period of indenture was over, former female servants, even pregnant ones, generally had no difficulty finding husbands.[18]

In both the Chesapeake and New England, as well as in England, part of a midwife's sworn duty was to obtain from an unmarried laboring woman

FIGURE 5.2: A courtroom scene with a judge, a pregnant woman, a guilty-looking man, and an angry wife. Engraving by T. Cook after W. Hogarth. Wellcome Library, London.

the name of her baby's father so that he could be charged and made to pay support. At the end of the eighteenth century, in some areas, an unmarried pregnant women might still plead guilty to the charge of fornication and name the father of her child to the midwife. However, the majority of these cases never entered the court records because the charges were dropped, and the men married the mothers of their children.[19]

One striking change that occurred in New England at the end of the seventeenth century was the rise in premarital pregnancies. Whereas 2 percent of brides were pregnant when they married in New Haven County, Connecticut, in the 1670s, by the 1690s, 19 percent were pregnant when they wed. By the time of the American Revolution, 30 to 40 percent of brides in many New England towns were pregnant. A combination of factors was responsible, among them a decline in Puritan values and a more permissive attitude displayed by parents.[20]

Young men and women experimented with one another, not only during courtship, but even before a formal courtship commenced. They did so, however, with the approval of their parents, and in their parents' homes (fig. 5.3). Knowing that it would be difficult to prevent their offspring from sexual experimentation, parents allowed their daughters' suitors to spend the night. This permitted the parents, or other relatives, to supervise. If a young woman

FIGURE 5.3: As a young man kisses a young lady's hand, a second woman shuts the door against another man attempting to enter the room. Engraving by Petit after Boilly. Wellcome Library, London.

became pregnant under these circumstances, at least her family knew the father's identity. Parents, and sometimes the community, could put pressure on the man; if he would not wed the pregnant woman, then she could bring a paternity suit against him with the knowledge that he could not easily contest it. As Richard Godbeer notes, "permissive courtship functioned for the families concerned as a pragmatic accommodation between the greater sexual freedom that young people now enjoyed and the desire of parents to maintain protective surveillance over their children."[21]

This custom of allowing courting couples to sleep together—often with the understanding that they would remain clothed—was known as bundling. European visitors noted and commented on the practice, which occurred mainly in the northern and middle colonies during the mid-eighteenth century. Journals kept by individuals during that time show that young men and women spent much unsupervised time together in activities such as sleighing, husking, and gathering at parties and dances, as well as simply visiting one another while doing errands. Overnight stays can be seen as an extension of this culture that permitted young men and women to socialize with one another with such ease. Moreover, it shows how New Englanders allowed for a more permissive sexual culture for young adults while maintaining parental supervision.[22]

For the most part, this parental and community supervision ensured that young men took responsibility for their behavior. Between 1785 and 1797, more than a third of the births attended by Maine midwife Martha Ballard were conceived out of wedlock. However, most of these mothers had married by the time they went into labor. In some instances, the couple had intended to marry before they engaged in sexual relations; in other cases, community pressure compelled the father to wed his pregnant lover. When young men refused to take responsibility, they could be taken to court to reach a settlement. Sometimes, too, a threatened court action propelled the father-to-be to marry.[23]

In contrast to the premarital pregnancy rates in New England and the middle colonies, which rose throughout the eighteenth century, premarital pregnancy rates in Philadelphia rose until the late colonial period, when one in three brides was pregnant at the time of the wedding, and then dropped following the Revolution, with one in five brides pregnant. It dropped still further in the nineteenth century, to one in six. However, bastardy rates—that is, births to women who did not marry the fathers—increased during this period in Philadelphia. Moreover, the parents of these illegitimate babies came from all social classes and from various ethnicities. This was probably because Philadelphia embraced an urban pleasure culture that emerged in the 1760s and emulated that of European cities, with theaters, gambling, prostitution, and opportunities for casual sexual encounters.[24]

Because an unmarried woman who had a baby out of wedlock often faced economic problems and public opprobrium, women in this situation often tried to conceal their pregnancies as long as possible. Some women attempted abortions. Knowledge of herbal abortifacients was widespread in both Europe and America, and it was possible to obtain them from doctors, midwives, and others who had knowledge of medicinal plants. Cornelia Dayton suggests that the "*idea* of taking an abortifacient" was familiar to young New England women, even if the knowledge of how to prepare such a potion was not.[25] In late-seventeenth-century and eighteenth-century London, both contraceptives and abortifacients were widely advertised, indicating that there must have been a market for these items. Abortion was not illegal, as long as it occurred before "quickening," when the mother first felt movement from the fetus. Without reliable tests for pregnancy, a woman could not even be certain she was pregnant before she felt such movement.[26]

It is difficult to know how common abortion was in the seventeenth or eighteenth centuries because it was not usually discussed and was seldom reported. The few examples that appear are mostly from court documents, either as part of another case, or because a problem occurred with the abortion. One case in eighteenth-century Connecticut reveals the part that abortion played in the regulation of sexuality among young people in the town. In 1745, officials in Windham County, Connecticut, began looking into the death of nineteen-year-old Sarah Grosvenor three years earlier. It is not known why it took so long for the case to come to the court's attention. Sarah died after John Hallowell, a "practitioner of physick," performed an abortion on her with instruments. At the instigation of her lover, twenty-seven-year-old Amasa Sessions, Sarah first tried taking an abortifacient he had procured from Hallowell. The "manual operation" was performed because the abortifacient proved ineffective. Sarah concealed her pregnancy from those around her, and all arrangements to rid her of the baby were made furtively because, although abortion itself was not illegal, it was used to cover up the prior act of fornication, which was both a crime and a sin. Only when it became necessary did Sarah reveal her secret to her sister and to some relatives around her own age. Sarah's parents, as well as some older adults in the town, remained unaware of her condition until she became ill from the abortion. While dying, Sarah confessed the details of her story to her good friend Abigail Nightingale. Sessions and Hallowell were eventually indicted—not for the abortion—but for causing Sarah's death. The grand jury dismissed the case against Sessions. Hallowell, however, was convicted and sentenced to be whipped and to stand in the town gallows. He avoided the punishment by escaping to Rhode Island.[27]

Some women successfully hid out-of-wedlock pregnancies, but then, in desperation, killed their newborns. Because it was difficult to determine whether or not a baby had been born alive, it became a crime to conceal a pregnancy. If a woman gave birth in secret, and the baby was stillborn, she could be prosecuted for infanticide. England passed such a law in 1624 and Scotland in 1690, and various German states passed infanticide laws throughout the seventeenth century. In parts of early modern Europe, more women were executed for infanticide than for any other crime. For example, in Geneva between 1595 and 1712, 31 women were charged with infanticide, and 25 were executed. During this same period, 122 were charged with witchcraft, but only 19 were executed.[28]

By the eighteenth century, however, sins that had been criminalized were starting to lose their criminal status. Arguing that it might reduce infanticide, lawmakers in parts of Prussia in 1765 decriminalized out-of-wedlock pregnancy. As new views about women developed in the eighteenth century, authorities were less inclined to see them executed.[29] In 1786, Charles Biddle, vice president of the Supreme Executive Council of Pennsylvania, noted that "the punishment of death is too great for an unmarried woman who destroys her child. They are generally led to it from a fear of being exposed."[30] Under a new law passed in Pennsylvania that year, in cases of suspected infanticide the burden was placed on the state to prove the baby had been born alive. Even then, however, it was far more likely that a woman found guilty would be imprisoned, not executed. Seventeenth-century authorities believed women were inherently sinful, and that their transgressions weakened society. To counter the threat to society, lawmakers ordered that the bodies of sinners be subjected to public displays of corporal punishment in order to instruct the community. In the eighteenth century, pregnant single women were frequently seen as the victims of seducers, and Enlightenment thought was changing notions of how criminals should be treated.[31]

In suspected cases of infanticide, midwives were often called on to examine the women's bodies to determine if they had recently given birth. Midwives also testified in alleged cases of rape. For example, Caterina Brighenti of Venice had her seven-year-old daughter examined by a midwife after she noticed that the child had an unusual discharge. The midwife concluded that the girl had been raped and had contracted a venereal disease. The case was then brought to the attention of the magistrates.[32]

It was often difficult to secure a conviction for a charge of rape, as the law generally required proof that the man had used force, that the woman had yelled and resisted, and that there were witnesses to these events. In addition, rape was a capital crime, and juries and witnesses were often loath to see a man executed for it. British North America followed English common law regarding rape, which reflected Sir Matthew Hale's famous comment that the crime "is an accusation easily to be made and hard to be proved, and harder to be defended by the party accused, tho never so innocent."[33]

In both the seventeenth and eighteenth centuries, theologians and lawmakers viewed rape as a form of sexual misbehavior—similar to fornication or adultery—in which a man who did not control his passions was considered a detriment to society. Governments during this time believed in the need to regulate sexual behavior as a way of maintaining or improving the social order.[34] Thus, it was not enough to prosecute fornicators and rapists. The state had to maintain order by making certain that individuals were properly married and that children were born in wedlock. These concerns about premarital sexuality

FIGURE 5.4: A secret marriage behind curtains, which is being watched by some men and women from outside. Engraving (n.d.). Wellcome Library, London.

and irregular or secret marriages led governments to enact new laws regulating marriage (fig. 5.4). In England, the government passed the Marriage Act of 1653, which required minors to have the consent of their parents in order to marry, but it was repealed in 1660 when the monarchy was restored.[35] More important for regularizing marriages in England, however, was Hardwicke's Marriage Act of 1753. The purpose of this act was to prevent clandestine marriages by demanding that couples follow specific and public procedures to make their marriages legal (fig. 5.5).

Prior to the passing of this act, marriages made in several ways were considered legal, although those involving property generally followed several distinct steps, including a written prenuptial contract; a public betrothal; the posting, three times, of banns in church; a church wedding; and finally, consummation. For the poor, for those living in remote areas, and for those who simply wanted a quick union, there were other, simpler ways to wed. For one thing, spousals (oral promises to wed) were considered to be legally binding for life, especially if they were followed by consummation.[36] Those who desired to be wed by a clergyman, however, could find many who would perform a ceremony without asking uncomfortable questions. In the late seventeenth and early eighteenth centuries, young people in England began

FIGURE 5.5: The drafting and signing of a marriage contract by Abraham Bosse, 1633. Wellcome Library, London.

to defy their parents over whom and when they would marry. Those who chose to elope found clergymen who were willing to marry them. Similarly, those desiring speedy or inexpensive weddings for other reasons were able to locate clergymen to perform marriage ceremonies without questions, and usually for only a modest fee. The Fleet area of London was notorious for these quick marriages, and some unscrupulous clergymen would even backdate a marriage to legalize children who were already born.[37]

Hardwicke's Marriage Act of 1753 prevented young couples from marrying without their parents' approval. Some, however, went to Scotland, since the act did not apply there, and so Gretna Green became an infamous site for elopements. In addition to requiring parental consent for those younger than twenty-one to wed, the act required a church wedding (fig. 5.6), not merely an oral contract, in order for a marriage to be legal. It also called for marriages to be registered in church parish books and put the enforcement of marriage laws under civil, rather than church, courts. A major purpose of the act was to prevent fortune hunters from marrying into families of wealth and property.[38]

FIGURE 5.6: A marriage ceremony is conducted in a church, with the couple holding hands and the guests looking on intently. Engraving, n.d. Wellcome Library, London.

Catholic countries also attempted to eradicate clandestine marriages and premarital sexual relations. In some areas, however, traditional practices took a long time to change. For example, in the rural parishes of Salzburg, Austria, between 1670 and 1680, the illegitimacy rate was 30 percent, indicating that betrothed couples continued to engage in sexual relations prior to being wed.[39]

In the eighteenth century, revolutions, changes in government, and Enlightenment thought brought about additional changes in the marriage laws of some countries. Revolutionary France passed civil acts governing both marriage and divorce in 1792. A year later, under Joseph II, the Habsburg Monarchy also reformed marriage laws. The Marriage Patent (*Ehepatent*) placed the state in charge of resolving all marriage-related issues, although it permitted religious ceremonies. As one historian notes, this act created a "civil-religious hybrid of marriage regulation," and it applied to all citizens, Catholic, Protestant, and Jewish.[40]

Within the North American British colonies, marriage laws and procedures varied. Puritans considered marriage a civil ceremony, rather than a sacrament, but they were very strict about controlling it. In seventeenth-century Massachusetts, marriage laws required couples to have the consent of parents or a magistrate in order to marry. Moreover, couples had to post banns for three weeks before the marriage took place. Realizing that betrothed couples faced sexual temptation, however, those in authority advised them to marry within a month of their betrothal.[41]

In contrast, Quakers in both England and America underwent a lengthy procedure before being permitted to marry within the meeting. By the 1660s, English Quakers needed parental approval to marry. By the early 1700s, the process for obtaining permission to marry involved several steps. First, couples were advised not to form a deep attachment until they received parental approval to begin their courtship. Unlike Puritans, who believed sin needed to be eradicated from their children, Quakers believed that parents needed to nourish the inner light present in their children. Therefore, to ensure that parents were neither too permissive nor too coercive, couples had to announce their intention to marry at both of the men's and women's monthly meetings. Each meeting then appointed committees to investigate the couple in order to make sure that neither had prior ties that would prevent a marriage, that they were Quakers of good character, and that they had examined their reasons for wanting to marry and felt holy love for one another. While waiting for the meetings to make a determination, the couple was not permitted to engage in sexual relations. In fact, the young man and woman had to persuade the meetings that their love was pure and spiritual. The couple then appeared before the meetings again to hear their determinations. If the monthly meetings decided in the couple's favor, then they married, usually at the meeting-house of the woman's family. Quaker couples married without the use of ministers, and members of the meeting signed their marriage certificates.[42]

The importance that Quakers placed on family obligated them to provide their sons with land and their daughters with equivalent marriage portions. By the eighteenth century, the daughters of poor Quakers in southeastern Pennsylvania often did not marry within the meeting. Because their fathers could not afford to provide for them, poor daughters were more likely to marry non-Quakers, if they married at all. Although female elders normally visited these women before they married out of meeting and counseled them to reconsider their actions, they were not usually successful. The women's meeting was in charge of overseeing the conduct of young women, overseeing their courtship behavior, and disciplining them. In one instance, the women of Chester Meeting criticized the behavior of one young woman "for keeping idle, dissolute company to the scandal of her sex."[43]

The wilderness and sparse population of frontier areas in the American colonies, along, with a lack of clergy, made it more difficult to regulate marriage. Couples in backcountry areas sometimes lived together until they found a clergyman

FIGURE 5.7: Camp scene with American Indians. Wellcome Library, London.

who would marry them. Some men took "temporary wives" when traveling with Native Americans. Nicholas Cresswell, a young, single man who emigrated from England in 1774 and traveled through "Indian Country" in 1775, was initially reluctant to sleep with an Indian woman. However, he soon decided it was "absolutely necessary to take a temporary wife" when traveling with Indians. The Indian women helped their temporary partners with the horses, made the evening fires, and cooked for them (fig. 5.7). Cresswell thought "conscientious people" might disapprove of such temporary alliances with Native American women, but he became fond of the woman he slept with for a little over a month.[44]

The regulation of marriage and changes in marriage laws led to new laws on divorce in some areas, but in England a divorce law was not passed until 1857. In the mid-seventeenth century, it became possible to obtain a divorce through a private act of Parliament, but this was a very expensive procedure. Mainly noblemen whose wives had been unfaithful and who wanted to be able to remarry and legally father an heir requested parliamentary divorces. Only 131 of these acts came before Parliament between 1670 and 1799, and only 17 of them passed before 1750. Couples could obtain private separation agreements, which provided wives with a financial maintenance and gave them a measure of economic freedom, but which did not permit remarriage. Among the poor, however, "self-divorce" by desertion was probably the most common method of leaving a marriage.[45]

In France, a divorce law was passed in 1792, but it was abolished in 1816 with the return of the monarchy. Divorce was permitted under the Habsburg marriage reforms passed in the 1780s. In 1796, Rachele Luzzato of Trieste became one of the first Jewish women to obtain a civil divorce in Europe. Rachele argued that her husband, Lucio, had brought her to financial ruin, had deserted her, and had put her life in danger by exposing her to his venereal disease. The legal battle took two years to resolve, but in the end, her arguments satisfied both civil and Jewish law, so that Rachele was able to achieve both a civil separation and a religious divorce.[46]

In the American colonies, divorce had been possible only in New England, except by act of Parliament or the colony's legislature, but new laws were passed after the Revolution, as the former colonies became part of the United States. For example, the Pennsylvania Divorce Act of 1785 gave a man or woman the ability to apply to the Supreme Court of Pennsylvania for a divorce. Prior to this act, divorce in Pennsylvania was only available by petitioning the assembly, and few divorces were granted. Although this law allowed couples to divorce more easily than in other states, the grounds for divorce were limited to adultery, bigamy, desertion, impotence, and the false rumor of the death of one's spouse. In addition, a woman could apply for a divorce from bed and board, with alimony, similar to a legal separation, as a result of "cruel and barbarous treatment" by her husband.[47]

The absence of love was not sufficient cause to legally end a marriage, though couples did desert or "self-divorce" for this reason throughout the American colonies and in frontier areas. The divorce law was intended to provide men and women with a way to legally end a marriage because one partner was harming the other or was not fulfilling his or her duty. Pennsylvania legislators were not condoning licentious behavior or giving couples an easy way out of a marriage. The man or woman who petitioned for the divorce was expected to be an upright, moral citizen of the republic. The testimony of family and neighbors was crucial in proving the worthiness and decency of the libelant and the disreputable character of the spouse.

In 1801, Eve Page petitioned for a divorce from her husband, Robert. The wording of her plea indicates that she understood the goal of the divorce law and the need for a well-regulated society. She claimed that her husband had committed adultery numerous times with different women. Moreover, his conduct was "so flagitious the object of the marriage contract is entirely defeated." Couched in republican language, she asked that her plea be granted, "that the innicent victims of the baseness of the said Robert may find comfort and that an example may be made to deter others from offending in a manner so fatal to the order of society & the happiness of individuals."[48]

A charge of adultery, usually committed by the wife, was the most common reason for the granting of both divorces and legal separations in most countries, since it affected the family so directly and could lead to questions about who had fathered the children born to the wife. For the most part, divorce, even where it was legal, remained uncommon. Many governments, however, whether they permitted couples to divorce or not, did attempt to regulate and prosecute sexual behavior they deemed immoral. The English government, for example, passed the Adultery Act of 1650. Whereas prior to this act, adultery had been tried and regulated by church courts, with the passing of this legislation, not only adultery, but also fornication, incest, and prostitution became criminal acts, while adultery and incest became capital crimes. Yet few people were actually prosecuted under this act, as it required the testimony of a witness or a confession, and husbands and wives were not permitted to testify against each other. This law did permit women to remarry, if their husbands had been absent for more than three years. As one historian notes, this law should be understood as a "public proclamation of state's authority over marriage."[49] This law, along with others passed under the Puritan regime, was then repealed when the monarchy was restored in 1660.

In the seventeenth and eighteenth centuries, the only legitimate sex act was that between husband and wife. Although a husband and wife should love one another, the main purpose of marital sex was to produce children. As a consequence, premarital, extramarital, and nonprocreative sex acts were considered both immoral and illegal. In the early modern world, Christian theologians and lawmakers considered sodomy and bestiality particularly heinous because both the Old and New Testaments explicitly condemned the acts—both were viewed as "unnatural."[50]

The extent to which the crimes were punished, however, varied from locale to locale. Few women were charged with either sodomy or bestiality, since it usually had to be proved that penetration had occurred. Bestiality was more likely to be tried in rural areas. In Sweden between 1635 and 1754, 1,486 men and 14 women were charged with bestiality. Five hundred or more people were executed, along with the animals involved in the crimes. During the same period in Sweden, only eight men were charged with sodomy. In other parts of Europe, bestiality charges usually amounted to no more than one per decade.[51] Even in Puritan New England, where ministers preached against "unnatural" sex, few were charged or executed for these crimes.

Because no children were produced as a result of homosexual acts, and because such acts during this time period generally involved an older, married man and a servant or a younger man, charges were not actively pursued most of the time. In addition, men in the early modern world were not labeled as homosexuals, as it was believed that any man and woman could be involved in a range of sexual activities (or sins), and it was often assumed that men who had sex with other men also had sexual relations with women.[52] During the late seventeenth century, however, homosexual subcultures began to develop and thrive in many European cities. In the Netherlands, approximately 250 men and boys were charged and tried for sodomy, after authorities discovered such a subculture in Utrecht, Amsterdam, and some other Dutch cities. One hundred of them may have been executed; others were imprisoned and tortured in interrogations.[53]

In 1690, the Society for the Reformation of Manners was formed as a response to the perceived decadence of English society. The societies used informers, who made lists of offenders who could then be brought up on charges. Between 1726 and 1727, there were 1,363 prosecutions of "molly houses," venues where homosexual men could meet and interact. The most famous of these was Mother Clap's, which was raided in 1726. Margaret "Mother" Clap was convicted of running a disorderly house and encouraging acts of sodomy there. She was fined and sentenced to two years imprisonment and may have died while in prison.[54] In 1772, following the notorious trial of Captain Jones for sodomy, homosexuality was publicly debated for the first time in English newspapers.

In the eighteenth century, an effort was also made to reform prostitutes. Some English reformers believed that prostitution was a necessary evil because, they thought, denying men access to prostitutes might lead them to the "horrid vice" of sodomy. Nevertheless, they believed that prostitution should be less visible and that some prostitutes could be taken off the streets to be educated and reformed. To that end, reformers founded institutions, such as the Magdalen Hospital in London. More prostitutes were remanded to these institutions after acts passed in 1752 and 1774, but only a small number of women were actually admitted to the institutions.[55]

In Pennsylvania, attempts were also made to suppress prostitution and other forms of vice. In 1764, the Pennsylvania Assembly passed An Act for Suppressing Idleness, Drunkenness, and Other Debaucheries, with This Government. In 1775, the city of Philadelphia eliminated the biannual market fair, because people used the opportunity to gather together and get drunk, gamble, and seek sexual outlets. Yet, late-eighteenth-century Philadelphia was filled with prostitutes and bawdy houses.[56] One Brazilian visitor noted in 1793 that "the prostitutes in Philadelphia are so many that they flood the streets at night, in such a way that even looking at them in the streets without men you can recognize them."[57]

The availability of prostitutes in the city was noted in divorce depositions, too, as witnesses testified about husbands' adultery. A witness in one divorce case stated that the defendant, William Burk, invited him to go along with Burk and his friends "to a Whore-House." In another case, Henry Wilkinson invited Samuel Addes to go with him "to houses of ill-fame, where girls of easy virtue were."[58]

As in London, by the close of the eighteenth century, reform efforts in Philadelphia and other cities were underway to improve society by making conditions better for prisoners, the mentally ill, and prostitutes, who were now frequently viewed as the victims of seducers. One organization that aimed to reform prostitutes was the Magdalen Society of Philadelphia, founded in 1800. This organization sought to transform the lives of "fallen women" by giving them shelter and religious instruction, and teaching them to live "respectably." The first women to be sheltered as Magdalens stayed there for several months before going to live with upstanding families as nursemaids or domestic servants. The effort to reform these women was considered a success by the moral reformers, as they were able to become a part of respectable society, some of them marrying or becoming teachers. However, as with the London asylums, the Magdalen Society in Philadelphia only dealt with a very few women.[59]

In addition to laws and the actions of reformers, sexual behavior and practices were regulated by medical beliefs. In some instances, such as in the case of rape, medical beliefs influenced the interpretation of laws. Although medical authorities expressed their views, sometimes in widely circulated literature, it is difficult to know the actual sexual behavior of most people, unless it was discussed in court documents or in the private journals some people kept.[60]

Many seventeenth- and eighteenth-century authorities believed that both husband and wife should enjoy their physical relationship and believed that pregnancy only occurred if a woman had an orgasm. Yet some physicians advised against having sexual relations too often. They thought the loss of too much sperm depleted the strength and mental abilities of men and also produced sickly children. Theologians also counseled that too frequent marital sex was wrong. The influential Puritan preacher, William Gouge, for instance, wrote in his *Domesticall Duties* that, just as a man could eat to excess, he could "play the adulterer with his own wife."[61] The eighteenth-century writer Daniel Defoe shared these sentiments in his 1727 essay, "Conjugal Lewdness: or Matrimonial Whoredom." Defoe was sympathetic to the moral reform societies that were fighting against lewd behavior and activities, but he also felt couples should show restraint in marital sexual relations. Having sex too often, he thought, weakened the offspring. He added that couples should not have sex while the woman was menstruating, pregnant, or had just given birth, because this could also lead to problems and weaknesses in their babies.

In addition to laws, social mores, and medical beliefs, taboos also regulated sexual behavior. For instance, many societies had taboos regarding menstrual blood, which warned against having sexual relations when the woman was menstruating. Jewish women were supposed to sleep apart from their husbands at the first sign of menstruation, and they were expected to visit the *mikvah*, or ritual bath, after their menstrual periods and after childbirth before resuming marital relations (fig. 5.8).[62] Menstrual blood was often perceived as vile and polluting, but many also associated menstruation with magic. Thus, menstrual blood was used in love potions, it could be used to help women conceive or to prevent conception, and some believed it was powerful enough to prevent natural disasters. This belief in the magical powers of menstrual blood declined in the seventeenth century, but the taboo remained, and menstruating women were still not permitted to perform some tasks or enter certain areas.

FIGURE 5.8: Etching illustrating the uncleanliness of the mother after giving birth, according to Jewish law. Leviticus 12:2–5 in the Bible states that a mother should be considered unclean for 40 days after giving birth to a boy and for 80 days after giving birth to a girl. Etching by Philipp Gottfried Harder after Johann Jacob Scheuchzer. Wellcome Library, London.

Until late in the nineteenth century, for example, Primitive Methodists would not allow menstruating women to enter their chapels. Some authorities considered menstrual blood to be dangerous to a woman's sexual partner, while others noted that biblical injunctions expressly prohibited sexual intercourse with a menstruating woman, under penalty of death.[63]

Many Native American tribes also considered menstrual blood to be polluting, or even toxic. As a consequence, menstruating women were thought to be very powerful, and they had to be isolated, as even a look from a menstruating woman could make a person sick or cause harm. The degree to which menstruating women were isolated depended upon the tribe. Among the Chickasaw, for example, menstruating women went to special structures (moon houses), but menstruating Shawnee and Mingo women stayed in their own houses and even prepared food for others, although they were not permitted to eat it.[64]

Many Native American tribes held rituals to observe a young woman's first menstrual period. After this first period was finished, they considered her to be ready for marriage. Although marriage was significant and considered to be a transition to adulthood, it was not necessarily the first time a man or woman had sexual intercourse. In many tribes, women and men engaged in premarital sex, meeting at night to experiment.[65]

With the formation of colonies abroad, Europeans were exposed to the indigenous inhabitants of the conquered countries and their customs. In addition, they transported Africans to their colonies as slaves. With this interaction between various races and cultures, sexuality and marriage underwent additional regulation. Many Europeans, through their often-faulty observations of Native Americans, believed that they were naturally licentious. Although this encouraged some European men to force themselves on Native American women, others were horrified at the thought of being intimate with people they considered to be savages. During times of tension between the English and Indians, the fears and misunderstandings increased. Following the outbreak of war in New England in 1675, for example, English settlers claimed that Indians engaged in rape and other sexual barbarism. However, the Indians generally abstained from sex during war, and they took captives in order to replace family members. Therefore, it is unlikely that Native Americans would break tribal taboos by raping their war prisoners.[66]

The Christian churches (both Catholic and Protestant) that were established in European colonies were concerned with regulating sexuality. Sometimes they accommodated local customs, but at other times they tried with various degrees of success to eradicate them. For example, European churches and clergy demanded as a condition for baptism that an Indian man with more than one wife choose just one to marry. For men who had made political alliances through marriages, this was an impossible situation.

Since most of the Europeans who had traveled to colonies were men, interracial relationships frequently developed between them and the indigenous women they encountered. Some of these relationships were consensual, though some were coerced. Unlike the Spanish in their colonies and the French in theirs, however, Englishmen in North America did not, in great numbers, have sexual relationships with Indian women. Although Englishmen were not immune to the charms of Native American women, they feared such entanglements. Cohabiting with so-called savages, some believed, might lead Englishmen living in the wilderness to become savages themselves. In addition, they suspected that such alliances might be a way for Indians to gain access to colonial settlements and destroy them. A factor the English probably did not consider was that, in many cases, the Indians themselves saw few advantages to sexual liaisons with them.[67]

Colonial authorities expressed concerns that white traders and settlers could cause disturbances in backcountry areas when they mistreated Indian women. English and colonial officials worried that abuse of Indian women might cause diplomatic problems. For example, in 1710, after receiving a report about a trader who had beaten and forced an Indian woman to live with him, the commissioners for Indian trade in South Carolina sternly demanded that their agents monitor the behavior of traders.[68]

To prevent such disturbances, and to discourage the development of illicit relationships and intermarriage with indigenous women, European governments sent women to their colonies to become the wives of the men already settled there. The English government sent a ship of women to Jamestown early in the seventeenth century. In New France several hundred *filles du roi* (king's girls) arrived from France between 1662 and 1673 to marry settlers there. The Crown supplied the dowries for these young women, who were mostly orphans. In the early eighteenth century, France sent young women to Louisiana. Many of them were prostitutes or criminals, as not many other women were as willing to settle in such a remote, frontier area.[69] In each of these places, the aim was to promote stability through the institutions of marriage and family, as well as to prevent European men from cohabiting with indigenous women and creating mixed-race offspring.

European men were more likely to have sexual relationships with African women held in bondage than with the indigenous women, although most of the time these were nonmarital relationships. Babies born to slave women, whether fathered by slave men or white men, simply meant another slave for the master to put to work, to sell, or to free. In contrast, when an unmarried free woman gave birth, the child had to be supported. If the father was unable or unwilling to do so, then support of the child became the responsibility of the community.

Prior to the mid-seventeenth century, there were no laws preventing marriage between whites and free blacks in the American colonies, nor did the courts react more harshly against interracial couples than they did to same-race couples. A law passed in Virginia in 1662 punished "any Christian" who committed fornication with a black man or woman by making them pay double the fine that intraracial couples would have to pay. A law passed in 1691 in Virginia made interracial marriages illegal, also clearly expressing the desire to keep white women from entering into relationships with black men. After the passage of this law, there was a great increase in interracial sex cases that came before the Virginia courts, almost all of them involving white women.[70]

Nevertheless, white men continued to have sexual relations with female slaves without fear of prosecution. However, in the eighteenth-century Chesapeake, men usually kept these relationships secret. Although planters there emulated the libertine culture of London, they did not consider sex with black slaves to be gallant or well-bred behavior, and in fact, they believed it could be harm them both physically and culturally. In contrast, South Carolina men were open about their relationships with slave women, despite laws in that colony against miscegenation, and in the West Indies, planters were strikingly casual about their relationships with female slaves.[71]

By the mid-eighteenth century, new notions of gender and sexuality were developing. For instance, it was believed that men had to struggle to control their sexual impulses, while women were naturally less passionate. In fact, it was now supposedly up to women to control the passions of men, and women who did not do so were often blamed for the results. This new construct for gender and sexuality applied mainly to middle- and upper-class white women. Often lower-class women and women of color were still viewed as being filled with lust and as instigators of sexual activity. As in previous centuries, slaves and female servants often had to cope with rape and coerced sex from men who believed them to be naturally licentious, and who deemed them "available," due to their station. Whatever her social status, gossip could still destroy a woman's reputation and make it difficult for her to marry, gain employment, or receive support. In some places, such as Pennsylvania, women could divorce their adulterous husbands; however, to do so, they had to prove to the community around them that they were dutiful spouses, blameless and above reproach.[72]

CHAPTER SIX

Sex, Medicine and Disease

GEORGE ROUSSEAU

SEX FOR WHAT ... ?

In matters of sex, the Enlightenment physicians found themselves devoting their attention increasingly to biological sex and gender. This was not merely because their profession was enlarging and they looked to make their mark in new fields, or that they were publishing more extensively than previously, but also because the times seemed to demand it, as sex was being widely discussed. Yet even the slightest suggestion of immodesty or appearance of prurience in their writings could tip them over the line of decency, eliciting charges of quackery or imperiling their standing among the golden-caned fraternity. It was a truth as valid in the British Isles as across the channel in Catholic France and Spain, or in the Protestant Low Countries, German lands, or Scandinavia.[1]

Particularly in the realms of reproduction, pleasure, and longevity—that trinity that had such magisterial impact on the differences between sex and gender—medicine claimed to be steering the ship of life. It was the branch of secular knowledge dedicated to sustaining life at its two crucial moments—birth and impending death—through health and disease, and it could still accomplish this because it had new things to say.[2] It probably still killed more than it cured, as Addison and Steele famously quipped in their *Spectator* early in the century, and as others nodded in assent,[3] but medicine was nevertheless newly acknowledged as capable of emancipating humankind from the fear, want, and suffering in which it had lingered for centuries. As Samuel Johnson pithily noted, and as Roy Porter said in the title of his recent study, it was "the greatest benefit to mankind."⁴

Biological sex lay at the base of these wants, especially the physical body, the *corpora fabrica,* which enabled it.⁵ The body had always been important, but one of the Enlightenment's great legacies was its discovery that "body" was fundamental to establishing and sustaining the social order: men and women of sense and sensibility (the two main virtues that the Enlightenment extolled) could become virtuous citizens enacting moral and practical improvement *only* if their bodies were willing partners in the process.⁶ Biological sex, as the doctors were coming to recognize, enabled these goals, and for the most part the public endorsed the view. But first it had to understand what biological sex *was.*

Crucial for attaining these goals was basic comprehension of the difference between the two sexes, and it fell to the ancient physicians to explain

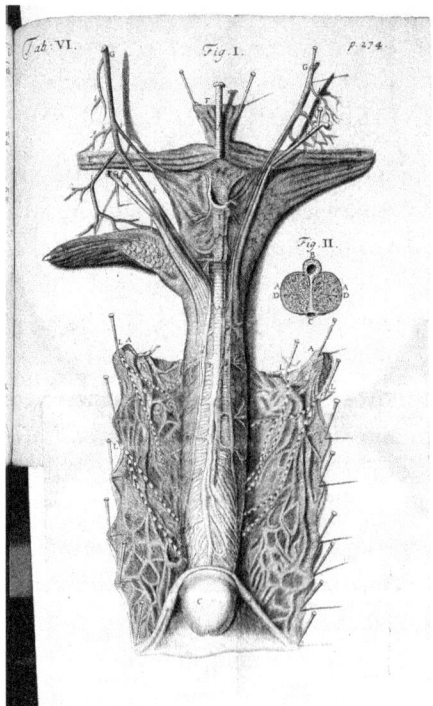

FIGURE 6.1: Forepart of the human penis, prepared with mercury, by James Drake. Engraving by M. van Gucht after Thos. Foster Delin, in *Anthropologia Nova, or a New System of Anatomy* (London, 1707). Wellcome Library, London.

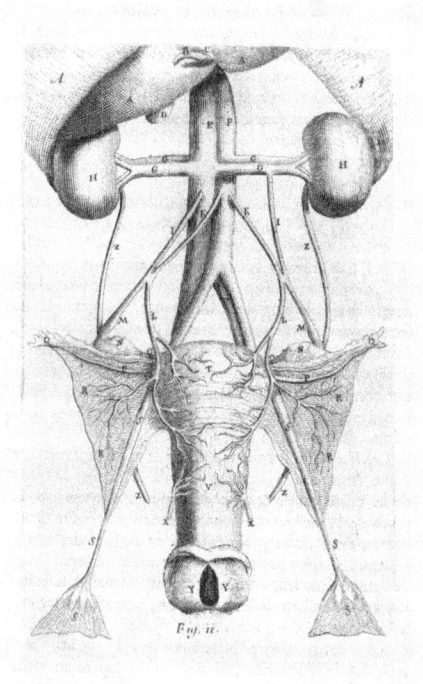

FIGURE 6.2: Diagram of female internal organs, including kidneys and vagina, from *Des Maladies des Femmes Grosses et Accouchées*, by François Mauriceau, 1668. Wellcome Library, London.

why two, and not one or three, were necessary. These ancients seem to have written on everything pertinent to the matter, but on the differences of the two sexes' anatomical apparatus they were less than definitive. It was left to Renaissance doctors to clarify the predominant "one-sex model": that is, two sexes, hot/dry (male), cold/wet (female), one grid, with female anatomy, especially reproductive apparatus, nearly identical to male in the form of a virtual copy (figs. 6.1 and 6.2).[7] The presence of a one-sex model in the Renaissance has been much contested. However, there is no longer any doubt that the doctors demolished it in the eighteenth century, replacing it with two differentiated bodies of man and woman.

These were anatomically and physiologically distinguished by their degrees of heat and bodily temperature: the male hotter and drier, the female colder and moister. The older pre-1700 models also placed weight on the different humoral balances between males and females, but these were dropping out as the concept of Galenic humors waned. And even if certain anatomical and physiological similarities lingered from the one-sex model, they paled in comparison to the differences.[8] As the eighteenth century wore on, these differences swelled, the voices that might have touted the older views now submerged. The discrete minds and bodies of men and women, separate entities even Descartes had considered distinct, continued to be contrasted, with few exceptions, as did observed differences between the sexes in the domains of rationality and will. Disparities between muscular male vigor and female weakness in the nerves were emphasized, for example, yet the main anatomic difference lay in the genitals, among men, whose organs were more robust and predictable than their weaker counterparts among soft, passive, receptive women.[9]

But these reproductive organs were not to be confused, copied, or imitated: it was *contra natura* to do so, as often bandied about even on the Restoration stage, especially the idea that it was unnatural for men to be playing women's parts, because their reproductive organs differed so markedly.[10] As the century wore on, concepts of chemical and neurological differences replaced the earlier, almost primordial, importance attached to bodily heat; and if the heart's function in circulating blood had been paramount around 1700, especially as it pumped in weaker feminine hearts and through their more delicate nerves, by 1800, newly gendered brains assumed greater significance than ever before in medical, and human, history.

Two sexes—male and female—came to represent the biological norm, tested even by newfangled explanations of hermaphrodites and other sexual anomalies (fig. 6.3).[11] The anxiety over male and female bodies was marked but less pronounced among physicians than among compilers of eighteenth-century erotica. Female breasts, for instance, were still considered among doctors as anatomical sites for lactation, at least publicly, rather than as the eroticized breasts of male fantasy. The male phallus was still just another anatomical organ, even if reproductively crucial, rather than a dark symbolic force; it had not yet become a Blakean "worm in the night invading 'the rose's bed.'" If "third sexes"—as Lord Hervey naughtily quipped about them as neither male or female, and as "Herveys," as his antagonist Lady Mary Wortley waspishly chimed in retort to his sexual phylogeny[12]—had previously been explained as freaks caused by supernatural intervention, they were now understood along anatomical lines determined by the mechanics of temperature, chemical difference, and nervous constitution (fig. 6.4). Monsters too were being refashioned along lines of gender. By 1800 or 1820, sex and gender differences themselves had altered, from the old humoral explanations carried over from the days of Bacon and Milton to whole new categories of explanation.[13]

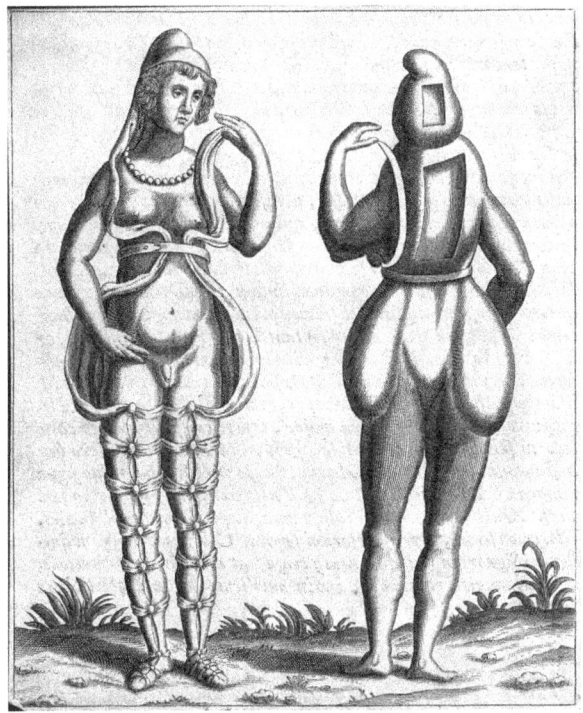

FIGURE 6.3: A hermaphrodite, front and back views, wearing a loose costume. Engraving, about 1690. Wellcome Library, London.

Even so, the mysteries of generation endured, and widespread interest greeted the discoveries of Dutch anatomists, such as that of Regnier de Graaf when he saw female ovarian follicles containing eggs in his dissections of the 1670s, and that of Leeuwenhoek when he detected sperm cells inside male semen with the aid of his microscope.[14] Each discovery inflamed existing controversies about generation, especially the proportional roles of the father and mother. For centuries the female body, whether or not viewed as an authentic replica of the male, had been mentalized as a passive container for male fluid.[15] Because the model persisted for so long, it inhibited open-minded investigation and tended to delimit the female organs of reproduction. Saddled to a lingering "one-sex model," anatomists about 1670–1720 often gave identical names to female reproductive organs and male brains: the uterus, for example, was known as the "female brain," while other parts of the womb were neglected, particularly their solids, fluids, and musculatures (*ecorchées*), because they did not fit male structures.[16] Indeed, a view formed that the female's soft, womb-like constitution predisposed her to domestic life rather than intellectual or professional

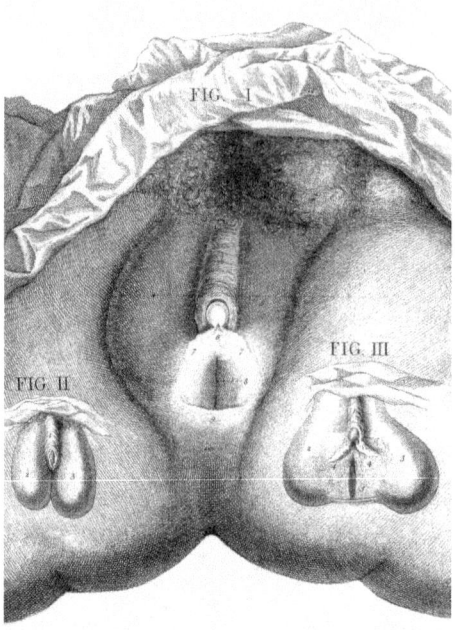

FIGURE 6.4: Folding plate of hermaphrodite genitalia, in James Parsons, *The Nature of Hermaphrodites,* London, 1741. Wellcome Library, London.

pursuits.[17] Yet, as the humoral model declined and was replaced by a mechanistic one, two opposed views about the mystery of reproduction gathered force: the preformationist and animalculist.[18] De facto they were old theories much tested in the seventeenth century, as when Dutch reproductive anatomist Charles Drelincourt debated them, but now they rocketed to the front rank of debate.[19] The first, the preformationist, as its name suggests, carried over from ovism the belief that new life is *already* fully formed within the egg and merely requires sperm to enliven it—rendering equally important the input of both sexes.[20] The second, the animalculist, diminished the ovist (the egg) role by claiming that male sperm alone contains the preformed human life, as verified by the microscopes of some of its practitioners.[21] Debates about the merits of each position endured into the nineteenth century, silenced only when compound microscopes resolved the matter in favor of the preformationists.

Controversy was not limited to the roles of the egg and sperm; the part played by the genders in reproduction itself was contentious, not merely about what each sex gave to the other during the coital act, but about the mechanics of birthing and diverse types of abortion.[22] For example, there was agreement that gynecological health was paramount for the total well-being of the woman, but little consensus about the biology of female sexual maturation during youth and adolescence: how menstruation physically developed and then somehow left women defective and disabled;[23] why some males seemed incapable of impregnating women due to their impotence;[24] and, alternatively, why fertility rates differed so much among couples and what complex conditions conspired to bring about barrenness and sterility in women. Questions like these lent an impression to lay people that anatomy, or at least anatomical physiology, lay at the heart of the New Science as much as Newtonian astronomy or physics; nor did debates about the value of diet and sleep, for instance, ensure their resolution. This was the point of James Drake's *New System of Anatomy*, a popular work frequently reprinted between 1707 and 1750, which aimed to demonstrate that generation was poorly understood despite the discoveries of the leading Dutch anatomists.[25] Even Aphra Behn's quasi-comical poem about the folly of youthful male impotence, "The Disappointment," reveals how its teachings had been absorbed into public discussion about these matters during the Restoration:

> Faintness its slack'ned Nerves invade:
> In vain th'enraged Youth essay'd
> To call its fleeting Vigor back,
> No motion 'twill from Motion take; ...
> In vain he Toils, in vain Commands
> The Insensible fell weeping in his hands.[26]

The transformation from a humoral model to a theory based on the chemistry of fluids and solids, aided by Newtonian principles, produced invigorated explanations of the mechanics of sexual intercourse and reproduction. The moment of union between sperm and egg was rendered a fit subject to be explored and, occasionally, satirized by writers such as Laurence Sterne in the opening paragraphs of *Tristram Shandy*, when describing how Walter Shandy's "homunculus" (fig. 6.5) enters Mrs. Shandy's genital cavity. The new model also embedded views of temperament and what we would call personality.[27] It also enlisted reproductive chemistry—the view that sperm are most vigorous when there is "an abundance of volatile salts in the body"; and it enlisted the physics of motion[28] in claiming that the rapid movement of animal spirits (the unseen fluid made in the heart and brain that flows through the blood and nerves) produces vigorous and healthy semen and gives rise to high fertility. Animal spirits were considered to be unseen vital particles in the blood. As a popular

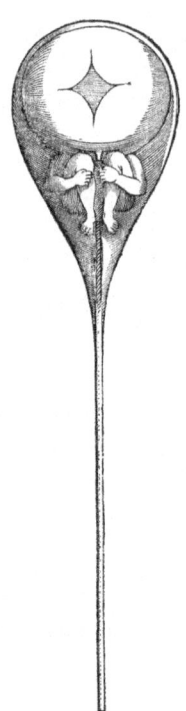

FIGURE 6.5: Spermatozoon and homunculus. Woodcut, in Nicolas Hartsoeker, *Essay de Dioptrique*, Paris, 1694. Wellcome Library, London.

medical handbook noted, when the motion of these spirits slows, "it dries up the Semen, and makes us [males] effeminate"[29]—effeminate in the sense that males are incapable of reproducing themselves because they are unable to fulfill the primary masculine role, yet also effeminate in temperament: that is, effeminate males and, by logical extension, masculine females whose animal spirits had dried up and rendered them barren.

Orgasm's biological function, especially in females, was even more contested than egg and sperm. Ever since Augustinian times the human's inability to control sexual desire revealed a fallen condition: this was the postlapsarian sin on which orthodox Christianity was built. But the physical pleasure derived from orgasm (whether solitary or in union) was biologically unclear: was it merely a fact of reproductive life—what we might call physical realism—or further postlapsarian proof of the failure of human will?[30] Enlightenment doctors demonstrated that answers to these questions were more metaphysical than real, explaining that orgasm was a necessary physiological process for human health in both females and males.³¹ In women, it regulated the blood and quality of the "seed" (eggs), and it was therefore necessary for healthy adults to have frequent orgasms. Without them, women, especially young women, would fall into chlorosis, or "green sickness," longing for males and the vitality sexual intercourse produced. Female orgasm, the doctors demonstrated, not only produced healthy "seed" (eggs), which was necessary for generation, but also elicited the pleasure enabling the race to perpetuate itself. Hence, pleasure served a social purpose exceeding its biological function. Small wonder that some doctors then described coition, as Freud would later, as an "intercourse" likened to minor epilepsy: a "shaking" of such proportions that pleasure gave birth to seed. This view was ripe, of course, with possibilities for exploitation in erotic literature.³²

Other doctors were puzzled by appearances of abundant salivation in women, which were often accompanied by nervous symptoms. Was salivation also sexually charged, they wondered? Excessive salivation could seem to suggest sexual preparation, as in brute creatures, and the doctors also noticed that it appeared in fever-producing diseases and was also caused by the ingestion of excessive mercury, as when used as a cure for venereal disease. But others noticed how frequently it arose during pregnancy and related it to reproductive biology, speculating that its production in the mouth during the whole course of pregnancy may have played a reproductive function. Spontaneous ovulation, or the production of seed without pleasure, had also been known to occur, but it was not the normal route to reproduction, nor was it found in males.

Eighteenth-century doctors also enlarged the role of imagination in the reproductive act, showing that it played a part at almost every step of the way, from the first issue of seed to the birth of the child. The role of the eyes was significant in initiating the process. As Spanish friar and physician Father Feijoo demonstrated, the eyes were principal among the body's organs for inflaming the imagination with sexual desire.³³ Having been aroused, imagination transmitted the images to the genital organs, producing orgasms by raising pictures in the mind of the desired partner, as well as creating in already pregnant women cravings for all sorts of foods, objects, and elements. An example can be seen in the character of Mrs. Peregrine Pickle in Tobias Smollett's comic novel, when she yearns for pineapples during her pregnancy.³⁴ A generation before the book's appearance in 1751, popular medical guides reported that pregnant women routinely crave these foods: "Our Women indulge themselves ... when they are with Child ... under the affected Notion of longing for all they like, they devour vast Quantities of Fruits,"³⁵ and—the author might have observed—they produce babies with the signs of melons, cucumbers, peaches, and pineapples on their bodies.

Orgasm for pleasure, without intended propagation, was contested: morally and ethically, by the Church and at home. It had been for centuries, most recently and eloquently by the French physician André du Laurens when he observed in the 1690s that pleasure alone accounts for the risks of pregnancy women take: he called them the "pricks and goads of voluptuousness."[36] The physical pleasure producing orgasm was usually associated with reproduction, even if tacitly, yet arguments about "pleasure for health" assumed a common end in marriage and reproduction. Once pleasure was cultivated as an end in itself, in popular sex manuals like Venette's *The Mysteries of Conjugal Love*,[37] by Restoration libertines, by hedonists like Pepys and Boswell, who autobiographically acknowledged its joys, and eventually by the followers of Casanova's and Cagliostro's secret orgies, the picture vis-à-vis pleasure's medicine changed. Some doctors, like Erasmus Darwin, taught that robust sex within marriage was necessary for continuous reproduction; and that the genitals of both sexes, like their analogous parts in plants and flowers, must be kept vital and ready for procreation; and that foreplay was a necessary component for reaching orgasm—even that sexual pleasure was compatible with feminine delicacy and purity.[38] They might not have condemned those hedonistic couples who reveled in its pleasures, even when nude, as apparently the two married Blakes did: William and Catherine, husband and wife, stark naked in their Lambeth summer house, recreated the fabled Swedenborgian Eden in their own garden, if we are to believe Marsha Schuchard.[39]

But there were limits. If medical doctors were to preserve their integrity and fulfill their professional role, it was necessary to tread delicately. "Doctors" like Franz Anton Mesmer, who plied his electric shock in French salons in the name of cure, were well aware of the sexual titillation his zap instilled (fig. 6.6).[40] Others, like James Graham, who touted the joys of orgiastic pleasure and who was a spiritual libertine if ever there was one, were deemed to be charlatans no matter how persuasively they emphasized the marriage bed.[41] His treatment was "electrified" and sought to enhance fertility among already married couples, but he was suspect from the start. When his popularity soared in the 1780s and made him rich, the establishment denounced him as a fraud, who not merely authored cheap sex manuals passed off as medical science, but claimed to serve "the public" while filling his pockets with gold. The stunt reduced him to the status of earlier quacks like John Marten, posing as a physician and writing didactically to disguise his intention to arouse pornographically.[42] Yet even "doctors" who went into league with merchants selling their goods were usually found out. One

MESMER'S TUB;
Or, a Faithful Representation of the Operations of Animal Magnetism.

The following is a translation of the original description accompanying the above curious old print, which is of especial interest at the present day, when mesmerism has been advanced to the dignity of a science: "Mr. Mesmer, M.D., of the Medical Faculty of Vienna, Austria, is the sole inventor of animal magnetism. This method of curing a number of ailments (such as paralysis, gout, scorbute, and accidental deafness) consists in the application, by Mr. Mesmer, of a fluid or agent, which he administers occasionally through one of his fingers—or else by means of an iron rod—to those who come to seek his aid. He uses also a large tub, to which are fixed pieces of cord which the patients tie round their limbs, or iron hooks which they apply to that part of the body in which they suffer; the patients, especially women, have fits, which bring about their recovery. The magnetizers (those to whom Mr. Mesmer has confided his secret, and numbering at least one hundred among the gentlemen of the Court) place their hands upon the ailing parts and rub them, thereby aiding the influence of the cords and hooks. There is a tub for the poor twice a week, and music is played in the entrance-hall to cheer the patients. People of all sorts and conditions flock to this celebrated physician, from Field Marshals to artisans. It is a scene to move the coldest heart to see men who have attained the highest honours in society magnetizing aged paupers. As to Mr. Mesmer, he is the picture of benevolence, of a serious disposition, and speaks little, seeming always to be absorbed in profound reflections."

FIGURE 6.6: Mesmer's Tub. Wellcome Library, London.

doctor celebrated that chocolate would revive the juices of both sexes, "who have been too free in expending their Spirits in Embraces; from which Cause I have seen some fall into Swoons, and recover'd by Chocolate, taken plentifully."[43]

Solitary orgasm was perilously vulnerable: having no goal in procreation, it required, first and foremost, an aroused sexual organ. Much ink was expended in the eighteenth century in explaining how this organ, whether male or female, became aroused and ejaculated.[44] The nervous model, initiated in the 1670s and well on the way to adoption by the 1720s, demonstrated that the accumulation of nerves in the sexual organs exceeded those of all organs except the brain. Hence, they were the natural bodily site of nervous arousal. Next was temperature, not merely the heat of the aroused sexual organ, but the geographical temperature of the place's climate.[45] Warm climates were judged to be prone to arousal, the opposite for cold. The final stimulus was repetition: the more often solitary orgasm occurred, the more it was practiced, until it became an incurable habit. Many doctors claimed, following Samuel-Auguste Tissot, the Swiss Protestant anthropological doctor, that compulsive repetition led to madness.[46] Add the moral issues—that solitary orgasm aborted life, wasted precious God-given seed, and was taboo, and it becomes evident why the anti-onanism campaigns were so fierce.[47] Celibate bodies anatomically incapable of nervous arousal and emission, rather than solitary for psychological reasons, were little discussed other than as antisocial aberrations. The health penalty for solitary orgasm was large and, according to most doctors, growing every year. If not leading to insanity, then it caused such "loss of seed" that the human body became depleted, withered, and prematurely died. According to medical gospel it was a high price to pay.

PATHOLOGIES OF SEXUAL IMBALANCE

Medical discussions of arousal and orgasm extended beyond procreation to include pathologies of excess. Carnal appetite and imagination, having run wild in tandem, were thought to produce "manias"—erotomania (inflamed desire); monomania (the uncontrollable propensity to reach orgasm); and nymphomania (fig. 6.7) (women incapable of forgoing heterosexual intercourse), the label Bienville gave to it in 1771—all manias of sexual excess.[48]

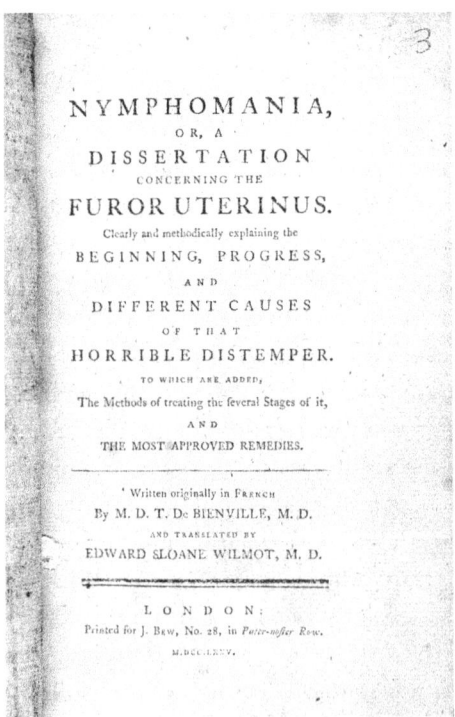

FIGURE 6.7: Title page from M.T.D. de Bienville, *Nymphomania, or, a Dissertation Concerning the Furor Uterinus* (London, 1775). Wellcome Library, London.

These states had been configured during the Renaissance but much reinvigorated in the Enlightenment under the weight of the new nervous knowledge. That is, the emphasis on nervous bodies permitted understanding of how such manias formed in the first place. The old pre-Enlightenment theories often resorted to supernatural explanations; after about 1700 these were *au fond* mechanistic and nervous. Expressed syllogistically, the process amounted to this: the imagination raised up through experience an object of desire, and nerves in the brain transmitted this image of desire through the nervous conduits of the body to the nervous constellation in the genitals. These sexual organs became aroused, blood accumulated there, and emission occurred (loss of seed). The more often ejaculation occurred, the more orgasm was desired. Soon the person was habitually addicted to a life of constant arousal and emission and fell into the state of one of the manias. The immediate effect of emission was release and relief, its long-term condition low spirits (depression) as the result of physiological depletion of the crucial animal spirits. Our current models are not so far removed from these mechanistic ones of the Enlightenment, except that we have replaced their edifice of animal spirits with neurochemical transmitters and synapses.

The penalty for erotomania, having arisen from solitary excess, was primarily mental and led to depression and madness. All sorts of social consequences followed—ostracism, failure, and poverty—but in most cases monomaniacs enacted their orgasms with multiple others, a perfidious state of affairs producing clap and other life-threatening, sexually transmitted, maladies.[49] The medical explanation for transmission, as distinct from the acquisition, of venereal diseases, was via heat. Females who frequently consorted intimately with men overheated their bodies, and as the woman's heat increased she transmitted it to the man's penis and urethra, causing him to be burned or "brent," the old names of clap being "brents" or "brennings."

Nicholas Robinson, a prominent physician who wrote abundantly on these matters, explained how this "Excoriation of the Urethra" occurs: the burning female genitals mix with the male genitals to produce "discoloured Running," followed by "Chancres with callous Lips, Christallines, [and] Strangulation of the [Penis] Glans."[50] But there were other explanations, especially when it became evident that clap, or Great Pox of whatever general venereal nature, was a sexual malady rather than any sort of divine punishment for sin. French physician Jean Astruc, who had written a best-selling history of the malady, explaining how it migrated from the New World to Europe, emphasized the mixture of semen from many men in one woman's uterus.[51] His model minimized heat (temperature) and had the merit, so his argument went, of accounting for its transmission through this mixture from prostitute to husband, husband to wife, and wife to children, down through the generations.[52] Yet a society of "clapped" men and women in every social class will capitalize on their infirmity. It did so in venereal pills and potions ranging over the whole spectrum of affordability, from John Burrows's "vegetable cures" (1772) to Velno's "Vegetable Syrup."[53] The eighteenth-century trade in pills and potions for the clap has filled many modern books and will produce others, their main point being that penalties for the "sexual manias," even when mild, were then as far-flung as their panaceas. Some medics refused to pronounce about these matters, while others made it their stock in trade. However appalling venereal diseases were for the victims, they had one social virtue: they forced sex into the open as a matter for public discourse, which it had barely been in previous generations.

Life with the clap, the "foul disease of modernity" as it was once called, was grim. Whether captured through promiscuous Boswell's painful symptoms or poet Blake's moving strophes about the harlot in *Songs of Experience,* its physical realities were grotesque. Having no successful cure, clap was attributed to almost everything on earth and mythologized as the disease of modernity that swept up all social ills in a single malady. As late as 1796 William Buchan, the author of much domestic medical advice, was still lamenting its grotesque myths, as would others after 1800.[54] It elicited the worst forms of xenophobia in countries that labeled it in the names of their political foes. In England it was called the "French pox," in France the "English Disease," and all sorts of opprobrious names were attached to describe it, for example, "leprosy" rather than the medically sanctioned "gonorrhoea" already assigned it by the doctors. Men blamed it on female promiscuity; instead of regulating their own reckless abandon they turned their women into scapegoats.[55] Most women were treated in poor houses or prisons until two hospitals for syphilis opened in London with reforming missions in mind—the Lock Hospital (1746) and the Lock Asylum for Women (1792)—but only a fraction of those afflicted were ever seen there.[56] The French followed in 1780 with the Vaugirard Hospice for children infected with venereal disease and the Hospice des Vénériens for adults in 1792. Down through the century the afflicted were incarcerated, men in the Bicêtre, women in the Salpetrière. Incarceration was the principal remedy rather than enlightened treatment of the symptoms, and these horrendous and crowded conditions killed the afflicted more than the malady itself. Therapies for sexually transmitted diseases had proliferated but not advanced.[57] Besides, how was the ordinary patient to know which panacea to choose from an armory of hundreds? In a milieu where sexuality had run rampant and birth control was unknown, clap was destined to be the killer of the century.

The devotees of repetitive orgasm spilled over to realms other than clap and the "love manias," such as male and female sodomy, but the last (sodomy) was far less medicalized than mythologized. Church, state, medicine, and moral-reform groups joined forces to attribute its existence to fallen souls, or rotted minds, which had turned bestial. In Swift's *Gulliver's Travels* (IV:vii), Lemuel hears that sodomy is a malady of "our side of the globe," unknown among the Houhyhnms who dwell somewhere in the eastern seas.[58] Yet everywhere grotesque animal metaphors dominated discussions of the type. When medicalized, the explanations varied, some doctors claiming it was a hereditary condition, although they had no notion how it was acquired, and they thought it could be identified by signs in the male physique, such as an affected gait, dangling limbs, tight clothing, and the habit of kissing in public.[59] Others, plugging a chemical model, attributed it to too many salts in the system accumulating in the brain and deranging normal sexual desire, and still others located it in local climate, especially temperature.[60] By midcentury the anonymous author of *Satan's Harvest Home* had compiled a long list of physical signs to detect sodomites, including kissing and limp wrists.[61] But there is no evidence the medical doctors enlisted any of these theories when advising their male patients, and even less that they considered "sodomy"—by this or any other name—as a medically treatable condition in itself. Female versions, often called "tribadism," received even less medical attention during the Enlightenment. The "Sapphist's" body was never labeled to the extent of that of the male sodomites, or "mollies," in their more vernacular parlance.[62]

According to the physicians, health penalties also existed for too little sexual activity. We have already observed that adult sexual health, in both genders, was viewed as a delicate balance between the "retention and expulsion of seed."[63] The proponents of controlled masturbation (those who refused, for example, to join anti-onanism campaigns) demonstrated how the regular emission of males was conducive to robust manliness. Males who never discharged semen were destined to ill health. Among women a failure to expel seed was even more dangerous, leading to illness during adolescence and possible death during maturity. The maladies arising depended on the cycle of life, with marriage viewed as the best medical solution (considered apart from its majestic social value) to all these ills.[64] Alternative lives of prostitution, poverty, illegitimate children, disease, and death, especially in cities, were dire. Once in the grace of marriage, health was gendered along lines of procreation, with healthy female adulthood viewed as a continuous round of pregnancy

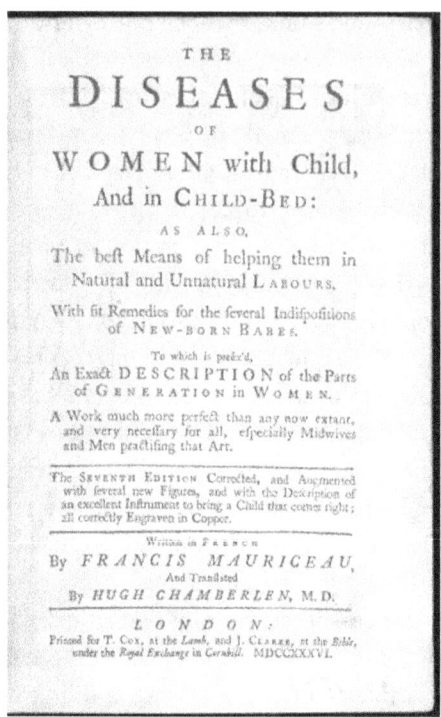

FIGURE 6.8: Title page from François Mauriceau, *The Diseases of Women with Child* (1736). Wellcome Library, London.

and child-bearing that staved off illness. For example, women who were continuously pregnant were rarely thought to acquire gout, as Francis Mauriceau noted in his *The Diseases of Women with Child* (1736) (fig. 6.8), or if they did, were cured by their next pregnancy, and insulated from life-threatening diseases.[65] Doctors harbored no idea of a normative, healthy, female adult who was neither married nor childbearing. Males were less affected, it seems, by the medical hazards of celibacy, provided they curbed their promiscuity, but the single woman was monolithically viewed by doctors in medical contexts of marriage and health. She may have cut a more complex figure among social commentators and writers of fiction, yet the doctors had no medical model that extolled her health when in the state of celibacy.

Medical theory also pronounced on less pressing topics, without the fullness of debate associated with modern medicine. For example, sexual frustration was construed in terms of its somatic effects, but not its psychological consequences. Cross-dressing, especially among committed cross-dressers such as Charlotte Charke and Hannah Snell, was understood as a social anomaly but not elevated to the status of medical pathology.[66] Fiction and nonfiction, especially written by female authors, gave voice to these subjects, but not medical theory, which tended to be conservative and formulated to enforce social norms rather than resist them or go against their grain. Male sexual frustration was an implausible medical category in an era when prostitutes were available under every arch. Indeed, most males (excluding only the clergy perhaps) who remained celibate were suspect, considered candidates for the growing sodomy label, even if it was then less a medical category than a detestable social stigma.

The writer Oliver Goldsmith, who was one of the century's most underrated talents and who had been medically trained himself in France, is a good example. His sexual biography has lingered in darkness from the eighteenth century on, in part because his visits to prostitutes have never been documented. To us it seems a strange reason to lack a rounded biography. But more recently historical biographers of the twentieth century, determined not to pronounce without hard evidence, and much under the sway of Freud's influence about the part sexuality played in every life—Michelangelo to Thomas Mann—were stymied by Goldsmith's life. There was no evidence whatever of sodomy. He never married. He was not known to frequent prostitutes. Was he asexual in an era when "asexuality" had no profile? The safe course was not to speculate.

Alternatively, the sexuality of youth began to receive attention as thinking about the child underwent a huge revolution, documented by Philippe Ariès (1962).[67] But it was usually sexuality delimited to abandoned street urchins and destitute prostitutes just arrived in the state of puberty; little comment was generated within canonical medical theory about the guiltless youthful sexual jouissance with which the nineteenth century would become preoccupied in the aftermath of Rousseau's *Émile*. The predominant physicalist view was that sex in old age, like sex among youths, required physical heat. Provided bodily heat endured, the obstacles to sex were few;[68] where heat was absent, its defect constituted a "horrid frost," as John Armstrong versified, withdrawing "vigorous heat" from the frigid, decaying, and senescent body icy to the touch.[69]

Other perils of sexual decrepitude were noted. A wife's voracious appetite could lead her husband into premature senility, as even the amorously enthusiastic Venette had warned. Mortality figures improved dramatically at the end of the century and, provided one lived beyond the age of five, and then again above thirty-five, an old age well beyond sixty was not rare. Among this aging male group, bodily heat sometimes endured and occasionally enabled procreation into the seventies, but more often it did not, and instead, the image of the old fool appeared as desperate, even disgusting (likewise, women were freakishly reported to have borne children in their sixties).[70] Cornaro, the

Renaissance Italian much translated into English, provided the basic formula: "Old Men, who have but little Natural Heat, require but a little Food, and too much [sex] overcharges them."[71] Lessius, the wise sixteenth-century author of *Hygiasticon,* a treatise on health in old age still much read in our period, endorsed the same view.[72] Even ancient paeans to fallen penises among the elderly were recited, as in the celebrated one often quoted in the eighteenth century and attributed to the sixth century C.E. Maximiamus Etruscus:

Ah! Fallen Member! Who were't once to me,
The best Improver of best Luxury ...
My only Entertainment, only Guest,
My sweetest Darling, my Delight, my Health.[73]

But Dr. Edward Strother, a sober English commentator, urged caution: "Old Men naturally love their Glass to a Pitch of Mirth" and "may be allow'd—to comfort themselves with an occasional toss in the hay too."[74]

In the broad spectrum of medical practitioners, among them physicians, surgeons, barbers, apothecaries, wet-nurses, bonesetters, charlatans, empirics, and quacks, none loomed more menacingly in the sexual domain than the male midwife.[75] The reasons were historically complicated. Male midwives had been delivering children for decades, but as gender and class rigidified in the eighteenth century, midwifery was transformed into a suspect profession.[76] The simplest solution was the restitution of female midwives and the enlargement of the role of wet nurses, which would solve the main danger of *touch*. Touch, especially the touching of private female parts, was the bone of contention: how could male midwives resist the temptation to touch these private parts? The matter was debated, in drawing rooms in town as well as by hearths in the country, as well as bandied wittily in works such as *The Lady's Decoy* (1738). More pedantically, Dr. Philip Thicknesse, a dour Scottish physician who claimed to be an authority on the issue, argued that they could not.[77] Meanwhile, university-trained all-male doctors certified by degrees and acknowledged by colleges of medicine continued to deliver learned opinions and prescribe medications, often without ever having seen the patient. But danger lurked if they touched female patients. It was forbidden yet no doubt occurred during their examinations of pregnant women.[78]

Even so, as the eighteenth century evolved, female midwives came under renewed attack from male physicians for their ignorance. Male midwives denounced them as murderous "witches" exploiting their limited, provincial experience. Untrained and unlearned, they knew nothing, so the argument went, beyond folklore and the reach of their naked eyes. This is what Dr. William Cadogan, vehement among their detractors, claimed: "The Preservation of Children should become the Care of *Men* of Sense because this business has been too long fatally left to the Management of Women."[79]

Gradually these male midwives in Britain, called *accoucheurs* in France, returned to birthing chambers, and by the second half of the century they were common fixtures in the Protestant North, especially in the German lands. In Mediterranean Catholic countries, where female modesty counted for more than expertise, male midwives were still not accepted. The development could not have occurred so rapidly without the fears of chronic depopulation for which the female midwives had also been blamed, so high had the mortality rates in childbirth soared before 1700.[80] Moreover, once male midwives returned to the scene, they brought with them newfangled technologies, such as the fictional Dr. Slop's forceps, based on Dr. John Burton's invention of the prior decade.[81] But fear of their predatory nature remained high in households like Shandy Hall: by the time the infant Tristram Shandy is delivered in Sterne's imagination they were still viewed as pernicious, for their concupiscence as well as technology.[82] Yet it is hard to know which Mrs. Shandy fears more, Dr. Slop's immodesty, or his forceps. Her anxiety sharpens Sterne's multifaceted medical conceit in the book. The idea is that if a male midwife attends her birthing chamber, her life and her infant's will be imperiled. So she forbids him, only to be overruled by her compulsively misogynist husband Walter, who has summoned Dr. Slop. Sterne's double irony lies in his further turn of the screw, demonstrating that her caution counts for little. Eventually "homunculus" Tristram is delivered by Dr. Slop's defective forceps, his nose snipped and his sexual organs damaged.

"Sexual patients," those reduced to illness through deeds of sin and love, were plentiful and sought out local practitioners out of desperation but rarely called for physicians, as the cost was too high. Concurrently, some pregnant mothers of means, like Elizabeth Shandy, the archetypal conceiving mother reliant on the expert hands of her male deliverer, feared predatory midwives as threats to their modesty. Mrs. Shandy typified the new rift growing between female patients and male physicians, with the distance augmenting between mothers who were losing their right to special knowledge about the birthing process and doctors claiming *they* were the experts. But female patientdom was hardly limited to these varieties, as equally numerous were healthy women who fell into illness once or twice a decade, before or after their childbearing years, and required medical attention.[83] For them the concept and function of the "medical practitioner," especially physicians and surgeons, was changing. As medicine slowly grew increasingly professionalized, the figure of the doctor, with his exalted standing in the community, his high style of living, his plush housing, his golden cane, his carriage and six, was romanticized and idealized. Smollett's novels describe the trend, replete with the doctors' sexual peccadilloes and a stinging satirical bite from a physician-author who knew the profession from the inside.[84] Marriage records also reveal much about the physician's image, with mothers eager to marry off their daughters to eligible candidates for financial reasons. Compare the earnings of doctors in England in 1700 and 1800 and the reason for the huge rise in numbers is evident.[85] The new social niche for the doctor anticipated the romance of soldierly status a century later.

Medical practitioners rarely used their writing as pretexts to court women, or sought to arouse them sexually through words, unless they were medical romancers like John Marten, aiming to produce a sort of veiled prose pornography disguised as legitimate medical theory.[86] Doctors' usual publications were didactic writing, in whatever prose form, works such as Tissot's well-read treatise on onanism, or the many books cited in this chapter about venereal disease.[87] Tissot's matter-of-fact tone, coupled to Swiss Protestant piety, apparently persuaded readers of his ulterior reason: the personal loathing he harbored for male masturbation. The same is true for the works of physicians with appointments in hospitals, the military, and universities: their motives were rarely impugned when they wrote about sex. When, in 1748, Doctor John Profily published case studies addressed to wives aiming to recognize venereal infections given to them by their husbands, he selected the dialogic form, using eighty-one dialogs between a wife and her physician to gain the victim's confidence and puncture the widespread secrecy about venereal infection.[88] The dialog form is intimate; it brings its participants into close proximity with no place to hide. Yet read a chapter in Marten's prose *Gonosologium,* and one could guess that the reader of 1709 must have suspected a "con." He cleverly disguised his sexual counsel for those with difficulty under the cloak of marriage, but the chapter dealing with the husband whose organ hangs down to his knees, for example, and the advice given to the desperate wife who needs some technological armament to harness her husband's tool to enter smoothly without choking her, is barely disguised pornography intending to arouse.[89] The only other possible response was laughter, but Marten was too heavily invested in sex to see himself as a jesting satirist.

ATTEMPTED INTEGRATIVE THEORIES OF SEX AND SEXUALITY

If eighteenth-century medicine was incapable of making the trailblazing discoveries of its predecessor, it nevertheless integrated its new theories more uniformly into mainstream culture. Conversely, its medical theories of the body and disease tended to reflect mainstream society's beliefs. Whereas Harvey's circulation of the blood, Descartes' pineal gland, and the often-threatening discoveries of the microscopists defied professional medicine and challenged normative cultural assumptions, their successors in the next century were tamer, especially in realms sexual.

A strong case can be made, not so much that the medical theories of the eighteenth century were integrated, as that mainstream culture held a firmer sway over their development in the first place than it previously had. This was certainly the case over theories of *sex*. As the curtain came down at the end of the century, a stunning example is found in the curious figure of Ebenezer Sibly (1750–1799), an English healer turned astrologer. Whether he was a charlatan, quack, or inspired devotee depended on one's point of view at the time. He sustained himself discoursing about the stars and inventing "lunar tinctures" for fainting females.[90] If Sibly embodies the sexual domain, it is in the blurred border separating orthodox from alternative medicine, murkier then than it is today.

Little is known about Sibly biographically. Nothing he left explains why, for example, he wrote his medical works as he did, but one book, *The Medical Mirror* (fig. 6.9), demonstrates his preoccupation with the topics discussed in this chapter.[91] Its subtitle about the "impregnation of the human female" hones in on his plan to puff his potions, especially tinctures for sexually frustrated young women. He begins with a chapter occupying almost half the book that presents him as God-fearing, mainstream Church of England, and spouting Scripture. It was a strategy calculated to court female readers to read on to the second half, where they would discover his potions. His first section is so explicit about the dynamics of sexual intercourse, cloaked under "the mechanisms of impregnation" explained by a good Christian that he appears no less prurient than John Marten had earlier.

Sibly's metaphor of the "mirror" invites readers to "behold the true picture of cure."[92] Yet it is "truth" in one crucial sphere—the one about "female impregnation," because it "is better understood than some medical men are willing to allow" (figs. 6.10, 6.11, and 6.12).[93] No tyranny of immodesty seems to have deterred him, and his status as outsider emboldened him despite his sense that no physician would attack "his brethren" for modesty in describing female parts. He locates further defect in this same area in that "no branch of physiology has been more exposed to censure and mistake than the mechanics of impregnation."[94] Within a few pages, his description of the genital organs is so vivid that it must have aroused readers of both sexes, which, in

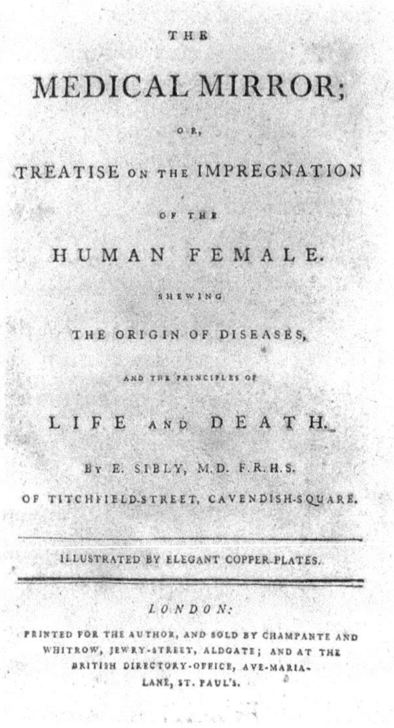
THE

MEDICAL MIRROR;

OR,

TREATISE ON THE IMPREGNATION

OF THE

HUMAN FEMALE.

SHEWING

THE ORIGIN OF DISEASES,

AND THE PRINCIPLES OF

LIFE AND DEATH.

BY E. SIBLY, M.D. F.R.H.S.

OF TITCHFIELD-STREET, CAVENDISH-SQUARE.

ILLUSTRATED BY ELEGANT COPPER-PLATES.

LONDON:

PRINTED FOR THE AUTHOR, AND SOLD BY CHAMPANTE AND WHITROW, JEWRY-STREET, ALDGATE; AND AT THE BRITISH DIRECTORY-OFFICE, AVE-MARIA-LANE, ST. PAUL'S.

FIGURE 6.9: Title page to the 1794 edition of Ebenezer Sibly, *The Medical Mirror; or Treatise on the Impregnation of the Human Female* (London, 1794). Wellcome Library, London.

turn, prompts one to wonder if his aim was to reach males, as well as females. For example, his long disquisitions on the vaginal cavity are too descriptive to preserve narrative modesty, as when expounding that the vagina, "being contrived by its organization for the purpose of exciting titillation and pleasure, it can and does accommodate itself to whatever size is necessary to embrace the male organ, in the act of copulation";[95] or, when spilling much ink on the "great distention [sic] of the vagina when receiving the male organ."[96] These "swellings and contractions," in both sexes, seem to extend beyond the mechanics of impregnation.

Sibly further trumpets his theme as the origin of diseases that arise at the moment of coition, whose split-second precision vivify "the principles of life and death."[97] His book was still in demand when being reprinted a half century later, in 1840.[98] A *vade mecum* promising to enhance female fertility, in an age when women of means feared barrenness far more than death, stood to make

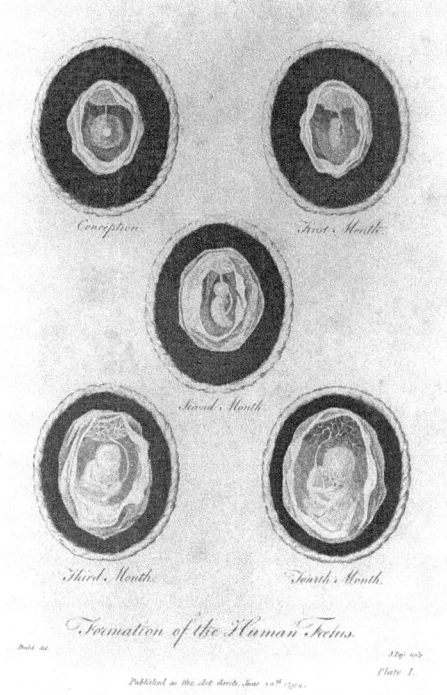

FIGURE 6.10: Ebenezer Sibly, *The Medical Mirror; or Treatise on the Impregnation of the Human Female* (London, 1794). Wellcome Library, London.

its author a mint. Records of Sibly's earnings do not survive, but his *Medical Mirror* speaks vividly for itself. It would be erroneous to claim Sibly for the ovist camp, or to pretend he was a biologist in the sense that university-trained doctors then were. But his writings display such constant name-dropping of medical authorities that he may well have impressed readers in 1799 or 1800 with his expertise. He also typifies how far apart the two genders had grown since the libertine salad days of the English Restoration. "Boys who have been subjected to castration never acquire either that strength of body or capability of mind which dignifies the complete male."[99] The "complete male" may be no more than a deft sleight of hand strategically placed to entice readers of both sexes; or it can be interpreted as assuming a substratum about gender identification, assuring readers that they, at least, were "complete" males or "complete" females.

Read the "medical mirror" cover to cover and you find little sense that the sexes share anything, certainly not their respective anatomies, and Sibly entices

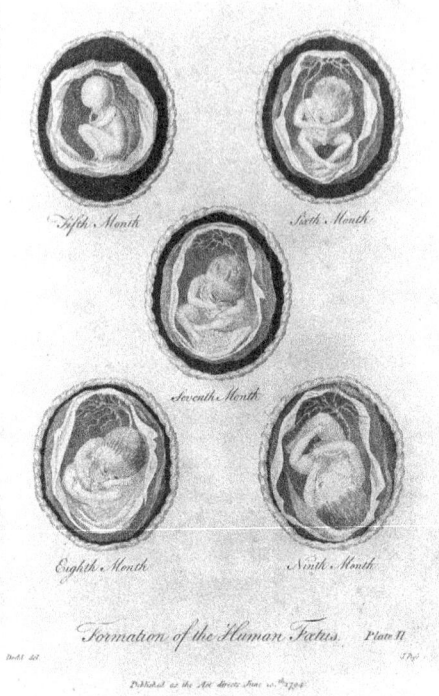

FIGURE 6.11: Ebenezer Sibly, *The Medical Mirror; or Treatise on the Impregnation of the Human Female* (London, 1794). Wellcome Library, London.

his readers to think sex and gender are far apart. In this view he represents some of the heartland of the eighteenth century's sexual revolution. One of our contemporaries recently placed his finger on the same spot: Jan Morris, the travel writer born a man who married a woman, had five children, and then underwent surgery to become a woman.[100] Anyone who lives close to a half-century in one sex, and now almost equal time in another, will have expended much effort to learn what is involved in the disparity. Morris's conclusions pinpoint our era: "It was ... the eighteenth century which first imposed upon western civilization rigid conceptions of maleness and femaleness, and made the idea of sexual fluidity in some way horrific."[101]

Sibly and his cohorts would have agreed that to confuse the sexes in any way was demeaning. More emphatically, in the eighteenth century, according to Morris, "Sex was like a biological pointer, but the gauge upon which it flickered was that very different device, gender."[102] It was gender indeed that made the difference, and the whole of Morris's discussion is based on this further

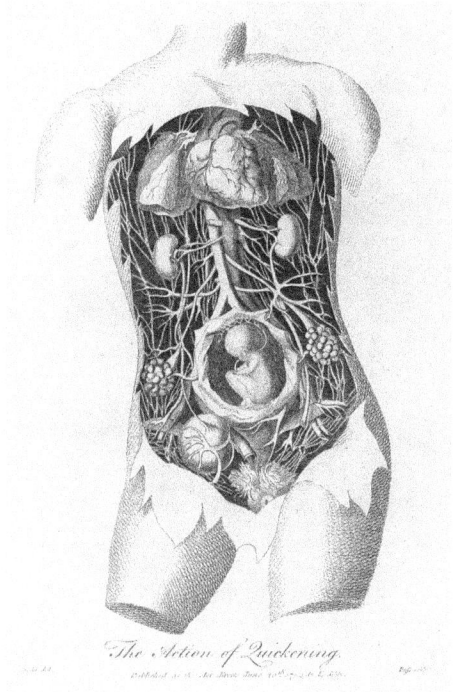

FIGURE 6.12: Ebenezer Sibly, *The Medical Mirror; or Treatise on the Impregnation of the Human Female* (London, 1794). Wellcome Library, London.

disparity: "if sex was a matter of glands or valves, gender was psychological, cultural or in my own view spiritual."[103]

Such distinct categories could not be facilely claimed in 1700, let alone the physical-versus-psychological disparity. The anatomy–culture divide or, to change the metaphor slightly, the body–mind split, was almost entirely of that century's making. It had been noted, of course, in the era of Descartes, but the eighteenth century gave it meaning and endowed it with substance. By 1800, or 1820, the differences of the two were being taken for granted. Sex and gender in the medical domain had come a long way from what they were in the time of Boyle and Boerhaave.

CHAPTER SEVEN

Sex, Popular Beliefs and Culture

HEIKE BAUER

Popular representations of sexuality in the eighteenth century were closely tied in with the Enlightenment invention of the rational human. Here, as postcolonial critic Gayatri Spivak has shown, the search for "universal truths" that lay at the core of Enlightenment thinking was deeply bound up with a distinction between the "civilized" West and a "primitive" other that negated the subaltern from the outset.[1] But the rational human was not just marked in terms of "race." Matters of "sex"—understood in terms of sexual behavior as well as biological difference—played an important role in establishing the limits of civilization, both in assessments of non-Western cultures following the discovery of the Americas and in the demarcation of national cultures within Europe. As Felicity A. Nussbaum has explained, the eighteenth century was the period "when sexual and racial differences evolve[d] into their modern shapes within emergent notions of national identity."[2]

Depictions of sex became one of the tools by which the new cartographies were mapped out throughout Europe. Within the specialist realms, groundbreaking new taxonomies, such as the *Systema Naturae* (1735) and the *Anthropomorphia* (1760) of Swedish physician and biologist Carl Linnaeus, who made the case for the centrality of reproduction for all life—made the subject of sex pivotal to scientific investigation (fig. 7.1).[3] Within the public

FIGURE 7.1: Types of "primitive" man, as imagined by seventeenth-century anthropologists. 1. Troglodyta Bontii. 2. Lucifer Aldrovandi. 3. Satyrus Tulipii. 4. Pygmaeus Edwardi. Engraving from Carl Linnaeus, *Anthropomorphia*, 1760. Wellcome Library, London.

sphere, the investment in defining the "West" helps to explain why we find similar, if nationally inflected, discourses about sex across the shifting political boundaries of eighteenth-century Europe.[4] For instance, while a rhetoric of sexual stereotyping used to discredit political enemies played some role in the process of the nationalization of Europe—for example, the French term for sodomy was *le vice allemand* (the German vice)—debates in Britain, France, the German states, Scandinavia, the Low Countries, Italy, and Spain nevertheless all focused on similar concerns about the exigencies of sex, which crystallized around issues such as sodomy, prostitution, and the upholding of gender norms.

Michel Foucault, whose *History of Sexuality* has initiated the ongoing critical debate about sexuality and identity, has argued that in the Enlightenment we find a shift from a theology of sex that understood sexual behaviors as "the meeting line of the body and the soul" and which conceptualized perceived aberrant behaviors as sinful, towards a secular, rational ethics of sex that would eventually replace God with Nature and hence associate sexual deviancy not with sinfulness, but with unnaturalness.[5] Part of the process of secularizing sex was, according to Foucault, the need to articulate sex, to "tell everything," so that desire could be rendered "morally acceptable and technically useful."⁶ Eighteenth-century popular culture played a crucial role in this process. For "it is in a variety of forms of sexual talk and action," as Peter Cryle and Lisa O'Connell have so convincingly argued, "that enlightenment vernacularized and dispersed itself, finding new ways into new public spheres, organizing itself into a variety of practises of the body, contributing to regimes of gendered identity, defining the limits of European culture in colonial contexts, and joining the culture of commerce and entrepreneurship which was so important to the period."⁷ The fictions, memoirs, and plays of the time allow us to trace some of the intersections between popular and apparently rarefied philosophical, legal, and political discourses about sexuality, as well as revealing the part played by popular culture itself for development of the Enlightenment ideologies of sex and the human. This chapter will examine some of the prevailing popular ideas about sex across an eighteenth-century European world where sexuality was conceived as a matter of humanity.

POPULARIZING SEX

Ideas about sex were primarily popularized as ideas about sexual difference. Social satirists such as William Congreve in *The Ways of the World*, one of the most famous Restoration plays, first performed in the theater in Lincoln's Inn field in London in 1700, explored the behavioral codes of courting couples in the context of contemporary social convention.⁸ Some critics have drawn a strict distinction between eighteenth-century popular culture and the rarefied philosophical debates of the Enlightenment and argued that what was happening in the late seventeenth century was not so much "a shift in sensibility ... as a shift in the model of what was deemed to be knowledge. In the process, learned culture was hived off from popular culture."⁹ For Douglas Chambers, the sociopolitical implications of developing scientific, philosophical, and other expert fields of knowledge during the Enlightenment led to a separation between learning, understood in terms of scholarly education, and culture, defined in terms of public entertainment. However, Morag Shiach has convincingly shown that such a neat distinction is problematic, as "the articulation of the importance of popular culture for the dominant culture often involves notions of 'social control' and 'effects,'" which in turn bind the popular and the learned.¹⁰ This point is reinforced by eighteenth-century debates about the everyday exigencies of femininity and masculinity, which within the literary sphere were linked to questions about the function of literature itself. Many writers shared the belief that "all art had to be morally useful."¹¹ John Dryden, for instance, made a typical case for the *raison d'être* of satire, in terms of its social function, when he argued that it must "instruct the people by discrediting vice."[12] This does not mean that social needs dictated artistic production, but that popular culture was part of the production and transmission of conflicting ideologies about sex and society.[13]

The rise of the novel is a characteristic feature of the eighteenth-century cultural landscape. While in England, as James Raven has shown, "in the early 1690s, shackled by the post-Restoration licensing laws, printing was a restricted medium, confined to London, Cambridge, Oxford and York; by 1800, print issued from hundreds of presses operating in London and almost every small town in the country."[14] The development of the railways further enhanced the dissemination of the new material, especially in Scandinavian countries such as Sweden, where book transports into the provinces before the introduction of the railway in the 1850s had been mostly confined to the summer months, when boats could navigate the open waters along the coast and inland waterways.[15] Boats still continued to play an important role in linking the colonies of the New World to European culture: the sales record of the most popular novels sold in America between 1750 and 1800 illustrates that by the second half of the eighteenth century, a wider European literary market had expanded to North America. Best-selling texts include Miguel de Cervantes's *Don Quixote* (1605–1615); Alain-René Le Sage's *The Devil on Two Sticks* (1707), and his *Gil Blas* (1715–1735); Daniel Defoe's *Robinson Crusoe* (1719); Samuel Richardson's *Pamela* (1740), and his *Clarissa* (1748); Samuel Johnson's *Rasselas* (1759); Tobias Smollett's *Humphrey Clinker* (1771), *Roderick Random* (1748), and *Peregrine Pickle* (1751); Laurence Sterne's *Tristram Shandy* (1760–1767); Jean-Jacques Rousseau's *Emilius and Sophia* (1762); Oliver Goldsmith's *Vicar of Wakefield* (1766); Johann Wolfgang von Goethe's *Sorrows of Young Werther* (1774); and Frances Burney's *Evelina* (1778).[16] The works encapsulate the development of the novel genre—from Cervantes's homosocial early modern adventure to the pressures of femininity experienced by Burney's romantic heroine. Often subtitled "histories" (or, in their more deliberately expository form, "secret histories"), the French *nouvelles,* Spanish *novelas,* and English novels ostensibly focused on individual lives, as the titles suggest, but were in fact concerned with larger moral and political concerns about vice, virtue, and the social order.

As books became commercialized commodities, the printed word became accessible to a far wider audience, and this in turn had implications for the gendering of writing and reading. Given their strong cultural links including, of course, shared language—the increasing use of the vernacular was crucial to the popularity of printed texts—it is not surprising that Anglo-French texts dominated the American market.[17] However, the sales record fails to convey that within Europe, and in particular within Britain, women writers had a substantial economic stake in the new marketplace.[18] The visibility of women as both writers and readers of fiction steadily increased over the century, while male-authored texts also paid particular attention to representations of femininity. For instance, one of the founding texts of the new novel genre, the best-selling *La Princesse de Clèves,* published anonymously in 1662, was written by the Frenchwoman Marie-Madeleine de Lafayette.[19] It was translated into English in 1678, and adapted for the English stage in 1681. The English literary market was dominated by women such as Aphra Behn, whose work explored questions of virtue and the social pressures of femininity, in what Paula Backscheider and John J. Richetti have called an "erotic world of aristocratic hedonism and often enough of sensational and even brutal violence."[20] Her sales figures were rivaled only by those of John Dryden. *Love in Excess* (1719), written by Behn's contemporary Eliza Haywood, ranked as one of the four best-selling books in early-eighteenth-century England, alongside Defoe's *Robinson Crusoe,* Jonathan Swift's *Gulliver's Travels* (1726), and Richardson's *Pamela.*[21]

The literary market was not confined to urban printing centers. Sarah Prescott has shown that many women writers operated successfully from the provinces, and overall a significant number of the new professional women writers undertook other money-making ventures—from starting their own oratories to opening coffeehouses—to earn their living.[22] Haywood, a prolific writer, actress, translator, playwright, and publisher, was one of the few to live comfortably off her literary earnings. Her work examined the gendered conventions of female sexuality in novels such as *The British Recluse* (1722), which explored "what Miseries may attend a Woman, who has no other Foundation for Belief in what her Lover says to her than the good Opinion her Passion has made her conceive of him."[23] However, Haywood was also famous for her more unusual portrayals of women as successful sexual predators. In her widely read novel *Fantomina* (1725), the female heroine unscrupulously employs a range of disguises, including that of prostitute and mistress, to continue to entrance and have sex with the gentleman Beauplaisir, who "varied not so much from his Sex as to be able to prolong Desire" for one and the same woman.[24]

Themes such as courtship, marriage, and faithfulness dominated the literary market. Critics sometimes categorize the literature of the eighteenth century according to the explicitness of its treatment of sexual matters into three genres: amatory fiction, erotic fiction, and pornography.[25] However, the distinction between "respectable" amatory fiction, tolerated erotic fiction, and avowedly indecent pornography is not helpful for covering the full range of writings that dealt with sexual matters. We only need to compare more salacious novels, such as *Fantomina,* with contemporary conduct literature, such as the *Letter of*

Genteel and Moral Advice to a Young Lady, written by the Reverend Wetenhall Wilkes (1741), to be persuaded by Vivien Jones's argument that, more often than not, the "moral discourse of chaste conduct evokes precisely the desire and fantasies it claims to police."[26] Wilkes describes in some detail the dangerous "double temptations of vanity and desire" that he considers intrinsic to male nature, in the process mapping out clearly the various ways in which a woman may attract a man through "look, gesture, smile or sentence."[27] Similarly, many popular depictions of women as mistresses deliberately blurred the boundaries of respectability. Mateo Alemán's picaresque novel *The Life of Guzmán of Alfarache,* which was first published in Spanish between 1599 and 1604 and continued to be widely read throughout the seventeenth and early eighteenth centuries, outselling even Cervantes's *Don Quixote,* describes the double role of the mother of the eponymous protagonist as both wife and mistress.[28] In the 1708 English translation, Guzmán explains how his mother successfully implemented a plan to enjoy simultaneously the privileged position as wife of an old knight—himself "a great Debauchee" who ensured her financial prosperity—and that of mistress of a virile gallant who could satisfy her sexual appetite.[29] The text ridicules contemporary ideas about female chastity, claiming that

> If only Virgins were to marry, I dare promise the World would soon be at an end, or at least it would not be supported by Marriage. Your tried Women contribute most to Generation, whereas Maids are so squeamish, t'is a long while before you can bring them to't, and so much time there is lost, that might, methinks, have been better spent.[30]

Here the inherent excess of human sexuality itself comes under scrutiny, as sex is seen to manifest itself in woman as the means to manipulate men in a way that suggests a high degree of female independence, while men are to suffer from an inability to be sexually continent.

Perhaps it is no surprise that some conservative Christian commentators were deeply concerned about the potentially corruptive impact of reading on women. Hannah More, a member of the Society for the Suppression of Vice, who strongly supported ideas of Christian morality, commented favorably on the "excellent variety" of "those books which are useful in general instruction,"[31] but she also warned that books constitute one of "the most pernicious sources of corruption."[32] For More, the dangers of reading were tied in to the excessive pursuits of pleasure she observed in contemporary society. "So little do our votaries of fashion understand of the true nature of pleasure," she wrote, "that one amusement is allowed to overtake another without any interval."³³ More particularly, she disapproved of what she called the "showy education of women," which

> tends chiefly to qualify them for the glare of public assemblies; secondly, they seem in many instances to be so educated, with a view to the greater probability of their being splendidly married; thirdly, it is alleged in vindication of those dissipated practices, that daughters can only be seen, and admirers to be procured at balls, operas, and assemblies: and that, therefore, by a natural and necessary consequence, balls, operas, and assemblies must be followed up without intermission till the object be effected.³⁴

More's writings are more than a call for modesty and sexual prudence. They tap into specific doubts about the increasing social and political participation of women who, as writers and readers, contributed to a popular culture that commoditized sex and in so doing increasingly blurred the carefully guarded boundaries between the feminine (private) and masculine (public) spheres.

Matters of sex played a different role in the antidogmatic, experience-oriented writings of eighteenth-century rakes and libertines. Recent scholarship has emphasized the European dimension of libertinage, showing that libertines crossed the full range of the sociopolitical spectrum.³⁵ What they shared was a kind of applied philosophical approach to life that put into practice Enlightenment theories of human "liberty," here understood in the broadest sense as a freedom of expression and experience. Sexual pursuits were crucial to the philosophy of this privileged, literary-artistic subculture. While libertine culture flourished especially in the aristocratic and courtesan salons of the growing cities, the sexual exploits of some of the most famous libertines are characterized by their travels throughout Europe and beyond.³⁶ Perhaps the best known example is Casanova, who recounted his life on the fringes of Europe's aristocratic circles in some detail in his *Memoirs*. He led a wandering existence after his notorious escape from prison in Venice in 1755, where he had been held on charge of contempt of religion, fleeing from Italy to Asia Minor via France, Spain, Germany, Holland, England, Poland, Greece, Turkey, and Russia, continuing to seduce women, and, occasionally, to be seduced by beautiful men.³⁷ The *Embassy Letters* of Lady Mary Wortley Montague (fig. 7.2) from 1716–18 show that sexual adventures were not only a male preserve. Written during Montague's time with her husband in Constantinople, where he held the post of British ambassador, the letters provide a rare glimpse at the diversity of female sexual experience.³⁸ Montague was much taken by the Sapphic culture she found in harems, retelling her encounters

FIGURE 7.2: Portrait of Lady Mary Wortley Montague; from an enamel miniature by Zink in the possession of Charles Colville. Lithograph by Villain, after A. Deveria. Wellcome Library, London.

with women such as Fatima, about whom she wrote, "I have seen all that has been call'd lovely either in England or Germany, and I must own that I never saw any thing so gloriously Beautiful."[39] Despite the fact that the same-sex adventures of Montague and, to a lesser extent, Casanova, may suggest that the politics of libertinism were sexually transgressive, the majority of libertine writing was firmly located within a heterosexual frame of reference. Scottish aristocrat James Boswell, for instance, was as famous for his drinking as he was for his numerous sexual encounters with female prostitutes in Edinburgh, Glasgow, and London.[40]

Over the course of the century, the more explicit focus on sexual adventure was replaced with a proto-Romantic focus on the emotions. The work of German poet, playwright, writer, and scientist Johann Wolfgang Goethe, who was made a nobleman in recognition of his success as a man of letters, signals this turning point. His work was inspired by his love affairs, including with a

FIGURE 7.3: Young Werther sits at his writing desk as a young boy brings him his pistol (which he will use to kill himself), while a young woman tries to prevent the boy from delivering the weapon. Line engraving by P. Bonato after A. Kauffman. Wellcome Library, London.

young pastor's daughter in Stesenheim, Alsace (motivating a cycle of poems that came to be known as *Stesenheimer Lyrik*), with Charlotte Buff, who inspired his *Sorrows of Young Werther,* and, later in life, with Christiane Vulpius.[41] *Young Werther* (fig. 7.3), an epistolary account of unrequited love that ends with the main character's suicide, led to what Bruce Duncan has called "Werther-Fever," a phenomenon that included not just enthusiasm for the novel but a desire to emulate its hero, which spread throughout Europe and to America.[42] Young men started to dress like their tragic fictional hero, in a blue swallow-tail coat, yellow waistcoat underneath, and high boots, while some young women adopted the white dress with pink bows worn by the fictional Lotte. *Young Werther*'s reception indicates a cultural shift in literary as well as popular sentiment toward affective responses to life and literature. Now "the whole literary enterprise justified itself," argues Duncan, "by its goal of educating, even creating a public of readers that would form the new public sphere."[43]

This did not mean that sexual allusion went out of fashion, but that it became associated with specific genres. In the first half of the eighteenth century, Thomas Stretser's pornographic text *A New Description of Merryland* (1741) famously satirized the exoticization of sex in writings by a new breed of professional explorers, cartographers, adventurers, and botanists. *Merryland* employs an elaborate geographical metaphor to describe female genitalia as a "country," which is opposed to the "antipodes" (arse) that, according to Stretser, are the preferred destination of some Italian, Dutch, and British explorers.[44] In the latter half of the eighteenth century, "exotic" sexual allure became increasingly associated with religion and rituals. In particular, the Catholic world of convents and monasteries inspired fictionalized sexual histories and sexualized depictions of female sexuality. Diderot's *La Religieuse* (written in 1760 and published posthumously in 1796), for instance, tells the story of torment, claustrophobia, and sexual excess experienced by the young Suzanne Simonin, who has been interned in a rural convent. The emergence of the gothic genre in turn established some of the most influential conventions of representations of sexual transgression. Matthew Lewis's *The Monk* (1796), one of the founding texts of the gothic genre, depicts from the British reader's point of view an exotic Spanish world where, under the mantle of Catholicism, strange sexual rituals are performed. These books, which featured perverse sexual practices ranging from prostitution to flagellation and sex between women, were popular sellers in the mainstream literary market.

Next to libertine, early Romantic and Gothic writings, a different kind of eighteenth-century writer sought to intervene specifically in political affairs by focusing on representations of sex. Here, the employment of sexual themes, especially in the form of metaphors of sexual corruption, served to make poignant comments about current political debates. One of the most famous examples of this type of writing is the work of Delarivière Manley, a best-selling early-eighteenth-century British novelist who wrote a number of *romans à clef* that provided scathing attacks on what she described as the sexual corruption of the Whigs. The first of these novels, *The Secret History of Queen Zarah and the Zarazians* (1705), primarily explored political corruption in terms of marriage, fidelity, and sexual intrigue. Its sequel, *Secret Memoirs and Manners of Several Persons of Quality, of Both Sexes, from the New Atlantis* (1709), extended the scope to include descriptions of incest and sodomy alongside adultery and seduction. *The New Atlantis* has been associated with the defeat of the Whigs in the elections of 1709, reinforcing the political potency of literature.[45] This kind of political engagement was echoed throughout Europe, as critics have well documented.[46] Events around the American Revolutions and the French

Revolution of 1789 directly affected writers such as Helen Maria Williams, whose *Letters from France,* published between 1790 and 1796, constitute one of the most influential British records of the French Revolution. Adriana Cracuin argues that the notion of revolution was itself gendered in feminine terms, as observers such as Williams focused on its female victims, as well as relying on "the feminized aesthetics of romance" when formulating their response.[47] But revolutionary events also inspired the production of that most overt example of the links between textual and sexual politics: Mary Wollstonecraft's manifesto of modern feminism, *A Vindication of the Rights of Women* (1792).

ECONOMICS OF PLEASURE

If sex was a political metaphor, the public politics of sex equally came under scrutiny as the explosion of writings about sex was part of a far wider-reaching economics of "pleasure."[48] Prostitution, or the trade in sex itself, was one of the most visible manifestations of sex in society.[49] As a profession, prostitution was typically divided into the grim reality of streetwalkers and the prostitutes who plied their trade in cheap brothels and bawdy houses, and the more affluent courtesans who entertained an exclusive clientele in their private salons. While the former were normally represented as anonymous commodities— Boswell's accounts of his adventures with London streetwalkers represents them as generic types—the notion of the courtesan captured the literary imagination in novels such as Defoe's *Roxana* (1724) and Henry Fielding's *Tom Jones* (1749).[50] John Cleland's *Fanny Hill: Memoirs of a Woman of Pleasure* (1749) famously imagines the life of a Marylebone-based female prostitute who leads an impoverished existence that is "pleasant nevertheless."[51] Her sexual encounters, written in the first-person singular, are depicted as (male) fantasies of desire and female sexual allure, as the following description of an encounter with a young man illustrates:

> The young fellow, overheated with the present objects, and too high mettled to be longer curb'd in by that modesty and awe which had hitherto restrain'd him, ventur'd, under the stronger impulse and instructive promptership of nature alone, to slip his hands, trembling with eager impetuous desires, under my petticoats. Oh then! the fiery touch of his fingers determines me, and my fears melting away before the glowing heat, my thighs disclose of themselves, and yield all the liberty to his hand: and now, a favourable movement giving my petticoats a toss, the avenue lay too fair, too open to be miss'd.[52]

The imagined account of Fanny Hill's own enjoyment of her trade provides tantalizing insights into popular constructions of male sexuality and female sexual excess. At the same time, it introduced a wide readership to sexual pleasures including sex between men, sex between women, and flagellation.

The pleasures of the relatively closed world of the bedroom or boudoir impacted on the design of real spaces in the eighteenth century city. In the American West, settlements such as San Francisco started to form, which, with the beginning of the gold rush in the 1840s, developed into chaotic places where prostitution and drunkenness flourished. In contrast, European cities, despite the high visibility of alcoholism and the proliferation of street prostitution, also turned their attention to a more ordered public pursuit of pleasure, expressed in the new fashion for parks and pleasure gardens took hold.[53] It is easy to see why Roy Porter considers the pleasure garden the very epitome of Georgian love of pleasure, as within London alone, around two hundred of them opened.[54] The development of Marybone (also known as Marrowbone and Maribone) Gardens indicates a common pattern of this kind of development, from its beginnings as rural park land on the very outskirts of London, where pastimes such as dueling and dog fighting were popular, to its increasing gentrification over the course the eighteenth century: in 1737, for instance, the Prince of Wales went bowling in the park.[55] But the parks were used by a wide section of the public. Vauxhall Gardens, reopened in 1732, provided cheap entertainment for anyone who, for the price of a shilling, wished to "stroll around the grottoes, statues, temples, waterfalls, listen to music [such as George Frideric Händel's newly-composed *Water Music*[56]] and watch the firework displays."[57] The opening of Ranelagh Gardens ten years later, which charged two shillings sixpence, was aimed at a more exclusive clientele that nevertheless included wealthier courtesans who could afford the admission price. Ranelagh also opened a garden in the Bois de Boulogne in Paris, where, for one livre and four sous, the public could enjoy amusements including the usual fireworks and concerts, but also masked balls, comedies, and balloon launchings.[58]

Alongside the static entertainment provided by the gardens, traveling fairs and other, older forms of entertainment continued to be popular throughout the eighteenth century, drawing in audiences from a cross section of the population (fig. 7.4). Here the performance of "sex" was usually linked to a display of perceived physical aberrations, such as bearded ladies and strong men. The so-called freak shows also sometimes advertised examples of extraordinary sexuality, specifically displaying "unusual" human genitals. At the 1777 fair at Saint-Germain, for instance, an eight-foot-one-inch-tall man from Westphalia, whose sizable penis was one of the attractions of the show.

FIGURE 7.4: Southwark Fair, a renowned place of amusement, with a variety of theatrical establishments. Engraving by T. Cook after W. Hogarth. London, 1796. Wellcome Library, London.

A contemporary French observer, Louis Petit de Bauchaumont, recorded in his *Mémoirs Secrets* (1777–1789) the appearance of "a 4-year-old child" at a similar event, "who, formed as fortunately as the most vigorous man beyond the finest proportions in the virile organ, has the diverse abilities of it such as erection and ejaculation."[59]

While this kind of explicitness was not exceptional, it was nevertheless relatively marginal within the eighteenth-century world of entertainment overall. On the theatrical stage, transgressive embodiments tended to be performed in terms of masquerades and cross-dressing. As the popular emergence of an operatic tradition swept across Europe from Italy and made famous female singers as well as men, the theater, too, was transformed when for the first time women actors were allowed on stage.[60] If the woman writer and the prostitute constitute opposite ends on the respectability scale of the eighteenth-century cultural market, the actress was located somewhere in between. Kristina Straub has examined the earliest professional female actors, and how the kinds of roles they were allowed to play were linked to contemporary gender anxieties. She reveals that the attitudes to cross-dressing women on stage changed as it became common convention from about the mid-eighteenth century to reveal the "true" sex of the actress.[61] Straub convincingly argues that this development is tied in to the increasing sexualization of theatrical performance, which made it necessary to emphasize the distinction between acceptably playful transgressions of gender and sexual transgressions that were condemned.[62]

While many of the plays were written specifically for the theater, Shakespearean drama remained popular, and literary best-sellers were also adapted for the stage. The adaptations of Behn's 1688 novel *Oroonoko*, for example, show that the theater was a whites-only world. When *Oroonoko* was adapted for the stage, it soon became the most popular play of the time. In the stage adaptation, the character of Inmoida was whitened, which was a fairly unusual practice and seems to have been reserved for women only. For certain male roles (but also some female ones), blackface continued to be a popular practice throughout the eighteenth century. It took until 1825 before the first black actor appeared on the English stage. This was Ira Aldridge, who, billed as a "man of colour," played in *Oroonoko* at the Royal Coburg Theatre.[63]

SEXUAL LIVES

In a climate where scandal and gossip constituted popular forms of entertainment, accounts of lived experience inspired much cultural production. As on the stage, it was important in real life that gender transgression, which was tolerated to an extent, was not confused with sexual transgression. The popularity of the memoirs of actresses such as Nell Gwynn and Margaret Wolffington, for example, was partly based on salacious assumptions about their private lives, derived from the sexual ambiguities they played out on stage, but these were tolerated, as they followed heteronormative narrative conventions. Adventures of women such as highway robber Mary Frith, better known as Moll Cutpurse, who was first brought to wider public attention in Thomas Dekker and Thomas Middleton's play *The Roaring Girl* (1608–1611), and whose life was later elaborated upon in the anonymous prose account of *The Life and Death of Mary Frith* (1662) (fig. 7.5), gained a firm place in the English national imagination. Charles Whibley's account of Moll Cutpurse, written more than a hundred years later, when the stability of the Victorian empire came under increasing pressure, deliberately harks back to a time of successful imperial expansion, as he associates Frith with "the heyday of England's greatness, four years after the glorious defeat of the Armada."[64] Frith was one of a number of eighteenth-century women who earned their living in male guise, and whose stories became well-known by

FIGURE 7.5: Portrait of Mary Frith (Moll Cutpurse) from *A Collection of Four Hundred Portraits*. London, 1880. Wellcome Library, London.

way of published accounts. After their exposure through such accounts, Anne Bonny and Mary Read were both tried for piracy in Jamaica in 1720, inspiring a number of widely popular histories of piracy, including *A General History of the Pyrates* (1724), which circulated throughout the eighteenth century.[65]

The seafaring female cross-dresser was not necessarily associated only with criminal conduct. By far the highest number of records relating to women "passing" as men in the English-speaking world of the first half of the eighteenth century belong to women who disguised themselves as male sailors or soldiers to undertake adventures and earn a living within the boundaries of the law. Julie Peakman has suggested that there is evidence of more than 20 women who served in the Royal Navy or the Marines in the course of the century.[66] The late-nineteenth-century feminist writer Ménie Muriel Dowie republished accounts of four such life stories of eighteenth-century adventurers including that of soldier Christian Davies, for whom "plain living and high thinking were never the notion"; Hannah Snell, another well-known soldier; whose alias was

James Knell, Mary Ann Talbot, a nobleman's daughter who, as John Taylor, worked as a "foot-boy, drummer, cabin-boy, and sailor"; and American Madame Velasquez who fought as Lieutenant Harry Buford for the Confederates. For Dowie, these narratives anticipated a successful "woman of the future" who is equal to men.[67] At the time of their first publications, however, these stories provided popular forms of entertainment. While cross-dressing was not illegal, the realities of the women who lived as men were often harsh. Mary Lacy, another cross-dressing woman sailor, whose account of her adventures, *The History of the Female Shipwright* (1773), was hugely popular, claimed that when her sex was discovered she escaped punishment and was simply sent ashore, though there is little evidence of a settled life afterward.[68] Snell, too, records that she was sent home when it was discovered that she was a woman. She took to performing her male persona onstage, now necessarily capitalizing on her female sex. That this way of earning a living remained precarious, however, is reinforced all too clearly by the fact that Snell died penniless at Bedlam Hospital, where she had been admitted for insanity.

FIGURE 7.6: Hannah Snell, a woman who passed as a soldier. Mezzotint by J. Young, 1789, after R. Phelps. 1789. Wellcome Library, London.

The relatively benign treatment of gender transgression was not extended to sexual conduct, as women who had sex with women were severely punished throughout Europe.[69] Their punishment constitutes arguably the most gruesome side of eighteenth-century popular entertainment. The case of Catharina Linck, who was prosecuted for lesbianism in 1721 in the town of Halberstadt in Saxony, amply illustrates this point.[70] At the trial, Linck, who was born sometime in the 1690s, argued that she had initially disguised herself as a man to lead a chaste life, joining a wandering religious sect for a time. Her story has much in common with narratives such as that of Snell, as Linck explains how she joined the army, deserted in 1708, was captured and sentenced to death, but was subsequently freed when her female sex was discovered. In 1717, she married a woman called Catharina Margaretha Mühlhahn, claiming that she tried to disguise her biological sex from her new wife with the help of a "leather sausage" that served as a false penis. However, when Mühlhahn's mother discovered the biological sex of her "son-in-law" and brought this to the attention of the authorities, both women were tried and convicted of sodomy. Mühlhahn, as accessory to Linck's crime, was sentenced to three years of imprisonment and hard labor and then banished for life from Saxony. Linck herself was sentenced to be beheaded and then burned.

In countries such as Britain, where the English Criminal Code recognized neither cross-dressing nor lesbianism, marriage between women was punished not as sodomy but as an economic crime such as fraud or vagrancy. Emma Donaghue, for instance, examines the case of a woman tried at the King's Bench in 1694 who was accused of trying to pass as a man so that she could marry her maid in order to obtain the maid's dowry.[71] The most famous case of this kind in England was that of Mary Hamilton, who had impersonated a man and married. Hamilton's story was reported by the novelist Henry Fielding in a widely read pamphlet entitled *The Female Husband* (1746), in which he embellished the facts of the story with misogynist warnings against excessive female sexuality. It is unclear how many women Hamilton had married during her life. She was tried for vagrancy in 1746 when her then "wife," a woman named Mary Price, reported Hamilton upon discovering her biological sex. As in the case of Linck, the fact that Hamilton had apparently used a dildo as part of her disguise played a key role in the trial and was used both to exonerate Price and to cement Hamilton's guilt. As the law did not recognize her sexual transgression, however, Hamilton was tried on economic grounds, for fraud and for impersonating a doctor. She was sentenced to public whipping in four market towns, followed by six months' imprisonment.

While there exist some famous male cross-dressers, notably the Chevalier d'Éon (fig. 7.7) and the Abbé de Choisy), public debates around the regulation of male sexuality focused mainly on sodomy and its perceived threat to society. Associated in the seventeenth century with anal intercourse—between two men, a man and a woman, or between a human and animal—in the course of the eighteenth century, sodomy came to denote specifically sex between men. Early erotic writings, such as the humorous play *Sodom, or the Quintessence of Debauchery* (1684), are among the first to indicate this shift.[72] The play has been ascribed to John Wilmot, second Earl of Rochester, an English libertine famous for his drunkenness and sexual adventures.[73] It charts the adventures of Sodom's king, Bolloxinion, who, on the advice of the "Buggermaster-General," abandons his queen, Cuntigratia, and introduces a rule of sodomy throughout the realm. The plot covers all the main themes and specific practices of current sexual debate, including descriptions of orgies, the use of dildos, masturbation, the devastating impact of venereal disease, and, of course, sodomy. While

FIGURE 7.7: Le Chevalier d'Éon, a man who passed as a woman. Stipple engraving by R. Cooper, 1821. Wellcome Library, London.

sodomy here is associated with the "human arse" generally, it is nevertheless assumed to be a practice between men.

The eighteenth-century reader would have been all too aware that sodomy was severely punished in most European states and in North America. In the first half of the eighteenth century, parts of Scandinavia and the Low Countries experienced some of the harshest persecution of sodomy in European history. Jonas Liliequist has collected data on convictions for sex with animals, which show that, in Sweden between the 1730s and 1778, "the last person convicted of bestiality was beheaded and burnt at the stake ... approximately six hundred to seven hundred persons, mostly male adolescents and young men, were executed."[74] The extensive focus of the Swedish prosecutions on bestiality has been relatively unusual and has been partly explained in terms of the country's rural isolation and an agrarian tradition in which boys worked in relative solitude as cattle herders during their formative years. In contrast, comparative studies of the Low Countries, where in a period of only two years, 1730–1732, the Courts of Holland executed at least 75 men for sexual acts with other men, tend to focus on the cultural signification of sodomy. Historians have argued that these persecutions indicate a new xenophobia that blamed a perceived increase in sex between men on the influence of French libertinism, which in turn was seen to undermine the moral values and hence political strength of Protestant Holland and its neighboring kingdoms.[75] In France itself, there were some attempts to decry sodomy as a foreign practice, as the anonymously published *La France devenue italienne avec les autres désordres de la cour* (France Becomes Italian with the Other Disorders of the Court) shows.[76]

By the mid-eighteenth century, philosophers started to turn their attention to developing what they thought was a new "rational" approach to crime that focused on the prevention, rather than merely the punishment, of "criminal" behavior. Here, the treatment of sex served as a measure for testing the "rational" legislation of the populace of the emerging modern states.[77] Montesquieu, in a chapter "On the Crime against Nature," (1748) made a typical Enlightenment plea for the prevention of sodomy, not because he wanted to decriminalize the practice, but because he believed that it was so hard to prove guilt objectively that sodomy trials carried the unenlightened risk of criminal injustice.[78] Similarly, the Italian criminologist Cesare Bonasa argued in 1764 that "punishment for a crime cannot be deemed truly just ... unless the laws have adopted the best possible means ... to prevent that crime."[79] These arguments did not, however, translate into more just legislation for all men and women: when eighteenth-century Pennsylvania amended its sodomy laws and replaced the death penalty with life imprisonment, the change applied to white citizens only.

Blacks and Indians found guilty of sodomy were still punished with the death penalty.[80]

The nationalization of sex and the racialization of sexuality typically went hand in hand, as seen in the literary accounts of the South Seas. Jorge Cañizares-Esguerra has examined in detail the ways in which "particular versions of masculinity, national identity and racial difference were constituted, transmitted and destabilized on the voyages" of explorers such as Captain James Cook.[81] The account of his South Sea voyages undertaken between 1768 and 1780 provides as much information on Polynesian sexual customs as on scientific accounts of the fauna and flora of the islands (fig. 7.8).[82] Such observations of "primitive" sexuality were commonly tied to discourses around development and civilization, in which establishing sexual difference was crucial to defining racial hierarchies. For Hannah More, the blurring of "racial" boundaries in

FIGURE 7.8: A young woman from the island of Otaheite (Tahiti) wearing a large skirt, encountered by Captain Cook on his third voyage (1777–1780). Engraving by F. Bartolozzi after J. Webber, 1780/1785. Wellcome Library, London.

matters of sex was a serious matter, as she claims that Asian influences directly led to the downfall of the Roman Empire.

> The modesty of the Roman matron, and the chaste demeanour of her virgin daughters ... fell a sacrifice to [Rome's] Asiatic conquests; after which the females were soon taught a complete change of character. They were instructed to accommodate their talents of pleasing to the more vitiated tastes of the other sex; and began to study every grace and every art which might captivate the exhausted hearts and excite the wearied and capricious inclinations of the men; till by a rapid and at length complete enervation, the Roman character lost its signature, and through a quick succession of slavery, effeminacy, and vice, sunk into that degeneracy of which some of the modern Italian states serve to furnish a too just specimen.[83]

More adds a distinct xenophobic touch to the more general distinction between Western and non-Western contexts. Voltaire, in turn, made a more typical argument for sexual difference, which implicitly dismissed the existence of sexual difference in African and Southeast Asian societies. He claimed that "the attraction of the two sexes for each other declares itself early on; but no matter what has been said about female Africans and the women of southern Asia, this inclination is generally much stronger in men than in women. It is a law that nature has established for all animals; it is always the male that assaults the female."[84] There were few non-white voices in Europe at the time. In 1789, the English public celebrated Olaudah Equiano, who had written an "'interesting narrative of his life'" that recounted his escape from slavery to freedom in London.[85] This was a best-seller, and Equiano's story became a *cause célèbre* of the abolitionist movement, despite the fact that the authenticity of his story was challenged.[86] Less well-known but perhaps more directly tied in to the culture of public pleasure was Dean Mohamet, an East Indian man who had come to London with his Irish wife, established the first public vapor bath, and had a successful, if not necessarily integrated social role.[87] Neither Equiano nor Mohamet overtly addressed how contemporary debates linked racial discourse and sexual difference, considering the distinction between men and women fundamental to "civilized humanity."

CONCLUSION

Volupteries of all ages and sexes—it is you alone that I offer this work. Nourish yourselves on its principles: they foster your passions; and these passions, with which cold and shabby moralists try to intimidate you, are simply the means used by nature to help human beings attain nature's goals. Listen solely to those delicious passions; their source is the only one that will lead you to happiness.[88]

The ethics of the sexual body had become a contentious matter by the close of the eighteenth century. For not only did the physicality of sex test the limits of the rational mind, but the existence and function of pleasure proved to be somewhat of a conundrum for philosophers seeking to understand human nature. In a cultural climate where the "truths" about sex formed important points of political debate, the idea of a-ethical sexual pleasure, developed by the Marquis de Sade, caused an outcry. Sade's law of desire, which viewed the body as an instrument of what Jacques Lacan subsequently called the "will-to-jouissance," constitutes perhaps the most famous legacy of eighteenth-century discourse on sex.[89] Lacan, in his much-quoted essay "Kant avec Sade," has famously linked Sade's notion of pleasure to Immanuel Kant's ethical reading of the sexual body, which explored the idea that the mind controls the body and argued, in contrast to Sade, that reason should control desire. Kant tried to locate sexual pleasure within the natural order and to understand its place within—or indeed the challenge it posed to—a Cartesian mind/body dichotomy. For Kant, the discussion of sexual conduct provided a way to test the principles of rational moral philosophy. For instance, in his *Lectures on Ethics* (1780), Kant argued that what he considered the *crimina carnis* (such as all same-sex acts and masturbation) are *contra naturam* because they do not serve the future of humanity.[90] In contrast, Sade developed a complex philosophy of pleasure, which argued precisely *for* the naturalness of perverse sexual behavior. As Caroline Warman has shown, Sade reappropriated John Locke's argument that there exist no innate ideas, but that all cognition is based on material sensation, according to which the body is the site of all knowledge.[91] Sade interpreted this idea to deduce that the sexual body is a blank canvas upon which natural instincts are acted out, and that as such it is amoral.

The legacies of Kant and Sade provide a fitting conclusion to this investigation. Alan Corkhill has explored the significance of their different discursive realms, arguing that "Kant was no lexicographer of carnal pleasures [but] he preferred to couch his philosophy of male and female sexuality in the clinical language of philosophical and semi-legalistic antimonies such as self-regarding duties and obligations vis-à-vis the moral law [while] for Sade the narrativization of sexual fantasies knew no bounds. His voluminous fiction is at once an instruction manual for the sexually uninitiated or inexperienced *and* pornography aimed at sexual arousal."[92] Kant is of course no longer primarily associated with the theorization of sex; however, Sade's perverse *Philosophy of the Boudoir* (1795) has become perhaps the best known theory of sexual behavior to come out of the Enlightenment. His writings are still associated with a particular concept of sexual behavior, partly due to the fact that nineteenth-century sexologists appropriated his ideas, coining a new terminology that entered different European languages as *sadism, sadisme, Sadismus,* and *sadismo*. Sade's own fate also indicates the limits of the new legal and philosophical attempts that sought to rationalize sex. First imprisoned for thirteen years in 1771 on charges of sodomy and other sexual transgressions at the instigation of his mother-in-law, he died during his second imprisonment on charges of being the author of pornographic fiction.[93] Kant and Sade provide unusual examples of how Enlightenment thought "vernacularized" itself from various specialized fields of investigation. Their shared concern with the *nature* of sexual conduct reinforces the view that the Enlightenment produced a new mode of thinking whereby, in the course of the eighteenth century, carnal pleasure was invested with psychosocial significance, turning the rational human into the sexual subject.

CHAPTER EIGHT

Prostitution

RANDOLPH TRUMBACH

In the first generation of the eighteenth century, a new sexual culture emerged in northwestern Europe, in which all individuals were divided into what was later called a heterosexual majority and a homosexual minority. This profoundly changed the nature and meaning of both male and female prostitution in England, France, and the Dutch Republic. By 1730, the prostitution of these northern European societies was quite different from the prostitution they had known before 1700. Heterosexual men went usually only to female prostitutes, whom they found either in brothels or in the streets, though occasionally they used male transvestite prostitutes whom they may have mistaken to be biological women. Homosexual men used only boys or men as prostitutes, who might themselves have been either homosexual or heterosexual. In the societies of southern Mediterranean Europe, the older pattern persisted, in which men might go either to female prostitutes or to male prostitutes (the latter were usually adolescent boys, but there was the occasional adult transvestite). This pattern of bisexual prostitution continued to be the norm in the Muslim world, as well as in the Asian societies of India, China, and Japan.

The radical Italian philosopher Alberto Radicati, observing England and Holland in the 1730s, saw quite clearly the difference between the north and the south: "throughout the Dominions of the Mahometans and Roman-Catholics, the Majority of whose Females are shut up in Seraglios and Convents, and where the Husbands are exclusively jealous, the men for Want of Women, addict themselves to the detestable Practice of Sodomy. Some may tell me, there are Sodomites also in England and Holland, tho' the women have there a very great Liberty. But I shall anticipate them by saying, First, that they are in very small Numbers in Comparison with those to be met with in the Countries I mentioned; and Secondly, That even most of those few who do it, are such as are unmarried, and are either poor, miserably timorous or ugly ..." An Englishman looking at Italian prostitution observed the same difference and claimed that in the south, a sexual equivalence was made between women and boys: "no sooner does a Stranger of Condition set his Foot in Rome, but he is surrounded by a Crowd of Panderers, who ask him if he chooses a Woman or a boy, and procure for him accordingly."[1]

Northern European visitors to Turkey in the late seventeenth and the early eighteenth centuries were struck by the frequency, the openness, and the prestige of sexual relations between men and boys. It could almost seem that the Turks preferred boys to women. But relations between Turkish men and women would have been largely hidden from the eyes of visiting European men because of the seclusion of women. Cornelis de Bruyn said that "they make no more of it than we do of the most innocent Galantries ... 'Tis the usual burden of their songs ... whereby they give a sufficient Evidence how much better pleas'd they are with that Beastly and Unnatural Passion, than they are with the natural use of women." Joseph Pitts noticed that it was "part of their ordinary Discourse to boast and brag of their detestable Actions. ... Tis common for Men to fall in love with Boys, as tis here in England to be in Love with Women; And I have seen many when they have been drunk, that have given themselves deep Gashes on their Arms with a Knife, saying, *Tis for the Love they bear to such a Boy*. ... I have seen many that have had their Arms full of great Cuts, as so many Tokens of their Love." Aaron Hill wrote that their favorite catamites were called "Pooshts" and were "as Common as their concubines," and that they rode "attended to the Wars or distant Governments, by rich and splendid Numbers of these young *Male Prostitutes*." Charles Thompson claimed that the young pages who served in the sultan's seraglio fell in love with each other and idealized their love: "they say abundance of fine things indeed upon this subject, and call it a step to the perfect Love of God, and say, they only admire his image and Beauty stamped upon his Creature." The officers of state watched "for a sight of these young fellows, as for a mistress, when they pass by to the Mosques or Baths ... and 'tis no uncommon Thing to see them made Sharers with their Masters in their Fortunes."

Some of what is described in these accounts by Europeans occurred between social equals and was not prostitution. The Ottoman Turkish sources make clear that the boys who waited on men in coffeehouses and bathhouses were often prostitutes. They were more likely to be tolerated than were the female prostitutes who frequently occupied the same public spaces. Public authority intervened only when a boy was raped. A male prostitute could, however, also be a boy or an adult man, called a *köçek* or transvestite dancer. Transvestite adult men were found in a wide range of societies in which sexual relations between males usually occurred between men and adolescent boys, since a boy sometimes did not make the transition from a passive boy who was penetrated, to an active man who was the penetrator, and such a boy became either a passive man who married a woman and secretly had relations with men (and in Turkey was known as an *ibne*), or grew up to be a man like the *köçek*. The sources for the Arab Islamic world document the same two kinds of male prostitution. Male prostitutes throughout the Islamic world were therefore usually boys but sometimes might be adult transvestites.[2]

In Japan, China, and India, most men had sexual relations with both males and females, with boys and transvestite adult men serving as prostitutes. Licensed male prostitution first appeared in Japan in the late sixteenth century. By the 1690s the Dutchman Engelbert Kaempfer found in a small temple town nine or ten houses in front of which sat boys of ten or twelve with their faces painted, offering themselves to visitors. In Edo the pleasure quarters provided both female and male prostitutes in the teahouses (fig. 8.1). A guidebook in 1768 counted at least 200 boy prostitutes in Edo, and there were similar numbers elsewhere. Adult male actors who were transvestite were the most expensive companions; their playhouses were usually located in the same city wards that offered teahouses with boys. Some teahouses catered mainly to Buddhist monks, who were forbidden to have relations with women but not with males. Erotic prints show that most men were interested in both males and females; in some, monks penetrate boys who are themselves penetrating a woman; or men are shown withdrawing from a boy so as to enter a woman. Utamoro Kitagawa produced two prints that illustrated the two kinds of male prostitutes. In one print a man lubricates his penis with his own saliva as he prepares to penetrate a boy (fig. 8.2). In the other print a man has fully penetrated an adult male transvestite (fig. 8.3). In China, the Kangixi emperor (1661–1722) made decrees against selling boys into prostitution, but boy brothels continued to flourish in the lanes of the Outer City of Beijing. As late as 1860, in Tianjin there were 35 brothels, with 800 boys catering to men who ranged across the social spectrum from laborers to scholars. Some boys feminized themselves and went so far as binding their feet. But some prostitutes grew up to father children. The men who played female roles in the Beijing opera were in demand as sexual companions, and some actors kept boys in their homes for wealthy clients. Among

FIGURE 8.1: Upstairs at a brothel. A maid combs out a hairpiece while guests play the finger game "ken." 1808. Wellcome Library, London.

FIGURE 8.2: A man has sex with a boy prostitute as a woman looks through a window. Kitagawa Utamoro.

FIGURE 8.3: A man has sex with an adult-male transvestite prostitute, 1802. Kitagawa Utamoro.

the rural poor there were frequent liaisons between men and adolescent boys; some boys were rewarded for their passivity, but there were also relationships that were closer to marriage. Public authorities punished sexual relations with prepubescent boys but presumed that boys over fifteen (when puberty began) had consented. These forms of male prostitution persisted in China at least until World War II. Eighteenth-century Hindu India is not easily documented, but there are enough references in the Urdu poetry of that century to suggest that the presence of the prostitution of women, boys, and *hijras* (or adult transvestite males) endured until the end of the twentieth century. Shakuntali Davi in 1976 noted that, "in India boy-brothels are very common in the bigger cities. The Bhindi Bazar and Foras Road area in Bombay have entire rows of houses." And in her 2005 film, *India's Third Gender,* the photographer Anita Khemka casually noticed that houses of prostitution could have either women, boys, or *hijras*—all this in a society in which (as estimated by Shivananda Khan) 60 percent of males have sex with other males, who are usually boys.[3]

Before 1700 in both northern and southern Europe, male prostitutes who were either boys or transvestite adults could be found. The best records are those for Italy, Spain, and Portugal. In fifteenth-century Florence, where at least two-thirds of all adult males were charged with sodomy, and where sex with boys must therefore have been the norm, prostitution shows up as part of the range of possible male sexual relations. Men typically gave the boys they courted or sodomized gifts of money or clothes, so it can be hard to say who was a prostitute and who was not. But *bardassa* was a word used to describe a young male prostitute, proving that the category was known to people at the time. Four boys worked as a prostitution ring and had 120 male clients among them. Some adult males were pimps for boys, and even a father could play this role. No adult transvestite prostitutes have turned up in the Florentine records, but in Venice in 1354 a man called Rolandina worked as a female prostitute around the Rialto. In Venice in 1585, Captain Annibale's landlady complained that he first installed over his bed a painting of a naked woman in an obscene pose, and then brought home female prostitutes and boys, providing us an excellent example of the typical taste of an adult man. Rome, with its overwhelmingly male population, has yet to be studied systematically, but the contrast at the end of the sixteenth century between St. Philip Neri and his friends struggling to be chaste, and Michelangelo Caravaggio pursuing boys and female prostitutes, makes the point.[4]

The records of the Spanish Inquisition from the sixteenth to the eighteenth centuries document the prostitution of young males. Some boys were paid occasionally for sex, but some made prostitution their means of living. In Valencia in 1629, Francisco de Lindo said that he had "nothing left to sell or pawn but my arse." And when, in 1712, a fourteen-year-old surgeon's apprentice agreed to let a man "stick it up his arse" for one *real*, he knew where in the town they could go to do it safely. Some boys followed the troops, renting themselves to the soldiers as the female prostitutes did.[5] The Portuguese Inquisition records give evidence of boy prostitutes and the occasional adult transvestite.[6] After 1700, England was no longer part of this world of bisexual male prostitution, but before 1700 there are cases in the arrest records of transvestite adult male prostitutes like John Rykener in 1394, who called himself Eleanor, and Robert Chetwyn in 1556. The poems and plays of Ben Johnson, John Marston, Thomas Middleton, and Thomas Randolph offer evidence of boy prostitutes in the street, some of them dressed as women; and there was the claim that, in 1649, there were male brothels at the Mulberry Gardens.[7]

In the first generation after 1700, the modern pattern of male prostitution came into existence in London (and probably also in Paris and Amsterdam) as a result of the reorganization of men into a homosexual minority and a heterosexual majority. This pattern differed profoundly from the traditional one described earlier for Asia and the Christian and Muslim Mediterranean, where it continued to exist after 1700. In the modern pattern, most male prostitutes were not themselves sodomites or homosexuals in the sense that, while for pay they could have sexual relations with sodomites, they considered themselves to actually be interested only in women. Among men who were sodomites, sexual desire came in two forms: some desired adult men, and some wanted adolescent boys. Male prostitutes accordingly fell into those two classes. The adolescent boys sometimes made their way into the secret world of the molly houses and could be pressured into providing evidence against their clients. The adult prostitute was usually a soldier who was often approached as he stood as a sentry in the parks. Soldiers therefore were knowledgeable about the cruising patterns of sodomites and often used this knowledge to intimidate and to blackmail sodomites.

There was a third kind of male prostitute who probably did not cater to sodomites. He was an adult transvestite, who often could not be distinguished from the biological women with whom he sometimes worked. His clients were probably men who were seeking women. It is possible that the clients of these transvestite male prostitutes were divided into those who knew their partner was a biological male and those who did not—as was the case in twentieth-century Latin American society. The London transvestite prostitutes, like the boys and the soldiers, sometimes blackmailed their clients. These transvestite male prostitutes differed entirely from the ones who had mixed with the boy prostitutes before 1700. They were now seen as the most extreme example of what was supposed to be true of all the men in the new homosexual minority, who desired sex only with other males. All of these sodomites were deemed to be effeminate and to have made themselves into prostitutes. The name for these men in the street language of London was "molly": *sodomite* was the polite term. *Molly* had started out as a term for a female prostitute. Over the course of the next three centuries, most of the Anglophone street words for a homosexual man—queen, punk, gay, faggot, fairy, fruit—began as terms for a female prostitute before being used for a sodomite or homosexual man.[8]

Female prostitution in northern Europe, it would at first seem, did not undergo so radical a change after 1700 as male prostitution did. It is true that, after 1700, a woman's male clients would no longer be likely to be interested in adolescent boys as well. But it was also the case that after the division into a heterosexual majority and a homosexual minority first appeared in northwestern Europe (in England, France, and the Dutch Republic), and then over the next two centuries became dominant throughout Western culture in Europe and North and South America, that a substantial part of men from the heterosexual majority continued to have occasional sex with sodomites or homosexuals. This was so in London and New York through the first half of the twentieth century and continued into the 1990s in Latin America: in Brazil, Peru, Costa Rica, and Mexico. It has been estimated that 30 percent of heterosexual Mexican men engaged in this crossover behavior during the 1970s. No doubt because of this, and for other reasons as well, sex with a female prostitute became central to the establishment of a male heterosexual identity in Western societies after 1700.[9]

In late medieval Europe, female prostitution had been licensed and tolerated by most city governments, partly on the prudent assumption that this would wean men from sodomy with boys, who were always more available than women. But over the course of the sixteenth and seventeenth centuries, many jurisdictions closed down their brothels of women. This was in part from a concern that it was through the prostitute population that syphilis spread more widely in the general population. But this opposition seems to have arisen much more from a new sexual restraint inspired by the Reformation and the Counter-Reformation. Over the course of the eighteenth century, while there were always complaints about the public visibility of street prostitution, in the end, a new level of toleration was put into practice. By the end of the century in France, a new system of registration and inspection of female prostitutes came into existence, and throughout the nineteenth century, this was the predominant European practice, though it was never accepted in England. Reformers in eighteenth-century England, like the experienced magistrate Saunders Welch, wished to keep "vice hiding its head and skulking in corners," rather than "exposing its face at noon-day," because the consequence of a total suppression of whoring "might be the increase of a horrid vice too rife already, though the bare thought of it strikes the mind with horror." This is similar to the late medieval justification of regulated prostitution and yet profoundly different. During the Middle Ages, all men were presumed to feel attraction to both boys and women, and to be always the sexually active partner and penetrator. By the beginning of the eighteenth century, sodomites were a minority, all of whom were supposed to be passive and desirous of being penetrated. Their ways had, over the generation before 1758, when Welch wrote, been brought to public attention by a series of raids, trials, and executions. The majority of men had to be kept uncontaminated by contact with this passive minority. A man like Welch may well have known that a substantial minority of heterosexual men had occasional sex with sodomites. Female prostitution was the guarantee that the number of such men would not grow. But female prostitution had to be kept discreet and out of public view.[10]

In London and in French cities like Paris, Marseilles, and Montpellier, and in Dutch cities like Amsterdam, Leiden, and the Hague, female prostitution came to be tolerated as a means of ensuring the exclusive heterosexuality of men.[11] The account that follows is based largely on London, but for the statistics for the ages and original occupations of prostitutes, it draws on material from the Continent, where they were systematically noted. Historians of prostitution usually concentrate on the lives of the women, who were never more than a very small proportion of all women. For the sake of argument here, it is appropriate to start with the men who went to prostitutes and who were probably the majority of those who lived in cities of any size.

It is sometimes presumed that prostitution was an instance of the class exploitation of poor females by well-off gentlemen, but most acts of prostitution were between men and women drawn from the same poor urban groups. Prostitutes could be found easily enough either walking the streets or in the bawdy houses. There were probably never more than 3,000 of them at any one time, composed of a core who made their living exclusively in this way for three or more years, with a smaller group of younger women who occasionally picked up a man. It is likely that most men who lived in London at some point went to a prostitute. This is suggested by the high rates of venereal infection, especially among groups like sailors, of whom from 20 to 60 percent had to be treated by their ships' surgeons. Streetwalking, especially at night after oil-burning street lamps were introduced in the 1690s, became extremely common. London's principal route traced a path from the Royal Exchange in Cornhill to Cheapside, around St Paul's Churchyard, down Ludgate Hill, into Fleet Street, and the Strand; from there, it went through Charing Cross, down Whitehall, and into St James's Park. This route became the principal thoroughfare for London's prostitutes, who walked it day and night, soliciting passing men to accompany them into one of the nearby bawdy houses for a drink, or to go with them to their lodgings, or simply to make do with a dark place in the street, a courtyard, or the park.

The identities of many of the impoverished men who went to prostitutes in the 1720s can be established from the arrests of at least 600 who were found with a prostitute, usually in a bawdy house but sometimes in the street. This was far fewer than the number of women arrested; in a single year as many of them were seized by the constables, at least half of them for walking in the streets. These arrests were inspired by the voluntary Societies for the Reformation of Manners, which were most active from the 1690s to the 1730s. The societies concentrated on three forms of deviant behavior: first on cursing, swearing, and drunkenness; then on breaking the Sabbath; and finally on sexual immorality, especially of those like prostitutes and sodomites, whose behavior could be openly observed in the streets and in public taverns. The societies were obliged to use the justices of the peace to enforce their program, since the London church courts had stopped punishing sexual immorality and confined themselves to questions of marriage and defamation. The arrests of these 600 men were the final instances in London of the Protestant reforming mind that had closed down the public brothels across Europe in the sixteenth and seventeenth centuries. This Protestant zeal was soon to be replaced by a more secularized toleration of public prostitution as a necessary bulwark against the new minority of adult effeminate sodomites.

The growth in public consciousness of the new effeminate sodomy, which changed the policing of female prostitution, can be conveniently tracked through the use of the word *effeminate* in the London newspapers. Between 1680 and 1720, it was used to mean weak and to refer to collectives, so that one could write of an effeminate nobility or an effeminate nation, attributing effeminacy to the Persians or the Venetians. But between 1720 and 1750, in 20 percent of the cases, a new usage appeared, in which the word characterized some aspect of an individual Englishman. Thus, the term turned up especially in the advertisements that attempted to find a robber or a soldier who had run away from his regiment. Individuals were described as having an effeminate face, countenance, or looks, and, most often as having an effeminate voice or speech. In 1737, the word *effeminate* was for the first time clearly associated with sodomites, in this case used to describe the women's names taken by a band of sodomitical robbers who had come down to Bristol from London. An effeminate voice in a man became a burden, and by 1749, Samuel Angier, an expert in speech impediments, advertised that he could relieve "men speaking in an effeminate, and women in a masculine tone." The traditional usage continued to come strongly to the fore during moments of national crisis like the American or French Revolutions. But the new meaning of effeminacy as a characteristic of male sodomites was clearly demonstrated in the 1750s by the *Public Advertiser*'s notice (March 4, 1756) that "on Tuesday night last information being brought to John Fielding and Saunders Welch Esqrs, that an assembly of men of the effeminate kind, were to have a dance at a public house, a warrant was immediately granted ... and [the constable's officers] apprehended about fourteen persons of the above stamp." Such behavior Saunders Welch wished two years later to deter by a regulated, discreet prostitution.[12]

The societies were in decline in the 1730s and 1740s, but they revived in the 1750s and 1760s. In the societies of the second generation of the eighteenth century, after the new role of the effeminate adult sodomite had become established in the public mind, their policy and that of the magistrates in regard to female prostitution changed significantly. The societies still went after Sabbath-breakers, profane cursers, sellers of obscene prints, keepers of bawdy houses, common prostitutes, and sodomites, claiming that, in the years between 1757 and 1765, they had had ten thousand brought to justice. But they no longer stormed bawdy houses in search of men with prostitutes. Thirty-six men in the

City of London were arrested for being with a prostitute between 1784 and 1790, but only two of them had been in a bawdy house; the other thirty-four had been found having sex in the street or in Moorfields, a park, and they were in any case simply discharged. Public authority had come to accept the point of view of a magistrate like Saunders Welch that prostitution needed to be discreetly tolerated, since otherwise the effeminate sodomy of adult men might be encouraged. It still made sense to regulate the numbers and locations of bawdy houses and to limit the numbers of women in the streets—but men were no longer being punished for having sex with women in enclosed, relatively private spaces.

The arrests of these 600 men in the 1720s, when the new system of a heterosexual majority and a homosexual minority had begun to take root, provide us with the only systematic descriptions of prostitutes' clients. Two-thirds of the men arrested were identified by occupation. Seven percent were gentlemen, which was about equal to the number of leisured men in society, but it is likely that this underrepresents their participation in prostitution, since they would have had more money than poor men to spend on women. In the same decade, in a fashionable parish where many military officers lived, gentlemen made up 17 percent of the men who had fathered bastard children. Constables were probably less likely to raid bawdy houses frequented by gentlemen. It was not unusual for men of all social statuses to resist arrest, but gentlemen were likely to be armed and to be able to draw their swords, as one unknown gentleman did when he defended a house that stood in the principal entrance to the royal gardens.[13]

Of the 600 men arrested for consorting with prostitutes, those who were not gentlemen came from a range of ninety different occupations. Among these, tailors were the most heavily represented. Tailors worked together in shops that were all-male environments, and this seems to have produced a libertine culture well into the nineteenth century. They made fashionable clothes for themselves, patronized and flirted with milliners in the Royal Exchange, from among whom across Europe came the highest number of prostitutes, and crowded into the pits of the theaters when a girl was to sing a new bawdy song. Francis Place was apprenticed to a breeches maker, all of whose children were disreputable: the boys were thieves; the girls were whores. Place belonged to a gang of fifteen apprentices who spent their money on the prostitutes walking Fleet Street. The boys went to the cheaper low bawdy houses, where women without stays or handkerchiefs exposed breasts that sometimes hung down "in a most disgusting manner."[14] In contrast, weavers were much less likely to go to a bawdy house. They usually worked at home, assisted by their families, and this produced a different sexual ethos. Weavers, on the other hand, sometimes seduced, and then left pregnant and unmarried, the poor, illiterate Irish girls they employed as maids of all work, whereas tailors did not show up as a significant body of seducers. Prostitution and family life were usually in conflict. Men became venereally infected and brought the disease home to their wives and children. They spent on prostitutes the wages that should have supported their families. In one case, a bricklayer's laborer and a prostitute fought over her price: he offered her sixpence, but she would not take less than a shilling. They charged each other and were taken to the watchhouse, where the man's wife arrived and attacked him saying, "You dog, you brought me but twopence farthing last week." He had intended to spend five times as much on the prostitute. On the other hand, there were ragged whores who would take any customer behind a wall for twopence.[15]

Sailors, soldiers, and apprentices were the other large, identifiable body of prostitutes' clients among the 600 apprehended men. Sailors were especially hard to police since they were loyal to each other, and to their women. Wapping and Shadwell at the East End of London were full of bawdy houses for sailors, the English as well as the Portuguese, Greek, Spanish, and East Indians or lascars. These houses were more likely to be run by men, whereas women ran those in the West End. Sailors were quick to riot—especially in a year such as 1763, when the city was full of men released at the end of a war. Sailors who ventured into the West End and felt they had been cheated also rioted and demolished the bawdy houses. In the early seventeenth century, it had been apprentices, not sailors, who had pulled down bawdy houses. By the eighteenth century, apprentices apparently had a different relationship with prostitutes. The increase in streetwalking had made it easier for them to pick up a woman, and, after the 1730s, masters ceased to complain to the magistrates that their apprentices had been seduced by a whore or a bawdy-house keeper. From the early eighteenth century on, adolescents were warned of the physical and mental deterioration that masturbation would bring on, and from the court cases it is apparent that they frequently discussed mollies or effeminate sodomites among themselves and were very likely to resist attempts by such men to draw them into an ongoing relationship. Among sodomy, masturbation, and prostitution, boys and their employers seem to have agreed that prostitutes were the safest option. Even religious youths found it difficult to avoid these women, and a young man like Dudley Ryder tested his self-confidence by the degree to which he could successfully "attack a whore" in the street and talk to her.[16]

Soldiers, according to a common saying of the rakes themselves, treated their whores much worse than sailors did. The prostitution of the West End was given much of its low tone because most of the soldiers in London lived there in barracks or in their own lodgings, or quartered in public houses. Officers and their servants seduced young women, like the mantua-maker or dressmaker Elinor Snowden, turning them into prostitutes. Snowden, after serving an apprenticeship of four years, became pregnant first by Thomas Hayes and then by Colonel Bing of the Footguards, who had her twice in the guardroom of St James's Palace. The most notorious military rake of the century, Colonel Francis Charteris, who had to be pardoned by the king twice for rape, held the opinion that, wherever he "caught a fine sempstress or mantua-maker in the public streets after nine at night, whether banboxed or bundled, it might still be lawful to charge her in custody of the first hackney coach, and convey her to the next bagnio" (a bathhouse brothel).

The arrest records of these 600 men show that they were relatively conventional in their sexual tastes. Only twenty-seven of them were found "lying in state" that is, with two women; and there were only four cases of two men with one woman, though in one of these it involved a father and a son together with a

FIGURE 8.4: William Hogarth, *A Rakes Progress*, Plate III, 1735. Wellcome Library, London.

woman. One man had attempted "unheard of lewdness" with a woman, which probably meant anal intercourse. More unambiguous cases of anal intercourse turn up in the court cases in other years; in one case a cabinetmaker offered a woman nine shillings a week to let him sodomize her. Yet, no one was charged with fellatio; it was probably very rare; although one man tried unsuccessfully to avoid venereal disease by engaging in it. Another man in the 1720s was whipped: the rods were there for evidence; from the court cases it is apparent that flagellation occurred much more frequently than anal intercourse. "Showing lewd postures" was probably the most frequent unusual act, in which one or more naked women simulated various positions in sexual intercourse for one or more men to look at. In Hogarth's representation of a male libertine in a house of women (*A Rake's Progress*), one of the women is putting her clothes back on after having shown lewd postures (fig. 8.4). In the dark of a bawdy-house, a man might take a candle to inspect a woman's private parts. Sometimes the stripping and the flagellation went together, with either the men or the women being whipped. But stripping for sex was unusual: John Cleland in his novel *Fanny Hill* (1748–1749) claimed that only a young, debauched Italian man would do so. In most instances, the sexual act occurred indoors between one man and one woman; they were both at least partly clothed: throwing up a woman's skirts gave a man full access since women did not wear underpants; and the act performed was vaginal penetration, with the man probably on top.

Female prostitution was central to the development of male aristocratic libertinism. In its justification of the use of public women in the years between 1660 and 1710, libertinism had already passed through two stages of development and bequeathed a mixed legacy to the first generation of the new sexual system. The abandonment of some of these developments due to fears of effeminate sodomy, and the influence of sentimentalism and the appearance by 1750 of the ideal of the domestic family, produced a more unified libertine position, which held the field until it was modified by the growth of Evangelical religion and the reaction to the French Revolution. The first of the earlier stages can be found in the ideals of the Earl of Rochester: sexual pleasure that hurt no one else or one's own health was legitimate, and men liked both boys and whores. But Rochester was obscene, and the libertinism of men like William Congreve and Charles St. Evremonde that followed was more restrained and more stoical, taking Petronius as its model. The collection of Petronius's fragments only became fully available to the European world in the 1690s, and they (along with François Nodot's forged expansions) were first translated into English in 1694, 1708, and 1736. In 1708, it could be said of Petronius that "he, of all the ancients, seems only to have known, and to have had a taste of that true gallantry, which at this time finishes the character of politeness"; he wrote without "those gross words" other Latin authors used. The largely homosexual adventures of Encolpius, Ascyltus, and Giton were described simply as "the portraicture of the disorderly life of young people."

This kind of libertine relation to both female prostitutes and to boys became impossible by the 1740s, after nearly two generations of the existence of the new effeminate sodomite. Petronius was now discredited by his sodomy. Tobias Smollett had his hero in *Roderick Random* (1748) declare to Earl Strutwell, who tested Random's sexual taste by referring to Petronius, that Petronius was "so lewd and indecent, that he ought to find no quarter or protection among people of morals and taste." Aristocratic libertinism continued, however, to find in the ancient world a model of sexual relations freed from Christian asceticism. The monks who met at Medmenham's Abbey in the 1750s and sacrificed to Bacchus, Venus, and the Bona Dea, and took their sexual pleasures in the gardens, were said by John Wilkes to have "seemed at least to have sinned naturally," and to have brought in female prostitutes for their enjoyment. The libertines in 1786 still professed to be liberated by Richard Payne Knight's *Discourse on the Worship of Priapus,* in which he argued that sexual intercourse had been a common form of worship in the ancient world, and that Christianity had attacked the worship of Priapus more furiously than any other part of ancient polytheism. The libertines, however, preferred not to think of the consequences of their way of life for the young girls who filled the Lock Hospital for venereal disease. The Hospital's chaplain, the Rev. Martin Madan, who was himself a former libertine, was frustrated by the return of these girls to their old lives as prostitutes. He claimed that the sexual asceticism of the Church Fathers was not based on the Bible. His solution was to reinstate the polygamy of the Old Testament and compel each man to marry each girl he seduced. The well-meaning chaplain unintentionally delighted the libertines and appalled his Evangelical friends.

Aristocratic libertinism and its relation to female prostitution was effectively limited by the growth of the new ideals of romantic marriage and domesticity that made their way across northwestern Europe after 1750. In England, France, and the Dutch Republic, these values took root first among the aristocracy, and then in the middle classes by the century's end. In 1760, fifteen-year-old Lady Sarah Lennox was told that the duke of Marlborough was "so entirely given up to women that it's quite dreadful." The duke's father had also gone to women "after he was married, though he loved his wife." But Lady Sarah thought "that sort of love would not content me, for I have no notion of a man's loving his wife and following all those sort of people." This

FIGURE 8.5: A repentant young woman prays on her knees in front of a table on which is placed the *Book of Common Prayer*, about 1758. From *Thoughts on the Plan for a Magdalen-House for Repentant Prostitutes*. [Anon]. Wellcome Library, London.

kind of domesticity was hard for many men to accept. They compromised and domesticated the brothel: the women were examined by a surgeon for disease, they were not allowed to become drunk or talk bawdy, and the men came for supper and a night of pleasure. It was the regime of some Parisian houses, which Mrs. Goadby had emulated in London. The new ideals did make it possible for Protestant England to set up houses for redeeming prostitutes (fig. 8.5) and returning them to ordinary life on the model of the houses that had long existed in Roman Catholic countries. The Magdalen Hospital opened in 1758 and the Lock Asylum in 1789. The latter was an offshoot of the Lock Hospital, which had been founded in 1746 to cure the London poor of the venereal diseases they had contracted by resorting to prostitutes.

Finally, we come to the prostitutes themselves. Who were these women who walked the streets? Had they been born in the cities where they worked, or were they immigrants? How old were they? Did they go back and forth between prostitution and ordinary life? What kind of ordinary work did they do? How long were they prostitutes—and did they leave the life because they married, or did they die from the effects of a hard life? How did their families and their neighbors treat them? How had they first begun to sleep with men for money? How did the men treat them? What were they willing—and not willing—to do in sex? Did they lose religion? Were they conventional at heart? Our sources for London and for the French and Dutch cities offer answers to all these questions, but none of them are definitive.

The ages of English prostitutes cannot be established with any certainty. The information we do have is based on the women confined in houses of correction, but the magistrates regularly dismissed half of the women arrested, and these were probably the younger ones. French and the Dutch records leave no doubt that at least three-fourths of the prostitutes were between fifteen and twenty-four. In the eighteenth century, menarche (first menstruation) began no earlier than the age of fifteen (the age has steadily fallen over the course of the twentieth century). Physical development for boys was similar, with their voices changing at seventeen, as opposed to thirteen in the twentieth century. Prostitutes therefore were mainly adolescents. But they had begun to work as other working-class adolescents then did. In the English anecdotal material they were either servants or made clothes as milliners or mantua makers, but it is not possible to say what the relative percentages were between these two most frequent occupations of young single women. In France, the nature of work seems to have depended on the size of the town. At Montpellier, 40 percent of young working women were servants; at Marseilles, the numbers fell to 25 percent; and, at Paris in the late eighteenth century, it was 12 percent, and then 6 percent during the Revolution. Slightly more than half of the prostitutes in both Paris and Marseilles worked in the various sections of the garment industry.

During the Revolution, a great change seems to have occurred in Paris, as prostitution became a long-term occupation. Between 1789 and 1794, 24 percent of prostitutes gave their occupation as prostitute rather than saying that they were servant or milliner. These women were not going back and forth between conventional work and prostitution, and it is likely that this phenomenon marked the appearance of women who would consider prostitution their occupation in the nineteenth century. The average age of prostitutes in Paris fell over the course of the second half of the century, and this may also attest to the emergence of a group of full-time prostitutes. In London, families sometimes went to the magistrate to reclaim a daughter or a sister who had been seduced or coerced into prostitution, but families almost never appeared in court after 1750. This may mean that the mass of London's prostitutes were undergoing a change in status similar to the women in Paris and becoming full-time prostitutes. On the other hand, in the early eighteenth century in London there had always been some women who were categorized as old offenders because they had been arrested repeatedly and were known to the constables and the magistrates: it is occasionally possible to trace such women over as long a period as a decade.

Prostitutes in England, France, and the Dutch Republic were sometimes natives of their city, sometimes immigrants. English anecdotal material, such as Hogarth's *Harlot's Progress*, liked to present them as seduced by bawds as they got off the wagons that had brought them to town looking for work (fig. 8.6). But some girls had clearly been born in London. It has been estimated that at least one in every six persons in England had lived for some time in London, and there are stories of girls from the countryside who returned home after a London experience involving seduction, prostitution, and sometimes even the birth of a child. In Paris, the proportion of immigrants among prostitutes was high (70 percent), similar to the total number of immigrants in the city, but much lower in Marseilles (30 percent). The question of whether

FIGURE 8.6: William Hogarth, *Harlots Progress*, Plate I, 1732. Wellcome Library, London.

women had been seduced into prostitution is hard to resolve, and some historians of French prostitution would insist that the women had entered the life by their own choice.

In London, female prostitutes tended to rob their customers, while male prostitutes blackmailed their clientele. Prostitutes were rowdy in their speech and actions, usually because they were drunk. The prostitute played many different roles with men. She was seductress and boon companion, trickster and thief; she was dominated and abused, spat at, and anally penetrated. Actual physical violence against her was considered acceptable by men. Her private parts were a delight to a man's eye—a great unknown through which he moved with a candle in the darkness of the bawdy house—but he was also contemptuous of her for making her private parts public. Men needed her as the proof that they were not sodomites. It is very likely, however, that most women moved thorough these dramas without surrendering their conventionality, and some of them continued to have a marked religious identity. Most prostitutes remained poor, and any contracts they may have had with clients did not have any legal weight. Most women disappeared from the world of prostitution

FIGURE 8.7: William Hogarth, *Harlots Progress*, Plate III, 1732. Wellcome Library, London.

in their late twenties. Hogarth again romanticized prostitutes' lives by having them die (fig. 8.7), but this was not the usual end to their careers. It is unlikely, though, that many of them ever married. Francis Place claimed he could tell when a woman had been a prostitute, and he and his friends did not marry such women. It is therefore likely that reintegration into the ordinary world was never complete for women who had walked the streets as prostitutes for any extended period of time.

CHAPTER NINE

Erotica: Representing Sex in the Eighteenth Century

KATHERINE CRAWFORD

The School of Venus (1680), an English translation of the erotic French dialogue *L'Éscole des Filles* (1655), features Frances encouraging her younger cousin, Katherine, to have sex with Roger. Throughout, Frances extols the pleasures of coitus and downplays the dangers (pregnancy, damaged reputation, venereal disease) in a pedagogy of sex. Frances bases most of her "lessons" on experience:

> He considered me all over with admiration, sometimes he commended my Belly, sometimes my Thighs and Breasts, then the Nobs of my Cunt, which he found plum and standing out, which he often stroaked, then he considered my shoulders and Buttocks, then making me lean with my hands upon the Bed, he got astride upon me, and made me carry him; at last, he got off me, and thrust his Prick into my Cunt, sliding it down my Buttocks. I had no mind to let him Fuck me at first, but he made such moan to me, that I had no heart to deny him, he said he took a great deal of pleasure in rubbing the Inside of my Cunt, which he did, often thrusting his Prick up to the Head, then suddenly plucking it out again, the noise of which, it being like to that which Bakers make when they Kneed their Dow, pleased me extreamly.[1]

The School of Venus is an Enlightenment text in many ways. Enlightenment philosophers advocated education based on experience in order to develop reason and the critical faculties. Similarly, Frances educated Katherine by explaining her sexual encounters so that Katherine could make rational choices in her relationship with Roger. Frances scoffs at convention and morality as impediments to pleasure, reflecting Enlightenment ideas about religion and nature. Enlightenment thinkers were often suspicious of organized religion, arguing that nature, rather than God, determined the construction of the universe. *The School of Venus* makes scant reference to Christian morals, preferring an ethics of pleasure, in which the mark of good sex is the pleasure it brings. The text also raises questions about gender. Frances is a pedagogue, but is this really what one wants young girls to learn? Ambivalence about women and whether they were capable of participating in the Enlightenment were recurrent issues that expanded into debates about "others," as categorized by race, ethnicity, and class. Erotica such as *The School of Venus* reflected the conflicting impulses of the Enlightenment. It imagined readers as rational and teachable, as following nature, and as eschewing superstition, while articulating fear about the reader's capacity for reason, about the implications of pleasure, and about who could become Enlightened.

The argument of this chapter is that, in negotiating these different logics of the Enlightenment, eighteenth-century producers and consumers of erotica transformed the market for, volume of, and nature of erotica. The range of material is tremendous, and this chapter will only sample themes and problems addressed by the Enlightenment. These include the transformation of the rational premises of science into erotica, the emergence of pornographic possibilities embedded in materialist philosophy, the development of an eroticized critique of organized religion, the celebration of the "natural" as an element of sexual pleasure, the use of the erotic as political commentary, and the exploration of "humanity" in sexual terms. The point of view is European, but the relationship of European ideas to the erotica of other cultures is crucial to this story. Encounters with erotic traditions around the globe were enmeshed with racial assumptions, contributed to racial hierarchy, and were integral to the sexual dynamics of colonial occupation. To address these issues, we begin in Europe and then move briefly to several distinct non-Western cultures.

While erotica was not new in the eighteenth century, the Enlightenment as a philosophical movement changed its relation to culture. To understand how this came about, some terminology must first be made clear. Historians have divided sexual writing into obscenity, bawdy, pornography, and erotica. The categories overlap, but, in Roger Thompson's view, each has distinct valences.[2] Obscenity aims to disgust or shock the consumer. Bawdy works are humorous, often using the same sorts of sexual or scatological imagery as obscenity. Pornography has been defined as "the explicit depiction of sexual organs and sexual practices with the aim of arousing sexual feelings."[3] Erotica refers to materials that envision sex with a component of love or affection. Borrowing from Karen Harvey, this last definition will be both expanded and narrowed. Harvey argues that erotica is "material about sexual pleasure which depicted sex, bodies, and desire through illusions of concealment and distance: bodies were represented through metaphor and suggestion, and depictions of sexual activity were characterized by deferral and silence."[4] Harvey's notion of erotica is too restrictive, but her point that erotica works at angles—often operating through allusion and metaphor to create its effects—is helpful. Authorial intent is often less significant than how a piece was constructed. To that end, erotica here signifies written or visual materials featuring sexual activity in any of a range of modes—from the most literal (pornography), to the most allusive or figural (erotica). The lines are not always clear, but that is part of the changing face of eighteenth-century erotica.

Much of the change was in response to the Enlightenment premise that men (meaning men, and not usually men and women) could use reason and rationality to understand nature and the place of humanity. Science and medicine were central to these ends. Advances in anatomy and botany generated optimism among Enlightenment scientists, who published their findings and presented them at venues such as the Royal Academy. Scientific observers developed a language of sex while analyzing plant and animal biology. Authors of erotica appropriated the language and ideas generated by such discussion, satirizing and sexualizing botany and reproductive processes in particular.[5] Despite their apprehensions about nature, Enlightenment thinkers often regarded it as the fundamental touchstone. Sex was natural, the argument went, and impediments such as superstition and human tradition should be removed to allow sex to proceed naturally.

The progression from science to erotica around botany demonstrates this mode of sexualizing the Enlightenment. In his classification of plants, Carl Linnaeus (1707–1778) offered an orderly, rational scheme for understanding the natural world. In the *Species Plantarum* (1753), he emphasized the difference between plants with visible sex organs (classified as *Phanerogams*) and those with hidden ones (*Cryptogams*). Linnaeus used mild sexual language to describe plant reproduction: "husband" and "wife" shared the "nuptial bed."[6] Satires and erotic puns capitalized on the extant descriptive language. Several poems described the penis through the metaphor of the tree. Rarely bigger than nine or eleven inches, the "Tree of Life" has distinct characteristics: "The Stem seems to be of the *sensitive* Tribe, tho' herein differing from the more common

Sensitives; that whereas they are known to shrink and retire from even the gentlest Touch of a Lady's Hand, this rises on the contrary, and extends itself when it is so handled."[7] Mimicking botanists' descriptions, writers of erotica compared female genitalia to flowers and plants.[8] *The Natural History of the Frutex Vulvaria, or Flowering Shrub* (1732) used the language of plant botany to describe venereal disease.[9] The physician Julien Offray de La Mettrie discussed the female body in terms of generation in *L'homme plante* (*The Man Plant*, 1748).[10] Erotica at once accepted and mocked botany, while rendering sex within the language of science.

Manuals ostensibly in the service of facilitating reproduction formed a second type of scientific erotica. In 1642, Joannes Benedictus Sinibaldus described techniques for men to satisfy lusty women without debilitating themselves. Advice included how to adjust the size of the penis to "fit" the woman and warnings about the cooling effects of an overly long penis.[11] Recognizing the market value of Sinibaldus's text if it could find a larger audience, translators

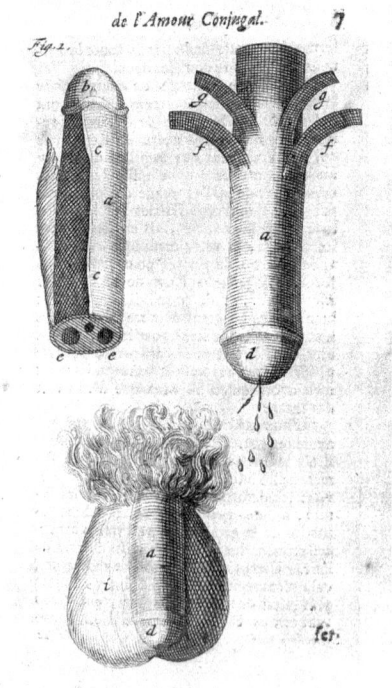

FIGURE 9.1: Nicolas Venette, *De la Génération de l'Homme* (Cologne: C. Joly, 1696). Wellcome Library, London.

produced abridged versions that highlighted the dirty bits. Using the excuse of encouraging procreative marriage, manuals like *Aristotle's Master-Piece* and Nicolas Venette's *De la génération de l'homme, ou Tableau de l'amour conjugal* (Mysteries of Conjugal Love Reveal'd) (fig. 9.1) provided information on foreplay, the mechanics of coitus, and sexual anatomy.[12] Reading of these manuals was widespread: Roger Thompson found references to them in colonial Massachusetts, and as Roy Porter and Lesley Hall have shown, editions of the *Master-Piece* and the *Tableau* appeared regularly throughout the eighteenth century. The basic message about happy, heterosexual reproduction persisted, with modifications, over decades, and in multiple languages.[13] As an Enlightenment education project, sex manuals had remarkable staying power.

Medical manuals offered erotic possibilities as well. Martin Schurig's medical anecdotes on sex included comparing penis length to nose size and describing copulation.[14] Works like Schurig's, in Latin, were aimed at a rarefied

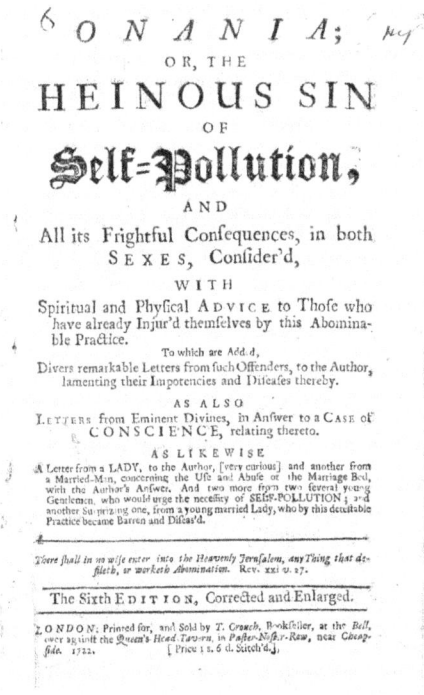

FIGURE 9.2: Title page of *Onania* depicting the effects of masturbation on the health of the individual, from *Onania: or the Heinous Sin of Self-Pollution* (London, 1722). Wellcome Library, London.

audience of educated men, but medical works in the vernacular provided erotica through medical warnings for a much wider reading public.[15] Termed medical soft-core pornography by Thomas Laqueur, John Marten's *Gonosologium Novum* graphically warned: "It is known, or should be known to all Physicians, that the *Venereal* Appetite, or Lust in Women, is nothing more than a tender sense and tickling of the extended *Clitoris*. ... The languishing of the *Venereal* Appetite in women, is frequently occasion'd by the smallness or want of *Genital Liquor.*"[16] Although it sounds tame now, the details about sex organs, impotence, and the mechanics of ejaculation earned Marten an indictment (which failed) at Queen's Bench in 1709. Marten was probably behind *Onania; or The Heinous Sin of Self Pollution* (fig. 9.2), the conceit of which was the revelation of the secret sexual vice of masturbation. Described in lurid detail and supplemented with letters ostensibly from readers describing their own masturbatory practices, the commentary was dressed up in learned garb:

> It is certain, that in some Women, especially those who are very salacious, and have much abused themselves by Self-Pollution, the *Clitoris* is so vastly extended, that, upon its thrusting out of the Passage, it is mistaken for a *Penis;* such have been called *Fricatrices;* by *Gaelius Aurelianus, Tribades:* By *Plautus, Subigatrices,* and accounted *Hermaphrodites,* because, as said before, they have been able to perform the Actions of Men with other Women.[17]

Like Marten, the Swiss physician Samuel-Auguste-David Tissot reported on masturbation, ostensibly in order to deter it, in such a fashion that readers might be inspired to try it for themselves.[18]

Venereal disease was trickier because its effects were likely to be antierotic, but texts often included sexually charged warnings that functioned as erotica. Marten's *Treatise of All the Degrees and Symptoms of Venereal Disease* (1704) contended that, "There is yet another way of getting the Infection ... the way I mean is by only a superficial contact or meer touch with the *Privities,* the Man no more than placing the erected *Yard* to the Womans *Labia,* without the least entrance into her Body."[19] Marten went on to blame (and describe) sodomy, oral sex, and French kissing for causing venereal disease. Jean Astruc did the same in his *De morbis venereis* (Treatise of the Venereal Disease, 1736). Information about how venereal disease might be contracted hinted at the larger erotic world: "likewise the *Venereal Disease* be by different ways communicated. ... By coition, either when a sound Woman converses with an infected Man, who has chancres in the glans, or a virulent Gonorrhoea ... or the corrupted seed, which is emitted in copulation, will adhere to the *pudendum,* the *vagina,* and the womb."[20] Authors intersposed medical information with coy references to sex and sexualized bodies. Medicine and science provided rational readings of the body and sexual imaginings of its doings.

Guides ostensibly for women but actually *about* them provided salacious descriptions under the guise of medical or anatomical information. John Maubray's *The Female Physician* (1724) purported to explain women to themselves, but the tour-book quality of the material was aimed at prurient readers. Section II included chapters such as "Of the Symptoms Peculiar to the State [of] Maidenhood," "Of Virginity," "Of Copulation," and "Remarks upon Copulation" (fig. 9.3).[21] Writers of erotica sometimes offered advice about midwifery. Claude Quillet's *Callipédie ou l'art d'avoir de beaux enfants* (1655) interspersed practical advice with suggestive descriptions of techniques. Under the guise of warning against unscrupulous practitioners who used access to women for nefarious purposes, *The Man-Midwife Unmasqu'd* (1738) recounted a story of seduction and debauchery that could be sung to the popular tune, "Lumps of Pudding."[22] Reproductive erotica presented heterosexual desire as natural because of its reproductive teleology, but sex manual erotica nonetheless offered to teach people how to improve their techniques.[23]

FIGURE 9.3: A physician examining a bare-breasted female patient. Mezzotint by Abraham De Blois after Jan Steen, n.d. Wellcome Library, London.

More broadly, Enlightenment assumptions about the status of nature provided the basis for an erotics of pleasure as the "natural" purpose of sex. Roy Porter noted that pleasure came to the fore in the eighteenth century.[24] Whereas the mind or soul had been considered more important than the body in earlier periods, Enlightenment attention to the physicality of embodiment redressed that imbalance somewhat (fig. 9.4). The development of sensationalist philosophy, in which sensory experience was considered foundational to knowledge, revalued bodily functions as natural and good.[25] One index of the imbrication of notions of the natural with pleasure in erotica was the recurrence of explorations of the female body. Some of these were metaphorical. Charles Cotton's *Erotopolis. The Present State of Betty-Land* (1684) and Thomas Stretzer's *A New Description of Merryland* (1741) were faux travelogues that described the female body and its genitalia as "foreign" lands. Stretzer discussed the MNSVNRS (Mons Veneris, or "little Mountain") at length, and is slightly more subtle in his coding of the anus, referring to it as PDX (short for the Latin *podex*). The male body came in for scrutiny in the *Libro del Perché* (The Book of Wherefore). Published at least six times in the eighteenth century, the *Libro del Perché* included an extended complaint by women to

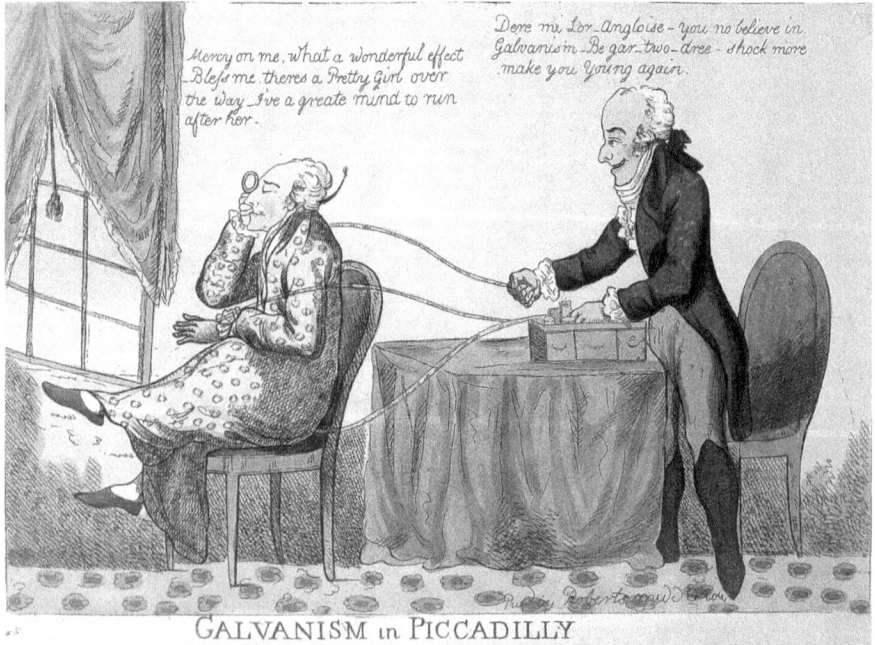

FIGURE 9.4: An affluent man, staring intently out a window, receives electrotherapy from a French pseudo-doctor. Colored etching. London: Roberts, n.d. Wellcome Library, ICV No. 11356.

Jupiter that the human penis was small in comparison to that of many animals. Other works were literal, if fictional. John Cleland's *Fanny Hill, or The Memoirs of a Woman of Pleasure* (1749) follows the innocent heroine as she discovers pleasures of all sorts—lesbianism, heterosexual intercourse, flagellation, male homosexual sodomy, and true love. Only the sodomy is looked on unfavorably. Pleasure is the yardstick in Fanny's encounters, and her transformation from naive girl to woman of pleasure is presented as the natural course of her experience.

But pleasure could be problematic (fig. 9.5). The Marquis de Sade's insistence on the priority of pleasure led him to discount any other possibility. In *Philosophy of the Bedroom* (1795), De Sade's stand-in, Dolmancé, lectures the ingénue Eugénie. Sexual pleasure is natural, Dolmancé says, and rational: "Start from one fundamental point, Eugénie: in libertinage, nothing is frightful, because everything libertinage suggests is also a natural inspiration; the most extraordinary, the most bizarre acts, those which most arrantly seem to conflict with every law, every human institution (as for Heaven, I have nothing to say), well, Eugénie,

FIGURE 9.5: Frontispiece to the Marquis de Sade's *Justine ou les Malheurs de la Vertu* (Holland: Libraries Associes, 1791), Wellcome Library, London.

even those are not frightful, and there is not one amongst them all that cannot be demonstrated within the boundaries of Nature."[26] Dolmancé defends sodomy as natural because nature never intended all sexual acts to be procreative. Physical pleasure is evidence of the natural purpose of sex. The lengthy group-sex encounters (which feature such an array of positions that even de Sade gets bored describing them) are meant to illustrate the primacy of pleasure. Shocking though his arguments were (and are), Sade was in tune with Enlightenment ideas about how the world ought to be organized. Nature was the guide, and man ought to use his powers of reason to conform his behavior to nature.

De Sade's adherence to Enlightenment values—and his concurrent extremity in relation to them—was the result of his taking philosophical materialism to its logical end, relative to erotic representation. Some Enlightenment philosophers had developed a mechanized understanding of matter in which everything—including the human body—was made of matter in motion. Erotica utilizing materialist presumptions figured prominently in libertine presentations of sex, in which matter was responsive to "desire." The language of desire produced a libertine ethic valorizing pleasure as natural and, in proper Enlightenment fashion, rejecting anything that impinged on pleasure as unnatural and therefore bad. Family, marriage, and Christian sexual ethics were prominent on the libertine list of structures that intruded on the seeking of sexual pleasure. The treatment of bodies as objects to be arranged and manipulated to provide pleasure figures prominently in materialist erotica. *L'Académie des Dames* (1680; Latin, 1660) used a dialogue to discuss differently sized, shaped, and positioned sex organs. The main characters are cousins who fall in love, signaling that family is secondary to pleasure. The French text is replete with pleasure as the result of mechanical, material facts of sex: "Car à force de remuer les fesses, je dissipais le reste de la douleur, outre que le chemin était déjà battu. Durant ces mouvements, je chatouillais légèrement la peau des testicules, je les pressais tous deux avec les doigts, je les irritai tellement par ce badinage, qu'ils répandirent avec profusion cette divine liqueur dont ils sont dépositaires." [Because of the force of moving the buttocks, I dispelled the rest of the pain, over and above the way that had already been beaten. During these movements, I tickled the skin of the testicles lightly, and pressing both with my fingers, I stimulated them with this stretching until they spilled out with profusion this divine liquor of which they are the depositories.][27] Materialist erotica rejected spiritual claims for sex in favor of purely somatic responses.

Materialist aspects appeared in several different guises in eighteenth-century erotica. Dutch erotica, although heavily dependent on French materialist pornography for texts, tended to invoke materialism to condemn it. As Wijnand W.

Mijhardt notes, the Dutch tradition was limited and mild in its development. The Dutch did produce some erotica, such as *D'openhertige juffrouw* (The Outspoken Mistress, 1679), *Het Amsterdamsch hoerdam* (Amsterdam Whores, 1681), and *De hedendaagshe haagsche en Amsterdamsezalet-juffers* (The Salon-Mistresses of Contemporary Amsterdam and the Hague, 1696). But libertine ideas made only rare appearances, and works such as *De Belydanis van een lichtmis* (Confessions of a Rake, 1770) avoided excessive explicit sexuality.[28] In other traditions, the body as object or mechanism is on stark display. This is apparent in *Thérèse Philosophe* (1748): "L'arrangement des organes, les dispositions des fibres, un certain mouvement, des liqueurs, donnent le genre des passions, les dégrés de force dont elles nous agitent contraignent la raison, déterminant la volonté dans les plus petites, comme dans les plus grandes actions de notre vie." [The arrangement of the organs, the disposition of the fibers, a certain movement, the liquids, give birth to the passions, the degrees of force with which they agitate us constrain the reason, determining in the will of the smallest, as in the most grand actions of our life.][29] To Thérèse, the body is utterly mechanical, and sexual positions are governed by the laws of matter in motion. The materialist ethos, as summed up by the Italian cryptolibertine Tommaso Crudeli (1703–1745), is very straightforward: "We obey and follow nature when we approach a woman who charms us."[30]

As Margaret Jacob has commented, "Materialism removed the dominance of the spirit and made matter and spirit essentially one, thus leaving the clergy useless as arbitrators of a separate spiritual realm."[31] Materialism shaped Enlightenment critiques of organized religion that appeared in erotica. While some maintained that religious belief was valuable—Jean-Jacques Rousseau, among others, advocated deism—some rejected all religion as irrational. The physician Julien Offray de la Mettrie (*L'homme machine* [Man a Machine], 1747) argued that all things were matter obedient to the laws of nature. He considered religious belief to be nonsense. Such attitudes provided a fertile environment for anticlerical erotica. A venerable tradition, anticlerical writing increased in volume and vehemence with the development of reading publics over the eighteenth century. By century's end, occasional tales of randy monks and lascivious nuns gave way to full-blown anticlerical pornography.

Local circumstances resulted in the uneven development of anticlerical erotica. The dominance of the Papacy in much of Italy limited the published expression of anticlerical erotica, but some did appear. Niccolò Forteguerri's *Ricciardetto* (1738) featured a priest attempting to seduce a newly married woman. In Luigi Batacchi's *Il Zibaldone* (The Miscellany), the parish priest Barletta contracts venereal disease from his maid. In Holland, occasional anticlerical works appeared (including one that was aimed at the Jesuits), but officials generally suppressed them as dangerous to the political order. Anti-Catholicism as a mode of sexual discourse was unacceptable, because approximately 40 percent of the Dutch population was Catholic. Spain policed erotica more closely. Anticlerical erotica risked running afoul of the Inquisition, and so the pattern of revealing sex by condemning it marked much Spanish erotic writing. Spanish erotica came primarily in the form of bawdy poems and satires, many of which were parodic and featured scatological or sexual humor. Older compilations, replete with anticlerical tidbits (such as the anonymous *Carajicomedia*, 1519), gained new life in the eighteenth century. Erotic content varied widely. Sexually explicit jokes were popular, one featuring the Devil slipping on some lard and falling on a shepherd's erect member. Other works, including Feliciana Enríquez de Guzmán's *Tragicomedia: Los Jardines y Campos Sabeos* (1619), lingered over sexually explicit descriptions cast as warnings against lust. Spanish erotica avoided being overtly defiant of the religious powers-that-be, and stringent licensing regulations forbidding criticism of Catholicism limited homegrown Spanish erotica.[32]

In contrast, Protestant English writers generated volumes of anticlerical—particularly anti-Catholic—erotica. Explications of Catholic errors lapsed periodically into sexual innuendo, as in *Popery Display'd* (1713): "Let a Spanish or Italian Husband consider how well he would like it to have his Wife perpetually seeking the Society of other Men … that she associates her self with them with all sorts of Familiarities."[33] Bawdy satires, such as *A Full and True Account of a Dreaded Fire That Lately Broke Out in the Pope's Breeches* (1713), drew on traditions of poking fun at the clergy.[34] As Peter Wagner has noted, publishers took advantage of the appeal of anti-Catholic feeling and printed works allegedly penned by Catholic apostates such as Christian Gottlieb Koch, Antonio Gavin, and Anthony Egan.[35] Accounts of priests seducing English girls contributed to the willingness to link clerics and sexual debauchery.[36] Anti-Catholicism occasionally wedded vitriol against Catholics with sadistic sexuality. Several pamphlets suggested castrating Catholic priests to prevent them from committing sexual misdeeds.[37] Others condemned religious flagellation but invited erotic inspection of the human body as part of penitential discipline, as Jean Louis de Lolme's *The History of Flagellants* (1776):

> By most of the antient [sic] Monastic Rules, religious persons were forbidden to inspect any part of their naked bodies, for fear of the wicked thoughts to which such imprudence might give rise: now, how is it possible for persons who intirely strip, in order to take discipline, to help, however great their piety may be, having a fight of those parts

of themselves which they have been directed never to look on? How can Nuns avoid, in those instants, having at least a glance of those excellent beauties which they are forbidden to survey?[38]

The line between a treatise (ostensibly) condemning whipping and erotic fiction that featured flagellation as titillation was a thin one. Erotica about nuns varied from mild to graphic. In *Nunnery Tales*, Charlotta's beloved, Villaret, comes to the convent grate. Charlotta experiences a flush of "Pleasure," and the author comments: "She was too innocent to imagine there was any other Effect of Love than Marriage."[39] The suggestive language invited the reader to tease out the sexual premise, a prominent technique in English anticlerical erotica. Tales of handsome but feckless gallants, jealous priests, amorous nuns, and initially innocent but pliable nubile young novices abound. The association of women closed off from the world, left to their own devices, and/or to the machinations of men determined to gain access to them created abundant imaginative space for sexual misdeeds.

French Enlightenment erotica lumped together organized religion and the monarchical political structure as twin poles of irrational traditionalism. Erotica grew more vicious and pornographic as the authority structures in France came under attack. Early anticlerical erotica, such as *Vénus dans le cloître, ou la religieuse en chemise* (1683), describes clerical misbehavior, emphasizing the hypocrisy of supposed celibates seducing innocent victims. Other standard fare included *Les Jésuites de la maison professe* (1696), which featured the innocent but unhappy Ninon seduced by her lecherous Jesuit confessor.[40] Salacious Jesuits figure in comparatively rare Dutch anticlerical works such as *Historische Print en Dicht Tafereelen* (1735). Prints illustrating this piece featured Jesuits, entranced by female nudity and sodomizing an unconscious woman.[41] By the 1740s, French anticlerical erotica had moved from soft-core seduction to ribald critique of clerical sexuality. *Histoire de Dom B ..., Portier des Chartreux*, for instance, is saturated with clerical corruption.[42] Saturnin's introduction to sex comes as the result of spying on a priest having sex with his stepmother, and with his sister recounting various sexual episodes in the convent. A series of misadventures results in the priest (rather than the horny Saturnin) taking Suzon's virginity. Saturnin's life in the monastery includes orgies, secret mistresses, and rape in the confessional. He eventually catches a venereal disease from his sister, loses his genitals, and ends his days as the porter at the monastery. Pierre-Jean-Baptiste Nougaret's *La Capucinade* (1765) attacked monks and priests for their sexual misdeeds and hypocrisy.[43] *Ma Conversion* (1783), probably by Mirabeau, featured sex with a nun, a sodomitical priest, and seduction of a female confessant. Most editions included explicit engravings depicting lecherous clerics and their nefarious sexual deeds. Denis Diderot's *La religieuse* (1796) told the story of a Mother Superior seducing an innocent novice, Susan, who flees the convent with her double-dealing confessor. Representations of misbehaving clerics corroded confidence in the religious establishment while titilating readers.

Erotica functioned similarly in undermining respect for political figures and institutions by tarring them with immorality and sexual scandal. Political turmoil could be a source of erotica, spurred on by it, or both. Typically, political erotica castigated rulers for actual or alleged sexual misdeeds. Moral lessons appended to much early political erotica justified its scabrous content. John Oldham's *Sardanapalus* (around 1676) implicitly compared Charles II to the legendary Assyrian king who supposedly ruined his kingdom through sexual debauchery. Sardanapalus, whom Oldham describes "swiving" himself to death on a funeral pyre, became a symbol of sexual misdeeds corrupting the body politic. Charles II was notorious for his affairs, which were thought to contribute to his absolutist tendencies and moral corruption. Like Sardanapalus, Charles allowed his sexual desires to overwhelm his judgment.[44] While scabrous attacks on political figures were rare in Holland, *Het gestoorde naaijpartijdje van Wilden de Vijfden* (The Disturbed Fornicating Party of William V) criticized the stadtholder for losing his reason in the face of sexual license. Casanova's memoirs described Catherine II of Russia as astonishingly dissolute, and accusations of sexual excess figured prominently in attacks on the Russian court.[45] Pamphlets such as the *Secret Memoirs of the Court of Petersburgh toward the Close of the Reign of Catherine II* circulated as far as the English colonies in America. Other erotica aimed at the privileged aristocracy. Aphra Behn's prose-fiction, *Love-Letters between a Nobleman and His Sister* (1684–1687), focused on aristocratic libertinage, with the nobleman Philander orchestrating the seduction of Silvia, who he then abandoned. Two works by Delarivier Manley, *The New Atalantis* (1709) and *The Adventures of Rivella* (1714), were thinly veiled tales of sexual political scandal. William King's satire, *The Toast* (1736), attacked the Duchess of Newcastle. Erotic political commentary functioned as public critique of the powers of the day, and many consumers learned a type of critical language from the genre.

The effects of a public educated by political erotica are most evident in France. During Louis XV's minority (1715–1722), graphic sexual attacks on the regent, Philippe d'Orléans, accompanied the political vicissitudes of his regime. Erotic commentary speculated about what happened at Philippe's private dinner parties and whether Philippe was having a sexual relationship with his own daughter.[46] One song claimed:

Philippe is a pretty boy
Who rolls over like a pig
The night with the Parabere [his favorite mistress at the time]
... His fat daughter Berry
Is always armed with a large penis [or dildo]
F ... 'd from the front and the back.[47]

Sustained political erotica continued and escalated during Louis XV's reign. *Les Mémoires Secrets d'une Femme Publique* and the *Anecdotes sur Mme la Comtesse du Barry* (the latter probably by Mathieu-François Pidansat de Mairobert) were two of the many titles that ridiculed Louis XV's dependence on his mistresses (especially Madame de Pompadour and Madame du Barry), and castigated the king for his profligacy. Under Louis XVI, attacks shifted from the king to his wife, Marie-Antoinette. The *Essais historiques sur la vie de Marie-Antoinette* conflated du Barry and Marie-Antoinette. Political erotica such as *The Austrian Woman on the RAMPAGE, or the Royal Orgy* (1789), *The Royal Bordello* (1789), and *The Vaginal Fury of Marie-Antoinette, Wife of Louis XVI* (1791) undermined the credibility of the monarchy. French erotica depicted Louis XVI as inept, inviting the public to laugh at the king for his inability to satisfy Marie-Antoinette sexually. The queen's alleged sexual crimes and the king's failure to control her merged with political crimes in public discourse. Erotica did not cause the French Revolution, but it did make killing Louis XVI easier to imagine by encouraging skepticism about monarchical rule.

Because French erotica was so aggressively political, later erotica played it safer. Erotica and pornography after the French Revolution featured coitus without nearly the volume of political commentary. Sexual attacks on political figures continued, but they receded as a prominent strain in erotica. This shift was facilitated by Enlightenment grapplings with the "otherness" of race and ethnicity. As Europeans expanded their influence around the globe, indigenous erotica and erotica deploying cultural or ethnic "others" combined to create an erotic hierarchy around sexual representation.

The foundations of this hierarchy lay first in eroticizing "others." Montesquieu's *Persian Letters* (1721) offered suggestive glimpses of harem life in the course of its veiled critique of French despotism. Crébillon fils's *The Sofa* (*Le Sopha*, 1742) is set in India. The narrator, Amanzei, recounts his time reincarnated as a sofa that was destined to last until a perfect union is consummated upon him. Along the way, he sees a hypocritical adulteress caught with her lover and killed, a prostitute taken up by a cold imperial steward, a sweet girl who forces herself on her timid lover, a virtuous woman seduced by her spiritual guide, and the torturous doings of a ne'er-do-well libertine. Only when two young lovers, Zeinis and Phileas, approach each other without hypocrisy or lust and with mutual love and admiration is Amanzei released from his furniture purgatory.[48] As with *The Persian Letters*, *The Sofa* is in part political critique: the sultan to whom Amanzei tells the story is weak-minded and libidinous—like Louis XV. But the exotic setting is not just a protective cover. Crébillon fils also depicted the "other" as sensual and lacking in reason when confronted with sexual possibilities. For Diderot, the exotic setting of *The Indiscreet Jewels* (*Les Bijoux indiscrets*, 1748) enabled both critique of Louis XV and a startling misogyny.[49] The sultan, Mangogul, presides over a society in which even the most seemingly chaste women of his court are lascivious liars. The mechanism for discovering sexual hypocrisy is a magic ring that enables Mangogul to make vaginas confess their experiences. No woman is safe when her jewel talks, but in the course of extracting confessions, Mangogul exposes the decadence of the court. The Abbé Prévost set his *The Story of a Modern Greek Woman* (*Histoire d'une Grecque moderne*, 1740) in Constantinople.

FIGURE 9.6: Women dancing to music in Cairo, Egypt. Colored lithograph by Louis Haghe after David Roberts (London: F. G. Moon, 1849). Wellcome Library, London.

His narrator becomes obsessed with Théophé, who manipulates male desire by alternately exposing herself (emotionally and physically) and retreating from the men who pursue her. Her vicissitudes raise questions about her veracity. In the context of Enlightenment debates over whether some, such as servants and women, were capable of reason, insistent images of non-Europeans as sexually debauched and untrustworthy undermined arguments for including them in the Enlightenment (fig. 9.6).

The integrity of non-Western erotica notwithstanding, European sexual values, including the eroticization of "others," figured centrally in European imperialism. This is evident with respect to China, where the European eighteenth century corresponds roughly to the High Qing era (1683–1839). Scholars consider this period the apogee of Manchu rule, which began with the destruction of the Ming loyalist resistance and ended with the Opium Wars and the Western military intervention that reconfigured the Chinese political landscape. The period was marked by economic transformation, demographic growth, revived interest in classical scholarship, and high levels of governmental involvement in daily life. The state encouraged female chastity, banned female erotic entertainers from palace precincts and official compounds, and frowned on erotic writing.[50] Pornography and sex manuals still circulated, but both, staples in the Ming period, became less available. Whereas Europeans gained access to erotica in the eighteenth century, the Qing made it more inaccessible, in part to dampen criticism of Chinese sexual mores.

These mores were nevertheless evident in erotica that drew on Chinese typologies. Keith McMahon has studied the recurrent types of men (misers, polygamists, ascetics, wastrels, spoiled sons) and women (shrews, scholar-beauties, virtuous wives, doting mothers, prostitutes) in eighteenth-century fiction. The types grew out of a Chinese sexual culture in which privileged men enjoyed legal access to multiple sexual partners, with one woman designated as the first wife, and others occupying a strict household hierarchy. Most Chinese marriages were monogamous, but polygamy signaled high status. Writers contrasted the potent polygamist with desexualized, effeminate, or uncontrolled sexual spendthrifts. The Chinese *ars erotica* encouraged men to have sex with many women, but to control "expenditure" of semen. Taoist and Buddhist manuals advised that sex redirected semen to the head, restoring and enhancing mental energy. Eroticism was coherent with the theory of the *Taiji* and its central notion of yin and yang. *Taiji* described human perception of natural phenomena (including sex) as the unity of opposites. Male and female antitheses united in sex is an obvious expression of this. But attention to the implications of yin and yang was invoked in erotic instruction manuals that advocated patterns of alternating long and short thrusts, told men to be attentive to female pleasure, and advised moderation in quantity of ejaculation.[51]

Sexual roles reflected gender and class hierarchy in erotica, as is apparent in Chinese prose-fiction texts. In *Liaodu Yuan* (The Cure for Jealousy, ca. 1749), the erotics are produced by the shrewish wife forbidding her husband contact with other women. After she is captured by bandits, the first wife learns to share her husband with his "mountain" wife, who uses her greater agility (because her feet are unbound) to save the first wife. In *Lin er Bao* (The Son of Good Fortune; early Qing), the hero is a common man who ends up with two wives. Although of equal social rank, one of the women takes the subordinate marital position out of gratitude to the other woman. Erotic novels such as *Jinxiang Ting* (Pavilion of Embroidered Fragrance; early Qing), played up special aptitudes of different women, announcing that each had a special niche and thus, no reason for jealousy.[52]

Like erotica that dealt with polygamy, other tales presented traditional erotic practices. *Lüye xianzong* (Trails of Immortals in the Green Wilds) features the prostitute Jinzhonger, who wants to convince Wen Ruyu to buy her freedom. Bald Miao is peaking at Ruyu and Jinzhonger: "Her feet were short and tiny ... and made a very delightful sight. Then he looked at Ruyu's penis. It was nearly six inches long, thick and strong, and thrust in and out of Jinzhonger's *yin*-gate like a huge serpent boring into its den. ... Then he saw Ruyu suddenly lift up both of Jinzhonger's legs and wildly thrust way, faster and faster with each stroke." Bald Miao can not bear it any more and races back to his concubine to satisfy his desire. Erotica centered on "beauty-scholars" features effeminate male intellectuals attracted to talented female scholars. The women, intellectually equal or superior to men, often take on male appearance (by cross-dressing) or habits (such as writing in the style of a man). In texts such as *Haoqui zhuan* (The Fortunate Union), the man is described as being as beautiful as a woman, so that the stories seem to be about two men in love, rather than heterosexual romances. Lesbian scenes appear occasionally, and almost always as preludes to heterosexual coitus.[53]

Despite efforts by the Qing, Western intervention in China increased dramatically, and erotica played its part. While some Chinese texts had been translated, Europeans denounced Chinese sexual practices.[54] Language about disorders caused by polygamy, wasting seed, and sexual brutality was saturated with presumptions of rationality on a European model. The Enlightenment provided the rhetoric.

But rhetoric could provide a space for erotica framed against European sexual values. As Dror Ze'evi has argued, travel accounts of the Ottoman world provided a model for erotica that turned the sexually perverse "other" against European claims.[55] Depictions of Turks and Arabs emphasized effeminate, sodomitical, and lascivious typologies. Travel accounts like the one by Paul Rycaut deplored Turkish homoerotics and found indigenous women to be lascivious.[56] François, Baron de Tott similarly wrote critical erotic accounts of both male homosexuality and female licentiousness.[57] The Chevalier Chardin claimed Persian women deserved the rigors of the harem because they were relentlessly lewd, cruel, and "wicked."[58] Lady Mary Wortley Montagu (1689–1762) was more positive. Having visited Turkey as the wife of the British ambassador, she described the homoerotics of the harem and the hammam (bathhouse) from the inside for generations of British travelers and writers.[59] As print culture spread, Arab erotica retaliated by sexualizing Europeans through similar means. Descriptions of Europeans as effeminate and sexually uncontrolled abounded.[60] The freedom of European women prompted critical commentary that doubled as erotica.[61] Abd al Rahman al-Jabarti's shocked response to unveiled European women led him to assume—in some detail—that the French copulated indiscriminately.[62] Enlightenment practices of assessing others and new publics created under the auspices of Enlightenment sociability encouraged the politics of Ottoman erotica turned against the West.

When the British established a colonial presence in India, a cultural clash over sexuality, expressed in Enlightenment terms, worked more restrictively. The British regarded Indians as lascivious and cited child marriage and polygamy as evidence. Edward Sellon considered half-caste Indian girls available for purchase, while Muslim girls were especially inexpensive and compared favorably to European prostitutes: "They do not drink, they are scrupulously cleanly in their person, they are sumptuously dressed ... they are well educated, and sing sweetly."[63] For their part, Indians regarded British habits such as allowing women to bare their shoulders and mixed-company dancing as unacceptably promiscuous.[64] It was not the first time that Indian erotic culture had been shaped by divergent attitudes attendant on political domination. Ancient Hindu epics such as the *Ramayana* (probably around 1400 B.C.E.) presented marital sex as focused on mutual pleasure. The *Upanishads* (around 500 B.C.E.) also advocated sexually tolerant attitudes. More graphically, the *Kama Sutra,* thought to be the work of Mallanaga Vatsyayana, described sexual union as one of the four *purusharthas,* or goals in life.[65] Hinduism also supported the development of Tantric sex as a mode of enlightenment. The Khajuraho temple and the cave temple at Ajanta featured explicit visual depictions of sexual encounters. Erotica was ingrained in Indian spiritual culture. The arrival of Muslim influence and the Delhi sultanate, however, limited expression of Indian sexuality. Pressure on non-Muslims was uneven but came to include inducements to respect Muslim notions of public sexual propriety, including (limited) purdah for women. The British intervention and gradual takeover of India under the auspices of the East India Company in the late eighteenth century brought Protestant sexual values into the mix, and British efforts to "reform" the so-called lascivious Indian traditions began in earnest. At the same time, Indian erotic texts such as the *Kama Sutra,* eventually translated by Sir Richard Burton, began circulating in the West, contributing to notions of the erotic, exotic "Orient." Scandalized Europeans consulted the erotica of India, even as they denounced it as symptomatic of an inferior and barbaric culture.[66] Enlightenment European style largely prevailed.

With all its contradictions, the European Enlightenment shaped the presumptions of colonial encounters in erotica. Conversely, indigenous erotic traditions challenged European sexual certainties. The Western propensity to both decry and succumb to the promises of erotica played out repeatedly in the nineteenth century. Enlightenment erotica produced and then gave way to colonial images of normative (read, European) sexuality. The colliding, unresolved imperatives of eighteenth-century erotica created the need to stratify, classify, and stigmatize erotic expression in ways that still mark the global context of erotica.

NOTES

Chapter 1

My thanks to Merril Smith and Katherine Crawford for reading through this chapter and for their suggestions.

1. See Michel Foucault, *The History of Sexuality: Volume 1, An Introduction*, translated by Robert Hurley (New York: Pantheon, 1978).
2. One of the great early pioneers was Vern Bullough; among others, see his *Sexual Variance in Society and History* (New York: Wiley Interscience, 1976), and *Sex, Society and History* (New York: Science History, Neale Watson, 1976); Vern Bullough, Dorr Legg, Barret Elcano, James Kepner, eds., *An Annotated Bibliography of Homosexuality Transvestism, and Transsexualism* (New York: Garland Publishers, 1976). Other earlier explorers include Reay Tannahill, *Sex in History* (London: H. Hamilton, 1980); R.E.L. Masters, *Sex Crimes in History* (New York: Julian Press, 1963); Gordon Rattray Taylor, *Sex in History* (London: Thames & Hudson, 1953); and George Ryley Scott, *Phallic Worship* (Privately printed, 1941).
3. Only but a few examples can be provided here: Kathryn Babayan and Afsaneh Najmabad, eds., *Islamicate Sexualities: Translations Across Temporal Geographies of Desire* (Cambridge, MA: Harvard University Press, 2008); Samir Habib, *Female Homosexuality in the Middle East: Histories and Representations* (London: Routledge, 2007); Durba Ghosh, *Sex and the Family in Colonial India: The Making of Empire* (Cambridge: Cambridge University Press, 2006); Ze'evi Dror, *Producing Desire: Changing Sexual Discourse in the Ottoman Middle East, 1500–1900* (Berkeley: University of California Press, 2006); Cuncun Wu, *Homoerotic Sensibilities in Late Imperial China* (London: Routledge, 2004).
4. Historians also seem to chose the words over which they argue; so while they argue over terms such as "heterosexuality" and "homosexuality," seeing them as achronistic terms that cannot be applied historically before particular times, often they continue to use other modern-day terminology to describe the past. However, since

even the word "sex" was used differently during different time periods, and the term "sexuality" was not used at all during some earlier periods, it is impossible to describe the past without using modern-day language.
5. G. R. Quaife, *Wanton Wenches and Wayward Wives: Peasants and Illicit Sex in Early Seventeenth-Century England* (London: Croom Helm, 1979).
6. Laura Gowing, *Domestic Dangers: Women, Words and Sex in Early Modern England* (Oxford: Clarendon Press, 1996).
7. Richard Godbeer, *Sexual Revolution in Early America* (Baltimore: John Hopkins University Press, 2002).
8. Sandra Adams, "Chinese Sexuality and the Bound Foot," in *Sexual Perversions, 1670–1890*, ed. Julie Peakman (Basingstoke: Palgrave, 2009), 246–74.
9. Angus McLaren, *A History of Contraception* (Oxford: Blackwell, 1990).
10. For the development of these discussions, see Edward Stein, ed., *Forms of Desire: Sexual Orientation and the Sexual Constructionist Controversy* (New York: Garland, 1990).
11. But a few examples can be found in Jonathan Ned Katz, *Love Stories: Sex Between Men Before Homosexuality* (Chigaco: University of Chicago Press, 2001); Rictor Norton, *Mother Clap's Molly House: The Gay Subculture in England, 1700–1830* (London: GMP, 1992); Judith M. Bennett, "'Lesbian-Like' and the Social Hstory of Lesbianisms," *Journal of the History of Sexuality* 9 (2000): 1–24; Julie Peakman, *Lascivious Bodies: A Sexual History of the Eighteenth Century* (London: Atlantic, 2004).
12. *Leggi e Memoire Venete sulla Prostituzione*, c. 1870, recalls many incidents recorded by "Pisanus Fraxis," Henry Spencer Ashbee, *Bibliography of Prohibited Books Vol. III* (1879; New York: USA: Jack Brussell, 1962), 32–59.
13. Michel Rey, "Police and Sodomy in Eighteenth-Century Paris: From Sin to Disorder," in *The Pursuit of Sodomy: Male Homosexuality in Renaissance and Enlightenment Europe*, ed. Kent Gerard and Gert Hekma (New York: The Haworth Press, 1989).
14. Norton, *Mother Clap's Molly House*.
15. Rey, "Police and Sodomy," 137.
16. Theo Van de Meer, "Tribades on Trial: Female Same-Sex Offenders in Late Eighteenth-Century Amsterdam," *Journal of the History of Sexuality* 1 (1991), 424–445.
17. For a discussion on this, see my introduction to *Sexual Perversion, 1670–1890* (Basingstoke: Palgrave, 2009).
18. Peakman, *Lascivious Bodies*, 276–77.
19. According to Wagner, Balthazar Beckers (or Bekkers) was the author; this has been contested by Michael Stolberg who believes it was penned by John Marten. Stolberg also argues that the date previously assumed by historians of 1710 is incorrect. I have used Stolberg's date. Also see Peter Wagner, "The Veil of Medicine and Morality: Some Pornographic Aspects of the *Onania*," *Eighteenth-Century Studies* 6 (1983): 179–84; Robert H. MacDonald, "The Frightful Consequences of Onania," *Journal of the History of Ideas* 28 (1967): 423–31; Michael Stolberg, "Self-Pollution, Moral Reform, and the Venereal Trade: Notes on the Sources and Historical Content of *Onania* (1716)," *Journal of the History of Sexuality* 9, no. 1–2 (2000): 37–61.

20. S.A.D. Tissot, *Onanism, or a Treatise upon the Disorders produced by Masturbation, or, the Dangerous Effects of Secret and Excessive Venery*, trans. A. Hume (London: J. Pridden, 1766), 24.
21. According to Vern and Bonnie Bullough, Tissot's views were widely accepted. Vern L. Bullough and Bonnie Bullough, *Sexual Attitudes* (London: Prometheus Books, 1995), 71.
22. Little is known about Bienville, although it is believed he lived in Holland and wrote several other scientific works.
23. Jonas Liliequist, "Peasants Against Nature: Crossing the Boundaries between Man and Animal in Seventeenth and Eighteenth Century Sweden," in *Forbidden History: The State, Society and the Regulation of Sexuality in Modern Europe*, ed. John C. Fout (Chicago: University of Chicago Press, 1990), 57–88; for the British case, see Peakman, *Lascivious Bodies*, 258.
24. Peakman, *Lascivious Bodies*, 271–73.
25. Ibid., 266–69.
26. Anthony E. Simpson, "Age of Consent," in *Sexual Underworlds of the Enlightenment*, ed. G. S. Rousseau and Roy Porter (Manchester: Manchester University Press, 1987), 181–205.
27. Matthew H. Sommer, *Sex, Law, and Society in Late Imperial China* (Cambridge: Cambridge University Press, 2000), 5.
28. Thomas Laqueur, *Making Sex* (Cambridge, MA: Harvard University Press, 1990).
29. Helen King, *Hippocrates Women: Reading the Female Body in Ancient Greece* (London: Routledge, 1998).
30. Quoted in Vernon A. Rosario, *The Erotic Imagination: French Histories of Perversity* (Oxford: Oxford University Press, 1997), 17.
31. Roy Porter and Lesley Hall, *Facts of Life: The Creation of Sexual Knowledge in Britain, 1650–1950* (New Haven, CT: Yale University Press, 1995), 36, 298.
32. Peter Wagner, *Eros Revived: Erotica of the Enlightenment in England and America* (London: Secker and Warburg, 1988), 11.
33. K. C. Wang and Lien-te Wu, *History of Chinese Medicine* (Tientsin: Tiensin Press, 1932), 114–15.
34. Gary P. Leupp, *Male Colours: The Construction of Homosexuality in Tokugawa Japan* (Berkeley: University of California Press, 1999), 3.
35. Min Tiam, "Male *Dan*: The Paradox of Sex, Acting and Perception of Gender Impersonation in Traditional Chinese Theatre," 17, no. 1 *Asian Theatre Journal* (2000): 78–97.
36. Saunders Welch, *A Proposal to Render Effectual a Plan to Remove the Nuisance of Common Prostitutes from the Street of This Metropolis* (London, 1758); Baron von Uffenbach *London in 1710*, trans. W. Quarrell and Margaret Moore (London: Faber, 1934).
37. Georges Duby, Natalie Zemon Davis, Michelle Perrot, and Arlette Farge, eds., *A History of Women in the West: Renaissance and Enlightenment Paradoxes* (Cambridge, MA: Harvard University Press, 1992), 470.
38. Melissa Hope Ditmore, *Encyclopedia of Prostitution and Sex Work* (London: Greenwood Press, 2006), 194.

39. Mary Gibson, *Prostitution and the State in Italy, 1860–1915* (New Brunswick, NJ: Rutgers University Press, 1986), 3, 15.
40. Welch, *A Proposal*, 5.
41. Duby, Zemon Davis, Perrot, and Farge, *A History of Women in the West*, 465.
42. Sommer, *Sex, Law, and Society*, 210–320.
43. This is not to say that it did not have its influences from much earlier—classical and medieval references to erotica show continuities. One example must suffice here; disembodied winged penises popular in pen and ink drawings illustrating eighteenth-century pornography can to this day be found on ancient tombs in holy sites such as Delos.
44. Kearney attributes *La Puttana Errante* to Niccolò Franco (1515–1570); it is often incorrectly ascribed to Aretino.
45. Julie Peakman, *Mighty Lewd Books* (Basingstoke: Palgrave, 2003), 15–22.
46. PRO, SP, 35/55/102.
47. For a biographies of Curll, see Ralph Straus, *The Unspeakable Curll* (London: Chapman and Hall, 1927), and Paul Baines and Pat Rogers, *Edmund Curll Bookseller* (Oxford: Clarendon Press, 2007).
48. John Cleland, *Memoirs of a Woman of Pleasure* (London: G. Fenton, 1749), II:155–56. Plates depicting flagellation were incorporated into the book.

Chapter 2

1. Henry Abelove, "Some Speculations on the History of Intercourse During the Long Eighteenth Century in England," *Genders* 6 (1989): 125–30.
2. For a somewhat different yet important interpretation, see Randolph Trumbach, *Heterosexuality and the Third Gender in Enlightenment London: Vol. 1, Sex and the Gender Revolution* (Chicago: University of Chicago Press, 1998).
3. Simon Szreter, *Fertility, Class and Gender in Britain, 1860–1940* (Cambridge: Cambridge University Press, 1996), 32.
4. Laura Gowing, *Common Bodies: Women, Touch, and Power in the Eighteenth Century* (New Haven, CT: Yale University Press, 2003), 109.
5. Jacques Rossiaud, *Medieval Prostitution*, trans. Lydia Cochrane (Oxford: Blackwell, 1988), 21.
6. Anna Clark, "Twilight Moments," *Journal of the History of Sexuality* 14, no. 1/2 (2005): 139–60; Helmut Puff, *Sodomy in Reformation Germany and Switzerland 1400–1600* (Chicago: University of Chicago Press, 2003), 177; Michael Rocke, *Forbidden Friendships: Homosexuality and Male Culture in Renaissance Florence* (New York: Oxford University Press, 1996), 191.
7. Ruth H. Bloch, "Changing Conceptions of Sexuality and Romance in Eighteenth-Century America," *William and Mary Quarterly* 60, no. 1 (2003): 13–15.
8. Stephen Haliczer, *Sexuality in the Confessional: A Sacrament Profaned*, Studies in the History of Sexuality (New York: Oxford University Press, 1996), 128.
9. Charlene Black Villaseñor, "Love and Marriage in the Spanish Empire: Depictions of Holy Matrimony and Gender Discourses in the Seventeenth Century," *Sixteenth Century Journal* 32, no. 3 (2001): 646.

10. Ann Twinam, *Public Lives, Private Secrets: Gender, Honor, Sexuality and Illegitimacy in Colonial Spanish America* (Stanford, CA: Stanford University Press, 1999), 63.
11. Abigail Dyer, "Seduction by Promise of Marriage: Law, Sex, and Culture in Seventeenth-Century Spain," *Sixteenth Century Journal* 34, no. 2 (2003): 439–55.
12. Twinam, *Public Lives*, 12.
13. James Hoke Sweet, "Recreating Africa: Race, Religion, and Sexuality in the African-Portuguese World, 1441–1770," Ph.D. dissertation, City University of New York, 1999, 99.
14. Susan M. Deeds, "Double Jeopardy: Indian Women in Jesuit Missions of Nueva Vizcaya," in *Indian Women of Early Mexico*, ed. Susan Schroeder, Stephanie Wood, and Robert Haskett (Norman: University of Oklahoma Press, 1997), 262.
15. Clark, "Twilight Moments".
16. Patricia Seed, *To Love, Honor, and Obey in Colonial Mexico: Conflicts over Marriage Choice, 1574–1821* (Stanford: Stanford University Press, 1988), 96.
17. Rebecca Earle, "Letters and Love in Colonial Spanish America," *Americas: A Quarterly Review of Inter-American Cultural History* 62, no. 1 (2005): 21.
18. James R. Farr, *Authority and Sexuality in Early Modern Burgundy* (New York: Oxford University Press, 1995), 91.
19. Isabel Hull, *Sexuality, the State, and Civil Society in Germany, 1790–1815* (Ithaca, NY: Cornell University Press, 1996), 143.
20. John R. Gillis, *For Better, for Worse: British Marriages, 1600 to the Present* (New York: Oxford University Press, 1985), 88.
21. Sandra Clark, "The Economics of Marriage in the Broadside Ballad," *Journal of Popular Culture* 36, no. 1 (2002): 119–33; John R. Gillis, "'A Triumph of Hope over Experience': Chance and Choice in the History of Marriage," *International Review of Social History* 44, no. 1 (1999): 47–54; Steven King, "Chance Encounters? Paths to Household Formation in Early Modern England," *International Review of Social History* 44, no. 1 (1999): 23–46.
22. Gillis, *For Better, for Worse*, 28.
23. Tim Hitchcock, "Sociability and Misogyny in the Life of John Cannon," in *English Masculinities*, ed. Tim Hitchcock and Michèle Cohen (Harlow: Longman, 1999), 25.
24. Jean-Louis Flandrin, *Sex in the Western World: The Development of Attitudes and Behavior*, trans. Sue Collins (Chur: Harwood Academic Publishers, 1991), 275; Clark, "Twilight Moments," 135–40.
25. Andreas Gestrich, "After Dark: Girls' Leisure."
26. Eilert Sundt, *Sexual Customs in Rural Norway*, trans. Odin W. Anderson (Ames: Iowa State University Press, 1993), 54.
27. Yochi Fischer-Yinon, "The Original Bundlers: Boaz and Ruth, and Seventeenth-Century English Courtship Practices," *Journal of Social History* 35, no. 3 (2002): 683–705.
28. Richard Adair, *Courtship, Illegitimacy and Marriage in Early Modern England* (Manchester: Manchester University Press, 1996), 62.
29. Laura Gowing, "Secret Births and Infanticide in Seventeenth-Century England," *Past & Present*, no. 156 (1997): 92.

30. Leah Leneman and Rosalind Mitchison, "Girls in Trouble: The Social and Geographical Setting of Illegitimacy in Early Modern Scotland," *Journal of Social History* (1988): 483–97.
31. Lee A. Gladwin, "Tobacco and Sex: Some Factors Affecting Nonmarital Sexual Behavior in Colonial Virginia," *Journal of Social History* 12, no. 1 (1978): 69.
32. Richard Godbeer, "Courtship and Sexual Freedom in Eighteenth-Century America," *Magazine of History* 18, no. 4 (2004): 8.
33. David Gaunt, "Illegitimacy in Seventeenth- and Eighteenth-Century Sweden," in *Bastardy and Its Comparative History*, ed. Peter Laslett, Karla Oosterveen, and Richard M. Smith (Cambridge, MA: Harvard University Press, 1980), 95; Anders Brandstrom, "Illegitimacy and Lone-Parenthood in Xixth Century Sweden," *Annales de Demographie Historique*, no. 2 (1998): 95.
34. Erica-Marie Benabou, *La Prostitution Et La Police Des Moeurs Au Xviiieme Siecle* (Paris: Perrin, 1987), 79–80; Georg'ann Cattelona, "Control and Collaboration: The Role of Women in Regulating Female Sexual Behavior in Early Modern Marseille," *French Historical Studies* 18, no. 1 (1993).
35. Godbeer, "Courtship and Sexual Freedom," 10.
36. John Knodel, *Demographic Behavior in the Past* (Cambridge: Cambridge University Press, 1988), 211.
37. Jan Kok, "The Moral Nation: Illegitimacy and Bridal Pregnancy in the Netherlands from 1600 to the Present," *Economic and Social History in the Netherlands* 2 (1990): 22.
38. Barry Reay, "Sexuality in Nineteenth-Century England: The Social Context of Illegitimacy in Rural Kent," *Rural History* 1, no. 2 (1990): 219.
39. Ann-Sofie Kalvemark, "Illegitimacy and Marriage in Three Swedish Parishes in the Nineteenth Century," in *Bastardy and Its Comparative History*, ed. Peter Laslett, Karla Oosterveen, and Richard M. Smith (Cambridge, MA: Harvard University Press, 1980), 220.
40. Adair, *Courtship, Marriage, and Illegitimacy*, 109.
41. Maryanne Kowaleski, "Single Women in Medieval and Early Modern Europe: The Demographic Perspective," in *Singlewomen in the European Past*, ed. Judith Bennett and Amy Froide (Philadelphia: University of Pennsylvania Press, 1999), 53.
42. Thomas W. Laqueur, "Sexual Desire and the Market Economy During the Industrial Revolution," in *Discourses of Sexuality from Aristotle to Aids*, ed. Domna C. Stanton (Ann Arbor: University of Michigan Press, 1992), 192.
43. Kowalski, "Singlewomen," 59.
44. Peter Laslett, "Introduction: Comparing Illegitimacy over Time and between Cultures," in *Bastardy and Its Comparative History*, ed. Peter Laslett, Karla Oosterveen, and Richard M. Smith (Cambridge, MA: Harvard University Press, 1980).
45. Rosella Rettaroli, "Age at Marriage in Nineteenth-Century Italy," *Journal of Family History* 15, no. 4 (1990): 409–25.
46. Kok, "The Moral Nation," 22.
47. Brandstrom, "Illegitimacy and Lone-Parenthood," 95.
48. Hull, *Sexuality, State, and Civil Society*, 127.

49. Jeremy Hayhoe, "Illegitimacy, Inter-Generational Conflict and Legal Practice in Eighteenth-Century Northern Burgundy," *Journal of Social History* 38, no. 3 (2005): 685.
50. Gladwin, "Tobacco and Sex," 69.
51. Tanya Evans, "'Unfortunate Objects': London's Unmarried Mothers in the Eighteenth Century," *Gender & History* 17, no. 1 (2005): 131.
52. David I. Kertzer, "Gender Ideology and Infant Abandonment in Nineteenth-Century Italy," *Journal of Interdisciplinary History* 22, no. 1 (1991): 18.
53. Jean Meyer, "Illegitimates and Foundlings in Pre-Industrial France," in *Bastardy and Its Comparative History*, ed. Peter Laslett, Karla Oosterveen, and Richard M. Smith (Cambridge, MA: Harvard University Press, 1980), 251.
54. Alain Lottin, "Naissances Illegitimes Et Filles-Mère à' Lille Au Xviiie Siècle," *Revue d'Histoire Moderne et Contemporaine* 17, no. 2 (1970): 251.
55. Kok, "The Moral Nation," 7–35.
56. Hans Marks, "On the Art of Differentiating: Proletarianization and Illegitimacy in Northern Sweden, 1850–1930," *Social Science History* 18, no. 1 (1994), 100.
57. Hayhoe, "Illegitimacy, Inter-Generational Conflict and Legal Practice," 682.
58. Lottin, "Naissances Illegitimes Et Filles-Mere a' Lille Au Xviiie Siecle," 305.
59. John R. Gillis, "Servants, Sexual Relations, and the Risks of Illegitimacy in London, 1801–1900," *Feminist Studies* 5, no. 1 (1979): 142–73.
60. Lottin, "Naissances Illegitimes Et Filles-Mere a' Lille Au Xviiie Siecle," 315.
61. Sharon Block, *Rape and Sexual Power in Early America* (Chapel Hill: University of North Carolina Press, 2006), 163.
62. Anna Clark, *Women's Silence, Men's Violence: Sexual Assault in England, 1770–1845* (London: Pandora, 1987), 80.
63. Evans, "'Unfortunate Objects,'" 142; Clark, *Women's Silence, Men's Violence*, 82.
64. Andrew Blaikie, *Illegitimacy, Sex, and Society: Northeast Scotland, 1750–1900* (Oxford: Clarendon Press, 1993), 215; W. R. Lee, "Bastardy and the Socio-Economic Structure of South Germany," *Journal of Interdisciplinary History* 7 (1977), no. 3: 403–425; Marks, "On the Art," 116.
65. Hayhoe, "Illegitimacy, Inter-Generational Conflict and Legal Practice," 680.
66. Jona Schellekens, "Courtship, the Clandestine Marriage Act, and Illegitimate Fertility in England," *Journal of Interdisciplinary History* 25, no. 3 (1995): 433–44.
67. Rebecca Probert, "Chinese Whispers and Welsh Weddings," *Continuity and Change* 20, no. 2 (2005): 211–38.
68. Andrew Blaikie, "Scottish Illegitimacy: Social Adjustment or Moral Economy?" *Journal of Interdisciplinary History* 29, no. 2 (1998): 26.
69. Rachel G. Fuchs, *Poor and Pregnant in Nineteenth-Century Paris* (New Brunswick, NJ: Rutgers University Press, 1992), 19, 36.
70. Knodel, *Demographic Behavior in the Past*, 124.
71. Gillis, *For Better, for Worse*, 79–130.
72. Samuel Pyeatt Menefee, *Wives for Sale: An Ethnographic Study of British Popular Divorce* (Oxford: Blackwell, 1981).
73. Olivier Blanc, *Les Libertines: Plaisir Et Liberté Au Temps Des Lumières* (Paris: Perrin, 1997), 27.

74. Mary Elizabeth Robinson and J. Fitzgerald Molloy, *Memoirs of Mary Robinson, "Perdita"* (London: Gibbings, 1895).
75. Julie de Lespinasse, *Letters of Mlle. De Lespinasse*, trans. Katherine Prescott Wormeley (Boston: Hardy, Pratt and Co., 1903), 91.
76. Reay, "Sexuality in Nineteenth-Century England: The Social Context of Illegitimacy in Rural Kent," 243; Knodel, *Demographic Behavior in the Past*, 223.
77. Margaret R. Hunt, *The Middling Sort: Commerce, Gender, and the Family in England, 1680–1780* (Berkeley: University of California Press, 1996).
78. Earle, "Letters and Love," 17–46.
79. Randolph Trumbach, *The Rise of the Egalitarian Family* (New York: Academic Press, 1978), 291.
80. As Trumbach points out in his later work, *Heterosexuality*, 393.
81. Donna T. Andrew, "'Adultery a-La-Mode': Privilege, the Law and Attitudes to Adultery 1770–1809," *History* 82, no. 265 (1997): 5–23.
82. Catherine Cusser, *No Tomorrow: The Ethics of Pleasure in the French Enlightenment* (Charlottesville: University of Virginia Press, 1999), 4.
83. James Grantham Turner, *Schooling Sex: Libertine Literature and Erotic Education in Italy, France, and England 1534–1685* (New York: Oxford University Press, 2003), 17.
84. Michel Feher, "Introduction," in *The Libertine Reader: Eroticism and Enlightenment in Eighteenth-Century France*, ed. Michel Feher (New York: Zone Books, 1997), 19.
85. G. J. Barker-Benfield, *The Culture of Sensibility: Sex and Society in Eighteenth-Century Britain* (Chicago: University of Chicago Press, 1992), 40–52.
86. Jonathan Irvine Israel, *Enlightenment Contested: Philosophy, Modernity, and the Emancipation of Man, 1670–1752* (Oxford: Oxford University Press, 2006), 281.
87. Jonathan Israel, *Radical Enlightenment* (Oxford: Oxford University Press, 2001), 66.
88. Israel, *Radical Enlightenment*, 88.
89. For analysis of the anti-clerical aspects of Wilkes' libertinism, see John Sainsbury, "Wilkes and Libertinism," *Studies in Eighteenth-Century Culture* 26 (1998): 151–74.
90. Arthur H. Cash, *John Wilkes: The Scandalous Father of Civil Liberty* (New Haven, CT: Yale University Press, 2006), 35.
91. Clark, *Scandal: The Sexual Politics of the British Constitution* (Princeton University Press, 2004), 44–45.
92. Bryant T. Ragan, "The Enlightenment Confronts Homosexuality," in *Homosexuality in Modern France*, ed. Jeffrey Merrick and Bryant T. Ragan (Oxford: Oxford University Press, 1996), 8–15.
93. Boyer de d'Argens, *Thérése Philosophe*, ed. Guillaume Pigeard de Gurbert (Paris: Babel, 1992), 125; Denis Diderot, *Rameau's Nephew and D'alembert's Dream*, trans. Leonard Tancock (Harmondsworth: Penguin, 1966), 228–29.
94. Robert Darnton, *The Forbidden Best-Sellers of Pre-Revolutionary France* (New York: W.W. Norton, 1995), 298.
95. Jacqueline Hecht, "From 'Be Fruitful and Multiply' to Family Planning: The Enlightenment Transition," *Eighteenth-Century Studies* 32, no. 4 (1999): 536–51;

Christine Théré, "Women and Birth Control in Eighteenth-Century France," *Eighteenth-Century Studies* 32, no. 4 (1999): 552–64.

96. John C. O'Neal, *The Authority of Experience: Sensationalist Theory in the French Enlightenment* (University Park: Pennsylvania State University Press, 1996), 158.
97. Feher, "Introduction," 19.
98. Choderlos de Laclos, *Les Liaisons Dangereuses* (London: The Nonesuch Press, 1940).
99. Denis Diderot and Jean Le Rond d Alembert, *Encyclopédie, Ou, Dictionnaire Raisonné Des Sciences, Des Arts Et Des Métiers*, 17 vols. (Paris: Briasson [etc.], 1751), 1:369.
100. D. G. Charllon, *New Images of the Natural in France* (Cambridge: Cambridge University Press, 1984), 28.
101. Jean-Jacques Rousseau and Judith H. McDowell, *La Nouvelle Héloïse, Julie, or the New Eloise: Letters of Two Lovers, Inhabitants of a Small Town at the Foot of the Alps* (University Park: Pennsylvania State University Press, 1968).
102. Barker-Benfield, *The Culture of Sensibility*, 227.
103. Anthony Fletcher, *Gender, Sex, and Subordination in England, 1500–1800* (New Haven, CT: Yale University Press, 1995).
104. Bloch, "Changing Conceptions of Sexuality," 38–40.
105. Irene Hardach-Pinke, "Managing Girls' Sexuality among the German Upper Classes," in *Secret Gardens, Satanic Mills: Placing Girls in European History, 1750–1960*, ed. Mary Jo Maynes, Brigitte Soland, and Christine Benninghaus (Bloomington: Indiana University Press, 2005), 108.
106. "A Lady," *The Twin Sisters; or, the Effects of Education*, 3 vols. (London: 1788), 1:53.
107. Dr. Gregory, *Dr. Gregory's Legacy to His Daughters* (London: 1806), 5.
108. Barker-Benfield, *The Culture of Sensibility*, 341.
109. Bloch, "Changing Conceptions of Sexuality," 38–40.
110. Thomas W. Laqueur, *Solitary Sex: A Cultural History of Masturbation* (New York: Zone Books, 2003), 59.
111. Hull, *Sexuality, State, and Civil Society*.
112. Thomas Malthus, *On Population* (London, 1798), ch. 7.

Chapter 3

1. M. McIntosh, "The Homosexual Role," *Social Problems* 16 (1968): 182–92; M. Foucault, *The History of Sexuality, Volume I: An Introduction*, trans. Robert Hurley (New York: Pantheon, 1978); J. Weeks, *Coming Out: Homosexual Politics in Britain, from the Nineteenth Century to the Present* (London: Quartet, 1977); R. A. Padgug, "Sexual Matters: On Conceptualizing Sexuality in History," *Radical History Review* 20 (1979): 3–33; K. Plummer, ed., *The Making of the Modern Homosexual* (London: Hutchinson, 1981); A. Bray, *Homosexuality in Renaissance England* (London: Gay Men's Press, 1982); D. Halperin, *One Hundred Years of Homosexuality* (New York: Routledge, 1989); Halperin, "How to Do the History of Male Homosexuality," *GLQ* 6 (2000): 87–123.

2. J. Butler, *Gender Trouble: Feminism and the Subversion of Identity* (New York: Routledge, 1990); E. Kosofsky Sedgwick, *Epistemology of the Closet* (Berkeley: University of California Press, 1990); T. Laqueur, *Making Sex: Body and Gender from the Greeks to Freud* (Cambridge, MA: Harvard University Press, 1990).
3. D. Halperin, "Is There a History of Sexuality?" *History and Theory* 28 (1989): 257–74.
4. These lines by Foucault are quoted by virtually all sexual theorists, although "temporary aberration" is a mistranslation of Foucault's term *relaps*, meaning someone who has relapsed into heresy, which is better translated as "sinner." See G. Robb, *Strangers: Homosexual Love in the Nineteenth Century* (New York: W.W. Norton, 2003), 42.
5. R. Norton, *The Myth of the Modern Homosexual: Queer History and the Search for Cultural Unity* (London: Cassell, 1997).
6. L. J. Boon, "Those Damned Sodomites: Public Images of Sodomy in the Eighteenth Century Netherlands," in *The Pursuit of Sodomy: Male Homosexuality in Renaissance and Enlightenment Europe*, ed. K. Gerard and G. Hekma (New York: Harrington Park Press, 1989), 246.
7. A. Richlin, "Not before Homosexuality," *Journal of the History of Sexuality* 3, no. 4 (1993): 523–73.
8. T. Hubberd, ed., *Homosexuality in Greece and Rome: A Sourcebook of Basic Documents* (Berkeley: University of California Press, 2003).
9. D. M. Robinson, *Closeted Writing and Lesbian and Gay Literature: Classical, Early Modern, Eighteenth-Century* (Aldershot: Ashgate Publishing, 2006).
10. B.-U. Hergemöller, *Sodom and Gomorrah: On the Everyday Reality and Persecution of Homosexuals in the Middle Ages* (London: Free Association Books, 2001).
11. M. B. Young, *King James and the History of Homosexuality* (New York: New York University Press, 2000).
12. A. Bray, *Homosexuality in Renaissance England* (London: Gay Men's Press, 1982).
13. K. Borris and G. Rousseau, eds., *The Sciences of Homosexuality in Early Modern Europe* (New York: Routledge, 2008).
14. See Halperin's Introduction to K. O'Donnell and M. O'Rourke, eds., *Love, Sex and Intimacy Between Men, 1550–1800* (Basingstoke: Palgrave Macmillan, 2003), 12.
15. R. Trumbach, "London's Sodomites: Homosexual Behaviour and Western Culture in the 18th Century," *Journal of Social History* 11, no. 1 (1977): 1–33; R. Trumbach, "Sodomitical Subculture, Sodomitical Roles, and the Gender Revolution of the Eighteenth Century: The Recent Historiography," *Eighteenth Century Life* 9 (1985): 109–21; R. Trumbach, "The Birth of the Queen: Sodomy and the Emergence of Gender Equality in Modern Culture, 1660–1750," in *Hidden from History*, ed. M. Duberman et al. (New York: Meridian/Penguin Books, 1989), 129–40; R. Trumbach, *Sex and the Gender Revolution, Volume 1: Heterosexualitiy and the Third Gender in Enlightenment London* (Chicago: University of Chicago Press, 1998); R. Trumbach, "London," in *Queer Sites: Gay Urban Histories since 1600*, ed. D. Higgs (London: Routledge, 1999), 89–111; R. Trumbach, "Modern Sodomy: The Origins of Homosexuality, 1700–1800," in *A Gay History of Britain: Love*

and *Sex Between Men Since the Middle Ages,* ed. M. Cook (Oxford and Westport: Greenwood, 2007).
16. Trumbach, "Modern Sodomy," 78–79.
17. G. S. Rousseau, "English Literature: Restoration and Eighteenth Century," in *The Gay and Lesbian Literary Heritage,* ed. C. J. Summers (New York: Henry Holt, 1995), 228–36.
18. L. Senelick, "Mollies or Men of Mode? Sodomy and the Eighteenth-century London Stage," *Journal of the History of Sexuality* 1, no. 1 (1990): 33–67.
19. Young, *King James,* 146.
20. D. Foxon, *Libertine Literature in England, 1660–1745* (New Hyde, NY: 1964), 7–10.
21. Bray, *Homosexuality in Renaissance England.*
22. R. Norton, ed., "A Sodomite Club in Warrington, 1806," *Homosexuality in Eighteenth-Century England: A Sourcebook,* May 5, 2008. Available at http://rictornorton.co.uk/eighteen/1806lanc.htm (accessed April 9, 2009).
23. R. Norton, ed., "Sodomy in Bristol," in *Homosexuality in Eighteenth-Century England: A Sourcebook,* December 10, 2003, updated February 28, 2007. Available at http://rictornorton.co.uk/eighteen/bristol.htm (accessed April 9, 2009); S. Poole, "'Bringing Great Shame upon This City': Sodomy, the Courts and the Civic Idiom in Eighteenth-century Bristol," *Urban History* 34, no. 1 (2007): 114–26. The following review is based on Bray, *Homosexuality in Renaissance England*; R. Norton, "Recovering Gay History from the Old Bailey," *London Journal* 30, no. 1 (2005): 39–54; R. Norton, *Mother Clap's Molly House: The Gay Subculture in England 1700–1830,* 2nd rev. ed. (Stroud, Glos.: Chalford Press, 2006[1992]); and the works by Trumbach cited in note 15. Many of the primary documents are reproduced on my Web site, *Homosexuality in Eighteenth-Century England: A Sourcebook,* updated March 15, 2009. Available at http://rictornorton.co.uk/eighteen/ (accessed April 9, 2009).
24. Trumbach, "London."
25. D. J. Noordam, "Sodomy in the Dutch Republic, 1600–1725," in *The Pursuit of Sodomy: Male Homosexuality in Renaissance and Enlightenment Europe,* ed. K. Gerard and G. Hekma (New York: Harrington Park Press, 1989), 207–28.
26. T. van der Meer, "The Persecutions of Sodomites in Eighteenth-century Amsterdam: Changing Perceptions of Sodomy," in *The Pursuit of Sodomy: Male Homosexuality in Renaissance and Enlightenment Europe,* ed. K. Gerard and G. Hekma (New York: Harrington Park Press, 1989), 263–307.
27. Details of more than 250 trials are summarized by L. W. A. M. von Römer, "Uranism in the Netherlands up to the Nineteenth Century with Special Emphasis on the Numerous Persecutions of Uranism in 1730: A Historic and Bibliographic Study," trans. M. A. Lombardi-Nash, in *Sodomites and Urnings: Homosexual Representations in Classic German Journals,* ed. and trans. M. A. Lombardi-Nash (New York: Harrington Park Press, 2006), 127–219.
28. R. Norton, ed., "Newspaper Reports: The Dutch Purge of Homosexuals, 1730," *Homosexuality in Eighteenth-Century England: A Sourcebook,* September 13, 2000, updated February 28, 2003. Available at http://www.rictornorton.co.uk/eighteen/1730news.htm (accessed April 9, 2009).

29. A. H. Huussen Jr., "Sodomy in the Dutch Republic during the Eighteenth Century," in *'Tis Nature's Fault: Unauthorized Sexuality during the Enlightenment*, ed. R. P. Maccubbin (New York: Cambridge University Press, 1987), 169–78; G. Hekma, "Amsterdam," in *Queer Sites: Gay Urban Histories since 1600*, ed. D. Higgs (London: Routledge, 1989), 61–88.
30. Noordam, "Sodomy in the Dutch Republic."
31. Boon, "Those Damned Sodomites."
32. von Römer, "Uranism in the Netherlands," 162.
33. T. van der Meer, "Sodomy and the Pursuit of a Third Sex in the Early Modern Period," in *Third Sex, Third Gender*, ed. G. Herdt (New York: Zone Books, 1996).
34. L. Mott, "Love's Labors Lost: Five Letters from a Seventeenth-century Portuguese Sodomite," in *The Pursuit of Sodomy: Male Homosexuality in Renaissance and Enlightenment Europe*, ed. K. Gerard and G. Hekma (New York: Harrington Park Press, 1989), 91–101.
35. D. Higgs, "Lisbon," in *Queer Sites: Gay Urban Histories since 1600*, ed. D. Higgs (London: Routledge, 1999), 112–37.
36. Ibid.
37. M. Rey, "Parisian Homosexuals Create a Lifestyle, 1700–1750: The Police Archives," in *'Tis Nature's Fault: Unauthorized Sexuality during the Enlightenment*, ed. R. P. Maccubbin (New York: Cambridge University Press, 1987), 186.
38. Ibid., 186.
39. Ibid., 179–80.
40. J. Merrick, "The Arrest of a Sodomite, 1723," *Gay and Lesbian Review Worldwide* 8, no. 5 (September 1, 2001), 29–30.
41. R. Oresko, "Homosexuality and the Court Elites of Early Modern France," in *The Pursuit of Sodomy: Male Homosexuality in Renaissance and Enlightenment Europe*, ed. K. Gerard and G. Hekma (New York: Harrington Park Press, 1989), 105–28.
42. O. Blanc, "The 'Italian Taste' in the Time of Louis XVI, 1774–92," in *Homosexualitiy in French History and Culture*, ed. J. Merrick and M. Sibalis (New York: Harrington Park Press, 2001), 69–84.
43. M. Rey, "Police and Sodomy in Eighteenth-century Paris: From Sin to Disorder," in *The Pursuit of Sodomy: Male Homosexuality in Renaissance and Enlightenment Europe*, ed. K. Gerard and G. Hekma (New York: Harrington Park Press, 1989), 129–46.
44. Ibid., 145.
45. J. Steakley, "Sodomy in Enlightenment Prussia: From Execution to Suicide," in *The Pursuit of Sodomy: Male Homosexuality in Renaissance and Enlightenment Europe*, ed. K. Gerard and G. Hekma (New York: Harrington Park Press, 1989), 163–75.
46. A. A. Kuzniar, ed., *Outing Goethe and His Age* (Palo Alto, CA: Stanford University Press, 1996); R. D. Tobin, *Warm Brothers: Queer Theory and the Age of Goethe* (Philadelphia: University of Pennsylvania Press, 2000).
47. R. Brooks, "'Vices Once Adopted': Theorising Male Homoeroticism in German-language Legal and Forensic Discourses, 1752–1869," *Reinvention: A Journal of*

Undergraduate Research 1, no. 2 (2008). Available at http://www2.warwick.ac.uk/go/reinventionjournal/issues/volume1issue2/Brooks.
48. Trumbach, "The Birth of the Queen."
49. Norton, *The Myth of the Modern Homosexual*, 245–48.
50. C. A. Lyons, "Mapping an Atlantic Sexual Culture: Homoeroticism in Eighteenth-century Philadelphia," *William and Mary Quarterly* 60, no. 1 (2003): 119–54.
51. W. Benemann, *Male-Male Intimacy in Early America: Beyond Romantic Friendships* (New York: Harrington Park Press, 2006).
52. D. Higgs, "Rio de Janeiro," in *Queer Sites: Gay Urban Histories since 1600*, ed. D. Higgs (London: Routledge, 1999), 138–63.
53. J. Marten, *A Treatise of All the Degrees and Symptoms of the Venereal Disease, in Both Sexes* (London: Sixth Edition corrected and enlarg'd, 1709), 68–69.
54. T. van der Meer, "European Oral Sex," e-mail to History of Sexuality List, May 1, 2001, Histsex Archives. Available at http://homepages.primex.co.uk/~lesleyah/hsxarc31.htm (accessed April 9, 2009).
55. von Römer, "Uranism in the Netherlands."
56. For example, in 1772 Charles Gibson kissed a nineteen-year-old man at a London inn, then went out back with him to urinate, where he took hold of his penis and admired it; then they went into the pub's privy, where Gibson pushed the other man down on the seat and masturbated him until he came; then kissed him "very heartily" while putting the man's hands on his own penis; then began tickling, rubbing, kissing, and sucking the other man's penis until it was again erect, then turned around and sat down naked on the man's lap, directing his penis into his body. Afterwards, he asked the other man to change positions with him.
57. Norton, "Recovering Gay History from the Old Bailey."
58. R. L. Dawson, "The *Mélange de poésies diverse* (1781) and the Diffusion of Manuscript Pornography in Eighteenth-century France," in *'Tis Nature's Fault: Unauthorized Sexuality during the Enlightenment*, ed. R. P. Maccubbin (New York: Cambridge University Press, 1987), 229–43.
59. A. Carter, *The Sadeian Woman* (London: Virago, 1979).
60. J. Peakman, *Lascivious Bodies: A Sexual History of the Eighteenth Century* (London: Atlantic Books, 2004).
61. H. Gladfelder, "In Search of Lost Texts: Thomas Cannon's *Ancient and Modern Pederasty Investigated and Exemplify'd*," *Eighteenth-Century Life* 31, no. 1 (2007): 22–38; H. Gladfelder, ed., "The Indictment of John Purser, Containing Thomas Cannon's *Ancient and Modern Pederasty Investigated and Exemplify'd*," *Eighteenth-Century Life* 31, no. 1 (2007): 39–61.
62. K. L. Cope, ed., *Eighteenth-Century British Erotica*, Set 1, Vol. 2: *Edmund Curll and Grub-Street Highlights* (London: Pickering & Chatto, 2002), 403–46.
63. J. Peakman, *Mighty Lewd Books: The Development of Pornography in Eighteenth-Century England* (London: Palgrave Macmillan, 2003), 59; R. Norton, ed., "Memoirs of Antonina [Marie Antoinette], 1791," *Homosexuality in Eighteenth-Century England: A Sourcebook*, July 24, 2002. Available at http://rictornorton.co.uk/eighteen/antonina.htm.

64. L. Crompton, "The Myth of Lesbian Impunity: Capital Laws from 1270 to 1791," in *The Gay Past: A Collection of Historical Essays*, ed. S. J. Licata and R. P. Petersen (New York: Harrington Park Press, 1985), 11–25.

65. B. Eriksson, "A Lesbian Execution in Germany, 1721: The Trial Records," in *The Gay Past: A Collection of Historical Essays*, ed. S. J. Licata and R. P. Petersen (New York: Harrington Park Press, 1985), 27–40.

66. R. Norton, *Eighteenth-Century British Erotica*, Set 1, Vol. 5: *Sodomites, Mollies, Sapphists and Tommies* (London: Pickering & Chatto, 2002), 107–10.

67. E. Donoghue, *Passions between Women: British Lesbian Culture, 1668–1801* (London: Scarlet Press, 1993).

68. R. Norton, ed., "The Case of Catherine Vizzani, 1755," *Homosexuality in Eighteenth-Century England: A Sourcebook*, December 1, 2005. Available at http://rictornorton.co.uk/eighteen/vizzani.htm (accessed April 9, 2009).

69. F. Easton, "Gender's Two Bodies: Women Warriors, Female Husbands and Plebian Life," *Past and Present* 180, no. 1 (2003): 131–74.

70. S. Baker, "Henry Fielding's *The Female Husband*: Fact and Fiction," *PMLA* 74, no. 3 (June 1959): 213–24; T. Castle, "'Matters Not Fit to Be Mentioned': Fielding's *The Female Husband*," *English Literary History* 49 (1982): 602–23.

71. L. Faderman, *Surpassing the Love of Men: Romantic Friendship and Love Between Women from the Renaissance to the Present* (London: Women's Press, 1985).

72. M. Vicinus, *Intimate Friends: Women Who Loved Women, 1778–1928* (Chicago: University of Chicago Press, 2004), 6.

73. E. Mavor, *The Ladies of Llangollen: A Study of Romantic Friendship* (Joseph, 1971).

74. Donoghue, *Passions between Women*.

75. Cited by Faderman, *Surpassing the Love of Men*, 110.

76. Norton, *Eighteenth-Century British Erotica*, Set 1, Vol. 5, 355–79.

77. Donoghue, *Passions between Women*, 242; see also S. Lanser, "'Au sein de vos pareilles': Sapphic Separatism in Late Eighteenth-century France," in *Homosexualitiy in French History and Culture*, ed. J. Merrick and M. Sibalis (New York: Harrington Park Press, 2001), 105–16.

78. R. Trumbach, "London's Sapphists: From Three Sexes to Four Genders in the Making of Modern Culture," in *Body Guards: The Cultural Politics of Gender Ambiguity*, ed. J. Epstein and K. Straub (London: Routledge, 1991), 112–41.

79. For example, Donoghue, *Passions between Women*, 20–21.

80. H. Whitbread ed., A. Lister, *I Know My Own Heart: The Diaries of Annje Lister 1791–1840*, (London: Virago, 1988); H. Whitbread ed., A. Lister, *No Priest But Love: Excerpts from the Diaries of Anne Lister, 1824–1826*, (New York: New York University Press, 1992); A. Clark, "Anne Lister's Construction of Lesbian Identity," *Journal of the History of Sexuality* 7, no. 1 (1996): 23–50; R, Norton, "Anne Lister, The First Modern Lesbian," August 1, 2003, updated June 13, 2008. Available at http://rictornorton.co.uk/lister.htm (accessed April 9, 2009).

81. Norton, *Mother Clap's Molly House*, 91–92.

82. Anonymous, "Les petits bougres au manège" (1790), trans. M. West, in *We Are Everywhere: A Historical Sourcebook of Gay and Lesbian Politics*, ed. M. Blasius and S. Phelen (New York: Routledge, 1997), 37–39.

83. M. Delon, "The Priest, the Philosopher, and Homosexuality in Enlightenment France," in *'Tis Nature's Fault: Unauthorized Sexuality during the Enlightenment*, ed. R. P. Maccubbin (New York: Cambridge University Press, 1987), 122–31.
84. von Römer, "Uranism in the Netherlands," 138.
85. Documents totalling more than 40,000 words are reproduced by R. Norton, "The First Public Debate about Homosexuality in England: The Case of Captain Jones, 1772," *Homosexuality in Eighteenth-Century England: A Sourcebook*, December 19, 2004, updated April 3, 2007. Available at http://rictornorton.co.uk/eighteen/jones1.htm (accessed April 9, 2009). For a full discussion see Norton, *Mother Clap's Molly House*, 282–306.
86. L. Crompton, introd. and ed., "Jeremy Bentham's Essay on 'Paederasty,'" *Journal of Homosexuality* 3 (1978): 383–405; and 4 (1978): 91–107.
87. A. D. Harvey, *Sex in Georgian England*, rev. ed. (London: Phoenix Press, 2001), 125–26.
88. G. Haggerty, *Men in Love: Masculinity and Sexuality in the Eighteenth Century* (New York: Columbia University Press, 1999).
89. Bray, *Homosexuality in Renaissance England*, 112.

Chapter 4

1. W. P. de Silva, "Sexual Variations," *British Medical Journal* 318 (1999): 654.
2. Roy Porter, *English Society in the Eighteenth Century* (Harmondsworth: Penguin, 1982), 278.
3. Karen Harvey, "The Century of Sex? Gender, Bodies, and Sexuality in the Long Eighteenth Century," *The Historical Journal* 45, no. 4 (2002): 900; see also Julie Peakman, *Lascivious Bodies: A Sexual History of the Eighteenth Century* (London: Atlantic, 2004), 281.
4. Julie Peakman, ed., *Sexual Perversions, 1670–1890* (Basingstoke: Palgrave Macmillan, 2009), 1–49.
5. Giles Jacob, "Buggery," in *A New Law-Dictionary: Containing the Interpretation and Definition of Words and Terms Used in the Law, etc.* (London: E. & R. Nutt & R. Gosling, 1729).
6. He actually referred to Exodus (22:19) and Leviticus (20:15 and 20:16). Daniel Jousse, *Traite de la justice criminelle de France* (Paris, 1771), t. 4, 122.
7. Pierre Francois Muyart de Vouglans, *Les Loix Criminelles de France, dans leur ordre naturel, etc.* (Paris, 1780), 244; Gaston Dubois-Desaulle, *Etude sur la Bestialite au point de vue Historique, Medical et Juridique* (Paris: Charles Carrington, 1905), 226.
8. *Riforma della legislazione criminale toscana del dì 30 novembre 1786* (Siena, [1786]), 53.
9. *Die Peinliche Gerichtsordnung Kaiser Karls V.: Constitutio Criminalis Carolina*. Kritisch herausgegeben von J. Kohler und W. Scheel (Berlin, 1900); Friedrichs Wilhelms, Königes in Preussen, verbessertes *Land-Recht des Königreichs Preussen*, etc. [27 June, 1721.] Königsberg, 1721. B. VI, s. 154.
10. Kathryn Preyer, "Crime, the Criminal Law and Reform in Post-Revolutionary Virginia," *Law and History Review* 1, no. 1 (1983): 58–59.

11. John M. Murrin, "'Things Fearful to Name': Bestiality in Colonial America," *Pennsylvania History* 65, supplement (1998): 18, 16.
12. Sir Edward Coke, *Institutions of the Laws of England*, part 3 (London: W. Rawlins, 1680), 58–59.
13. William Blackstone, *Commentaries on the Laws of England*, vol. 2 (Philadelphia, 1893), 215–16.
14. Sir George Mackenzie, *Lawes and Customs of Scotland in Matters Criminal* (Edinburgh, 1699), 81.
15. David Hume, *Commentaries on the Law of Scotland*, vol. 2 (Edinburgh, 1797), 336.
16. Jonas Liliequist, "Sexual Encounters with Spirits and Demons in Early Modern Sweden: Popular and Learned Concepts in Conflicts and Interation," in *Christian Demonology and Popula Mythology: The Role of Aesthetic Imagination in Human Society*, ed. Gabor Klaniczay, Eva Pocs, and Eszter Csonka-Takacs (Budapest: CEU Press, 2005), 153–55.
17. "Artikul Voinskij," in *Zakonodatel'stvo perioda stanovlenija absolutizma*, ed. A. G. Man'kov (Moscow, 1986), 358.
18. A. Pavlov, *Nomokanon pri Bol'shom Trebnike* (Odessa, 1872), 66; National Library of Russia, f. 775, no. 2060, p. 11rev.; f.573, SPBDA 130, p. 21.
19. Joseph R. Rosenberg, *Bestiality* (Los Angeles: Medco Books, 1968), 28.
20. James D. Steakey, "Sodomy in Enlightenment Prussia: From Execution to Suicide," in *The Pursuit of Sodomy: Male Homosexuality in Renaissance and Enlightenment Europe*, ed. Kent Gerard and Gert Hekma (New York: Routledge, 1989), 164.
21. Polly Morris, "Sodomy and Male Honour: The Case of Somerset, 1740–1850," in *The Pursuit of Sodomy: Male Homosexuality in Renaissance and Enlightenment Europe*, ed. Kent Gerard and Gert Hekma (New York: Routledge, 1989), 389.
22. Arend H. Huussen Jr., "Prosecution of Sodomy in Eighteenth Century Frisia, Netherlands," in *The Pursuit of Sodomy: Male Homosexuality in Renaissance and Enlightenment Europe*, ed. Kent Gerard and Gert Hekma (New York: Routledge, 1989), 257.
23. P. G. Maxwell-Stuart, "'Wild, Filthie, Execrabil, Detestabill, and Unnatural Sin': Bestiality in Early Modern Scotland," in *Sodomy in Early Modern Europe*, ed. Thomas Betteridge (Manchester: Manchester University Press, 2002), 89.
24. Dubois-Desaulle, *Etude sur la Bestialite*, 211.
25. Henry Bamford Parkes, "Morals and Law Enforcement in Colonial New England," *The New England Quarterly* 5, no. 3 (1932): 445.
26. Andre Fernandez, "The Repression of Sexual Behavior by the Aragonese Inquisition between 1560 and 1700," *Journal of the History of Sexuality* 7, no. 4 (1997): 480–81.
27. Jonas Liliequist, "State Policy, Popular Discourse, and the Silence on Homosexual Acts in Early Modern Sweden," in *Scandinavian Homosexualities: Essays on Gay and Lesbian Studies*, ed. Jan Löfström (New York: Haworth Press, 1998), 15–52.

28. Jonas Liliequist, "Peasants against Nature, Crossing the Boundaries between Man and Animal in Seventeenth- and Eighteenth-Century Sweden," *Journal of the History of Sexuality* 1 (1991): 393–423.
29. Liliequist, "Sexual Encounters with Spirits and Demons," 160–65; Liliequist, "Peasants against Nature," 399, esp. 408–411.
30. John D'Emilio and Estelle B. Freedman, *Intimate Matters: A History of Sexuality in America* (Chicago: University of Chicago Press, 1997), 17. For contemporary fears, see Midas Dekkers, *Dearest Pet: On Bestiality* (London: Verso, 1992), 75–91.
31. A. D. Harvey, *Sex in Georgian England* (London: Duckworth, 1994), 123. About English anxieties, see Erica Fudge, "Monstrous Acts: Bestiality in Early Modern England," *History Today* 50, no. 8 (2003): 20–25; Erica Fudge, *Perceiving Animals: Humans and Beasts in Early Modern English Culture* (Basingstoke: Macmillan, 2000), esp. chapter 5; Keith Thomas, *Man and the Natural World: Changing Attitudes in England 1500–1800* (Harmondsworth: Penguin, 1984); Dudley Wilson, *Signs and Portents: Monstrous Births from the Middle Ages to the Enlightenment* (New York: Routledge, 1993).
32. Coke, *Institutions of the Laws of England*, 58–59. Coke gives an example of a "great lady" who conceives after having sex with a baboon.
33. Arthur N. Gilbert, "Buggery and the British Navy, 1700–1861," *Journal of Social History* 10, no. 1 (1976): 93 no. 39.
34. Danielle Jousse, *Traite de la justice criminelle*, t. 4, 122.
35. Dubois-Desaulle, *Etude sur la Bestialite*, 213.
36. Maxwell-Stuart, "'Wild, Filthie, Execrabil, Detestabill, and Unnatural Sin,'" 87.
37. Murrin, "'Things Fearful to Name,'" 14–15.
38. See Muyart de Vouglans, *Les Loix Criminelles de France*, 244.
39. D'Emilio and Freedman, *Intimate Matters*, 17.
40. Murrin, "'Things Fearful to Name,'" 10.
41. TsGIA SPB, f. 1740, op. 1, no. 19, p. 1rev.
42. Liliequist, "Peasants against Nature," 407–8.
43. Dubois-Desaulle, *Etude sur la Bestialite*, 125–214.
44. Fernandez, "The Repression of Sexual Behavior," 479.
45. Maxwell-Stuart, "'Wild, Filthie, Execrabil, Detestabill, and Unnatural Sin,'" 87.
46. Thomas, *Man and the Natural World*, 98.
47. Murrin, "'Things Fearful to Name,'" 9.
48. D'Emilio and Freedman, *Intimate Matters*, 17.
49. Murrin, "'Things Fearful to Name,'" 11.
50. Hani Miletski, "A History of Bestiality," in *Bestiality and Zoophilia: Sexual Relations with Animals*, ed. Andrea M. Beetz and Anthony L. Podberscek (West Lafayette, IN: Purdue University Press, 2005), 7.
51. J. Stengers and A. Van Neck, *Histoire d'unegrande peur: la masturbation* (Brussels: Éditions de l'Université de Bruxelles, 1984), 29–32.
52. *Die Peinliche Gerichtsordnung Kaiser Karls V.: Constitutio Criminalis Carolina*. Kritisch herausgegeben von J. Kohler und W. Scheel (Berlin, 1900).

53. Benedicto Carpzov, *Practicae Novae Imperialis Saxonicae. Rerum Criminalium*, Pars II (Witengergae, 1670), 210.
54. See especially, Augustin Leyser, *Meditationes ad Pandectas*, vol. 1 (Leipzig/Wolfenbüttel, Meisner, 1748), 589 seqq.
55. John D'Emilio and Estelle B. Freedman, "Family Life and the Regulation of Deviance," in *Sexualities in History: A Reader*, ed. Kim M. Philips and Barry Reay (New York: Routledge, 2002), 141.
56. Murrin, "'Things Fearful to Name,'" 20.
57. On that, see Francz X. Eder, "Sexualized Subjects: Medical Discourses on Sexuality in German-Speaking Countries in the Late 18th Century and in the 19th Century," in *Civilization, Sexuality and Social Life in Historical Context: The Hidden Face of Urban Life—International Conference, Budapest, 1995*, ed. Judith Forrai (Budapest: SOTE UP, 1996), 17–29.
58. Thomas Laqueur, *Solitary Sex: A Cultural History of Masturbation* (New York: Zone Books, 2003), 16; see chapter 2 and 3 on *Onania*.
59. This idea is mostly based on the presumption that there were no such sources as *Onania* in previous centuries, and the sources in general kept silence about it. See Edward Shorter, *The Making of the Modern Family* (New York: Basic, 1977), 119.
60. Lawrence Stone, *The Family, Sex and Marriage in England 1500–1800* (New York: Harper and Row, 1977), 515; Isabel V. Hull, *Sexuality, State and Civil Society in Germany 1700–1815* (Ithaca, NY: Cornell University Press, 1996), 260–61.
61. Tim Hitchcock, *English Sexualities, 1700–1800* (New York: St. Martin's Press, 1997), 56–57.
62. About that, see Patrick Singy, "Friction of the Genitals and Secularization of Morality," *Journal of the History of Sexuality* 12, no. 3 (2003): 345.
63. Ibid., 349–63.
64. Brian D. Carroll, "'I Indulged My Desire Too Freely': Sexuality, Spirituality, and the Sin of Self-Pollution in the Diary of Joseph Moody, 1720–1724," *The William and Mary Quarterly* 60, no. 1 (2003): 170.
65. See also on *Onania*, Michael Stolberg, "Self-Pollution, Moral Reform, and the Venereal Trade: Notes on the Sources and Historical Context of Onania (1716)," *Journal of the History of Sexuality* 9, no. 1/2 (2000): 37–61.
66. Peter Wagner, "The Veil of Medicine and Morality: Some Pornographic Aspects of the *Onania*," *The British Journal for Eighteenth-Century Studies* 6 (1983): 179–84.
67. The Russian edition appeared in 1793, then two subsequent editions in 1822 and 1823, and four other editions by the end of the nineteenth century. It was known and read. Russian political philosopher Alexandr Radischev warned young people to restrain their desires and read Tissot's book in order to know all the "horrors" of masturbation. See Alexandr Radischev, "O Cheloveke, Ego Smertnosti i Bessmertiji," in *Sobranie Sochinenij*, vol. 2, ed. Alexandr Radischev (Moscow-Leningrad, Izdatel'stro Akademiji Naul SSSR, 1941), 70.
68. See Tissot's other works, "Avis au peuple sur sa santé" (Losanne, 1761); "Dissertation sur les parties sensibles et irritables des animaux" (Losanne, 1757); "Mémoire sur le mouvement du sang et sur les effets de la saignée" (Losanne, 1757); "Dissertatio

de febribus biliosis" (Losanne, 1768), "Tentament de morbis ex manustupratione ortis" (Losanne, 1760); "De valetudine litteratorum" (Losanne, 1766): "Epistolae medico-practiae" (Losanne, 1770); "Traité de l'épilepsie" (Paris, 1772); and "Traité des nerfs et de leurs maladies" (Paris, 1782).
69. For the situation in Germany, see Franz X. Eder, "Discourse and Sexual Desire: German-Language Discourse on Masturbation in the Late Eighteenth Century," *Journal of the History of Sexuality* 13, no. 4 (2004): 428–45; and for the situation in Britain, see Harvey, *Sex in Georgian England,* 116–22.
70. D'Emilio and Freedman, *Intimate Matters,* 20.
71. Carroll, "'I Indulged My Desire Too Freely,'" 155–65.
72. Ibid., 167.
73. David Stevenson, "Recording the Unspeakable: Masturbation in the Diary of William Drummond, 1657–1659," *Journal of the History of Sexuality* 9, no. 3 (2000): 233.
74. Hitchcock, *English Sexualities,* 28–29, 14.
75. Ivan Dolgorukov, *Povest' o Rozhdeniji Mojem, Proishozhdeniji i Vsej Zhizni …,* vol. 1 (St. Petersburg: Nauka, 2004), 42, 747.
76. Jean-Jacques Rousseau, *Confessions,* ed. P. Coleman (Oxford: Oxford University Press, 2006), 106.
77. See this point at Kathleen Verduin, "'Our Cursed Natures': Sexuality and the Puritan Conscience," *New England Quarterly* 56 (1983): 222–24.
78. Carroll, "'I Indulged My Desire Too Freely,'" 159, esp. no. 21.
79. Ibid., 160.
80. Dolgorukov, *Povest' o Rozhdeniji Mojem,* 42.
81. On the Galenic model of the body physiology, see Thomas Laqueur, *Making Sex: Body and Gender from the Greeks to Freud* (Cambridge, MA: Harvard University Press, 1990): 25, 115; Anthony Fletcher, *Gender, Sex, and Subordination in England, 1500–1800* (New Haven, CT: Yale University Press, 1995), 33–59, 83–98; and Ava Chamberlain, "The Immaculate Ovum: Jonathan Edwards and the Construction of the Female Body," *William and Mary Quarterly* 57 (2000): 289–301.
82. Rousseau, *Confessions,* 106.
83. See in detail about the text, Manuela Mourao, "The Representation of Female Desire in Early Modern Pornographic Texts, 1660–1745," *Signs* 24, no. 3 (1999): 583–84.
84. Gervaise de Latouch, *L'Histoire de Dom Bourge, portier de Chartreaux* ([Paris]: le Grand livre du mois, 1993).
85. Lyndal Roper, "'Evil Imaginings and Fantasies': Child-Witches and the End of the Witch Craze," in *Gender in Early Modern German History,* ed. Ulinka Rublack (Cambridge: Cambridge University Press, 2002), 116–17.
86. Robert Sumser, "'Erziehung,' the Family, and the Regulation of Sexuality on the Late German Enlightenment," *German Studies Review* 15, no. 3 (1992): 463.
87. Bernard Mandeville, *The Modest Defense of Public Stews* (London, A. Moore, 1724). See, G. J. Barker-Benfield, *The Culture of Sensibility. Sex and Society in Eighteenth Century Britain* (Chicago: University of Chicago Press, 1992), 126.
88. Harvey, *Sex in Georgian England,* 118.

89. Jan Oosterhoff, "Sodomy at Sea and at the Cape of Good Hope during the Eighteenth Century," in *The Pursuit of Sodomy: Male Homosexuality in Renaissance and Enlightenment Europe,* ed. Kent Gerard and Gert Hekma (New York: Routledge, 1989), 233–34.
90. National Library of Russia (hereafter NLR). Manuscripts Department, f. 728, Sof. 1183, p. 98 rev. About Russian confessional guides, see Marija V. Karogodina, *Ispoved' v Rossiji v XIV-XIX vv.* (St. Petersburg: Dmitry Bulanin, 2006).
91. NLR, f. 728, Sof. 1183, p. 32 rev.; A. Pavlov, *Nomokanon pri Bol'shom Trebnike* (Odessa, 1872), 80.
92. See, for example, L. Habert, *Pratique de sacrament de penitence pour l'administer utilement* (Paris, 1748). For Catholic discourse on masturbation, see Pierre Hurteau, "Moral Discourse on Male Sodomy and Masturbation in the Seventeenth and Eighteenth Centuries," *Journal of the History of Sexuality* 4, no. 1 (1993): 1–26.
93. Michael Ray, "Police and Sodomy in 18th Century Paris," in *The Pursuit of Sodomy: Male Homosexuality in Renaissance and Enlightenment Europe,* ed. Kent Gerard and Gert Hekma (New York: Routledge, 1989), 138–39.
94. Eder, "Discourse and Sexual Desire," 444.
95. Randolph Trumbach, *Sex and Gender Revolution, Vol. 1: Heterosexuality and the Third Gender in Enlightenment London* (Chicago: University of Chicago Press, 1998), 63–64.
96. A. A. Brille, "Necrophilia," *Journal of the Criminal Psychopathology* 2 (1941): 433–53; and vol. 3, 51–73; Janos Boros, Ivan Munnich, and Marton Szegedi, eds., *Psychology and Criminal Justice: International Review of Theory and Practice* (Berlin: de Gruyter, 1998), 243.
97. Johann G. von Reichell, *Rassuzhdenija o Prestupleniji i Nakazaniji,* vol. 1 (St. Petersburg, 1779), 420. NLR, f. 885, no. 48-1.
98. Camille Naish, *Death Comes to the Maiden: Sex and Execution 1431–1933* (London: Routledge, 1991), 8, 82.
99. V.A.C. Gatrell, *The Hanging Tree: Execution and the English People 1770–1868* (Oxfrod: Oxford University Press, 1996), 264–65.
100. Edward Nye, *Literary and Linguistic Theories in Eighteenth-Century France* (Oxford: Oxford University Press, 2000), 221–22.
101. William Cobbett, *The Cannibal's Progress, or the Dreadful Horrors of French Invasion* (London: Wright, Cadel and others, 1798), 9. See, for example, German pamphlet, Dr. Vincent, *The Lamentations of Germany* (London, 1638), which is full of horrible details of cannibalism, rape, necrophilia, and so on.
102. Philippe Aries, *L'Homme devant la Mort* (Paris: Editions du Seuil, 1977), 373.
103. Ian Gibson, *The English Vice: Beating, Sex and Shame in Victorian England and After* (London: Duckworth, 1978), 1–15.
104. Julie Peakman, *Mightly Lewd Books: The Development of Ponrpgraphy in Eighteenth-Century England* (Basingstoke: Palgrave, 2003).
105. Henry Spencer Ashbee, *Index of Forbidden Books* (London: Sphere Books, 1969), 147–51.

106. Lawrence Stone, "Libertine Sexuality in Post-Restoration England: Group Sex and Flagellation among the Middling Sort in Norwich in 1706–1707," *Journal of the History of Sexuality* 2, no. 4 (1992): 517–19.
107. Harvey, *Sex in Georgian England*, 35–37.
108. For other types of variations, see Peakman, *Lascivious Bodies*, 262–80.
109. Stone, "Libertine Sexuality," 522.
110. Hitchcock, *English Sexualities*, 29.
111. About voyeuristic motifs in art, see Mirjam Westen, "The Woman on a Swing and the Sensuous Voyeur: Passion and Voyeurism in French Rococo," in *From Sappho to De Sade: Moments in the History of Sexuality*, ed. Jan N. Bremmer (London: Routledge, 1991), 69–83.
112. See pictures in Gilles Neret, *Erotica Universalis* (Bonn: Benedikt Taschen, 1994), 118–19, 124, 335.
113. Entry for July 1, 1663, of Pepys diary in Robert Latham and William Matthews, eds., *The Diary of Samuel Pepys*, vol. 4 (London: Penguin, 2003), 209.

Chapter 5

1. James McMullin v. Wilkin and Hickman, ADI file 1792 and 1794, Chester County Archives, Chester County, PA. Merril D. Smith, *Breaking the Bonds: Marital Discord in Pennsylvania, 1730–1830* (New York: New York University Press, 1991), chapter 4.
2. Hambleton, "The Regulation of Sex in Seventeenth-Century Massachusetts" 89–115.
3. Patricia Crawford, *Blood, Bodies and Families in Early Modern England* (Harlow, England: Pearson Longman, 2004), 61.
4. Mary Beth Norton, *Founding Mothers and Fathers*, chapter 4; Else L. Hambleton, *Daughters of Eve: Pregnant Brides and Unwed Mothers in Seventeenth-Century Massachusetts* (New York: Routledge, 2004).
5. Richard Godbeer, *Sexual Revolution in Early America* (Baltimore: John Hopkins University Press, 2002), 25.
6. Cotton Mather, *Bonifacius: An Essay upon the Good*, ed. D. Levin (Cambridge, 1966), 85, quoted in Godbeer, *Sexual Revolution*, 89.
7. Kathleen M. Brown, *Good Wives, Nasty Wenches, and Anxious Patriarchs: Gender, Race, and Power in Colonial Virginia* (Chapel Hill: University of North Carolina Press, 1996), 147–48.
8. Goodbeer, *Sexual Revolution*, 26–27.
9. Crawford, *Blood, Bodies, and Families*, 68–69; Renato Barahona, *Sex Crimes, Honor, and the Law in Early Modern Spain: Vizcaya, 1528–1735* (Toronto: University of Toronto Press, 2003), 30, 111; Laura Gowing, "Language, Power, and the Law: Women's Slander Litigation in Early Modern Europe," in *Women, Crime, and the Courts in Early Modern England*, ed. Jennifer Kermode and Garthine Walker (Chapel Hill: The University of North Carolina Press, 1994), 26–27; Sheilagh Ogilvie, "How Does Social Capital Affect Women: Guilds and

Communities in Early Modern Europe," *American Historical Review* 109, no. 2 (2004): 354–55.
10. Brian P. Levack, *The Witch-Hunt in Early Modern Europe*, 3rd ed. (London: Pearson Longman, 2006), 141–42.
11. Ibid., 145–46, 152–53.
12. Quoted in Carol R. Karlsen, *The Devil in the Shape of a Woman: Witchcraft in Colonial New England* (New York: Vintage Books, 1989) p. 141.
13. Levack, *The Witch-Hunt in Early Modern Europe*, 147.
14. Karlsen, 43–45; John Putnam Demos, *Entertaining Satan: Witchcraft and the Culture of Early New England* (New York: Oxford University Press, 1982), 387–94; Levack, *The Witch-Hunt in Early Modern Europe*, 268–69.
15. Merry E. Wiesner-Hanks, *Christianity and Sexuality in the Early Modern World: Regulating Desire, Reforming Practice* (New York: Routledge, 2000), 122.
16. Ibid., 84.
17. Patricia Crawford, "The Construction and Experience of Maternity in Seventeenth-Century England," in *Women as Mothers in Pre-Industrial England: Essays in Memory of Dorothy McLaren*, ed. Valerie Fildes (London: Routledge, 1990), 9–10.
18. Brown, *Good Wives*, 189–94; Mary Beth Norton, 335–38.
19. Hambleton, *Daughters of Eve*, 13–15; Laurel Thatcher Ulrich, *A Midwife's Tale: The Life of Martha Ballard, Based on Her Diary, 1785–1812* (New York: Knopf, 1990), 147–56.
20. Godbeer, *Sexual Revolution*, 228–29.
21. Ibid., 246.
22. Ibid., 247–51, 255.
23. Ibid., 257; Ulrich, *A Midwife's Tale*, 147–50.
24. Clare A. Lyons, *Sex among the Rabble: An Intimate History of Gender and Power in the Age of Revolution, Philadelphia, 1730–1830* (Chapel Hill: University of North Carolina Press, 2006), 60–61.
25. Cornelia Hughes Dayton, "Taking the Trade: Abortion and Gender Relations in an Eighteeenth-Century New England Village," *William and Mary Quarterly* 48, no. 1 (1991): 24–25.
26. Crawford, 71.
27. Cornelia Hughes Dayton, *Blood, Bodies, and Families*, "Taking the Trade," 19–23.
28. Wiesner-Hanks, *Christianity and Sexuality*, 83–84.
29. Ibid., 93. For an eighteenth-century infanticide case in which authorities were forced almost against their will to execute a woman for murdering her twin infants, see Merril D. Smith, "'Unnatural Mothers': Infanticide, Motherhood, and Class in the Mid-Atlantic, 1730–1830," in *Over the Threshold: Intimate Violence in Early America*, ed. Christine Daniels and Michael V. Kennedy (New York: Routledge, 1999).
30. Charles Biddle, *Autobiography of Charles Biddle* (Philadelphia, 1881), 202.
31. Smith, "'Unnatural Mothers,'" 176–77.

32. Nadia Maria Filippini, "The Church, the State, and Childbirth: The Midwife in Italy during the Eighteenth Century," in *The Art of Midwifery: Early Modern Midwives in Europe*, ed. Hilary Marland (London: Routledge, 1993), 156.
33. Hale, 635, quoted in Cornelia Hughes Dayton, *Women Before the Bar: Gender, Law and Society in Connecticut, 1639–1789* (Chapel Hill: University of North Catolina Press, 1995); Matthew Hale, *Historia Placitorum coronae: The History of the Pleas of the Crown* (London, 1736), 1, 61, 635.
34. Sharon Block, *Rape and Sexual Power in Early America* (Chapel Hill: University of North Carolina Press, 2006), 28–37.
35. Wiesner-Hanks, *Christianity and Sexuality*, 74.
36. Lawrence Stone, *The Family, Sex and Marriage in England 1500–1800*, abridged ed. (New York: Harper & Row, 1979), 30.
37. Stone, *The Family, Sex and Marriage*, 30–32.
38. Ibid., 32–33.
39. Wiesner-Hanks, *Christianity and Sexuality*, 121.
40. Lois C. Dubin, "Jewish Women, Marriage Law, and Emancipation: A Civil Divorce in Late-Eighteenth-Century Trieste," *Jewish Social Studies: History, Culture, Society* 13, no. 2 (2007): 66.
41. Hambleton, *Daughters of Eve*, 115–17.
42. Barry Levy, *Quakers and the American Family: British Settlement in the Delaware Valley* (New York: Oxford University Press, 1988), 73, 132–34.
43. Quoted in ibid., 212.
44. Cresswell, *Blood, Bodies, and Families*, 93, 100, 103–6, 122, quoted in Godbeer, *Sexual Revolution*, 184–85.
45. Lawrence Stone, *The Road to Divorce: England 1530–1987* (New York: Oxford University Press, 1990), 152; Stone, *The Family, Sex, and Marriage*, 34–35.
46. This case is explained in detail in Dubin, "Jewish Women, Marriage Law, and Emancipation."
47. Smith, *Breaking the Bonds*, 14.
48. "Divorce Papers, Plea of Eve Page," *Divorce Papers, 1785–1815*. Records of the Supreme Court (Eastern District) (Harrisburg, PA: Pennsylvania Historical and Museum Commission); Smith, *Breaking the Bonds*, 23–24.
49. "May 1650: An Act for suppressing the detestable sins of Incest, Adultery and Fornication," *Acts and Ordinances of the Interregnum, 1642–1660* (1911), 387–89. Available at http://www.british-history.ac.uk/report.aspx?compid=56682 (accessed May 26, 2008); Mary Elizabeth Fissell, *Vernacular Bodies: The Politics of Reproduction in Early Modern England* (New York: Oxford University Press, 2006), 173.
50. See Leviticus 20:13, 15–16; and Romans 1:26–27; John M. Murrin, "'Things Fearful to Name': Bestiality in Colonial America," *Explorations in Early American Culture Pennsylvania History. A Journal of Mid-Atlantic Studies* 65 (1998): 8.
51. Wiesner-Hanks, *Christianity and Sexuality*, 89.
52. Randolph Trumbach, "Sex, Gender, and Sexual Identity in Modern Culture: Male Sodomy and Female Prostitution in Enlightenment London," *Journal of the History of Sexuality* 2, no. 2 (1991): 192.

53. Murrin, "'Things Fearful to Name,'" 8; Wiesner-Hanks, *Christianity and Sexuality*, 89.
54. Rictor Norton, ed., "The Trial of Margaret Clap, 1726," in *Homosexuality in Eighteenth-Century England: A Sourcebook*, updated June 5, 2002. Available at http://www.rictornorton.co.uk/eighteen/clap.htm.
55. Trumbach, "Sex, Gender and Sexual Identity in Modern Culture" 196–201.
56. Lyons, *Sex among the Rabble*, 61–62.
57. da Costa Pereira, 65, cited in Lyons, *Sex among the Rabble*, 192.
58. Divorce Papers, Deposition of Griffith Jones, Burk v. Burk, 1797; and Chester County Divorce Papers, Deposition of Peter A. Brown, Wilkinson v. Wilkinson, 1810.
59. Lyons, *Sex among the Rabble*, 323–25.
60. Two examples of men who recorded their many sexual encounters are Virginia planter William Byrd and Jamaican overseer Thomas Thistlewood.
61. Gouge, 303, quoted in Crawford, *Blood, Bodies, and Families*, 61.
62. Hasra R. Diner and Beryl L. Broderly, *Her Works Praise Her* (New York: Basic Books, 2003), 18. Many Jewish women continue to follow this ritual.
63. Crawford, *Blood, Bodies, and Families*, 26–29, 47 no. 82; 29–30.
64. Carol Berkin, *First Generations: Women in Colonial America* (New York: Hill and Wang, 1996), 65–66.
65. Ibid., 66.
66. Godbeer, *Sexual Revolution*, 108.
67. Ibid., 155–67.
68. Ibid., 180.
69. Jennifer M. Spear, "'They Need Wives': Métissage and the Regulation of Sexuality in French Louisiana, 1699–1730," in *Sex, Love, Race: Crossing Boundaries in North American History*, ed. Martha Hodes (New York: New York University Press, 1999), 46–50.
70. Godbeer, *Sexual Revolution*, 202–3.
71. Ibid., chapter 6.
72. Lyons, *Sex among the Rabble*, 293.

Chapter 6

1. Roy Porter, *Quacks: Fakers and Charlatans in English Medicine* (Stroud: Tempus, 2000); Dorothy Porter and Roy Porter, *Patient's Progress, Doctors and Doctoring in Eighteenth-Century England* (Oxford: Polity Press, 1989).
2. Peter Gay, *The Enlightenment: An Interpretation* (New York: Knopf, 1967), 2:3–54, which open Gay's second volume with medicine as the basis of his "science of freedom."
3. Donald Bond, *Joseph Addison, and Richard Steele, The Spectator* (Oxford: Clarendon Press, 1965), 1:96, 2:124, 4:58–62, and 4:551–5. Roy Porter, *The Greatest Benefit to Mankind: A Medical History of Humanity* (New York: W.W. Norton, 1998).
4. Porter, *The Greatest Benefit to Mankind*.

5. A useful introduction to the subject is found in Katherine Crawford, *European Sexualities, 1400–1800* (Cambridge: Cambridge University Press, 2007).
6. Jean H. Hagstrum, *Sex and Sensibility: Ideal and Erotic Love from Milton to Mozart* (Chicago: University of Chicago Press, 1980).
7. Thomas Laqueur, *Making Sex: Body and Gender from the Greeks to Freud* (Cambridge, MA: Harvard University Press, 1990).
8. Laqueur, *Making Sex*, 149–73; Crawford, *European Sexualities*, 109–10.
9. Regnier de Graaf, "Regnier De Graaf on the Human Reproductive Organs …" *Journal of Reproduction and Fertility* 17 (supp.) (Oxford: Blackwell Scientific, 1972).
10. James Drake, *Anthropologia Nova; or, a New System of Anatomy* (London: Smith and Walford, 1707).
11. The new views are reflected in the English version of Meibom's *Tractatus de Hermaphroditis* (1718); see A. Pettit and P. Spedding, eds., *Eighteenth-Century British Erotica*, vol. 2, ed. Kevin Cope (London: Pickering and Chatto, 2002), 3–98; Londa L. Schiebinger, *The Mind Has No Sex? Women in the Origins of Modern Science* (Cambridge, MA: Harvard University Press, 1989).
12. G. S. Rousseau, "'Homoplatonic, Homodepressed, Homomorbid': Some Further Genealogies of Same-Sex Attraction in Western Civilization," in *Love, Sex, Intimacy and Friendship, 1550–1800*, ed. K. O'Donnell and M. O'Rourke (Basingstoke: Palgrave Macmillan, 2003).
13. W. F. Bynum, "Cullen and the Nervous System," in *William Cullen and the Eighteenth Century Medical World*, ed. A. Doig et al. (Edinburgh: Edinburgh University Press, 1993).
14. de Graaf, "Regnier De Graaf on the Human Reproductive Organs …"
15. Crawford, *European Sexualities*, 108–11.
16. Katharine Park, *Secrets of Women: Gender, Generation, and the Origins of Human Dissection* (New York: Zone Books, 2006); Jacques Roger and K. R. Benson, *The Life Sciences in Eighteenth-Century French Thought* (Stanford, CA: Stanford University Press, 1997).
17. The French physicians hammered away at this point; see Pierre Roussel, *Système Physique et Moral de la Femme* (Paris: Lannette, 1775), who incorporated it into his philosophy, and its discussion in Anne C. Vila, *Enlightenment and Pathology, Sensibility in the Literature and Medicine of Eighteenth-Century France* (Baltimore: Johns Hopkins University Press, 1998), 225–57. See also Sarah Knott and Barbara Taylor, ed., *Women, Gender and Enlightenment* (Basingstoke: Palgrave Macmillan, 2007).
18. Joseph Needham, *A History of Embryology*, 2nd ed. (Cambridge: Cambridge University Press, 1959); Clara Pinto Correia, *The Ovary of Eve, Egg and Sperm and Preformation* (Chicago: University of Chicago Press, 1997); Roger and Benson, *The Life Sciences*.
19. Albrecht von Haller, *Réflexions sur le Système de la Génération* (Geneva: Barrillot, 1751); Correia, *The Ovary of Eve*.
20. Martin Schurig, *Parthenologia Historico-Medica, Hoc Est, Virginitatis Consideratio* (Dresden: Christophori Hekelii, 1729); Martin Schurig and Friedrich Heckel, *Gynµcologia Historico-Medica* (Dresden: Libraria Hekeliana, 1730).

21. Correia, *The Ovary of Eve*.
22. Angus McLaren, *Reproductive Rituals: The Perception of Fertility in England from the Sixteenth to the Nineteenth Century* (London: Methuen, 1984); Angus McLaren, "The Pleasures of Procreation," in *William Hunter and the Eighteenth-Century Medical World*, ed. W. F Bynum and Roy Porter (Cambridge: Cambridge University Press, 1985); Raewyn Connell, *Gender and Power: Society, the Person and Sexual Politics* (Cambridge: Polity, 1987).
23. Shail (2004); Michael Stolberg, "Menstruation and Sexual Difference in Early Modern Medicine," in *Menstruation: A Cultural History*, ed. Andrew Shail (Basingstoke, Hampshire: Palgrave, 2005).
24. Angus McLaren, *Impotence: A Cultural History* (Chicago: University of Chicago Press, 2007).
25. Drake, *Anthropologia Nova*, a text Laurence Sterne knew well.
26. Cited by Angeline Goreau in Philippe Ariès, *Western Sexuality: Practice and Precept in Past and Present Times* (Oxford: Blackwell, 1985), 111.
27. G. S. Rousseau, ed., *Children and Sexuality: The Greeks to the Great War* (Basingstoke: Palgrave Macmillan, 2007), 364–67.
28. Martin Schurig, *Spermatologia Historico-Medica* (Frankfurt, 1720); Nicholas Robinson, *A New System of the Spleen, Vapours, and Hypochondriack Melancholy* (London: J. J. and P. Knapton, 1729), 108.
29. Robinson, *A New System of the Spleen*, 108.
30. Roy Porter and Marie Mulvey Roberts, eds., *Pleasure in the Eighteenth Century* (Basingstoke: Macmillan, 1996).
31. Lester S. King, *The Medical World of the Eighteenth Century* (Chicago: University of Chicago Press, 1958).
32. See, for example, *Pleasures of Coition* (1721) in K. L. Cope, ed., *Eighteenth-Century British Erotica*, Set 1, Vol. 2, *Edmund Curll and Grub-Street Highlights* (London: Pickering & Chatto, 2002), 99–156.
33. Benito Jerâonimo Feijoo, *An Essay on Woman* (London: W. Bingley, 1768), cited in Rebecca Haidt, *Embodying Enlightenment: Knowing the Body in Eighteenth-Century Spanish Literature and Culture* (Basingstoke: Macmillan, 1998), 57–63 and chap. 2, 63–79.
34. G. Rousseau, *Nervous Acts: Essays on Literature, Culture and Sensibility* (Basingstoke: Palgrave Macmillan, 2004), 113–40.
35. Edward Strother, *The Family Companion for Health* (London: F. Fayram; and J. Leake, 1729), 35.
36. Cited in Crawford, *European Sexualities*, 124.
37. See Nicholas Venette, *De la Generation de l'homme; ou, Tableau De L'amour Conjugal* (Cologne: Claude Joly, 1696); Nicholas Venette, *The Mysteries of Conjugal Love Reveal'd* (London, 1712); Nicolas Venette, *Conjugal Love, or, the Pleasures of the Marriage Bed* (New York: Garland, 1984).
38. Roy Porter and Mikulâaés Teich, *Sexual Knowledge, Sexual Science: The History of Attitudes to Sexuality* (Cambridge: Cambridge University Press, 1994); Julie Peakman, "Medicine, the Body and the Botanical Metaphor in Erotica," in *From Physico-Theology to Bio-Technology: Essays in the Social and Cultural History*

of Biosciences, ed. Kurt Bayertz and Roy Porter (Amsterdam: Rodopi, 1998), 197–223.

39. M. K. Schuchard, *Why Mrs Blake Cried: William Blake and the Sexual Basis of Spiritual Vision* (London: Century, 2006).
40. Robert Darnton, *Mesmerism and the End of the Enlightenment in France* (Cambridge, MA: Harvard University Press, 1968); mesmerism continued well into the nineteenth century.
41. James Graham, *The Guardian Goddess of Health, Or, the Whole Art of Preventing and Curing Diseases* (London, 1780); James Graham, *An Abstract from a Book by J. Graham. Intituled "Medical Transactions at the Temple of Health in London"* (1781); James Graham, *Dr. Graham's General Directions as to Regimen* (1782); James Graham, *Now or Never!* (1783); James Graham, *A Clear, Full, And Faithful Portraiture, ... and Ardent Recommendation Of A ... Virgin Princess ... To A Certain Youthful Heir-Apparent,* 2nd ed. (Bath, 1792); Roy Porter, "The Sexual Politics of James Graham," *British Journal for Eighteenth-Century Studies* 5 (1982): 199–206; Hannah Baynes, *James Graham: "Doctor of Medicine and Lover of His Species" or Simply a Quack?* (London: Wellcome Institute for the History of Medicine, 1997). "Spiritual libertine," as applied to Graham, is Peter Otto's term, cited in P. M. Cryle and Lisa O'Connell, *Libertine Enlightenment: Sex, Liberty, and Licence in the Eighteenth Century* (Basingstoke: Palgrave Macmillan, 2004), 204–20.
42. John Marten, *Gonosologium novum; or, A new system of all the secret infirmities and diseases natural, accidental, and venereal in men and women* (London: N. Crouch et al., 1709).
43. Strother, *The Family Companion,* 144.
44. Anonymous, *Aristotle's Compleat Master-Piece: Displaying the Secrets of Nature in the Generation of Man,* 15 ed. (London: 1723); Roy Porter, "Spreading Carnal Knowledge or Selling Dirt Cheap? Nicolas Venette's Tableau De L'amour," *Journal of European Studies* 14 (1984): 233–55.
45. Anonymous, *Onania; or, the Heinous Sin of Self-Pollution, and All Its Frightful Consequences, in Both Sexes* (London: T. Crouch, 1722); Castitatis Philo, *Onania Examined, and Detected* (London: Marshall & Roberts, 1724).
46. S.A.D. Tissot, *An Essay on the Disorders of People of Fashion* (London: Richardson and Urquhart, 1771) and his view in Tissot, *Onanism: Or, a Treatise Upon the Disorders Produced by Masturbation, or, the Dangerous Effects of Secret and Excessive Venery* (London: J. Pridden, 1766) discussing those prone to this "vice."
47. See Thomas W. Laqueur, *Solitary Sex: A Cultural History of Masturbation* (New York: Zone Books, 2003) for its development.
48. For nymphomania see D. T. de Bienville and Edward Sloane Wilmot, *Nymphomania, or a Dissertation Concerning the Furor* (Uterinus, London: J. Bew, 1775); G. S. Rousseau, "Nymphomania, Bienville and the Rise of Erotic Sensibility," in *Sexuality in Eighteenth-Century Britain,* ed. G. Bouce (Manchester: Manchester University Press, 1982).
49. As Le Rebours warned her readers; see Marie-Angelique Le Rebours, *Avis Aux M*Res Qui Veulent Nourrir Leurs Enfans* (Utrecht: Lacombe, 1767).

50. Robinson, *A New System of the Spleen*, 41–43, the most thorough discussion in English of its generation.
51. Jean Astruc, *A Treatise of the Venereal Disease* (London: W. Innys, 1737); and Daniel Turner, *Syphilis ... Containing Farther Observations on the Venereal Disease* (London: John Clarke, 1739).
52. Astruc also claimed that wet-nurses could transmit it to their charges; see V. A. Fildes, *Breasts, Bottles and Babies: A History of Infant Feeding* (Edinburgh: Edinburgh University Press, 1986).
53. For these and dozens of others see Linda Merians, *The Secret Malady, Venereal Disease in Eighteenth-Century Britain and France* (Lexington: University Press of Kentucky, 1996), 85–102; John Profily, *An Easy and Exact Method of Curing the Venereal Disease* (London: J. Robinson, 1748).
54. William Buchan, *Observations Concerning the Prevention and Cure of the Venereal Disease* (London, 1796); Merians, *The Secret Malady*; Kevin Siena, *Sins of the Flesh: Responding to Sexual Disease in Early Modern Europe* (Toronto: Centre for Reformation and Renaissance Studies, 2005); Laura J. Rosenthal, *Infamous Commerce, Prostitution in Eighteenth-century British Literature and Culture* (Ithaca, NY: Cornell University Press, 2006).
55. Kevin Siena, *Poverty and the Pox: Venereal Disease in London Hospitals, 1600–1800* (2001); for Italy see David Gentilcore, *Medical Charlatanism in Early Modern Italy* (Oxford: Oxford University Press, 2006), 196–99.
56. D. I. Williams and W. F. Bynum, *The London Lock: A Charitable Hospital for Venereal Disease 1746–1952* (London: Royal Society of Medicine Press, 1995).
57. For the proof see Buchan's preparations (*Observations Concerning the Prevention and Cure of the Venereal Disease*).
58. Jonathan Swift, *Gulliver's Travels*, ed. Louis A. Landa (New York: Riverside, 1960), 213.
59. Anonymous, *Satan's Harvest Home: Or the Present State of Whorecraft, Adultery, Fornication, Procuring* (London: Dod; Lewis, 1749); G. S. Rousseau, "The Pursuit of Homosexuality in the Eighteenth Century: 'Utterly Confused Category and/or Rich Repository?'" in *'Tis Nature's Fault: Unauthorized Sexuality During the Enlightenment*, ed. R. P. Maccubbin (Cambridge: Cambridge University Press, 1987), 140–42.
60. Strother, *The Family Companion*, 28–30; John Armstrong, *The Oeconomy of Love: A Poetical Essay* (London: T. Cooper, 1736).
61. Anonymous, *Satan's Harvest Home*.
62. Valerie Traub, *The Renaissance of Lesbianism in Early Modern England* (Cambridge: Cambridge University Press, 2002); A. H. Andreadis, *Sappho in Early Modern England: Female Same-sex Literary Erotics, 1550–1714* (Chicago: University of Chicago Press, 2001).
63. A point Armstrong continuously versified in *The Art of Preserving Health; a Poem* (Dublin: J. Smith & W. Powell, 1744).
64. As Samuel Johnson had claimed in the *Rambler* (1750) and others on the English stage.
65. Francis Mauriceau, *The Diseases of Women with Child* (London: T. Cox, 1736).

66. Rudolf Dekker and Lotte van de Pol, *The Tradition of Female Transvestism in Early Modern Europe* (Basingstoke: Macmillan, 1989).
67. Philippe Ariès, *Centuries of Childhood; a Social History of Family Life* (New York: Vintage Books, 1962); and Rousseau, *Children and Sexuality*, 1–57.
68. The point made by Robinson, *A New System of the Spleen*, 29.
69. Armstrong, *The Art of Preserving Health*, 30.
70. As reported by Marten, *Gonosologium novum,* and cited in Bradford K. Mudge, ed., *When Word Becomes Flesh: An Anthology of Eighteenth-Century Libertine Literature* (Oxford: Oxford University Press, 2004), 125.
71. Luigi Cornaro, *Sure and Certain Methods of Attaining a Long and Healthful Life* (London: Daniel Midwinter, 1722), 120.
72. Leonardus Lessius, *Hygiasticon, Or, a Treatise of the Means of Health and Long Life* (London: printed by the author, 1742); see also his later edition with new advice (*A Treatise of Health and Long Life* [Bath: James Leake, 1743]).
73. See Maximianus, *The Impotent Lover Describ'd in Six Elegies on Old-Age* (London: J. Sackfield, and T. Warner, 1718); and McLaren, *Impotence,* who discusses other "Fallen Members" on pp. 67–82.
74. Strother, *The Family Companion,* 29.
75. Roy Porter, "'The Secrets of Generation Display'd': Aristotle's Master-Piece in Eighteenth-Century England," in *'Tis Nature's Fault: Unauthorized Sexuality During the Enlightenment*, ed. R. P. Maccubbin (Cambridge: Cambridge University Press, 1987).
76. For the background in Britain see Paul-Gabriel Boucé, *Sexuality in Eighteenth-Century Britain* (Manchester: Manchester University Press, 1982); for France, Nina Gelbart, *The King's Midwife: A History and Mystery of Madame du Coudray* (Berkeley: University of California Press, 1998).
77. Anonymous, *The Lady's Decoy: Or, the Man-Midwife's Defence* (London: S. Slow, 1738); Philip Thicknesse, *Man-Midwifery Analysed, And the Tendency of That Practice Detected and Exposed* (London: R. Davis, 1764).
78. Adrian Wilson, *The Making of Man-Midwifery, Childbirth in England 1660–1770* (London: UCL Press, 1995); Thicknesse, *Man-Midwifery Analysed.*
79. William Cadogan, *An Essay upon Nursing, and the Management of Children* (London: J. Roberts, 1748), preface, cited in McLaren, *Reproductive Rituals,* 53; William Smellie, *A Treatise on the Theory and Practice of Midwifery* (London, 1752).
80. Western countries then concerned about falling population were not prepared to set up national programs for birth control even if they had the scientific capability.
81. For Dr. Burton see Louis Landa, "The Shandean Homunculus: The Background of Sterne's 'Litte Gentleman,'" in *Restoration and Eighteenth-Century Literature*, ed. Carroll Camden (Chicago: University of Chicago Press, 1963). Burton refined the forceps originally developed by several generations of the Chamberlen family in the seventeenth century.
82. For commentary during the years Sterne was composing the early volumes of *Tristram Shandy* (1759–1764) see Thicknesse, *Man-Midwifery Analysed*; the dangers they posed continue to be debated after 1800; see John Stevens, *Man-Midwifery*

Exposed, or the Danger and Immorality of Employing Men in Midwifery Proved; and the Remedy for the Evil Found (London, 1849).
83. R. Porter and D. Porter, *Patient's Progress: Doctors and Doctoring in Eighteenth-century England* (Oxford: Polity Press, 1989).
84. Rousseau, "Nymphomania Bienville."
85. P. J. Corfield, *Power and the Professions in Britain 1700–1850* (London: Routledge, 2000).
86. Marten, *Gonosologium novum,* is a lucid example; Porter, *Quacks.*
87. Tissot (1787); Nicholas Robinson, *A New Treatise of the Venereal Disease* (London: J. J. and P. Knapton, 1736); Profily, *An Easy and Exact Method*; Buchan, *Observations Concerning the Prevention and Cure of the Venereal Disease.*
88. Profily, *An Easy and Exact Method* (1748).
89. Marten (1709).
90. Ebenezer Sibly, *The Medical Mirror: Or Treatise on the Impregnation of the Human Female* (London: Champante and Whitrow, 1796); for his astrology see Ebenezer Sibly, *A Complete Illustration of the Celestial Science of Astrology* (London, 1788); Ebenezer Sibly, *A New and Complete Illustration of the Occult Sciences* (London, 1790); for his typical *vade mecum* see Ebenezer Sibly, *Everybody's Fortune Teller* (London, 1925).
91. Sibly, *The Medical Mirror,* reprinted several times by 1800.
92. Sibly, *The Medical Mirror,* preface.
93. Ibid., preface.
94. Ibid., 14.
95. Ibid., 15.
96. Ibid.
97. Ibid., 16.
98. They were still being reprinted in the twentieth century; see Sibly, *Everybody's Fortune Teller.*
99. Sibly, *The Medical Mirror,* 42.
100. Jan Morris, *Conundrum* (London: Faber, 1974).
101. Ibid., 36.
102. Ibid., 42.
103. Ibid.

Chapter 7

1. Gayatri Spivak, *A Critique of Postcolonial Reason: Towards a History of the Vanishing Present* (Cambridge, MA: Harvard University Press, 1999), 6.
2. Felicity A. Nussbaum, *The Limits of the Human: Fictions of Anomaly, Race and Gender in the Long Eighteenth Century* (Cambridge: Cambridge University Press, 2003), 1.
3. Lisa Cody, *Birthing the Nation: Sex, Science and the Conception of Eighteenth-Century Britons* (Oxford: Oxford University Press, 2005), 240–45.
4. Thomas Laqueur, *Making Sex: Body and Gender From the Greeks to Freud* (Cambridge, MA: Harvard University Press, 1992).

5. Michel Foucault, *The History of Sexuality, Volume 1: An Introduction*, trans. Robert Hurley (London: Penguin, 1990), 20.
6. Ibid., 20–21.
7. Peter Cryle and Lisa O'Connell, "Sex, Libertine and License in the Eighteenth Century," in *Libertine Enlightenment: Sex, Libertine and License in the Eighteenth Century*, ed. Peter Cryle and Lisa O'Connell (Basingstoke: Palgrave Macmillan, 2004), 2.
8. John E. Loftis, "Congreve's *Way of the World* and Popular Criminal Literature," *Studies in English Literature, 1500–1900* 36, no. 3 (1996): 561–78.
9. Douglas Chambers, *The Reinvention of the World: English Writing 1650–1750* (London: Arnold, 1996), 31. See also John Mullan and Christopher Reid, eds., "Introduction" to their *Eighteenth-Century Popular Culture: A Selection* (Oxford: Oxford University Press, 2000), 1–28.
10. Morag Shiach, *Discourse on Popular Culture: Class, Gender and History in Cultural Analysis, 1730 to the Present* (Cambridge: Polity Press, 1989), 7.
11. Moyra Haslett, *Pope to Burney, 1714–1779: Scriblerians to Bluestockings* (Basingstoke: Palgrave Macmillan, 2003), 1.
12. Vic Gattrell, *City of Laughter: Sex and Satire in Eighteenth-Century London* (London: Atlantic, 2006), 171.
13. Jeremy Black, *Culture in Eighteenth-Century England: A Subject for Taste* (London: Hambledon and London, 2005), xix.
14. James Raven, "The Book Trades," in *Books and Their Readers in Eighteenth-Century England: New Essays*, ed. Isabel Rivers (London: Leicester University Press, 2001), 1.
15. Sten G. Lindberg, "The Scandinavian Book Trade in the Eighteenth Century," in *The Book and the Book Trade in Eighteenth-Century Europe*, ed. Giles Barber and Bernhard Fabian (Hamburg: Dr Ernst Hauswedell & Co, 1981), 225–48.
16. Robert B. Winans, "Bibliography and the Cultural Historian: Notes on the Eighteenth-Century Novel," in *Printing and Society in Early America*, ed. William L. Joyce et al (Worcester: American Antiquarian Society, 1983), 178.
17. Black, *Culture in Eighteenth-Century England*, 132.
18. See Ros Ballaster, *Seductive Forms: Women's Amatory Fiction from 1684–1740* (Oxford: Clarendon Press, 1992); Catherine Gallagher, *Nobody's Story: The Vanishing Acts of Women Writers in the Marketplace, 1670–1820* (Berkley: University of California Press, 1994); Sarah Prescott, *Women, Authorship and Literary Culture, 1690–1740* (Basingstoke: Palgrave Macmillan, 2003); Jane Spencer, *The Rise of the Woman Novelist: From Aphra Behn to Jane Austen* (Oxford: Blackwell, 1986).
19. See Tara L. Collington and Philip D. Collington, "Adulteration or Adaptation? Nathaniel Lee's 'Princess of Cleve' and Its Sources," *Modern Philology* 100, no. 2 (2002): 196–226.
20. Paula R. Backscheider and John J. Richetti, "Introduction" to their *Popular Fiction by Women 1660–1730. An Anthology* (Oxford: Clarendon, 1996), 2.
21. Ibid., x.
22. Prescott, *Women, Authorship and Literary Culture*, 37.
23. Eliza Haywood, *The British Recluse; or, The Secret History of Cleomira, Supposed Dead: A Novel* (London: Brown and Chapman, 1722).

24. Eliza Haywood, *Fantomina: or, Love in a Maze. Being a Secret History of an Amour Between Two Persons of Condition* (London: Brown and Chapman, 1725).
25. Backscheider and Richetti, *Popular Fiction by Women*, ix–xxiii. Karen Harvey, *Reading Sex in the Eighteenth Century: Bodies and Gender in English Erotic Culture* (Cambridge: Cambridge University Press, 2004), 33.
26. Vivien Jones, "The Seductions of Conduct: Pleasure and Conduct Literature," in *Pleasure in the Eighteenth Century*, ed. Roy Porter and Marie Mulvey Roberts (Basingstoke: Macmillan, 1996), 108.
27. Reverend Mr Wetenhall Wilkes, "A Letter of Genteel and Moral Advice to a Young Lady," in *Women in the Eighteenth-Century: Constructions of Femininity*, ed. Vivien Jones (London: Routledge, 1990), 31–32.
28. Donald McGrady, "A Pirated Edition of *Guzman de Alfarache*: More Light on Mateo Aleman's Life," *Hispanic Review* 34, no. 4 (1966): 326–28.
29. Mateo Aleman, *The Life of Guzman of Alfarache, or, The Spanish Rogue*, trans. by several hands, 2 vols. (London: Bonwick, Freeman, Goodwin, 1708), 1:32.
30. Ibid., 1:40.
31. Hannah More, *Strictures on the Modern System of Female Education: With a View of the Principles and Conduct Prevalent Among Women of Rank and Fortune*, 2 vols. (London: Cadell and Davies, 1799), 1:170–71.
32. Hannah More, "On The Religion of the Fashionable World," in *The Works of Hannah More* (London, 1801), 221. See also Julie Peakman, *Lascivious Bodies: A Sexual History of the Eighteenth Century* (London: Atlantic, 2004), 29–30.
33. More, *Strictures on the Modern System*, 2:163.
34. Ibid., 2:166.
35. Peter Cryle and Lisa O'Connell, eds., *Libertine Enlightenment: Sex, Libertine and License in the Eighteenth Century* (Basingstoke: Palgrave Macmillan, 2004), 3–4; Peakman, *Lascivious Bodies*, 46–47.
36. Gattrell, *City of Laughter*, 316.
37. Peakman, *Lascivious Bodies*, 64–72.
38. See John C. Beynon, "Lady Mary Wortley Montague's Sapphic Vision," in *Imperial Desire: Dissident Sexualities and Colonial Literature*, ed. Philip Holden and Richard J. Ruppel (Minneapolis: University of Minnesota Press, 2003), 21–43; Felicity A Nussbaum, *Torrid Zones: Maternity, Sexuality, and Empire in Eighteenth-Century English Narratives* (Baltimore: John Hopkins University Press, 1995), 135–41.
39. Robert Halsband, ed., *The Complete Letters of Lady Mary Wortley Montagu*, 3 vols. (Oxford: Clarendon, 1965), 1:349.
40. James Boswell, *London Journal, 1762–1763*, ed. Frederick A. Pottle (repr.; Harmodsworth: Penguin, 1966).
41. Gattrell, *City of Laughter*, 316.
42. Bruce Duncan, *Goethe's* Werther *and the Critics* (Rochester: Camden House, 2005), 1.
43. Ibid., 9.
44. Thomas Stretser, *A New Description of Merryland* (London, 1741), chapter 2.

45. Nicola Parsons, "Secrecy and Enlightenment: Delarivière Manley's," in *Libertine Enlightenment: Sex, Libertine and License in the Eighteenth Century*, ed. Peter Cryle and Lisa O'Connell (Basingstoke: Palgrave Macmillan, 2004), 145–60.
46. See Adriana Cracuin, *British Women Writers and the French Revolution* (Basingstoke: Macmillan, 2005); J. A. Dowie, *To Settle the Succession of the State: Literature and Politics, 1678–1750* (Basingstoke: Macmillan, 1994); Robert A. Ferguson, *The American Enlightenment, 1750–1820* (Cambridge, MA: Harvard University Press, 1997).
47. Cracuin, *British Women Writers*, 99.
48. Lawrence Stone, *The Family, Sex and Marriage in England 1500–1800* (London: Weidenfels & Nicolson, 1987), 328–29. Roy Porter, "Enlightenment and Pleasure," in *Pleasure in the Eighteenth Century*, ed. Roy Porter and Marie Mulvey Roberts (Basingstoke: Macmillan, 1996), 1–18.
49. Laura Rosenthal, *Infamous Commerce: Prostitution in Eighteenth-century British Literature and Culture* (Ithaca, NY: Cornell University Press, 2006); Sophie Carter, *Purchasing Power* (Aldershot: Ashgate, 2004).
50. Boswell, *London Journal*.
51. John Cleland, *Fanny Hill: Memoirs of a Woman of Pleasure* (1749) (London: Mayflower, 1964), 201.
52. Ibid., 102.
53. John D'Emilio and Estelle B. Freedman, *Intimate Matters: A History of Sexuality in America* (New York: Harper & Row, 1988); Robert M. Isherwood, *Farce and Fantasy: Popular Entertainment in Eighteenth-Century Paris* (Oxford: Oxford University Press, 1986).
54. Roy Porter, "Material Pleasures in the Consumer Society," in *Pleasure in the Eighteenth Century*, ed. Roy Porter and Marie Mulvey Roberts (Basingstoke: Macmillan, 1996), 27–29.
55. Mollie Sands, *The Eighteenth-Century Pleasure Gardens of Marylebone 1737–1777* (London: The Society for Theatre Research, 1987), 5.
56. Ibid., 12.
57. Peakman, *Lascivious Bodies*, 6–7.
58. Isherwood, *Farce and Fantasy*, 207–8.
59. Cited in ibid., 48.
60. Roberta Monetemorra Marvin and Downing A. Thomas, eds., *Operatic Migrations. Transforming the Works and Crossing Boundaries* (Aldershot: Ashgate, 2006).
61. Kristina Straub, "The Guilty Pleasure of Female Theatrical Cross-Dressing and the Autobiography of Charlotte Charke," in *Body Guards: The Cultural Politics of Gender Ambiguity*, ed. Julia Epstein and Kristina Straub (London: Routledge, 1991), 142–66.
62. Kristina Straub, *Eighteenth Century Players and Sexual Ideology* (Princeton, NJ: Princeton University Press, 1992), 12–23.
63. David Worrall, *The Politics of Romantic Theatricality, 1787–1832* (Basingstoke: Palgrave Macmillan, 2007), esp. 68–106.

64. Charles Whibley, "Moll Cutpurse," in *A Book of Scoundrels* (London: William Heinemann, 1897), 59.
65. Emma Donaghue, *Passions Between Women: British Lesbian Culture, 1668–1801* (New York: Harper Collins, 1996), 96–97.
66. Peakman, *Lascivious Bodies*, 229.
67. Ménie Muriel Dowie, "Introduction" to her *Women Adventurers* (London: T. Fisher Unwin, 1893).
68. Mary Lacy, *The History of the Female Shipwright* (London: M. Lewis, 1773). See also Dianne Duggaw, "Women and Popular Culture: Gender, Cultural Dynamics and Popular Prints," in *Women and Literature in Britain 1700–1800,* ed. Vivien Jones (Cambridge: Cambridge University Press, 2000), 263–84.
69. The following account is based on my "Introduction" to Heike Bauer, ed., *Women and Cross-Dressing 1800–1939,* 3 vols. (London: Routledge, 2006), xvi–xix.
70. Brigitte Eriksson, "A Lesbian Execution in Germany, 1721: The Trial Records," in *The Gay Past: A Collection of Historical Essays,* ed. Salvatore J. Licata and Robert P. Petersen (New York: Harrington Park Press, 1985), 27–40. See also Martha Vicinus, "'They Wonder to Which Sex I Belong': The Historical Roots of the Modern Lesbian Identity," in *The Lesbian and Gay Studies Reader,* ed. Henry Abelove, Michèle Aina Barale and David Halperin (New York: Routledge, 1993), 432–52.
71. Donaghue, *Passions Between Women,* 64.
72. John Wilmot, *Sodom, or the Quintessence of Debauchery* (London, 1684).
73. Rictor Norton, *Mother Clap's Molly House: The Gay Subculture in England 1700–1830* (Stroud: Chalford Press, 1992), 47.
74. Jonas Liliequist, "Peasants against Nature: Crossing the Boundaries Between Man and Animal in Seventeenth- and Eighteenth-Century Sweden," in *Forbidden History: The State, Society, and the Regulation of Sexuality in Modern Europe,* ed. John Fout (Chicago: University of Chicago Press, 1992), 57.
75. Theo van der Meer, "Sodomy and the Pursuit of a Third Sex in the Early Modern Period," in *Third Sex, Third Gender: Beyond Sexual Dimorphism in Culture and History,* ed. Gilbert Herdt (New York: Zone Books, 1994), 137–212; Arend H. Hussen Jr., "Sodomy in the Dutch Republic During the Eighteenth Century," in *Hidden from History: Reclaiming the Gay and Lesbian Past,* ed. Martin Duberman, Martha Vicinus, and George Chauncey Jr. (London: Penguin, 1989), 141–49.
76. *La France devenue italienne* was first published in Roger the Rabutin, comte the Bussy, *Histoires amoureuse the Gaules, suivie des romans historico-satiriques du XVII siècle,* 4 vols., ed. Paul Boiteau and C. L. Livet (Paris, 1856–1876), 3:345–60. See Jeremy Merrick and Bryant T. Ragan Jr., eds., *Homosexuality in Early Modern France: A Documentary Collection* (Oxford: Oxford University Press, 1991), 119–24.
77. See Diana Donald and Frank O'Gorman, eds., *Ordering the World in the Eighteenth Century* (Basingstoke: Palgrave Macmillan, 2006).
78. Charles de Secondat, Baron de Montesquieu, *The Spirit of the Laws* (1748). Reprinted in Merrick and Ragan, *Homosexuality in Early Modern France,* 154.

79. Cesare Bonasa, *Crime and Punishment* (1764), in Mark Blasius and Shane Phelan, eds., *We Are Everywhere: A Historical Sourcebook of Gay and Lesbian Politics* (New York: Routledge, 1997), 11.
80. See Blasius and Phelan, *We Are Everywhere*.
81. Jorge Cañizares-Esguerra, *How to Write the History of the New World: Histories, Epistemologies, and Identities in the Eighteenth-Century Atlantic World* (Stanford, CA: Stanford: University Press, 2001), 169–200.
82. See Neil Rennie. "The Point Venus 'Scene,' Tahiti, 14 May 1769," in *The Global Eighteenth Century*, ed. Felicity A. Nussbaum (Baltimore: John Hopkins University Press, 2003), 239–50.
83. More, *Strictures*, 1:84–85.
84. Voltaire, *Philosophical Dictionary* (1764), in Merrick and Ragan, *Homosexuality in Early Modern France*, 156.
85. Olaudah Equiano, *The Interesting Narrative of the Life of Olaudah Equiano, or Gustavus Vassa, the African. Written by Himself* [1789], ed. Vincent Carretta (New York: Penguin, 1995).
86. Vincent Carretta, "Questioning the Identity of Olaudah Equiano, or Gustavus Vassa, the African," in *The Global Eighteenth Century*, ed. Felicity A. Nussbaum (Baltimore: John Hopkins University Press, 2003), 226–35.
87. Dean Mahomet, *The Travels of Dean Mahomet: An Eighteenth-Century Journey through India*, ed. Michael H. Fisher (Berkeley, CA: University of Berkeley Press, 1997), 161–69.
88. Marquis de Sade, "To the Libertines," in his *Philosophy of the Boudoir*, trans. Joachim Neugroschel (London: Penguin, 2006), 1.
89. Jacques Lacan, "Kant avec Sade," in *Écrits* (Paris: Editions du Seuil, 1966), 765–90.
90. Immanuel Kant, *Lectures on Ethics* (1780), trans. Louis Infield (London: Methuen, 1930).
91. Caroline Warman, *Sade: From Materialism to Pornography* (Oxford: Voltaire Foundation, 2002), esp. 69–86.
92. Alan Corkhill, "Kant, Sade and the Libertine Enlightenment," in *Libertine Enlightenment: Sex, Libertine and License in the Eighteenth Century*, ed. Peter Cryle and Lisa O'Connell (Basingstoke: Palgrave Macmillan, 2004), 65–66.
93. Francine du Plessis Gray, "Introduction," in *Philosophy of the Boudoir*, Marquis de Sade, trans. Joachim Neugroschel (London: Penguin, 2006), vii–xvi.

Chapter 8

1. Alberto Radicati, *A Phiosophical* [sic] *Dissertation upon Death*, trans. Joseph Morgan (London, 1732), 67–60, 78–79; Anonymous, *Satan's Harvest Home, Or the Present State of Whorecraft, Adultery, Fornication, Procuring* (London, 1749), 55.
2. Cornelis de Bruyn, *A Voyage to the Levant* (London, 1702), 101; Joseph Pitts, *A True and Faithful Account of the Religion and Manners of the Mohammetans* (London, 1704), 18; Aaron Hill, *A Full and Just Account of the Present State*

of the Ottoman Empire, 2nd ed. (London, 1710), 80–81; Charles Thompson, *The Travels of the late Charles Thompson Esq.*, 3 vols. (London, 1744), 2:83, and for the version quoted: Thomas Salmon, *Modern History or the Present State of All Nations*, 26 vols. (London, 1726), 302–3; Walter G. Andrews and Mehmet Kalpakli, *The Age of Beloveds, Love and the Beloved in Early-Modern Ottoman and European Culture and Society* (Durham, NC: Duke University Press, 2005), 48–51, 69–73, 276–89; Khaled El-Rouayheb, *Before Homosexuality in the Arab-Islamic World, 1500–1800* (Chicago: University of Chicago Press, 2005), 18, 32, 41–43; Stephen O. Murray and Will Roscoe, *Islamic Homosexualities* (New York: New York University Press, 1997), 15–54; Thijs Janssen, "Transvestites and Transsexuals in Turkey," in *Sexuality and Eroticism among Males in Moslem Societies*, ed. Arno Schmitt and Jahoeda Sofer (New York: Harrington Park Press, 1992), 14, 83–91; Stephen O. Murray, "Homosexuality in the Ottoman Empire," *Historical Reflections* 33 (2007): 101–16; Dorit Klebe, "Effeminate Professional Musicians in Sources of Ottoman-Turkish Court Poetry and Music of the Eighteenth and Nineteenth Centuries," *Music in Art* 30 (2005): 97–116.

3. Gary P. Leupp, *Male Colors, The Construction of Homosexuality in Tokugawa Japan* (Berkeley: University of California Press, 1995), 11–17, 65–78, 87–89, 129–36, 157–63; Gregory M. Pflugfelder, *Cartographies of Desire, Male-Male Sexuality in Japanese Discourse, 1600–1950* (Berkeley: University of California Press, 1999), 75–76, 110–24, 134–44, 154–57; Bret Hinsch, *Passions of the Cut Sleeve: The Male Homosexual Tradition in China* (Berkeley: University of California Press, 1990), 93–95, 133, 150–57; Matthew H. Sommer, *Sex, Law, and Society in Late Imperial China* (Stanford: Stanford University Press, 2000), 114–65; Matthew H. Sommer, "Was China Part of a Global Eighteenth-Century Homosexuality?" *Historical Reflections* 33 (2007): 117–33; Wenqing Kang, "Male Same-Sex Relations in China, 1900–1950," Ph.D. thesis, Santa Cruz, University of California, 2006; C. M. Naim, "The Theme of Homosexual (Pederastic) Love in Pre-Modern Urdu Poetry," in *Studies in the Urdu Gazal and Prose Fiction*, ed. Muhammad Umar Memom (Madison, WI: South Asian Studies, publication no. 5, 1979); Shakuntali Devi, *The World of Homosexuals* (New Delhi: Vikas, 1976), 94; Anita Khemka, *India's Third Gender*, dir. Thomas Wartman, Germany, 2005; Shivananda Khan, *Contexts, Race, Culture and Sexuality* (London: Naz Project, 1996), 36.

4. Michael Rocke, *Forbidden Friendships, Homosexuality and Male Culture in Renaissance Florence* (New York: Oxford University Press, 1996), 37–39, 106–7, 164–65, 175–76; Guido Ruggiero, *The Boundaries of Eros: Sex, Crime and Sexuality in Renaissance Venice* (New York: Oxford University Press, 1985), 136; Bette Talvacchia, *Taking Positions: On the Erotic in Renaissance Culture* (Princeton, NJ: Princeton University Press, 1999), 114; Meriol Trevor, *Apostle of Rome: St Philip Neri 1515–1595* (London: Macmillan, 1966), 46–47, 50–51, 70–73, 88, 95, 113, 158, 160, 221–22, 228, 254; Peter M. Robb, *The Man Who Became Caravaggio* (New York: Henry Holt, 2000); Mary Hewlett, "Women, Sodomy and Sexual Abuse in Late-Renaissance Lucca," Ph.D. thesis, Toronto, University of Toronto, 2000, is spoilt by her ideological presuppositions.

5. Rafael Carrasco, "Lazarillo on a Street Corner: What the Picaresque Novel Did Not Say about Fallen Boys," in *Sex and Love in Golden Age Spain*, ed. Alan Saint-Saëns (New Orleans: University Press of the South, 1996), 57–69; Cristian Berco, *Sexual Hierarchies: Public Status, Men, Sodomy, and Society in Spain's Golden Age* (Toronto: University of Toronto Press, 2007), 28 and passim.
6. Luiz Mott, "Pagode português, A subcultura gay em Portugal nos tempos inquisitorais," *Ciência e cultura* 40 (1988): 120–39; D. Higgs, *Queer Sites: Gay Urban Histories since 1600* (London: Routledge, 1999), 112–37; David Higgs, "Tales of Two Carmelites: Inquisitorial Narratives from Portugal and Brazil," in *Infamous Desire: Male Homosexuality in Colonial Latin America*, ed. Pete Sigal (Chicago: Chicago University Press, 2003), 152–66; David Higgs, "The Historiography of Male-Male Love in Portugal, 1550–1800," in *Queer Masculinities: Siting Same-Sex Desire in Early Modern World*, ed. Katherine O'Donnell and Michael O'Rourke (New York: PlagraveMacmillan, 2006), 37–57; in this last, Higgs shows the evidence for passive adult men who also married women, a standard role in societies in which most male-male acts were between men and boys. Such men were called *cinaedus* in ancient Rome and *ibner* in traditional Turkey, but Higgs is on the verge of turning them into gay men.
7. Ruth Mazo Karras and David Lorenzo Boyd, "'Ut cum muliere': A Male Transvestite Prostitute in Fourteenth Century London," in *Premodern Sexualities*, ed. Louise Fradenburg and Carla Freccero (New York: Routledge, 1996), 101–16; R. Mark Benbow and Alasdair D. K. Hawkyard, "Appendix C: Legal Records of Cross-Dressing," in Michael Shapiro, *Gender Play on the Shakespearean Stage: Boy Heroines and Female Pages*, (Ann Arbor, MI: University of Michigan Press, 1994), 226; Randolph Trumbach, "Renaissance Sodomy, 1500–1700," in *A Gay History of Britain: Love and Sex Between Men since the Middle Ages*, Matt Cook (Oxford: Greenwood, 2007), 61–62.
8. Randolph Trumbach, "Modern Sodomy: The Origins of Homosexuality, 1700–1800," in *A Gay History of Britain: Love and Sex Between Men since the Middle Ages*, ed. Matt Cook (Oxford: Greenwood, 2007); Randolph Trumbach, "The Heterosexual Male in Eighteenth-Century London and His Queer Interactions," in *Love, Sex, Intimacy and Friendship Between Men, 1550–1800*, ed. Katherine O'Donnell and Michael O'Rourke (New York: PalgraveMacmillan, 2003), 99–127; Randolph Trumbach, "Blackmail for Sodomy in Eighteenth-Century London," *Historical Reflections* 33 (2007): 23–39; for Latin American transvestite prostitutes: Don Kulick, *Travesti, Sex, Gender, and Culture among Brazilian Transgendered Prostitutes* (Chicago: University of Chicago Press, 1998); Anick Prieur, *Mema's House, Mexico City: On Transvestites, Queens, and Machos* (Chicago: University of Chicago Press, 1998); for a survey of studies of male prostitution, see Kerwin Kaye, "Sex and the Unspoken in Male Street Prostitution," *Journal of Homosexuality* 53 (2007): 37–73.
9. Matt Houlbrook, *Queer London* (Chicago: University of Chicago Press, 2005); George Chauncey, *Gay New York* (New York: Basic Books, 1994); Kulick, *Travesti, Sex, Gender, and Culture*; Carlos F. Cáceres, "Sexual Culture and Sexual Health among Young People in Lima in the 1990s," Ph.D. thesis, Berkeley, University of

California, 1996; Carlos F. Cáceres, "Male Bisexuality in Peru and the Prevention of AIDS," in *Bisexualities and AIDS*, ed. Peter Aggleton (London: Taylor and Francis, 1996); Carlos F. Cáceres, "Fletes in Parque Kennedy: Sexual Cultures among Young Men Who Sell Sex to Other Men in Lima," in *Men Who Sell Sex*, ed. Peter Aggleton (Philadelphia: Temple University Press, 1999); Jacobo Schifter, *Lila's House: Male Prostitution in Latin America* (New York: Harrington Park Press, 1998); Jacobo Schifter, *From Toads to Queens, Transvestism in a Latin American Setting* (New York: Harrington Park Press, 1999); Jacobo Schifter, *Public Sex in a Latin Society* (New York: Harrington Park Press, 2000); Joseph Carrier, *De Los Otros: Intimacy and Homosexuality among Mexican Men* (New York: Columbia University Press, 1995); Hector Carillo, *The Night is Young: Sexuality in Mexico in Time of AIDS* (Chicago: University of Chicago Press, 2002); Prieur, *Mema's House*; Joseph Carrier, "Mexican Male Bisexuality," in *Two Lives to Lead: Bisexuality in Men and Women*, ed. Fritz Klein and Timothy J. Wolf (New York: Harrington Park Press, 1985), 81.

10. Kathryn Norberg, "Prostitution," in *Encyclopedia of European Social History, from 1350 to 2000*, ed. Peter N. Stearns (New York: Charles Scribner, 2001); Kathryn Norberg, "Prostitutes," in *A History of Women in the West, vol. 3: Renaissance and Enlightenment Paradoxes,* ed. Natalie Zemon Davis and Arlette Farge (Cambridge, MA: Harvard University Press, 1993); Saunders Welch, *A Proposal to Render Effective a Plan to Remove the Nuisance of Common Prostitutes from the Streets of this Metropolis* (London, 1758).

11. For London: R. Trumbach, *Sex and Gender Revolution, vol. 1: Heterosexuality and the Third Gender in Enlightenment London* (Chicago: University of Chicago Press, 1998), 69–225; Tony Henderson, *Disorderly Women in Eighteenth Century London: Prostitution and Control in the Metropolis, 1730–1830* (New York: Longman, 1999); for France: Erica-Marie Benabou, *La prostitution et la police des moeurs au XVIIIe siècle* (Paris: Perrin, 1987); Norberg, "Prostitutes"; Collin Jones, "Prostitution and the Ruling Class in Eighteenth-Century Montpellier," *History Workshop* 6 (1978): 7–28; Susan P. Conner, "Prostitution and the Jacobin Agenda for Social Control," *Eighteenth-Century Life* 12 (1988): 42–51; Susan P. Conner, "Politics, Prostitution, and the Pox in Revolutionary Paris, 1789–1799," *Journal of Social History* 22 (1989): 713–34; Susan P. Conner, "Public Virtue and Public Women in Revolutionary Paris, 1793–1794," *Eighteenth-Century Studies* (1994–1995): 221–40; for the Dutch Republic: Lotte van de Pol, *Het Amsterdams hoerdom: prostitutie in de zeventiende en acchttiende eeuw* (Amsterdam: Wereldbibliotheek, 1996); Dirk Jaap Noordam, "Prostitutie in Leiden in de 18e eeuw," in *Leidse facetten*, ed. Diden Boer (Leiden: Waanders, 1982); Faramerz Dabhoiwala, "Koppellaarsters, Kruishoeren and the Kooi, Prostitution in the Hague, 1720–1749," BA essay, University of York, 1990.

12. These findings are based on a search of the Burney Collection of seventeenth and eighteenth century newspapers (Gale Publishing). Philip Carter, *Men and the Emergence of Polite Society, Britain, 1660–1800* (New York: Longman, 2001), and E. J. Cleary, *The Feminization Debate in Eighteenth-Century England: Literature, Commerce and Luxury* (New York: PalgraveMacmillan, 2004), seek to either limit or ignore the significance of the new meaning of effeminacy and fail to note that over time the new meaning eventually replaced the old.

13. Jennine Hurl-Eamon, "Policing Male Heterosexuality: The Reformation of Manners Societies' Campaign against the Brothels in Westminster, 1690–1720," *Journal of Social History* 37 (2004): 1017–35, does not appreciate that it is necessary to distinguish a traditional Protestant morality, which sought to treat the sexual behavior of men and women on equal terms and therefore intended to abolish brothels, from the modern heterosexuality of men like Saunders Welch, which tolerated discreet prostitution as a means of preventing effeminate sodomy. Hurl-Eamon improbably claims to be the first to use recognizances for this purpose six years after my results were published.
14. Francis Place, *The Autobiography,* ed. Mary Thale (Cambridge: Cambridge University Press, 1972), 71–82, 95–96.
15. Information about London prostitution is taken from Trumbach, *Sex and Gender Revolution,* unless otherwise noted.
16. Dudley Ryder, *The Diary ... 1715–1716,* ed. William Matthews (London: Methuen, 1939), 66–67, 71–72, 85, 88, 105.

Chapter 9

1. *The School of Venus* (1680) in *When Word Becomes Flesh: An Anthology of Eighteenth-Century Libertine Literature,* ed. Bradford K. Mudge (Oxford: Oxford University Press, 2004), 3–57, see 21. The French original, *L'Escole des filles* (1655), was probably the work of Michel Millot.
2. Roger Thompson, *Unfit for Modest Ears: A Study of Pornographic, Obscene, and Bawdy Works Written or Published in England in the Second Half of the Seventeenth Century* (Totowa, NJ: Rowman and Littlefield, 1979), ix–x.
3. Lynn Hunt, "Introduction," in *The Invention of Pornography: Obscenity and the Origins of Modernity,* ed. Lynn Hunt (New York: Zone Books, 1993), 10.
4. Karen Harvey, *Reading Sex in the Eighteenth Century: Bodies and Gender in English Erotic Culture* (Cambridge: Cambridge University Press, 2004), 20. See also 22, 33.
5. See Julie Peakman, *Mighty Lewd Books: The Development of Pornography in Eighteenth-Century England* (New York: Palgrave, 2003) for a more detailed analysis of these themes.
6. Carl von Linnaeus, *Systema naturae per regna tria naturae* (Lugduni Batavorum: Theodore Haak, 1735); *Species plantarum, exhibentes plantas rite cognitas, ad genera relatas, cum differentiis specificis* (Stockholm: Laurent Salvi, 1753). See also Philip Miller, *Catalogus plantarum officinalium quae in Horto Botanico Chelseyano* (London, 1730).
7. [Thomas Stretser], *Arbor Vitae: or The Tree of Life* (London: E. Curll, 1741); Anonymous, *Wisdom Revealed; or the Tree of Life, discover'd and describ'd. By a Studious enquirer into the mysteries of Nature. To which is added the Crab-Tree: or, Sylvia Discover'd* (London: E. Hill, 1741), 3–4.
8. See for instance *The Fruit Shop* (London: C. Moran, 1765).
9. Philogynes Clitorides [pseudo.], *The Natural History of the Frutex Vulvaria, or Flowering Shrub: As it is Collected from the Best Botanists Both Ancient and Modern* (London: W. James, 1732).

10. Julien Offray de La Mettrie, *L'homme plante* (Potsdam: Chretien Frederic Voss, 1748).
11. Joannes Benedictus Sinibaldus, *Geneanthropeiae sive de hominis generatione decateuchon* (Rome, 1642). The English translation was *Rare Verities, or the Cabinet of Venus Unlocked* (London: P. Briggs, 1658).
12. Editions consulted: Anonymous, *Aristotle's Master-Piece* (1684; London: F.C. for J. How, 1690) and Nicolas Venette, *La génération de l'homme, ou tableau de l'amour conjugal considéré dans l'état du mariage*, 2 vols. ([London], 1741), published originally in Amsterdam in 1687.
13. Roger Thompson, *Sex in Middlesex: Popular Mores in a Massachusetts County, 1649–1699*, forword by David D. Hall (Amherst: University of Massachusetts Press, 1986), 85–86, 93; Roy Porter and Lesley Hall, *The Facts of Life: The Creation of Sexual Knowledge in Britain, 1650–1950* (New Haven, CT: Yale University Press, 1995), 31–90. On earlier sex manuals, see Rudolph M. Bell, *How to Do It: Guides to Good Living for Renaissance Italians* (Chicago: University of Chicago Press, 1999).
14. Martin Schurig, *Spermatologia historico-medico* (Frankfurt, 1720).
15. John Marten, *Gonosologium novum; or, A new system of all the secret infirmities and diseases natural, accidental, and venereal in men and women* (London: N. Crouch et al., 1709); Thomas W. Laqueur, *Solitary Sex: A Cultural History of Masturbation* (New York: Zone Books, 2003), 29.
16. Marten, *Gonosologium novum*, 102.
17. [John Marten], *Onania: or, the heinous sin of self-pollution, and all its frightful consequences, (in both sexes,) considerd; with spiritual and physical advice*, 15th ed. (1712; London: J. Isted, 1730), 135. See Laqueur, *Solitary Sex*, 31 on Marten as the original author, although a number of hands had parts to play as new editions expanded.
18. Samuel-Auguste-David Tissot, *L'Onanisme; ou Dissertation physique sur les malades produites par la masturbation* (Lausanne, 1760; [Latin edition, 1759]). See also Bienville, *La Nymphomanie, ou Traité de la fureur uterine* (Amsterdam, 1771); English translation by Dr. Edward Sloane Wilmot, *Nymphomania, or, a Dissertation concerning the Furor Uterinus* (London: J. Bow, 1775).
19. John Marten, *A Treatise of all the Degrees and Symptoms of the Venereal Disease, in both Sexes*, 6th ed. (London: S. Crouch et al, 1708), 31.
20. Jean Astruc, *A Treastise of the Venereal Disease, in Six Books: Containing an Account of the Original, Propagation, and Contagion of this Distemper in General. Written Originally in Lanin by John Astruc, And now Translated into English by William Barrowby, M. B.*, 2 vols. (London: W. Innys and R. Manby, C. Davis, and J. Clarke, 1737), 1:141–42.
21. John Maubray, *The Female Physician, Containing all the Diseases incident to that Sex, in Virgins, Wives, and Widows; Together With their Causes and Symptoms, their Degrees of Danger, and respective Methods of Prevention and Cure* (London: James Holland, 1724). See also *The Ladies Dispensatory, or, Every Woman her Own Physician* (London: James Hodges, John James, 1739).
22. Anonymous, *The Man-Midwife Unmasqud: Being the Case of a Certain Young Lady, who apply'd to the noted Doctor D—for his Advice* (London: J. Dormer,

1738). See also Anonymous, *The Danger and Immodesty of The Present too general Custom of Unnecessarily Employing Men-Midwives* (London: J. Wilkie and F. Blyth, 1772).

23. This tension between nature and having to learn the natural was common both in Enlightenment erotica and in educational texts more generally. See for instance Jean-Jacques Rousseau, *Émile, or On Education*, intro. and trans. Allan Bloom (1762; New York: Basic Books, 1979), chapter 5.
24. Roy Porter, "Enlightenment and Pleasure," in *Pleasure in the Eighteenth Century*, ed. Roy Porter and Mulvey Roberts (Basingstoke: Macmillan, 1996), 1.
25. John C. O'Neal, *The Authority of Experience: Sensationalist Theory in the French Enlightenment* (University Park: Pennsylvania State University Press, 1996).
26. Marquis de Sade, *The Complete Justine, Philosophy of the Bedroom, and Other Writings,* trans. Richard Seaver and Austyn Wainhouse, intro. Jean Paulhan and Maurice Blanchot (New York: Grove Press, 1966), 273–74.
27. Nicolas Chorier, *L'Academie des dames ou la philosophie dans le boudoir du Grand Siècle*, ed. Jean-Pierre Dubost (1680; Arles: Éditions Philippe Picquier, 1999), 91.
28. Wijnand W. Mijnhardt, "Politics and Pornography in the Seventeenth- and Eighteenth-Century Dutch Republic," in *The Invention of Pornography: Obscenity and the Origins of Modernity*, ed. Lynn Hunt (New York: Zone Books, 1993), 283–300.
29. [Xavier d'Arles de Montigny], *Thérèse philosophe, ou Mémoires pour servir à l'Histoire de D. Dirrag, & de Mademoiselle Eradice* (The Hague [Paris], 1748), 23. The imprint is false, and the work is also sometimes attributed to Jean Baptiste de Boyer, Marquis d'Argens.
30. Tommaso Crudeli, *Arte di piacere in Rime e prose* (Paris, 1805), 151, quoted in Armando Marchi, "Obscene Literature in Eighteenth-Century Italy: An Historical and Bibliographical Note," in *'Tis Nature's Fault: Unauthorized Sexuality during the Enlightenment*, ed. Robert Purks Maccubbin, (Cambridge: Cambridge University Press, 1985), 244–60, see 247. The piece was originally published in 1769.
31. Margaret Jacob, "The Materialist World of Pornography," in *The Invention of Pornography: Obscenity and the Origins of Modernity*, ed. Lynn Hunt (New York: Zone Books, 1993), 162.
32. Theresa Ann Smith, *The Emerging Female Citizen: Gender and Enlightenment in Spain* (Berkeley: University of California Press, 2006), discusses the publishing situation generally. The Spanish debated the status of women, but avoided discussing sexual issues.
33. Anonymous, *Popery Display'd: or, The Church of Rome Described in her True Colors* (London: Joseph Downing, 1713), 25.
34. Anonymous, *A Full and True Account of a Dreaded Fire that Lately Broke Out in the Pope's Breeches* (London: J. Baker, 1713). See also Anonymous, *The Cloisters laid Open, Or, Adventures of the Priests and Nuns with Some Account of Confessions, and the lewd Use they make of them* (London: Meanwell, [1770]), which includes one of Boccaccio's more famous anticlerical stories. On the history of Aretino in England, see Ian Frederick Moulton, *Before Pornography: Erotic Writing in Early Modern England* (Oxford: Oxford University Press, 2000).

35. Peter Wagner, *Eros Revived: Erotica of the Enlightenment in England and America* (London: Secker and Warburg, 1988), 77. For Koch, see *De obscoenis pontificiorum decimis* (Flensurg, 1707). *The Frauds of Romish Monks and Priests Set forth in Eight Letters*, 4th ed. (London: Robert Clavell, 1704) is attributed to Gavin, as is *A Master-Key to Popery By the Reverend Mr. Anthony Gavin* (Dublin: J. Walthoe, 1725). The authorship of the latter is unclear. See Peakman, *Mighty Lewd Books*, 135–36. For Anthony Egan, *The Book of Rates Now Used in the Sin Custom House of the Church of Rome* (London, 1673).
36. Peakman, *Mighty Lewd Books*, 132–34.
37. See for instance, *Reasons Humbly Offer'd For a Law to Enact the Castration of Popish Ecclesiastics, As the Best Way to Prevent th[e] Growth of Popery in England* (London: A. Baldwin, 1700), and *The Priest Gelded: Or, Popery At The Last Gasp Shewing* (London: M. M'Culloh, 1747).
38. Jean Louis de Lolme, *The History of Flagellants, or the Advantages of Discipline; Being a Paraphrase and Commentary on the Historia Flagellantium of the Abbé Boileau, Doctor of the Sorbonne* (London: M. Hingeston, Yeats and Robertson; Fielding and Walker, [1776]), 327–28. This comment includes rather come-hither footnotes decrying the dangers of self-examination.
39. [Young nobleman], *Nunnery Tales, Written by a Young Nobleman, and Translated from his French Manuscript into English* (London: M. Lovemore, sold by Booksellers of London and Westminster, 1727), 69. See also [G. B.], *A Compleat History of the Intrigues of Priests and Nuns* (London: printed for John Marshall, 1732).
40. Anonymous, *Les jésuites de la maison professe de Paris, en belle humeur* (1696; Cologne: Pierre Marteau, 1725). A third edition appeared in 1761. See also Charles-Jacques-Louis-Auguste Rochette de la Morlière (chevalier), *Les lauriers ecclésiasiques, ou Campagnes de l'abbé de T . . .* (Luxuropolis: l'imprimerie ordinaire du Clergé, 1748). Of the publication information, obviously only the date is reliable.
41. Jean Baptiste Girard, *Historische print en Dicht Tafereelen, van Jan Baptist Girar en Juffrou Maris Catharina Cadiere* (1735).
42. Text consulted with Jacques-Charles Gervaise de Latouche (attributed), *Histoire de dom B . . ., portier des Chartreux, écrite par lui-même* (Rome: chez Philotanus, c. 1745). The first edition seems to have appeared in 1741 or 1742.
43. Pierre-Jean-Baptiste Nougaret, *La capucinade, histoire sans vraisemblance, par Frère P.-J. Niscret N**** (Partout, 1765).
44. Rachel Weil, "Sometimes a Scepter is Only a Scepter," in *Invention of Pornography: Obscenity and the Origins of Modernity*, ed. Lynn Hunt (New York: Zone Books, 1993), 124–53.
45. John T. Alexander, *Catherine the Great* (Oxford: Oxford University Press, 1989).
46. Katherine Crawford, *Perilous Performances: Gender and Regency in Early Modern France* (Cambridge, MA: Harvard University Press, 2004), chapter 5.
47. BN MS 12629, p. 83. One widely circulated version of the incest claim was in the first of the *Philippiques*. Lescure denies the rumor, blaming it on the Duchesse du Maine and arguing that Philippe was just demonstrative in public. See *Les Philippiques*, 240–41, 296–301.

48. Claude-Prosper Jolyot de Crébillon [Crébillon fils], *The Sofa*, trans. Bonamy Dobrée in *The Libertine Reader*, ed. Michel Feher (New York: Zone Books, 1997), 169–331.
49. See also Giambattista Casti, *Berretto magico* [*The Magic Cap*], which is a reworking of Diderot's text. For discussion, see Armando Marchi, "Obscene Literature in Eighteenth-Century Italy: An Historical and Bibliographical Note," trans. James Coke and David Marsh in *'Tis Nature's Fault: Unauthorized Sexuality during the Enlightenment*, ed. Robert Purks Maccubbin (Cambridge: Cambridge University Press, 1987), 244–60, see esp. 251.
50. This section draws heavily on Susan Mann, *Precious Records: Women in China's Long Eighteenth Century* (Palo Alto, CA: Stanford University Press, 1997). Not all Qing erotic repression succeeded. Efforts to eradicate foot binding came to naught. Chinese women regarded the practice as indicating purity and good breeding, while male comments on the erotics of "lotus-shaped feet" are legion. The removal of erotic entertainers from palace precincts did not end courtesan entertainments, which flourished until the Opium War. When the state tried to limit access to female entertainment quarters in the Lower Yangzi, it inadvertently encouraged the development of the private marketplace.
51. Keith McMahon, *Misers, Shrews, and Polygamists: Sexuality and Male-Female Relations in Eighteenth-Century Chinese Fiction* (Durham, NC: Duke University Press, 1995), 2, 11, 33. The *ars erotica* flourished in ancient China, going "underground" under the Song. Relatively few works appeared after that; see pp. 37–38. On the discourse of moderation, see pp. 39, 44–47. Much of this discussion is based on McMahon's analyses.
52. McMahon, *Misers, Shrews*, 66–69, 116, 129.
53. *Yu Jiao Li* (The Two Cousins) features two women fondling each other until the man joins them and heterosexual consummation closes the scene. McMahon, *Misers, Shrews*, 99, 116, 241.
54. See for instance, *Haoqui zhuan* (The Fortunate Union) and *Yu Jiao Li* (translated into French as *Les deux cousines*); McMahon, *Misers, Shrews*, 17.
55. Dror Ze'evi, *Producing Desire: Changing Sexual Discourse in the Ottoman Middle East, 1500–1900* (Berkeley: University of California Press, 2006).
56. Paul Rycaut, *The Present State of the Ottoman Empire* (1668; reprint, Frankfurt: Institute for the History of Arabic-Islamic Science, 1995). Rycaut was an ambassador to the Sublime Porte.
57. François, baron de Tott, *Memoirs*, 2 vols. (1785; facsimile, New York: Arno Press, 1973).
58. Jean Chardin, *Voyages du Chevalier Chardin en Perse, et autre lieux de l'Orient*, 4 vols. (Amsterdam: aux dépens de la Cie, 1735), 3:384.
59. Lady Mary Wortley Montagu, *Letters from the Levant*, ed. J. A. St. John (1763; London, 1838; reprint, New York, 1971).
60. Afsaneh Najmabadi, *Women with Mustaches and Men without Beards: Gender and Sexual Anxieties of Iranian Modernity* (Berkeley: University of California Press, 2005).
61. Fatima Müge Göçek, *East Encounters West: France and the Ottoman Empire in the Eighteenth Century* (New York: Oxford, 1987).

62. *Tarikh muddat al-Fransis bi-Misr*, ed. S. Moreh (Leiden, 1975), 12. Romantics, including Goethe, Byron, Hugo, and Lamartine, made use of erotic imagery of the east recurrently in their work. See Derek Hopwood, *Sexual Encounters in the Middle East: The British, the French and the Arabs* (Reading, NY: Ithaca Press, 1999), 28–48. The dual stereotype of Arabs as lazy and overly sensual persisted into the twentieth century, and perhaps persists still.
63. Captain Edward Sellon, *The Ups and Downs of Life*, ed. C. J. Scheiner (Hertfordshire: Wordsworth Editions, 1996), 55. See pp. 47–49 for Sellon's opinions of Indian women more generally.
64. Kenneth Ballhatchet, *Race, Sex and Class under the Raj: Imperial Attitudes and Policies and the their Critics, 1793–1905* (New York: St. Martin's, 1980), 5.
65. *Kama* referred to erotic or aesthetic pleasure. The other three purusharthas are *dharma* (virtuous living), *artha* (prosperity), and *moksha* (freedom or liberation). See Gavin Flood, *An Introduction to Hinduism* (Cambridge: Cambridge University Press, 1996), 17.
66. See also the efforts against African sexual customs. For the British interventions there, see Ronald Hyam, *Empire and Sexuality: The British Experience* (New York: St. Martin's Press, 1990).

BIBLIOGRAPHY

Primary Sources

Aleman, M. *The Life of Guzman of Alfarache, or, The Spanish Rogue*. 1708. London: Longman, 1821.

Anonymous. *Aristotle's Compleat Master-Piece, Displaying the Secrets of Nature in the Generation of Man*, 15th ed. London, 1723.

Anonymous. *Aristotle's Master-Piece*. London: F.C. for J. How, 1690.

Anonymous. *The Cloisters laid Open, Or, Adventures of the Priests and Nuns with Some Account of Confessions, and the lewd Use they make of them*. London, c. 1770.

Anonymous. *The Danger and Immodesty of The Present too general Custom of Unnecessarily Employing Men-Midwives*. London: J. Wilkie and F. Blyth, 1772.

Anonymous. *The Fruit Shop*. London: C. Moran, 1765.

Anonymous. *A Full and True Account of a Dreaded Fire that Lately Broke Out in the Pope's Breeches*. London: J. Baker, 1713.

Anonymous. *Les jésuites de la maison professe de Paris, en belle humeur*. Cologne: Pierre Marteau, 1725.

Anonymous. *The Lady's Decoy, Or, the Man-Midwife's Defence*. London: S. Slow, 1738.

Anonymous. *The Man-Midwife Unmasqud, Being the Case of a Certain Young Lady, who apply'd to the noted Doctor D—for his Advice*. London: J. Dormer, 1738.

Anonymous. *Nunnery Tales, Written by a Young Nobleman, and Translated from his French Manuscript into English*. London, 1727.

Anonymous. *Onania; or, the Heinous Sin of Self-Pollution, and All Its Frightful Consequences, in Both Sexes*. London: T. Crouch, 1722.

Anonymous. *Popery Display'd, or, The Church of Rome Described in her True Colors*. London: Joseph Downing, 1713.

Anonymous. *Satan's Harvest Home, Or the Present State of Whorecraft, Adultery, Fornication, Procuring*. London, 1749.

Anonymous. *Sodom, or the Quintessence of Debauchery*. London, 1684.
Anonymous. *A Treatise of Health and Long Life*. Bath: James Leake, 1743.
Anonymous. *Wisdom Revealed; or the Tree of Life, discover'd and describ'd. By a Studious enquirer into the mysteries of Nature. To which is added the Crab-Tree, or, Sylvia Discover'd*. London: E. Hill, 1741.
Armstrong, John. *The Art of Preserving Health; a Poem*. Dublin: J. Smith & W. Powell, 1744.
Armstrong, John. *The Oeconomy of Love: A Poetical Essay*. London: T. Cooper, 1736.
Astruc, Jean. *A Treatise of the Venereal Disease*. London: W. Innys, 1737.
Biddle, Charles. *Autobiography of Charles Biddle*. Philadelphia, 1881.
Bienville, D. T. de, and Edward Sloane Wilmot. *Nymphomania, or a Dissertation Concerning the Furor. Uterinus*. London: J. Bew, 1775.
Blackstone, W. *Commentaries on the Laws of England*, 4 vols. Oxford: Clarendon Press, 1768.
Bruyn, Cornelis de. *A Voyage to the Levant*. London, 1702.
Buchan, William. *Observations Concerning the Prevention and Cure of the Venereal Disease*. London, 1796.
Carpzov, B. *Practicae Novae Imperialis Saxonicae. Rerum Criminalium*. Pars II. Witengergae, 1670.
Chardin, Jean. *Voyages du Chevalier Chardin en Perse, et autre lieux de l'Orient*, 4 vols. Amsterdam: aux dépens de la Cie, 1735.
Cleland, John. *Memoirs of a Woman of Pleasure*. London: G. Fenton, 1749.
Cobbett, W. *The Cannibal's Progress, or the Dreadful Horrors of French Invasion*. London: Wright, Cadel et al., 1798.
Cornaro, Luigi. *Sure and Certain Methods of Attaining a Long and Healthful Life*. London: Daniel Midwinter, 1722.
Diderot, Denis, and Jean Le Rond d Alembert. *Encyclopédie, Ou, Dictionnaire Raisonné Des Sciences, Des Arts Et Des Métiers*, 17 vols., vol. 8, translated by Anoush Terjanian. Paris: Briasson [etc.], 1751.
Divorce Papers. Records of the Supreme Court. Eastern District. Pennsylvania Historical and Museum Commission. Harrisburg, PA, 1785–1815.
Drake, James. *Anthropologia Nova; or, a New System of Anatomy*. London: Smith and Walford, 1707.
Dubois-Desaulle, G. *Etude sur la Bestialite au point de vue Historique, Medical et Juridique*. Paris: Charles Carrington, 1905.
Egan, Anthony. *The Book of Rates Now Used in the Sin Custom House of the Church of Rome*. London, 1673.
Feijoo, Benito Jerâonimo. *An Essay on the Learning, Genius, and Abilities, of the Fair-sex, etc.* London: D. Steel, 1774.
Feijoo, Benito Jerâonimo. *An Essay on Woman*. London: W. Bingley, 1768.
Friedrichs Wilhelms. *Land-Recht des Königreichs Preussen*, etc. Königsberg, 1721.
Gavin, Antonio. *The Frauds of Romish Monks and Priests Set forth in Eight Letters*, 4th ed. London: Robert Clavell, 1704.
Gavin, Antonio. *A Master-Key to Popery By the Reverend Mr. Anthony Gavin*. Dublin: J. Walthoe, 1725.

[G. B.] *A Compleat History of the Intrigues of Priests and Nuns*. London: printed for John Marshall, 1732.

Girard, Jean Baptiste. *Historische print en Dicht Tafereelen, van Jan Baptist Girar en Juffrou Maris Catharina Cadiere*. 1735.

Gouge, William. *The Works of William Gouge ... Domesticall Duties*. London, 1627.

Graham, James. *An Abstract from a Book by J. Graham. Intituled "Medical Transactions at the Temple of Health in London."* 1781.

Graham, James. *A Clear, Full, And Faithful Portraiture, ... and Ardent Recommendation Of A ... Virgin Princess ... To A Certain Youthful Heir-Apparent*, 2nd ed. Bath, 1792.

Graham, James. *Dr. Graham's General Directions as to Regimen*. 1782.

Graham, James. *The General State of Medical and Chirurgical Practice, Ancient and Modern, Exhibited*. Bath: R. Cruttwell, 1778.

Graham, James. *The Guardian Goddess of Health, Or, the Whole Art of Preventing and Curing Diseases*. London, 1780.

de la Grande-Chancel, Joseph. *Les Philippques de La Grande-Chancel*, edited by M. de Lescure. Paris: Pouler-Malassis et De Broise, 1858.

Gregory, John. *Dr. Gregory's Legacy to His Daughters*. London, 1806.

Haller, Albrecht von. *Réflexions sur le Système de la Génération*. Geneva: Barrillot, 1751.

Haywood, Eliza. *The British Recluse; or, The Secret History of Cleomira*. London, 1722.

Haywood, Eliza. *Fantomina, or, Love in a Maze*. London, 1724.

Hill, Aaron. *A Full and Just Account of the Present State of the Ottoman Empire*, 2nd ed. London: 1710.

Jacob, G. *A New Law-Dictionary, Containing the Interpretation and Definition of Words and Terms Used in the Law, etc*. London: E. & R. Nutt & R. Gosling, 1729.

Koch, Christian Gottlieb. *De obscoenis pontificiorum decimis*. Flensburg, 1707.

Kohler, J. *Die Peinliche Gerichtsordnung Kaiser Karls V., Constitutio Criminalis Carolina*. Berlin: Kritisch herausgegeben von J. Kohler und W. Scheel, 1900.

Lacy, M. *The History of the Female Shipwright*. London: M. Lewis, 1773.

[Lady, A]. *The Twin Sisters; or, the Effects of Education*, 3 vols., vol. 1. London, 1788.

La Mettrie, Julien Offray de. *L'homme plant*. Potsdam: Chretien Frederic Voss, 1748.

[Latouche, Jacques-Charles Gervaise de]. *Histoire de dom B ..., portier des Chartreux, écrite par lui-même*. Rome: chez Philotanus, c. 1745.

Le Rebours, Marie-Angelique. *Avis Aux M*Res Qui Veulent Nourrir Leurs Enfans*. Utrecht: Lacombe, 1767.

Lessius, Leonardus. *Hygiasticon, Or, a Treatise of the Means of Health and Long Life*. London: printed by the author, 1742.

Lessius, Leonardus. *A Treatise of Health and Long Life*. Bath: James Leake, 1743.

Leyser, A. *Meditationes ad Pandectas*. Leipzig: Wolfenbüttel, Meisner, 1748.

Linnaeus, Carl von. *Species plantarum, exhibentes plantas rite cognitas, ad genera relatas, cum differentiis specificis*. Stockholm: Laurent Salvi, 1753.

Linnaeus, Carl von. *Systema naturae per regna tria naturae*. Lugduni Batavorum, Theodore Haak, 1735.

Lolme, Jean Louis de. *The History of Flagellants, or the Advantages of Discipline; Being a Paraphrase and Commentary on the Historia Flagellantium of the Abbé Boileau, Doctor of the Sorbonne.* London: M. Hingeston, Yeats and Robertson; Fielding and Walker, [1776].

Mackenzie, G. *Lawes and Customs of Scotland in Matters Criminal.* Edinburgh, 1699.

Malthus, Thomas. *On Population.* London, 1798.

Marten, J. *A Treatise Of all the Degrees and Symptoms of the Venereal Disease, In both Sexes.* London: S. Crouch et al., 1708.

Marten, John. *Gonosologium novum; or, A new system of all the secret infirmities and diseases natural, accidental, and venereal in men and women.* London: N. Crouch et al., 1709.

Maubray, John. *The Female Physician, Containing all the Diseases incident to that Sex, in Virgins, Wives, and Widows; Together With their Causes and Symptoms, their Degrees of Danger, and respective Methods of Prevention and Cure.* London: James Holland, 1724.

Maubray, John. *The Ladies Dispensatory, or, Every Woman her Own Physician.* London: James Hodges, John James, 1739.

Mauriceau, Francis. *The Diseases of Women with Child.* London: T. Cox, 1736.

Maximianus. *The Impotent Lover Describ'd in Six Elegies on Old-Age.* London: J. Sackfield, and T. Warner, 1718.

Miller, Philip. *Catalogus plantarum officinalium quae in Horto Botanico Chelseyano.* London, 1730.

Montagu, Lady Mary Wortley. *Letters from the Levant*, edited by J. A. St. John. London, 1838.

[Montigny, Xavier d'Arles de]. *Thérèse philosophe, ou Mémoires pour servir à l'Histoire de D. Dirrag, & de Mademoiselle Eradice.* The Hague [Paris], 1748.

Nougaret, Pierre-Jean-Baptiste Nougaret. *La capucinade, histoire sans vraisemblance, par Frère P.-J. Niscret N***.* Partout, 1765.

[Philo, Castitatis]. *Onania Examined, and Detected.* London: Marshall & Roberts, 1724.

[Philogynes Clitorides]. *The Natural History of the Frutex Vulvaria, or Flowering Shrub, As it is Collected from the Best Botanists Both Ancient and Modern.* London: W. James, 1732.

Pitts, Joseph. *A True and Faithful Account of the Religion and Manners of the Mohammetans.* London, 1704.

Profily, John. *An Easy and Exact Method of Curing the Venereal Disease.* London: J. Robinson, 1748.

Radicati, Alberto. *A Phiosophical [sic] Dissertation upon Death*, translated by Joseph Morgan. London, 1732.

Riforma della legislazione criminale toscana del dì 30 novembre 1786. Siena, [1786].

Robinson, Mary Elizabeth, and J. Fitzgerald Molloy. *Memoirs of Mary Robinson, "Perdita."* London: Gibbings, J. B. Lippincott Co., 1895.

Robinson, Nicholas. *A New Treatise of the Venereal Disease.* London: J. J. and P. Knapton, 1736.

Rochette de la Morlière, Charles-Jacques-Louis-Auguste (chevalier). *Les lauriers ecclésiastiques, ou Campagnes de l'abbé de T. ...* Luxuropolis: l'imprimerie ordinaire du Clergé, 1748.

Roussel, Pierre. *Système Physique et Moral de la Femme*. Paris: Lannette, 1775.
Rycaut, Paul. *The Present State of the Ottoman Empire*. 1668. Reprint, Frankfurt: Institute for the History of Arabic-Islamic Science, 1995.
Salmon, Thomas. *Modern History or the Present State of All Nations*, 26 vols. London, 1726.
Schurig, Martin. *Parthenologia Historico-Medica, Hoc Est, Virginitatis Consideratio*. Dresden: Christophori Hekelii, 1729.
Schurig, Martin. *Spermatologia Historico-Medica*. Frankfurt, 1720.
Schurig, Martin, and Friedrich Heckel. *Gynµcologia Historico-Medica*. Dresden: Libraria Hekeliana, 1730.
Sellon, Captain Edward. *The Ups and Downs of Life*, edited by C. J. Scheiner. Hertfordshire: Wordsworth Editions, 1996.
Sibly, Ebenezer. *A Complete Illustration of the Celestial Science of Astrology*. London, 1788.
Sibly, Ebenezer. *Everybody's Fortune Teller*. London, 1925.
Sibly, Ebenezer. *A New and Complete Illustration of the Occult Sciences*. London, 1790.
Sibly, Ebenezer. *The Medical Mirror. Or Treatise on the Impregnation of the Human Female*. London: Champante and Whitrow, 1796.
Sinibaldus, Joannes Benedictus. *Geneanthropeiae sive de hominis generatione decateuchon*. Rome, 1642.
Smellie, William. *A Treatise on the Theory and Practice of Midwifery*. London, 1752.
Stevens, John. *Man-Midwifery Exposed, or the Danger and Immorality of Employing Men in Midwifery Proved; and the Remedy for the Evil Found*. London, 1849.
Stretser, T. *A New Description of Merryland*. London, 1741.
[Stretser, Thomas]. *Arbor Vitae, or The Tree of Life*. London: E. Curll, 1741.
Strother, Edward. *The Family Companion for Health*. London: F. Fayram; and J. Leake, 1729.
Thicknesse, Philip. *Man-Midwifery Analysed, And the Tendency of That Practice Detected and Exposed*. London: R. Davis, 1764.
Thompson, Charles. *The Travels of the late Charles Thompson Esq.*, 3 vols. London, 1744.
Tissot, S.A.D. *An Essay on the Disorders of People of Fashion*. London: Richardson and Urquhart, 1771.
Tissot, S.A.D. *Onanism: Or, a Treatise Upon the Disorders Produced by Masturbation, or, the Dangerous Effects of Secret and Excessive Venery*. London: J. Pridden, 1766.
Tissot, S.A.D. *L'Onanisme; ou Dissertation physique sur les malades produites par la masturbation*. Lausanne, 1760.
Tott, François, Baron de, *Memoirs*, 2 vols. 1785. Facsimile, New York: Arno Press, 1973.
Turner, Daniel. *Syphilis ... Containing Farther Observations on the Venereal Disease*. London: John Clarke, 1739.
Venette, Nicholas. *De la Generation de l'homme; ou, Tableau De L'amour Conjugal*. Cologne: Claude Joly, 1696.

Venette, Nicholas. *The Mysteries of Conjugal Love Reveal'd*. London, 1712.
Venette, Nicolas. *Conjugal Love, or, the Pleasures of the Marriage Bed*. New York: Garland, reprinted 1984.
Vincent, Dr. *The Lamentations of Germany*. London, 1638.
Von Uffenbach, Baron [trans. W. Quarrell and Margaret Moore]. *London in 1710*. London: Faber, 1934.
Welch, Saunders. *A Proposal to Render Effective a Plan to Remove the Nuisance of Common Prostitutes from the Streets of this Metropolis*. London, 1758.
Wilkes, Rev W. *A Letter of Genteel and Moral Advice to a Young Lady*. Dublin, 1741.
Wilmot, Edward Sloane. *Nymphomania, or, a Dissertation concerning the Furor Uterinus*. London: J. Bow, 1775.

Secondary Sources

Abelove, Henry. "Some Speculations on the History of Intercourse During the Long Eighteenth Century in England." *Genders* 6 (1989): 125–30.
Abelove, H., M. A. Barale, and D. M. Halperin D. eds. *The Lesbian and Gay Studies Reader*. London: Routledge, 1993.
Adair, Richard. *Courtship, Illegitimacy and Marriage in Early Modern England*. Manchester: Manchester University Press, 1996.
Aggleton, Peter, ed. *Bisexualities and AIDS*. London: Taylor and Francis, 1996.
Aggleton, Peter, ed. *Men Who Sell Sex*. Philadelphia: Temple University Press, 1999.
Alexander, John T. *Catherine the Great*. Oxford: Oxford University Press, 1989.
Andrew, Donna T. "'Adultery a-La-Mode': Privilege, the Law and Attitudes to Adultery 1770–1809." *History* 82, no. 265 (1997): 5–23.
Andrews, Walter G., and Mehmet Kalpakli. *The Age of Beloveds, Love and the Beloved in Early-Modern Ottoman and European Culture and Society*. Durham, NC: Duke University Press, 2005.
Aries, Philip. *L'Homme devant la Mort*. Paris: Editions du Seuil, 1977.
Ariès, Philippe. *Centuries of Childhood: A Social History of Family Life*. New York: Vintage Books, 1962.
Ariés, Phillipe, and André Béjin. *Western Sexuality, Practice and Precept in Past and Present Times*. Oxford: Blackwell, 1985.
Ashbee, Henry Spencer [Pisanus Fraxis]. *Bibliography of Prohibited Books*, vol. 3, 1879. Reprint, New York: Jack Brussell, 1962.
Babayan, Kathryn, and Afsaneh Najmabad, eds. *Islamicate Sexualities: Translations Across Temporal Geographies of Desire*. Cambridge, MA: Harvard University Press, 2008.
Backscheider, P., and J. Richetti. *Popular Fiction by Women 1660–1730*. Oxford: Clarendon, 1996.
Baines, Paul, and Pat Rogers. *Edmund Curll Bookseller*. Oxford: Clarendon Press, 2007.
Baker, S. "Henry Fielding's *The Female Husband*: Fact and Fiction." *PMLA* 74, no. 3 (1959): 213–24.
Ballaster, R. *Seductive Forms: Women's Amatory Fiction from 1684–1740*. Oxford: Clarendon Press, 1992.

Ballhatchet, Kenneth. *Race, Sex and Class under the Raj: Imperial Attitudes and Policies and the Their Critics, 1793–1905*. New York: St. Martin's, 1980.

Barahona, Renato. *Sex Crimes, Honor, and the Law in Early Modern Spain, Vizcaya, 1528–1735*. Toronto: University of Toronto Press, 2003.

Barber, Giles, and B. Fabian, eds. *The Book and the Book Trade in Eighteenth-Century Europe*. Hamburg: Dr. Ernst Hauswedell & Co, 1981.

Barker-Benfield, G. J. *The Culture of Sensibility: Sex and Society in Eighteenth Century Britain*. Chicago: University of Chicago Press, 1992.

Bauer, H., ed. *Women and Cross-Dressing 1800–1939*, 3 vols. London, Routledge, 2006.

Baynes, Hannah. *James Graham, "Doctor of Medicine and Lover of His Species" or Simply a Quack?* London: Wellcome Institute for the History of Medicine, 1997.

Bell, Rudolph M. *How To Do It: Guides to Good Living for Renaissance Italians*. Chicago: University of Chicago Press, 1999.

Benabou, Erica-Marie. *La prostitution et la police des moeurs au XVIIIe siècle*. Paris: Perrin, 1987.

Benemann, W. *Male-Male Intimacy in Early America: Beyond Romantic Friendships*. New York: Harrington Park Press, 2006.

Bennett, Judith M. "'Lesbian-Like' and the Social History of Lesbianisms." *Journal of the History of Sexuality* 9 (2000): 1–24.

Bennett, Judith M., and Amy M. Froide, ed. *Single Women in the European Past, 1250–1800*. Philadelphia: University of Pennsylvania Press, 1999.

Berco, Cristian. *Sexual Hierarchies: Public Status, Men, Sodomy, and Society in Spain's Golden Age*. Toronto: University of Toronto Press, 2007.

Berkin, Carol. *First Generations: Women in Colonial America*. New York: Hill and Wang, 1996.

Betteridge, Thomas, ed. *Sodomy in Early Modern Europe*. Manchester: Manchester University Press, 2002.

Black, J. *A Subject for Taste Culture in Eighteenth-Century England*. London: Hambledon, 2005.

Blaikie, Andrew. *Illegitimacy, Sex, and Society, Northeast Scotland, 1750–1900* (1994), 215, W. R. Lee, "Bastardy and the Socio-Economic Structure of South Germany," *Journal of Interdisciplinary History* 7, no. 3, pp. 403–425.

Blaikie, Andrew. "Scottish Illegitimacy, Social Adjustment or Moral Economy?" *Journal of Interdisciplinary History* 29, no. 2 (1998), pp. 221–241.

Blanc, Olivier. *Les Libertines, Plaisir Et Liberté Au Temps Des Lumières*. Paris: Perrin, 1997.

Blasius, M., and S. Phelen, eds. *We Are Everywhere: A Historical Sourcebook of Gay and Lesbian Politics*. New York: Routledge, 1997.

Bloch, Ruth H. "Changing Conceptions of Sexuality and Romance in Eighteenth-Century America." *William and Mary Quarterly* 60, no. 1 (2003): 13–42.

Block, Sharon. *Rape and Sexual Power in Early America*. Chapel Hill: University of North Carolina Press, 2006.

Bond, Donald. *Joseph Addison, and Richard Steele: The Spectator*, 5 vols. Oxford: Clarendon Press, 1965.

Boros, J., I. Munnich, and M. Szegedi, eds. *Psychology and Criminal Justice: International Review of Theory and Practice*. Berlin: de Gruyter, 1998.

Borris, Kenneth, and G. Rousseau, eds. *The Sciences of Homosexuality in Early Modern Europe*. London: Routledge, 2008.

Boswell, James. *London Journal, 1762–1763*, edited by Frederick A. Pottle. London: William Heinemann, 1966.

Boucé, Paul-Gabriel. *Sexuality in Eighteenth-Century Britain*. Manchester: Manchester University Press, 1982.

Brandstrom, Anders, "Illegitimacy and Lone-Parenthood in Xixth Century Sweden." *Annales de Demographie Historique [France]*, no. 2 (1998).

Bray, Alan. *Homosexuality in Renaissance England*. London: Gay Men's Press, 1982.

Bremmer, Jan N., ed. *From Sappho to De Sade: Moments in the History of Sexuality*. London: Routledge, 1991.

Brille, A. A. "Necrophilia." *Journal of the Criminal Psychopathology* 2 (1941): 433–53.

Brille, A. A. "Necrophilia." *Journal of the Criminal Psychopathology* 3 (1941): 51–73.

Brooks, R. "'Vices Once Adopted': Theorising Male Homoeroticism in German-language Legal and Forensic Discourses, 1752–1869." *Reinvention, a Journal of Undergraduate Research* 1, no. 2 (2008).

Brown, Kathleen M. *Good Wives, Nasty Wenches, and Anxious Patriarchs: Gender, Race, and Power in Colonial Virginia*. Chapel Hill: University of North Carolina Press, 1996.

Bullough, Vern. *Sex, Society and History*. New York: Science History, Neale Watson, 1976.

Bullough, Vern. *Sexual Variance in Society and History*. New York: Wiley Interscience, 1976.

Bullough, Vern L., and Bonnie Bullough. *Sexual Attitudes*. London: Prometheus Books, 1995.

Bullough, Vern, Dorr Legg, Barret Elcano, and James Kepner, eds. *An Annotated Bibliography of Homosexuality, Transvestism, and Transsexualism*. New York: Garland Publishers, 1976.

Butler, Judith. *Gender Trouble: Feminism and the Subversion of Identity*. London: Routledge, 1990.

Bynum, W. F. "Cullen and the Nervous System." In *William Cullen and the Eighteenth Century Medical World*, edited by A. Doig et al., 151–57. Edinburgh: Edinburgh University Press, 1993.

Bynum, W. F., and Roy Porter. *William Hunter and the Eighteenth-Century Medical World*. Cambridge: Cambridge University Press, 1985.

Cáceres, Carlos F. "Sexual Culture and Sexual Health among Young People in Lima in the 1990s." Ph.D. thesis, Berkeley, University of California, 1996.

Camden, Carroll. *Restoration and Eighteenth-Century Literature*. Chicago: University of Chicago Press, 1963.

Cañizares-Esguerra, J. *How to Write the History of the New World*. Stanford, CA: Stanford Universtiy Press, 2001.

Carillo, Hector. *The Night is Young: Sexuality in Mexico in Time of AIDS*. Chicago: University of Chicago Press, 2002.

Carretta, V., and P. Gould, eds. *Genius in Bondage: Literature of the Early Black Atlantic*. Lexington: University Press of Kentucky, 2001.

Carrier, Joseph. *De Los Otros: Intimacy and Homosexuality among Mexican Men*. New York: Columbia University Press, 1995.

Carroll, B. D. "'I Indulged My Desire Too Freely': Sexuality, Spirituality, and the Sin of Self-Pollution in the Diary of Joseph Moody, 1720–1724." *The William and Mary Quarterly* 60 (2003): 155–70.

Carter, Angela. *The Sadeian Woman*. London: Virago, 1979.

Carter, Philip. *Men and the Emergence of Polite Society: Britain, 1660–1800*. New York: Longman, 2001.

Carter, S. *Purchasing Power*. Aldershot: Ashgate, 2004.

Cash, Arthur H. *John Wilkes, The Scandalous Father of Civil Liberty*. New Haven, CT: Yale University Press, 2006.

Castle, Terry. "'Matters Not Fit to be Mentioned': Fielding's *The Female Husband*." *English Literary History* 49 (1982): 602–23.

Cattelona, Georg'ann. "Control and Collaboration: The Role of Women in Regulating Female Sexual Behavior in Early Modern Marseille." *French Historical Studies* 18, no. 1 (1993), pp. 13–33.

Chamberlain, A. Ava. "The Immaculate Ovum: Jonathan Edwards and the Construction of the Female Body." *William and Mary Quarterly* 57 (2000): 289–301.

Chambers, D. *The Reinvention of the World: English Writing 1650–1750*. London: Arnold, 1996.

Chauncey, George. *Gay New York*. New York: Basic Books, 1994.

Chorier, Nicolas. *L'Academie des dames ou la philosophie dans le boudoir du Grand Siècle*, ed. Jean-Pierre Dubost. Arles: Éditions Philippe Picquier, 1999.

Clark, A. "Anne Lister's Construction of Lesbian Identity." *Journal of the History of Sexuality* 7, no. 1 (1996): 23–50.

Clark, Anna. "Twilight Moments." *Journal of the History of Sexuality* 14, no. 1/2 (2005), pp. 139–164.

Clark, Anna. *Women's Silence, Men's Violence: Sexual Assault in England, 1770–1845*. London: Pandora, 1987.

Clark, Sandra. "The Economics of Marriage in the Broadside Ballad." *Journal of Popular Culture* 36, no. 1 (2002): 119–33.

Cleary, E. J. *The Feminization Debate in Eighteenth-Century England: Literature, Commerce and Luxury*. New York: PalgraveMacmillan, 2004.

Cleland, J. *Fanny Hill: Memoirs of a Woman of Pleasure*. London, 1749.

Cody, L. *Birthing the Nation: Sex, Science and the Conception of Eighteenth-Century Britons*. Oxford: Oxford University Press, 2005.

Coke, E. *Institutions of the Laws of England: Part III*. London: W. Rawlins, 1680.

Collington, T., and P. Collington. "Adulteration or Adaptation? Nathaniel Lee's 'Princess of Cleve' and Its Sources." *Modern Philology* 100, no. 2 (2002): 196–226.

Connell, Raewyn. *Gender and Power: Society, the Person and Sexual Politics*. Cambridge: Polity, 1987.

Conner, Susan P. "Politics, Prostitution, and the Pox in Revolutionary Paris, 1789–1799." *Journal of Social History* 22 (1989): 713–34.

Conner, Susan P. "Prostitution and the Jacobin Agenda for Social Control." *Eighteenth-Century Life* 12 (1988): 42–51.

Conner, Susan P. "Public Virtue and Public Women in Revolutionary Paris, 1793–1794." *Eighteenth-Century Studies* (1994–1995): 221–40.

Cook, Matt, ed. *A Gay History of Britain: Love and Sex Between Men since the Middle Ages*. Oxford: Greenwood, 2007.

Cope, Kevin L., ed. *Eighteenth-Century British Erotica*, Set 1, Vol. 2: *Edmund Curll and Grub-Street Highlights*. London: Pickering & Chatto, 2002.

Corfield, P. J. *Power and the Professions in Britain 1700–1850*. London: Routledge, 2000.

Corkhill, A. "Kant, Sade and the Libertine Enlightenment." In *Libertine Enlightenment: Sex, Libertine and License in the Eighteenth Century*, edited by Peter Cryle and Lisa O'Connell. Basingstoke: Palgrave Macmillan, 2004.

Correia, Clara Pinto. *The Ovary of Eve, Egg and Sperm and Preformation*. Chicago: University of Chicago Press, 1997.

Costa Pereira, Robe Hipolita da. *Diario de minha viagem para Filadelfia*. 1798–1799. Reprint, Rio de Janeiro, 1955.

Cracuin, A. *British Women Writers and the French Revolution*. Basingstoke: Macmillan, 2005.

Crawford, Katherine. *European Sexualities, 1400–1800*. Cambridge: Cambridge University Press, 2007.

Crawford, Katherine. *Perilous Performances: Gender and Regency in Early Modern France*. Cambridge, MA: Harvard University Press, 2004.

Crawford, Patricia. *Blood, Bodies and Families in Early Modern England*. Harlow: Pearson Longman, 2004.

Crébillon, Claude-Prosper Jolyot de. *The Sofa*, translated by Bonamy Dobrée. In *The Libertine Reader*, edited by Michel Feher. New York: Zone Books, 1997.

Cresswell, Nicholas. *The Journal of Nicholas Cresswell, 1774–1777*. Port Washington, NY, 1968.

Crompton, Louis, introd. and ed. "Jeremy Bentham's Essay on 'Paederasty.'" *Journal of Homosexuality* 3 (1978): 383–405, and 91–107.

Cryle, Peter M., and Lisa O'Connell. *Libertine Enlightenment: Sex, Liberty, and Licence in the Eighteenth Century*. Basingstoke: Palgrave Macmillan, 2004.

Cusser, Catherine, *No Tomorrow, The Ethics of Pleasure in the French Enlightenment*. Charlottesville, University of Virginia Press, 1999.

Dabhoiwala, Faramerz. "Koppellaarsters, Kruishoeren and the Kooi, Prostitution in the Hague, 1720–1749." BA essay, University of York, 1990.

Daniels, Christine, and Michael V. Kennedy, eds. *Over the Threshold: Intimate Violence in Early America*. New York: Routledge, 1999.

d'Argens, Boyer de. *Thérèse Philosophe*, ed. Guillaume Pigeard de Gurbert. Paris: Babel, 1992.

Darnton, Robert. *The Forbidden Best-Sellers of Pre-Revolutionary France*. New York: W.W. Norton, 1995.

Darnton, Robert. *Mesmerism and the End of the Enlightenment in France*. Cambridge, MA: Harvard University Press, 1968.

Dayton, Cornelia Hughes. "Taking the Trade: Abortion and Gender Relations in an Eighteeenth-Century New England Village." *William and Mary Quarterly* 43, no. 1 (1991): 19–49.

Dekker, Rudolf, and Lotte van de Pol. *The Tradition of Female Transvestism in Early Modern Europe*. Basingstoke: Macmillan, 1989.

D'Emilio, J., and E. Freedman. *Intimate Matters: A History of Sexuality in America*. New York: Harper & Row, 1988.

Demos, John Putnam. *Entertaining Satan: Witchcraft and the Culture of Early New England*. New York: Oxford University Press, 1982.

De Silva, W. P. "Sexual Variations." *British Medical Journal* 318 (1999): 654–56.

Devi, Shakuntali. *The World of Homosexuals*. New Delhi: Vikas, 1976.

Diderot, Denis. *Rameau's Nephew and D'alembert's Dream,* trans. Leonard Tancock. Harmondsworth: Penguin, 1966.

Diner, Hasia R., and Beryl L. Benderly. *Her Works Praise Her: A History of Jewish Women in America from Colonial times to the Present*. New York: Basic Books, 2003.

Ditmore, Melissa Hope. *Encyclopedia of Prostitution and Sex Work*. London: Greenwood Press, 2006.

Donald, D., and F. O'Gorman, eds. *Ordering the World in the Eighteenth-Century*. Basingstoke: Palgrave, 2006.

Donoghue, Emma. *Passions between Women: British Lesbian Culture, 1668–1801*. London: Scarlet Press, 1993.

Dowie, J. A. *To Settle the Succession of the State: Literature and Politics, 1678–1750*. Basingstoke: Macmillan, 1994.

Dowie, M. *Women Adventurers*. London: T. Fisher Unwin, 1893.

Duberman, M., et al., eds. *Hidden from History: Reclaiming the Gay and Lesbian Past*. Meridian: Penguin Books, 1989.

Dubin, Lois C. "Jewish Women, Marriage Law, and Emancipation: A Civil Divorce in Late-Eighteenth-Century Trieste." *Jewish Social Studies, History, Culture, Society* 13, no. 2 (2007): 65–92.

Duby, Georges, Natalie Zemon Davis, Michelle Perrot, and Arlette Farge, eds. *A History of Women in the West: Renaissance and Enlightenment Paradoxes*. Cambridge, MA: Harvard University Press, 1992.

Duncan, B. *Goethe's* Werther *and the Critics*. Rochester, NY: Camden House, 2005.

Dyer, Abigail. "Seduction by Promise of Marriage, Law, Sex, and Culture in Seventeenth-Century Spain." *Sixteenth Century Journal* 34, no. 2 (2003): 439–55.

Earle, Rebecca. "Letters and Love in Colonial Spanish America." *Americas: A Quarterly Review of Inter-American Cultural History* 62, no. 1 (2005), pp. 127–153.

Easton, Fraser. "Gender's Two Bodies: Women Warriors, Female Husbands and Plebian Life." *Past and Present* 180, no. 1 (2003): 131–74.

Eder, F. X. "Sexualized Subjects: Medical Discourses on Sexuality in German-Speaking Countries in the Late 18th Century and in the 19th Century." In *Civilization, Sexuality and Social Life in Historical Context: The Hidden Face of Urban Life. International Conference, Budapest, 1995,* edited by Judith Forrai, 17–29. Budapest: SOTE UP, 1996.

El-Rouayheb, Khaled. *Before Homosexuality in the Arab-Islamic World, 1500–1800*. Chicago: University of Chicago Press, 2005.

Epstein, J., and K. Straub, eds. *Body Guards: The Cultural Politics of Gender Ambiguity*. London: Routledge, 1991.

Eriksson, Brigitte. "A Lesbian Execution in Germany, 1721: The Trial Records." In *The Gay Past: A Collection of Historical Essays*, edited by Salvatore J. Licata and Robert P. Petersen, 27–40. New York: Harrington Park Press, 1985.

Evans, Tanya. "'Unfortunate Objects': London's Unmarried Mothers in the Eighteenth Century." *Gender & History* 17, no. 1 (2005), pp. 127–153.

Faderman, Lilian. *Surpassing the Love of Men: Romantic Friendship and Love Between Women from the Renaissance to the Present*. London: Women's Press, 1985.

Farr, James R. *Authority and Sexuality in Early Modern Burgundy*. New York: Oxford University Press, 1995.

Feher, Michel. "Introduction." In *The Libertine Reader: Eroticism and Enlightenment in Eighteenth-Century France*, edited by Michel Feher. New York: Zone Books, 1997.

Ferguson, R. A. *The American Enlightenment, 1750–1820*. Cambridge, MA: Harvard University Press, 1997.

Fernandez, A. "The Repression of Sexual Behavior by the Aragonese Inquisition between 1560 and 170." *Journal of the History of Sexuality* 7 (1997): 469–501.

Fildes, Valerie, ed. *Women as Mothers in Pre-IndustrialEngland: Essays in Memory of Dorothy McLaren*. London: Routledge, 1990.

Finger, Stanley, et al., eds. *Brain, Mind and Medicine in the Eighteenth Century*. New York: Springer International, 2007.

Fischer-Yinon, Yochi. "The Original Bundlers: Boaz and Ruth, and Seventeenth-Century English Courtship Practices." *Journal of Social History* 35, no. 3 (2002): 683–705.

Fissell, Mary Elizabeth. *Vernacular Bodies: The Politics of Reproduction in Early Modern England*. New York: Oxford University Press, 2006.

Flandrin, Jean-Louis. *Sex in the Western World: The Development of Attitudes and Behavior*, translated by Sue Collins. Chur: Harwood Academic Publishers, 1991.

Fletcher, Anthony. *Gender, Sex, and Subordination in England, 1500–1800*. New Haven, CT: Yale University Press, 1995.

Flood, Gavin. *An Introduction to Hinduism*. Cambridge: Cambridge University Press, 1996.

Fortune, 2 vols. London: Cadell and Davies, 1997.

Foucault, Michel. *The History of Sexuality: Volume I, An Introduction*, translated by Robert Hurley. New York: Pantheon, 1978.

Fout, J., ed. *Forbidden History: The State, Society, and the Regulation of Sexuality in Modern Europe*. Chicago: University of Chicago Press, 1992.

Foxon, D. *Libertine Literature in England, 1660–1745*. New York: New Hyde Park, 1964.

Fradenburg, Louise, and Carla Freccero, eds. *Premodern Sexualities*. New York: Routledge, 1996.

Fuchs, Rachel G. *Poor and Pregnant in Nineteenth-Century Paris*. New Brunswick, NJ: Rutgers University Press, 1992.

Fudge, E. *Perceiving Animals: Humans and Beasts in Early Modern English Culture*. Basingstoke: Macmillan, 2000.

Gallagher, C. *Nobody's Story: The Vanishing Acts of Women Writers in the Marketplace, 1670–1820*. Berkeley: University of California Press, 1994.

Gattrell, V. *City of Laughter: Sex and Satire in Eighteenth-Century London*. London: Atlantic, 2006.

Gatrell, V.A.C. *The Hanging Tree: Execution and the English People 1770–1868*. Oxford: Oxford University Press, 1996.

Gay, Peter. *The Enlightenment: An Interpretation*. New York: Knopf, 1967.

Gentilcore, David. *Medical Charlatanism in Early Modern Italy*. Oxford: Oxford University Press, 2006.

Gerard, Kent, and Gert Hekma, eds. *The Pursuit of Sodomy: Male Homosexuality in Renaissance and Enlightenment Europe*. New York: The Haworth Press, 1989.

Gerbi, Antonelle. *Nature in the New World: From Christopher Columbus to Gonazalo Fernández de Oviedo*. Pittsburg, PA: University of Pittsburg Press, 1985.

Gestrich, Andreas. "After Dark: Girls' Leisure, Work, and Sexuality in Eighteenth- and Nineteenth-Century Rural Southwest Germany." In *Secret Gardens, Satanic Mills: Placing Girls in European History, 1750–1960*, edited by Mary Jo Maynes, Brigitte Soland, and Christine Benninghaus. Bloomington: Indiana University Press, 2005.

Ghosh, Durba. *Sex and the Family in Colonial India: The Making of Empire*. Cambridge: Cambridge University Press, 2006.

Gibson, I. *The English Vice: Beating, Sex and Shame in Victorian England and After*. London: Duckworth, 1978.

Gibson, Mary. *Prostitution and the State in Italy, 1860–1915*. New Brunswick, NJ: Rutgers University Press, 1986.

Gilbert, A. N. "Buggery and the British Navy, 1700–1861." *Journal of Social History* 10 (1976): 72–98.

Gillis, John R. *For Better, for Worse: British Marriages, 1600 to the Present*. New York: Oxford University Press, 1985.

Gillis, John R. "Servants, Sexual Relations, and the Risks of Illegitimacy in London, 1801–1900." *Feminist Studies* 5, no. 1 (1979): 142–73.

Gillis, John R. "'A Triumph of Hope over Experience': Chance and Choice in the History of Marriage." *International Review of Social History* 44, no. 1 (1999): 47–54.

Gladfelder, H., ed. "The Indictment of John Purser, Containing Thomas Cannon's *Ancient and Modern Pederasty Investigated and Exemplify'd*." *Eighteenth-Century Life* 31, no. 1 (2007): 39–61.

Gladfelder, H. "In Search of Lost Texts: Thomas Cannon's *Ancient and Modern Pederasty Investigated and Exemplify'd*." *Eighteenth-Century Life* 31, no. 1 (2007): 22–38.

Gladwin, Lee A. "Tobacco and Sex, Some Factors Affecting Non-marital Sexual Behavior in Colonial Virginia." *Journal of Social History* 12, no. 1 (1978), pp. 57–75.

Göçek, Fatima Müge. *East Encounters West: France and the Ottoman Empire in the Eighteenth Century*. New York: Oxford, 1987.

Godbeer, Richard. "Courtship and Sexual Freedom in Eighteenth-Century America." *Magazine of History* 18, no. 4 (2004): 8–11.

Godbeer, Richard. *Sexual Revolution in Early America*. Baltimore: John Hopkins University Press, 2002.
Gowing, Laura. *Common Bodies: Women, Touch, and Power in the Eighteenth Century*. New Haven, CT: Yale University Press, 2003.
Gowing, Laura. *Domestic Dangers: Women, Words and Sex in Early Modern England*. Oxford: Clarendon Press, 1996.
Gowing, Laura. "Secret Births and Infanticide in Seventeenth-Century England." *Past & Present* 156 (1997), pp. 87–115.
Graaf, Regnier de. "Regnier De Graaf on the Human Reproductive Organs ..." *Journal of Reproduction and Fertility*, supp. no. 17. Oxford: Blackwell Scientific, 1972.
Habib, Samir. *Female Homosexuality in the Middle East: Histories and Representations*. London: Routledge, 2007.
Haggerty, George. *Men in Love: Masculinity and Sexuality in the Eighteenth Century*. New York: Columbia University Press, 1999.
Hagstrum, Jean H. *Sex and Sensibility: Ideal and Erotic Love from Milton to Mozart*. Chicago: University of Chicago Press, 1980.
Haidt, Rebecca. *Embodying Enlightenment: Knowing the Body in Eighteenth-Century Spanish Literature and Culture*. Basingstoke: Macmillan, 1998.
Haliczer, Stephen. *Sexuality in the Confessional: A Sacrament Profaned, Studies in the History of Sexuality*. New York: Oxford University Press, 1996.
Halperin, David. "How to Do the History of Male Homosexuality." *GLQ* 6 (2000): 87–123.
Halperin, David. "Is There a History of Sexuality?" *History and Theory* 28 (1989): 257–74.
Halperin, David. *One Hundred Years of Homosexuality*. London: Routledge, 1989.
Halsband, Rorbert, ed. *The Complete Letters of Lady Mary Wortley Montagu*. Cambridge, MA: Harvard University Press, 1965.
Hambleton, Else L. *Daughters of Eve: Pregnant Brides and Unwed Mothers in Seventeenth-Century Massachusetts*. New York: Routledge, 2004.
Hardach-Pinke, Irene. "Managing Girls' Sexuality among the German Upper Classes." In *Secret Gardens, Satanic Mills: Placing Girls in European History, 1750–1960*, edited by Mary Jo Maynes, Brigitte Soland, and Christine Benninghaus. Bloomington: Indiana University Press, 2005.
Harvey, A. D. *Sex in Georgian England*. London: Phoenix Press, 1994.
Harvey, K. "The Century of Sex? Gender, Bodies, and Sexuality in the Long Eighteenth Century." *The Historical Journal* 45 (2002): 899–916.
Harvey, Karen. *Reading Sex in the Eighteenth Century: Bodies and Gender in English Erotic Culture*. Cambridge: Cambridge University Press, 2004.
Haslett, M. *Pope to Burney, 1714–1779, Scriblerians to Bluestockings*. London: Palgrave, 2003.
Hayhoe, Jeremy. "Illegitimacy, Inter-Generational Conflict and Legal Practice in Eighteenth-Century Northern Burgundy." *Journal of Social History* 38, no. 3 (2005), pp. 673–683.
Hecht, Jacqueline. "From 'Be Fruitful and Multiply' to Family Planning: The Enlightenment Transition." *Eighteenth-Century Studies* 32, no. 4 (1999): 536–51.

Henderson, Tony. *Disorderly Women in Eighteenth Century London: Prostitution and Control in the Metropolis, 1730–1830*. New York: Longman, 1999.
Herdt, G. *Third Sex, Third Gender: Beyond Sexual Dimorphism in Culture and History*. New York: Zone Books, 1994.
Hergemöller, B.-U. *Sodom and Gomorrah: On the Everyday Reality and Persecution of Homosexuals in the Middle Ages*. Free Association Books, 2001.
Hewlett, Mary. "Women, Sodomy and Sexual Abuse in Late-Renaissance Lucca." Ph.D. thesis, University of Toronto, 2000.
Higgs, David, ed. *Queer Sites: Gay Urban Histories since 1600*. New York: Routledge, 1999.
Hilary Marland, ed. *The Art of Midwifery: Early Modern Midwives in Europe*. London: Routledge, 1993.
Hinsch, Bret. *Passions of the Cut Sleeve: The Male Homosexual Tradition in China*. Berkeley: University of California Press, 1990.
Hitchcock, T. *English Sexualities, 1700–1800*. New York: St. Martin's Press, 1997.
Hodes, Martha, ed. *Sex, Love, Race: Crossing Boundaries in North American History*. New York: New York University Press, 1999.
Holden, P., and Richard J. Ruppel, eds. *Imperial Desire: Dissident Sexualities and Colonial Literature*. Minneapolis: University of Minnesota Press, 2003.
Hopwood, Derek. *Sexual Encounters in the Middle East: The British, the French and the Arabs*. Reading, NY: Ithaca Press, 1999.
Houlbrook, Matt. *Queer London*. Chicago: University of Chicago Press, 2005.
Hubberd, T., ed. *Homosexuality in Greece and Rome: A Sourcebook of Basic Documents*. Berkeley: University of California Press, 2003.
Hull, Isabel. *Sexuality, the State, and Civil Society in Germany, 1790–1815*. Ithaca, NY: Cornell University Press, 1996.
Hume, D. *Commentaries on the Law of Scotland*. Edinburgh, 1797.
Hunt, Lynn, ed. *The Invention of Pornography: Obscenity and the Origins of Modernity*. New York: Zone, 1993.
Hunt, Margaret R. *The Middling Sort: Commerce, Gender, and the Family in England, 1680–1780*. Berkeley: University of California Press, 1996.
Hurl-Eamon, Jennine. "Policing Male Heterosexuality: The Reformation of Manners Societies' Campaign against the Brothels in Westminster, 1690–1720." *Journal of Social History* 37 (2004): 1017–35.
Hurteau, P. "Moral Discourse on Male Sodomy and Masturbation in the Seventeenth and Eighteenth Centuries." *Journal of the History of Sexuality* 4 (1993): 1–26.
Hyam, Ronald. *Empire and Sexuality: The British Experience*. New York: St. Martin's Press, 1990.
Isherwood, R. M. *Farce and Fantasy: Popular Entertainment in Eighteenth-Century Paris*. 1986. Oxford: Oxford University Press, 1996.
Israel, Jonathan. *Radical Enlightenment*. Oxford: Oxford University Press, 2001.
Israel, Jonathan Irvine. *Enlightenment Contested: Philosophy, Modernity, and the Emancipation of Man, 1670–1752*. Oxford: Oxford University Press, 2006.
Jacques, Rossiaud. *Medieval Prostitution*, trans. Lydia Cochrane. Oxford: Blackwell, 1988.

Janssen, Thijs. "Transvestites and Transsexuals in Turkey." In *Sexuality and Eroticism among Males in Moslem Societies*, ed. Arno Schmitt and Jahoeda Sofer. New York: Harrington Park Press, 1992.

Jocelyn, H. D., and B. P. Setchell, eds. *Regnier de Graaf on the human reproductive organs.* 1672. Oxford: Blackwell Scientific, 1972.

Jones, Collin. "Prostitution and the Ruling Class in Eighteenth-Century Montpellier." *History Workshop* 6 (1978): 7–28.

Jones, Vivien. *Women and Literature in Britain 1700–1800.* Cambridge: Cambridge University Press, 2000.

Jousse, D. *Traite de la justice criminelle de France,* 4 vols. Paris, 1771.

Joyce William, et al., eds. *Printing and Society in Early America.* Worcester: American Antiquarian Society, 1983.

Kalvemark, Ann-Sofie. "Illegitimacy and Marriage in Three Swedish Parishes in the Nineteenth Century." In *Bastardy and Its Comparative History*, edited by Peter Laslett, Karla Oosterveen, and Richard Smith. Cambridge, MA: Harvard University Press, 1980.

Kang, Wenqing. "Male Same-Sex Relations in China, 1900–1950." Ph.D. thesis, Santa Cruz, University of California, 2006.

Kant, I. *Lectures on Ethics,* translated by L. Infield. 1780. London, Methuen, 1930.

Karlsen, Carol F. *The Devil in the Shape of a Woman: Witchcraft in Colonial New England.* New York: Vintage Books, 1989.

Katz, Jonathan Ned. *Love Stories: Sex Between Men Before Homosexuality.* Chigaco: University of Chicago Press, 2001.

Kaye, Kerwin. "Sex and the Unspoken in Male Street Prostitution." *Journal of Homosexuality* 53 (2007): 37–73.

Kermode, Jennifer, and Garthine Walker, eds. *Women, Crime, and the Courts in Early Modern England.* Chapel Hill: The University of North Carolina Press, 1994.

Kertzer, David I. "Gender Ideology and Infant Abandonment in Nineteenth-Century Italy." *Journal of Interdisciplinary History* 22, no. 1 (1991), pp. 1–25.

Khan, Shivananda. *Contexts, Race, Culture and Sexuality.* London: Naz Project, 1996.

Khemka, Anita. *India's Third Gender*, dir. Thomas Wartman. Germany, 2005.

King, Helen. *Hippocrates Women: Reading the Female Body in Ancient Greece.* London: Routledge, 1998.

King, Lester S. *The Medical World of the Eighteenth Century.* Chicago: University of Chicago Press, 1958.

King, Steven. "Chance Encounters? Paths to Household Formation in Early Modern England." *International Review of Social History* 44, no. 1 (1999): 23–46.

Klaniczay, Gabor, Eva Pocs, and Eszter Csonka-Takacs. *Christian Demonology and Popular Mythology: The Role of Aesthetic Imagination in Human Society.* Budapest: CEU Press, 2005.

Klebe, Dorit. "Effeminate Professional Musicians in Sources of Ottoman-Turkish Court Poetry and Music of the Eighteenth and Nineteenth Centuries." *Music in Art* 30 (2005): 97–116.

Klein, Fritz, and Timothy J. Wolf, eds. *Two Lives to Lead, Bisexuality in Men and Women.* New York: Harrington Park Press, 1985.

Knodel, John. *Demographic Behavior in the Past*. Cambridge: Cambridge University Press, 1988.

Knott, Sarah, and Barbara Taylor, ed. *Women, Gender and Enlightenment*. Basingstoke: Palgrave Macmillan, 2007.

Kok, Jan. "The Moral Nation: Illegitimacy and Bridal Pregnancy in the Netherlands from 1600 to the Present." *Economic and Social History in the Netherlands [Netherlands]* 2 (1990), pp. 7–36.

Kowaleski, Maryanne. "The Demographic Perspective." In *Singlewomen in the European Past*, edited by Judith Bennett and Amy Froide. Philadelphia: University of Pennsylvania Press, 1999.

Kulick, Don. *Travesti, Sex, Gender, and Culture among Brazilian Transgendered Prostitutes*. Chicago: University of Chicago Press, 1998.

Kuzniar, A. A., ed. *Outing Goethe and His Age*. Palo Alto, CA: Stanford University Press, 1996.

Lacan, J. *Écrits*. Paris: Editions du Seuil, 1966.

Laclos, Choderlos de. *Les Liaisons Dangereuses*. Reprint, London: The Nonesuch Press, 1940.

Landa, Louis. "The Shandean Homunculus: The Background of Sterne's 'Little Gentleman.'" In *Restoration and Eighteenth-Century Literature*, edited by Carroll Camden, 49–68. Chicago: University of Chicago Press, 1963.

Landry, Donna, and Gerald MacLean. "Of Forceps, Patents, and Paternity: Tristram Shandy." *Eighteenth-Century Studies* 23 (1990): 522–43.

Laqueur, Thomas. *Making Sex, Body and Gender from the Greeks to Freud*. Cambridge, MA: Harvard University Press, 1990.

Laqueur, Thomas W. *Solitary Sex: A Cultural History of Masturbation*. New York: Zone Books, 2003.

Laslett, Peter. "Introduction: Comparing Illegitimacy over Time and between Cultures." In *Bastardy and Its Comparative History*, edited by Peter Laslett, Karla Oosterveen, and Richard M. Smith. Cambridge, MA: Harvard University Press, 1980.

Laslett, Peter, Karla Oosterveen, and Richard M. Smith, eds. *Bastardy and Its Comparative History*. Cambridge, MA: Harvard University Press, 1980.

Latouch, G. de. *L'Histoire de Dom Bourge, Portier de Chartreaux*. [Paris]: le Grand livre du mois, 1993.

Leneman, Leah, and Rosalind Mitchison. "Girls in Trouble: The Social and Geographical Setting of Illegitimacy in Early Modern Scotland." *Journal of Social History* (1988): 483–97.

Lespinasse, Julie de. *Letters of Mlle: De Lespinasse*, trans. Katherine Prescott Wormeley. Boston: Hardy, Pratt and Co., 1903.

Leupp, Gary P. *Male Colors: The Construction of Homosexuality in Tokugawa Japan*. Berkeley: University of California Press, 1995.

Levack, Brian P. *The Witch-Hunt in Early Modern Europe*, 3rd ed. London: Pearson Longman, 2006.

Levy, Barry. *Quakers and the American Family, British Settlement in the Delaware Valley*. New York: Oxford University Press, 1988.

Licata, S. J., and R. P. Petersen, eds. *The Gay Past: A Collection of Historical Essays*. New York: Harrington Park Press, 1985.
Liliequist, J. "Peasants against Nature: Crossing the Boundaries between Man and Animal in Seventeenth- and Eighteenth-Century Sweden." *Journal of the History of Sexuality* 1 (1991): 393–423.
Lister, A. *I Know My Own Heart: The Diaries of Annje Lister 1791–1840,* edited by H. Whitbread. London: Virago, 1988.
Lister, A. *No Priest But Love: Excerpts from the Diaries of Anne Lister, 1824–1826,* edited by H. Whitbread. New York: New York University Press, 1992.
Löfström, Jan, ed. *Scandinavian Homosexualities: Essays on Gay and Lesbian Studies*. New York: Haworth Press, 1998.
Lombardi-Nash, M. A., ed. and trans. *Sodomites and Urnings: Homosexual Representations in Classic German Journals*. New York: Harrington Park Press, 2006.
Lottin, Alain. "Naissances Illegitimes Et Filles-Mere à Lille Au Xviiie Siecle." *Revue d'Histoire Moderne et Contemporaine [France]* 17, no. 2 (1970).
Lyons, C. A. "Mapping an Atlantic Sexual Culture: Homoeroticism in Eighteenth-century Philadelphia." *William and Mary Quarterly* 60, no. 1 (2003): 119–54.
Lyons, Clare A. *Sex among the Rabble: An Intimate History of Gender and Power in the Age of Revolution, Philadelphia, 1730–1830*. Chapel Hill: University of North Carolina Press, 2006.
Maccubbin, R. P., ed. *'Tis Nature's Fault: Unauthorized Sexuality during the Enlightenment*. New York: Cambridge University Press, 1987.
MacDonald, Robert H. "The Frightful Consequences of Onania." *Journal of the History of Ideas* 28 (1967): 423–31.
Mahomet, S. D. *The Travels of Dean Mahomet*. 1794. Cork: Connor, 1997.
Man'kov, A. G., ed. *Zakonodatel'stvo perioda stanovlenija absolutizma*. Moscow: Nauka, 1986.
Mann, Susan. *Precious Records: Women in China's Long Eighteenth Century*. Palo Alto, CA: Stanford University Press, 1997.
Marks, Hans. "On the Art of Differentiating: Proletarianization and Illegitimacy in Northern Sweden, 1850–1930." *Social Science History* 18, no. 1 (1994).
Masters, R.E.L. *Sex Crimes in History*. New York: Julian Press, 1963.
Mavor, E. *The Ladies of Llangollen: A Study of Romantic Friendship*. Joseph, 1971.
McDowell, Judith H. *La Nouvelle Héloïse, Julie, or the New Eloise, Letters of Two Lovers, Inhabitants of a Small Town at the Foot of the Alps*. University Park: Pennsylvania State University Press, 1968.
McFarlane, C. *The Sodomite in Fiction and Satire, 1660–1750*. New York: Columbia University Press, 1997.
McGrady, Donald. "A Pirated Edition of *Guzmán de Alfarache*: More Light on Mateo Alemán's Life." *Hispanic Review* 34, no. 4 (1966): 326–28.
McIntosh, Mary. "The Homosexual Role." *Social Problems* 16 (1968): 182–92.
McLaren, Angus. *A History of Contraception*. Oxford: Blackwell, 1990.
McLaren, Angus. *Impotence: A Cultural History*. Chicago: University of Chicago Press, 2007.

McLaren, Angus. "The Pleasures of Procreation." In *William Hunter and the Eighteenth-Century Medical World*, edited by W. F. Bynum and Roy Porter, 323–41. Cambridge: Cambridge University Press, 1985.

McLaren, Angus. *Reproductive Rituals: The Perception of Fertility in England from the Sixteenth to the Nineteenth Century.* London: Methuen, 1984.

McMahon, Keith. *Misers, Shrews, and Polygamists: Sexuality and Male-Female Relations in Eighteenth-Century Chinese Fiction.* Durham, NC: Duke University Press, 1995.

Memom, Muhammad Umar, ed. *Studies in the Urdu Gazal and Prose Fiction.* Madison, WI: South Asian Studies, publication no. 5, 1979.

Menefee, Samuel Pyeatt. *Wives for Sale: An Ethnographic Study of British Popular Divorce.* Oxford: Blackwell, 1981.

Merians, Linda. *The Secret Malady: Venereal Disease in Eighteenth-Century Britain and France.* Lexington: University Press of Kentucky, 1996.

Merrick, J. "The Arrest of a Sodomite, 1723." *Gay and Lesbian Review Worldwide* 8, no. 5 (2001).

Merrick, J., and B. Ragan Jr. *Homosexuality in Early Modern France.* Oxford: Oxford University Press, 2001.

Merrick, J., and M. Sibalis, eds. *Homosexualitiy in French History and Culture.* New York: Harrington Park Press, 2001.

Midas Dekkers, M. *Dearest Pet: On Bestiality.* London: Verso, 1992.

Miletski, H. "A History of Bestiality." In *Bestiality and Zoophilia: Sexual Relations with Animals,* edited by Andrea M. Beetz and Anthony L. Podberscek. West Lafayette, IN: Purdue University Press, 2005.

Miller, C. *Stages of Desire: Gay Theatre's Hidden History.* London: Cassell, 1996.

Monetemorra, R., and D. A. Thomas, eds. *Operatic Migrations: Transforming Works and Crossing Boundaries.* Aldershot: Ashgate, 2006.

More, Hannah. *Strictures on the Modern System of Female Education: With a View of the Principles and Conduct Prevalent Among Women of Rank and Fortune,* 2 vols. London: Cadell and Davies, 1799.

Morris, Jan. *Conundrum.* London: Faber, 1974.

Mott, Luiz. "Love's Labors Lost: Five Letters from a Seventeenth-century Portuguese Sodomite." In *The Pursuit of Sodomy: Male Homosexuality in Renaissance and Enlightenment Europe,* edited by K. Gerard and G. Hekma. New York: Harrington Park Press, 1989.

Mott, Luiz. "Pagode português: A subcultura gay em Portugal nos tempos inquisitorais." *Ciência e cultura* 40 (1988): 120–39.

Moulton, Ian Frederick. *Before Pornography: Erotic Writing in Early Modern England.* Oxford: Oxford University Press, 2000.

Mourao, M. "The Representation of Female Desire in Early Modern Pornographic Texts, 1660–1745." *Signs* (1999): 573–602.

Mudge, Bradford K., ed. *When Word Becomes Flesh: An Anthology of Eighteenth-Century Libertine Literature.* Oxford: Oxford University Press, 2004.

Mullan, J., and C. Reid, eds. *Eighteenth-Century Popular Culture: A Selection.* Oxford: Oxford University Press, 2000.

Murray, Stephen O. "Homosexuality in the Ottoman Empire." *Historical Reflections* 33 (2007): 101–16.

Murray, Stephen O., and Will Roscoe. *Islamic Homosexualities*. New York: New York University Press, 1997.

Murrin, John M. "'Things Fearful to Name': Bestiality in Colonial America." *Explorations in Early American Culture Pennsylvania History. A Journal of Mid-Atlantic Studies* 65 (1998): 8–43.

Muyart de Vouglans, P.-F. *Les Loix Criminelles de France, dans leur ordre naturel, etc.* Paris, 1780.

Naish, C. *Death Comes to the Maiden: Sex and Execution 1431–1933*. London: Routledge, 1991.

Najmabadi, Afsaneh. *Women with Mustaches and Men without Beards: Gender and Sexual Anxieties of Iranian Modernity*. Berkeley: University of California Press, 2005.

Needham, Joseph. *A History of Embryology*, 2nd ed. Cambridge: Cambridge University Press, 1959.

Neret, G. *Erotica Universalis*. Bonn: Benedikt Taschen, 1994.

Noordam, Dirk Jaap. "Prostitutie in Leiden in de 18e eeuw." In *Leidse facetten*, edited by Diden Boer. Leiden: Waanders, 1982.

Norberg, Kathryn. "Prostitutes." In *A History of Women in the West*: vol. 3, Renaissance and Enlightenment Paradoxes, edited by edited by Natalie Zemon Davis and Arlette Farge. Cambridge, MA: Harvard University Press, 1993.

Norton, Mary Beth. *Founding Mothers and Fathers: Gendered Power and the Forming of American Society*. New York: Vintage Books, 1996.

Norton, Rictor, ed. *Eighteenth-Century British Erotica*, Set 1, vol. 5: *Sodomites, Mollies, Sapphists and Tommies*. London: Pickering & Chatto, 2004.

Norton, Rictor. *Homosexuality in Eighteenth-Century England: A Sourcebook*. Available at http://rictornorton.co.uk.

Norton, Rictor. *Mother Clap's Molly House: The Gay Subculture in England, 1700–1830*. London: GMP, 1992.

Norton, Rictor. *The Myth of the Modern Homosexual: Queer History and the Search for Cultural Unity*. London: Cassell, 1997.

Norton, Rictor. "Recovering Gay History from the Old Bailey." *London Journal* 30, no. 1 (2005): 39–54.

Nussbaum, Felicity A., ed. *The Global Eighteenth Century*. Baltimore: John Hopkins University Press, 2003.

Nussbaum, Felicity A. *The Limits of the Human: Fictions of Anomaly, Race and Gender in the Long Eighteenth Century*. Cambridge: Cambridge University Press, 2003.

Nussbaum, Felcity A. *Torrid Zones. Maternity, Sexuality, and Empire in Eighteenth-Century English Narratives*. Baltimore: John Hopkins University Press, 1995.

Nye, E. *Literary and Linguistic Theories in Eighteenth-Century France*. Oxford: Oxford University Press, 2000.

Oaks, Robert F. "'Things Fearful to Name': Sodomy and Buggery in Seventeenth-Century New England." *Journal of Social History* (1978): 268–81.

O'Donnell, Katherine, and Mi O'Rourke, eds. *Love, Sex and Intimacy and Friendship Between Men, 1550–1800*. Basingstoke: Palgrave Macmillan, 2003.

O'Donnell, Katherine, and Michael O'Rourke, eds. *Queer Masculinities: Siting Same-Sex Desire in the Early Modern World.* New York: PalgraveMacmillan, 2006.

Ogilvie, Sheilagh. "How Does Social Capital Affect Women: Guilds and Communities in Early Modern Europe." *American Historical Review* 109, no. 2 (2004): 325–59.

O'Neal, John C. *The Authority of Experience: Sensationalist Theory in the French Enlightenment.* University Park: Pennsylvania State University Press, 1996.

Padgug, R. A. "Sexual Matters: On Conceptualizing Sexuality in History." *Radical History Review* 20 (1979): 3–33.

Park, Katharine. *Secrets of Women, Gender, Generation, and the Origins of Human Dissection.* New York: Zone Books, 2006.

Parkes, H. B. "Morals and Law Enforcement in Colonial New England." *The New England Quarterly* (1932): 431–52.

Peakman, Julie. *Lascivious Bodies: A Sexual History of the Eighteenth Century.* London: Atlantic Books, 2004.

Peakman, Julie. "Medicine, the Body and the Botanical Metaphor in Erotica." In *From Physico-Theology to Bio-Technology: Essays in the Social and Cultural History of Biosciences*, edited by Kurt Bayertz and Roy Porter, Amsterdam: Rodopi, 1998: 197–223.

Peakman, Julie. *Mighty Lewd Books: The Development of Pornography in Eighteenth-Century England.* New York: Palgrave, 2003.

Peakman, Julie, ed. *Sexual Perversions, 1670–1890.* Basingstoke: Palgrave Macmillan, 2009.

Pflugfelder, Gregory M. *Cartographies of Desire: Male-Male Sexuality in Japanese Discourse, 1600–1950.* Berkeley: University of California Press, 1999.

Place, Francis. *The Autobiography*, edited by Mary Thale. Cambridge: Cambridge University Press, 1972.

Plummer, K., ed. *The Making of the Modern Homosexual.* London: Hutchinson, 1981.

Pol, Lotte van de. *Het Amsterdams hoerdom, prostitutie in de zeventiende en acchttiende eeuw.* Amsterdam: Wereldbibliotheek, 1996.

Poole, S. "'Bringing Great Shame upon This City': Sodomy, the Courts and the Civic Idiom in Eighteenth-century Bristol." *Urban History* 34, no. 1 (2007): 114–26.

Porter, Dorothy, and Roy Porter. *Patient's Progress: Doctors and Doctoring in Eighteenth-Century England.* Oxford: Polity Press, 1989.

Porter, Roy. *English Society in the Eighteenth Century.* Harmondsworth: Penguin, 1982.

Porter, Roy. *The Greatest Benefit to Mankind: A Medical History of Humanity.* New York: W.W. Norton, 1998.

Porter, Roy. "The Sexual Politics of James Graham." *British Journal for Eighteenth-Century Studies* 5 (1982): 199–206.

Porter, Roy. "Spreading Carnal Knowledge or Selling Dirt Cheap? Nicolas Venette's Tableau De L'amour." *Journal of European Studies* 14 (1984): 233–55.

Porter, Roy, and Lesley Hall. *Facts of Life: The Creation of Sexual Knowledge in Britain, 1650–1950.* New Haven, CT: Yale University Press, 1995.

Porter, Roy, and Marie Mulvey Roberts, eds. *Pleasure in the Eighteenth Century*. Basingstoke: Macmillan, 1996.

Porter, Roy, and Mikulâaés Teich. *Sexual Knowledge, Sexual Science: The History of Attitudes to Sexuality*. Cambridge: Cambridge University Press, 1994.

Prescott, S. *Women, Authorship and Literary Culture, 1690–1740*. Basingstoke: Palgrave, 2003.

Preyer, K. "Crime, the Criminal Law and Reform in Post-Revolutionary Virginia." *Law and History Review* (1983): 53–85.

Prieur, Anick. *Mema's House, Mexico City: On Transvestites, Queens, and Machos*. Chicago: University of Chicago Press, 1998.

Probert, Rebecca. "Chinese Whispers and Welsh Weddings." *Continuity and Change* 20, no. 2 (2005): 211–38.

Puff, Helmut. *Sodomy in Reformation Germany and Switzerland 1400–1600*. Chicago: University of Chicago Press, 2003.

Quaife, G. R. *Wanton Wenches and Wayward Wives: Peasants and Illicit Sex in Early Seventeenth-Century England*. London: Croom Helm, 1979.

Rattray Taylor, Gordon. *Sex in History*. London: Thames & Hudson, 1953.

Reay, Barry. "Sexuality in Nineteenth-Century England: The Social Context of Illegitimacy in Rural Kent." *Rural History [Great Britain]* 1, no. 2 (1990).

Reis, Elizabeth. *Damned Women: Sinners and Witches in Puritan New England*. Ithaca, NY: Cornell University Press, 1997.

Rettaroli, Rosella. "Age at Marriage in Nineteenth-Century Italy." *Journal of Family History* 15, no. 4 (1990): 409–25.

Richlin, Amy. "Not before Homosexuality." *Journal of the History of Sexuality* 3, no. 4 (1993): 523–73.

Richter, S. "Wet-Nursing, Onanism, and the Breast in Eighteenth-Century Germany." *Journal of the History of Sexuality* (1996): 1–22.

Rivers, I., ed. *Books and their Readers in Eighteenth-century England*. Leicester: Leicester University Press, 1982.

Robb, Graham. *Strangers: Homosexual Love in the Nineteenth Century*. London: Picador, 2003.

Robb, Peter M. *The Man Who Became Caravaggio*. New York: Henry Holt, 2000.

Robinson, D. M. *Closeted Writing and Lesbian and Gay Literature: Classical, Early Modern, Eighteenth-Century*. Aldershot: Ashgate Publishing, 2006.

Rocke, Michael. *Forbidden Friendships: Homosexuality and Male Culture in Renaissance Florence*. New York: Oxford University Press, 1996.

Roger, Jacques, and K. R. Benson. *The Life Sciences in Eighteenth-Century French Thought*. Stanford, CA: Stanford University Press, 1997.

Rosario, Vernon A. *The Erotic Imagination: French Histories of Perversity*. Oxford: Oxford University Press, 1997.

Rosenberg, Joseph R. *Bestiality*. Los Angeles: Medico Book, 1968.

Rosenthal, Laura J. *Infamous Commerce: Prostitution in Eighteenth-century British Literature & Culture*. Ithaca, NY: Cornell University Press, 2006.

Rousseau, G. S. *Nervous Acts: Essays on Literature, Culture and Sensibility*. Basingstoke: Palgrave Macmillan, 2004.

Rousseau, G. S., ed. *Children and Sexuality: The Greeks to the Great War*. Basingstoke: Palgrave Macmillan, 2007.

Rousseau, G. S. "English Literature: Restoration and Eighteenth Century." in *The Gay and Lesbian Literary Heritage*, edited by C. J. Summers, 228–36. New York: Henry Holt, 1995.

Rousseau, G. S. *Perilous Enlightenment*. Manchester: Manchester University Press, 1991.

Rousseau, G. S. "'Homoplatonic, Homodepressed, Homomorbid': Some Further Genealogies of Same-Sex Attraction in Western Civilization." In *Love, Sex, Intimacy and Friendship, 1550–1800*, edited by K. O'Donnell and M. O'Rourke, 12–52. Basingstoke: Palgrave Macmillan, 2003.

Rousseau, G. S. "Nymphomania, Bienville and the Rise of Erotic Sensibility." In *Sexuality in Eighteenth-Century Britain*, edited by G. Bouce, 95–120. Manchester: Manchester University Press, 1982.

Rousseau, G. S., and Roy Porter. *Sexual Underworlds of the Enlightenment*. Manchester: Manchester University Press, 1987.

Rousseau, G. S. *Tobias Smollett: Essays of Two Decades*. Edinburgh: T. & T. Clark, 1982.

Rousseau, Jean-Jacques. *Émile, or On Education*, introduction and translation by Allan Bloom. New York: Basic Books, 1979.

Rousseau, Jean-Jacques. *Confessions*, edited by P. Coleman. Reprint, Oxford: Oxford University Press, 2006.

Rublack, Ulinka, ed. *Gender in Early Modern German History*. Cambridge: Cambridge University Press, 2002.

Ruggiero, Guido. *The Boundaries of Eros: Sex Crime and Sexuality in Renaissance Venice*. New York: Oxford University Press, 1985.

Ryder, Dudley. *The Diary ... 1715–1716*, edited by William Matthews. London: Methuen, 1939.

Sade, Marquis de. *The Complete Justine, Philosophy of the Bedroom, and Other Writings*, edited by Jean Paulhan and Maurice Blanchot, translated by Richard Seaver and Austyn Wainhouse. New York: Grove Press, 1966.

Sade, Marquis de. *Philosophy of the Boudoir*, translated by J. Neugroschel. London, 2006.

Sainsbury, John. "Wilkes and Libertinism." *Studies in Eighteenth-Century Culture* 26 (1998): 151–74.

Saint-Saëns, Alan, ed. *Sex and Love in Golden Age Spain*. New Orleans: University Press of the South, 1996.

Salvatore, J. Licata, and Robert P. Petersen, eds. *The Gay Past: A Collection of Historical Essays*. New York: Harrington Park Press, 1985.

Sands, Mollie, *The Eighteenth-Century Pleasure Gardens of Marylebone 1737–1777*. London: Society for Theatre Research, 1987.

Schellekens, Jona. "Courtship, the Clandestine Marriage Act, and Illegitimate Fertility in England." *Journal of Interdisciplinary History* 25, no. 3 (1995): 433–44.

Schiebinger, Londa L. *The Mind Has No Sex? Women in the Origins of Modern Science*. Cambridge, MA: Harvard University Press, 1989.

Schiebinger, Londa. *Nature's Body: Sexual Politics and the Making of Modern Science*. London: Pandora, 1994.
Schifter, Jacobo. *From Toads to Queens: Transvestism in a Latin American Setting*. New York: Harrington Park Press, 1999.
Schifter, Jacobo. *Lila's House: Male Prostitution in Latin America*. New York: Harrington Park Press, 1998.
Schifter, Jacobo. *Public Sex in a Latin Society*. New York: Harrington Park Press, 2000.
Schroeder, Susan, Stephanie Wood, and Robert Haskett, eds. *Indian Women of Early Mexico*. Norman: University of Oklahoma Press, 1997.
Scott, George Ryley. *Phallic Worship*. Privately printed, 1941.
Sedgwick, Eve Kosofsky. *Epistemology of the Closet*. Berkeley: University of California Press, 1990.
Seed, Patricia. *To Love, Honor, and Obey in Colonial Mexico: Conflicts over Marriage Choice, 1574–1821*. Stanford, CA: Stanford University Press, 1988.
Senelick, L. "Mollies or Men of Mode? Sodomy and the Eighteenth-century London Stage." *Journal of the History of Sexuality* 1, no. 1 (1990): 33–67.
Shail, Andrew, and Gillian Howie, ed. *Menstruation: A Cultural History*. Basingstoke: Palgrave Macmillan, 2005.
Shapiro, Michael. *Gender Play on the Shakespearean Stage: Boy Heroines and Female Pages*. Ann Arbor, MI: University of Michigan Press, 1994.
Shiach, M. *Discourse on Popular Culture: Class, Gender and History in Cultural Analysis, 1730 to the Present*. Stanford, CA: Stanford University Press, 1983.
Shorter, E. *The Making of the Modern Family*. New York: Basic Books, 1977.
Siena, Kevin. *Sins of the Flesh: Responding to Sexual Disease in Early Modern Europe*. Toronto: Centre for Reformation and Renaissance Studies, 2005.
Siena, Kevin. *Venereal Disease in London Hospitals, 1600–1800*. Rochester, NY: University of Rochester Press, 2001.
Sigal, Pete, ed. *Infamous Desire: Male Homosexuality in Colonial Latin America*. Chicago: Chicago University Press, 2003.
Singy, P. "Friction of the Genitals and Secularization of Morality." *Journal of the History of Sexuality* 12 (2003): 345–64.
Smith, Merril D. *Breaking the Bonds: Marital Discord in Pennsylvania, 1730–1830*. New York: New York University Press, 1991.
Smith, Merril D., ed. *Sex and Sexuality in Early America*. New York: NewYork University Press, 1998.
Smith, Theresa Ann. *The Emerging Female Citizen: Gender and Enlightenment in Spain*. Berkeley: University of California Press, 2006.
Sommer, Matthew H. *Sex, Law, and Society in Late Imperial China*. Stanford: Stanford University Press, 2000.
Sommer, Matthew H. "Was China Part of a Global Eighteenth-Century Homosexuality?" *Historical Reflections* 33 (2007): 117–33.
Spencer, J. *The Rise of the Woman Novelist from Aphra Behn to Jane Austen*. Oxford: Blackwell, 1986.
Spivak, G. *A Critique of Postcolonial Reason: Towards a History of the Vanishing Present*. Cambridge, MA: Harvard University Press, 1999.

Stanton, Domna C., ed. *Discourses of Sexuality from Aristotle to AIDS*. Ann Arbor: University of Michigan Press, 1992.

Stearns, Peter N., ed. *Encyclopedia of European Social History, from 1350 to 2000*. New York: Charles Scribner, 2001.

Stein, Edward, ed. *Forms of Desire: Sexual Orientation and the Sexual Constructionist Controversy*. New York: Garland, 1990.

Stengers, J., and A. Van Neck. *Histoire d'une grande peur, la masturbation*. Brussels: Éditions de l'Université de Bruxelles, 1984.

Stevenson, D. "Recording the Unspeakable: Masturbation in the Diary of William Drummond, 1657–1659." *Journal of the History of Sexuality* (2000): 223–39.

Stolberg, Michael. "Menstruation and Sexual Difference in Early Modern Medicine." In *Menstruation: A Cultural History*, edited by Andrew Shail, 90–101. Basingstoke: Palgrave, 2005.

Stolberg, Michael. "Self-Pollution, Moral Reform, and the Venereal Trade: Notes on the Sources and Historical Content of *Onania*, 1716." *Journal of the History of Sexuality* 9, no. 1–2 (2000): 37–61.

Stone, L. *The Family, Sex and Marriage in England 1500–1800*. New York: Harper and Row, 1977.

Stone, L. "Libertine Sexuality in Post-Restoration England: Group Sex and Flagellation among the Middling Sort in Norwich in 1706–1707." *Journal of the History of Sexuality* 2 (1992): 511–26.

Stone, Lawrence. *The Road to Divorce: England 1530–1987*. New York: Oxford University Press, 1990.

Straub, Kristina. *Eighteenth Century Players and Sexual Ideology*. Princeton, NJ: Princeton University Press, 1992.

Straus, Ralph. *The Unspeakable Curll*. London: Chapman and Hall, 1927.

Sumser, R. "'Erziehung,' the Family, and the Regulation of Sexuality on the Late German Enlightenment." *German Studies Review* 15 (1992): 455–74.

Sundt, Eilert. *Sexual Customs in Rural Norway*, translated by Odin W. Anderson. Ames: Iowa State University Press, 1993.

Sweet, James Hoke. "Recreating Africa: Race, Religion, and Sexuality in the African-Portuguese World, 1441–1770." Ph.D. thesis, City University of New York, 1999.

Swift, Jonathan. *Gulliver's Travels*, edited by Louis A. Landa. New York: Riverside, 1960.

Szreter, Simon. *Fertility, Class and Gender in Britain, 1860–1940*. Cambridge: Cambridge University Press, 1996.

Talvacchia, Bette. *Taking Positions: On the Erotic in Renaissance Culture*. Princeton, NJ: Princeton University Press, 1999.

Tannahill, Reay. *Sex in History*. London: H. Hamilton, 1980.

Théré, Christine. "Women and Birth Control in Eighteenth-Century France." *Eighteenth-Century Studies* 32, no. 4 (1999): 552–64.

Thomas, Keith. *Man and the Natural World: Changing Attitudes in England 1500–1800*. Harmondsworth: Penguin, 1984.

Thompson, Roger. *Sex in Middlesex: Popular Mores in a Massachusetts County, 1649–1699*, foreword by David D. Hall. Amherst: University of Massachusetts Press, 1986.

Thompson, Roger. *Unfit for Modest Ears*. Totowa, NJ: Rowman and Littlefield, 1979.
Tiam, Min. "Male *Dan*: The Paradox of Sex, Acting and Perception of Gender Impersonation in Traditional Chinese Theatre." *Asian Theatre Journal* (2000): 78–97.
Tobin, R. D. *Warm Brothers: Queer Theory and the Age of Goethe*. Philadephia: University of Pennsylvania Press, 2000.
Traub, Valerie. *The Renaissance of Lesbianism in Early Modern England*. Cambridge: Cambridge University Press, 2002.
Trevor, Meriol. *Apostle of Rome, St. Philip Neri 1515–1595*. London: Macmillan, 1966.
Trumbach, Randolph. "London's Sapphists: From Three Sexes to Four Genders in the Making of Modern Culture." In *Body Guards: The Cultural Politics of Gender Ambiguity*, edited by J. Epstein and K. Straub, 112–41. London: Routledge, 1991.
Trumbach, Randolph. "London's Sodomites: Homosexual Behaviour and Western Culture in the 18th Century." *Journal of Social History* 11, no. 1 (1977): 1–33.
Trumbach, Randolph. "Modern Sodomy: The Origins of Homosexuality, 1700–1800." In *A Gay History of Britain, Love and Sex Between Men Since the Middle Ages*, edited by M. Cook. Oxford: Greenwood, 2007.
Trumbach, Randolph. *Sex and Gender Revolution. Vol. 1. Heterosexuality and the Third Gender in Enlightenment London*. Chicago: University of Chicago Press, 1998.
Trumbach, Randolph. "Sodomitical Subculture, Sodomitical Roles, and the Gender Revolution of the Eighteenth Century: The Recent Historiography." *Eighteenth Century Life* 9 (1985): 109–21.
Trumbach, Randolph. "Blackmail for Sodomy in Eighteenth-Century London." *Historical Reflections* (2007): 23–39.
Trumbach, Randolph. *The Rise of the Egalitarian Family*. New York: Academic Press, 1978.
Trumbach, Randolph. "Sex, Gender, and Sexual Identity in Modern Culture, Male Sodomy and Female Prostitution in Enlightenment London." *Journal of the History of Sexuality* 2, no. 2 (1991): 186–203.
Turner, James Grantham. *Schooling Sex: Libertine Literature and Erotic Education in Italy, France, and England 1534–1685*. New York: Oxford University Press, 2003.
Twinam, Ann. *Public Lives, Private Secrets: Gender, Honor, Sexuality and Illegitimacy in Colonial Spanish America*. Stanford, CA: Stanford University Press, 1999.
Ulrich, Laurel Thatcher. *A Midwife's Tale: The Life of Martha Ballard, Based on Her Diary, 1785–1812*. New York: Knopf, 1990.
Van de Meer, Theo. "Tribades on Trial: Female Same-Sex Offenders in Late Eighteenth-Century Amsterdam." *Journal of the History of Sexuality* 1 (1991).
Venette, Nicolas. *Conjugal Love, or, the Pleasures of the Marriage Bed*. Reprint, New York: Garland, 1984.
Verduin, K. "'Our Cursed Natures': Sexuality and the Puritan Conscience." *New England Quarterly* (1983): 220–37.
Vicinus, Martha. *Intimate Friends: Women Who Loved Women, 1778–1928*. Chicago: University of Chicago Press, 2004.

Vila, Anne C. *Enlightenment and Pathology: Sensibility in the Literature and Medicine of Eighteenth-Century France.* Baltimore: Johns Hopkins University Press, 1998.

Villaseñor, Charlene Black. "Love and Marriage in the Spanish Empire: Depictions of Holy Matrimony and Gender Discourses in the Seventeenth Century." *Sixteenth Century Journal* 32, no. 3 (2001).

Wagner, Peter. "The Veil of Medicine and Morality: Some Pornographic Aspects of the *Onania*." *The British Journal for Eighteenth-Century Studies* 6 (1983): 179–84.

Wagner, Peter. *Eros Revived: Erotica of the Enlightenment in England and America.* London: Secker and Warburg, 1988.

Wang, K. C., and Lien-te Wu. *History of Chinese Medicine.* Tientsin: Tiensin Press, 1932.

Warman, C. *Sade: From Materialism to Pornography.* Oxford: Voltaire, 2002.

Weeks, Jeffrey. *Coming Out: Homosexual Politics in Britain, from the Nineteenth Century to the Present.* London: Quartet, 1977.

Whibley, C. "Moll Cutpurse." In *A Book of Scoundrels.* London, 1897.

Wiesner-Hanks, Merry E. *Christianity and Sexuality in the Early Modern World: Regulating Desire, Reforming Practice.* New York: Routledge, 2000.

Williams, D. I., and W. F. Bynum. *The London Lock: A Charitable Hospital for Venereal Disease 1746–1952.* London: Royal Society of Medicine Press, 1995.

Wilson, Adrian. *The Making of Man-Midwifery: Childbirth in England 1660–1770.* London: UCL Press, 1995.

Wilson, D. *Signs and Portents: Monstrous Births from the Middle Ages to the Enlightenment.* New York: Routledge, 1993.

Worrall, D. *The Politics of Romantic Theatricality, 1787–1832.* Basingstoke: Penguin, 2007.

Wu, Cuncun. *Homoerotic Sensibilities in Late Imperial China.* London: Routledge, 2004.

Young, M. B. *King James and the History of Homosexuality.* New York: New York University Press, 2000.

Ze'evi, Dror. *Producing Desire: Changing Sexual Discourse in the Ottoman Middle East, 1500–1900.* Berkeley: University of California Press, 2006.

CONTRIBUTORS

Heike Bauer is a senior lecturer in English and gender studies and director of the Birkbeck Institute of Gender and Sexuality. She has research interests in the histories and theories of sexuality and gender (1800–1950), especially with regard to sexology, translation, gender, and discipline formation. Her main publications include a monograph, *English Literary Sexology: Translations of Inversion, 1860–1930* (2009), and a three-volume anthology of texts, *Women and Cross-Dressing, 1800–1930* (2006). She is currently working on a study of Magnus Hirschfeld, "race," and the history of sexuality.

Anna Clark is professor of history at the University of Minnesota, where she holds the Samuel Russell Chair in the Humanities. Her most recent books include *Desire: A History of European Sexuality* (2008) and *Scandal: The Sexual Politics of the British Constitution* (2004). She has written articles on the Chevalier d'Éon, Anne Lister, and lesbian identity, as well as "twilight moments" in the history of sexuality.

Katherine Crawford is an associate professor at Vanderbilt University, where she teaches the history of gender and sexuality. Her first book, *Perilous Performances: Gender and Regency in Early Modern France*, analyzed the gendering of politics in the French monarchy. Her second book, *European Sexualities, 1400–1800*, presented a synthetic account of the scholarship on family, religion, medicine, crime, and deviance with respect to sexuality. She is completing a book entitled *The Sexual Culture of the French Renaissance*, which argues that cultural contestation over sexuality produced crucial elements of French national identity.

M. G. Muravyeva is a university researcher at the Helsinki Collegium for Advanced Studies, University of Helsinki. She has extensively published works on the history of masculinities, prostitution, and sexual violence in modern Europe, as well as on gender history and theory in Russia. She is currently working on a book entitled *Criminalizing Sexualities in Eighteenth-Century Europe*.

Rictor Norton is an independent scholar living in London. His books include *Mother Clap's Molly House: The Gay Subculture in England, 1700–1830*, *The Myth of the Modern Homosexual*, and a biography of the gothic novelist Ann Radcliffe. He has edited three volumes of the Pickering & Chatto series *Eighteenth-Century British Erotica*, and has contributed entries on homosexual figures for the *Oxford Dictionary of National Biography*. He maintains an extensive Web site about homosexual history, which includes many primary sources for the history of homosexuality in eighteenth-century England.

Julie Peakman is a writer and historian. She runs an MA course on sex, medicine, and the body at Birkbeck College, University of London. Her recent books include *Lascivious Bodies. A Sexual History of the Eighteenth Century* and *Mighty Lewd Books: The Development of Pornography in Eighteenth-century England*. She has edited *Sexual Perversion, 1670–1890*, and eight volumes of *Whore's Bibliographies 1680–1815*. She is currently writing a sexual history of the world.

George Rousseau is a fellow of the Royal Historical Society and the recipient of several honorary degrees. He has been a professor at UCLA, Regius Professor of English Literature at King's College Aberdeen, and codirector of the Centre for the History of Childhood at Oxford University. He lives and writes in Oxfordshire. His books include a 1991 trilogy about Enlightenment culture: *Enlightenment Borders, Enlightenment Crossings,* and *Perilous Enlightenment*, as well as *Nervous Acts: Essays on Literature, Culture and Sensibility* (2004). His biography of Sir John Hill, entitled *Notorious*, is forthcoming.

Merril D. Smith is an independent scholar living in National Park, New Jersey. She is the editor and author of several books and articles, including *Sex and Sexuality in Early America, Encyclopedia of Rape, Women's Roles in Seventeenth-Century America,* and *Women's Roles in Eighteenth-Century America*.

Randolph Trumbach is professor of history at Baruch College and the Graduate Center, City University of New York. He has written *The Rise of the Egalitarian*

Family: Aristocratic Kinship and Domestic Relations in Eighteenth-Century England and *Sex and the Gender Revolution, Volume 1: Heterosexuality and the Third Gender in Enlightenment London*. He has also written extensively on the history of homosexual behavior, which will be the subject of a forthcoming *Volume 2*. He is currently engaged in a study of seventeenth- and eighteenth-century books of devotion.

INDEX

abnormal, abnormality, 12–13, 105
abnormal sexual cravings, 141–2
abortion, 111, 117, 118, 138, 244
Académie des dames, 30, 212
Accomplished Whore, 29
actresses, 12, 25, 48, 79–80, 163, 171–2
adolescents, 183, 184–90, 195, 197, 199
adultery, 8, 32, 41, 47–52, 82, 107–8, 112, 119, 125–8, 168, 230, 245, 250, 257
Africa, Africans, 2, 6–7, 37–8, 46, 130–1, 179, 227, 256
age of consent, 62, 225
ailments, 15, 23
Aldridge, Ira, 172
Alémán, Mateo, 164
Al-Jabarti, Abd al Rahman, 221
America, Americans, 4–7, 11, 23, 29, 33–41, 45, 73, 79, 87, 90–5, 98, 108–12, 114–19, 123–5, 130–2, 159, 162, 167–8, 170, 174, 177, 189, 192, 216, 224–9, 235, 237, 239, 243–6, 253–5, 258–9, 263
American colonies, 7, 41, 42, 43, 67, 73, 87, 93, 109–17, 122–5, 130–2, 162, 216

American Revolution, 115, 168
Amsterdam, 188, 190, 213, 224
anal sex, 10, 13, 36, 61–2, 73–4, 87, 176, 196, 201
    see also buggery; sodomy
anatomy, 19, 134, 157, 205, 207, 246
    and immodesty, 133, 151
    and sexuality, 135–40
    also see dissection
Andrew, Donna, 51
Angier, Samuel, 192
animalculists, 138–9
Anne, Queen, 77
Annibale, Captain, 188
anti-Catholicism, 214
apprentices, 4, 27, 34, 39, 45, 188, 193–5
Aragon, 89, 238
Arbor Vitae Or, The Natural History Of The Tree Of Life, 30
Aretino, Pietro, 29, 226, 263
Aretin's postures, 29, 226
aristocracy, 3, 4, 13, 36, 49–51, 55, 71, 163, 165–6, 196–7, 216, 297
    see also elites
Aristotle's Master-Piece, 49, 207
Ars erotica, 219
Ascyltus, 197

Augustus of Saxony, 86
Austrian states, 42, 46, 122
auto-asphixiation, 18
avisodomy, 93–4

Bacchus, 197
bagnio, 195
Baker, Thomas, 60
Bardasa, 187–8
Barry, Madame du, 217
bathhouse, 184–5, 195
bawds, 60, 200
bawdy, 76, 110, 205, 214
   houses, 62, 65, 127, 169, 191–6, 198, 201
   poems, 15, 30
   see also erotica; pornography
Beccaria, Cesare, 82
Beggar's Opera, 25
Behn, Aphra, 139, 163, 172, 216, 253
Beijing, 185
Bentham, Jeremy, 83, 237
berdache, 11, 73
Berkeley, Theresa, 103
Berlin, 28, 71
bestiality, 13, 17, 61, 74, 82, 85–94, 101, 126, 177, 237–9, 245
   agents of, 92–3
   as buggery, 87
   as a crime against nature, 89–90
   and law, 87–9
   statistics, 89
   terminology, 87
Bible, 12, 87, 88, 129, 197
Bienville, M.T.D. de, 16, 144, 225, 249, 251, 262
binarism, 58
Bing, Colonel, 195
biological sex, 133–7
bi-sexuals, bisexuality, 2, 59–61, 67, 80, 183, 188, 259
Blackstone, William, 88, 102, 238
blasphemy, 52, 101
Bloch, Ruth, 35, 55
blood, 16, 20, 21, 35, 67, 94

boarding schools, 10, 12, 98
body, bodies, 13, 16, 21, 86, 101, 119, 134–6, 205, 208, 212, 214
   dead bodies, 102
Boerhaave, Herman, 22, 157
Bona Dea, 197
Bonasa, Cesare, 177
Bonny, Anne, 173
Bon Pasteur asylum, 27
bordellos, *see* bawdy, houses
Borris, K., 59
Boswell, James, 15, 26, 142, 146, 166, 169
botany, 30, 205–6
Boucher, 93
bound feet, 8, 17–18
boys, 3, 9, 11, 24, 40, 41, 62, 100, 103, 113, 127, 155, 177, 183, 184–99
Branter, Samuel, 91
Bray, Alan, 58–9, 231–3
Brazil, homosexual subculture in, 73
"breeches role," 11, 79
Bretonne, Restif de, 28
Britain, British, 1, 11, 17–18, 27, 29, 49, 57, 63, 69, 77, 82–3, 151, 160, 163, 175
brothels, 4, 9–10, 25–8, 32, 65–6, 76, 94, 103, 169, 183, 185–8, 190–5, 198, 260
   male brothels, 10, 25, 65–7, 188
Bruyn, Cornelis de, 184, 257
Buddhism, 184
buggery, 10, 75, 82, 87–8, 92–3, 105, 237
Buggery Act, 61
Bundling, 4, 42, 116
Burton, John, 151
Burton, Richard, 222
Busby, Richard, 103
Butler, Judith, 58, 232
Butler, Lady Eleanor, 79–80
Byron, Lord, 11, 265

Caldwell, Edward, 91
Cannon, John, 15, 98, 104

Cannon, Thomas, 75
Cape of Good Hope, 100
Cape Town, 100
Caravaggio, Michael, 188
Carnal Prayer Mat, 31
Carolina, 87, 92, 94, 131–2
Caroll, Brian D., 99
Carpzov, Benedict, 94
Casanova, 86, 142, 165–6, 216
Catherine the Great, 86, 216
Catholics, Catholicism, 4, 5, 31, 34–5, 38, 49, 51, 53, 101, 122, 130, 133, 151, 161, 168, 183, 198, 242
celibacy, celibates, 5, 33, 51, 56, 143, 148–9, 215
  see also chastity; virgins, virginity
Chambers, Douglas, 161
chaparones, 3
Chardin, Chevalier, 221
Charke, Charlotte, 12, 79, 148
Charlemagne, 87
Charles II of England, 216
Charles V, 94
Charteris, Colonel Francis, 195
chastity, 3, 35, 38, 45, 48–9, 51, 110, 164, 219
  see also celibacy, celibates; virgins, virginity
Chesapeake colonies, laws in, 110, 114, 132
Chetwyn, Robert, 188
China, Chinese, 4, 8, 11–13, 18, 20, 25, 28–32, 183, 185, 187, 219–20
chlorosis, 141
Christ's Hospital School, 103
Christianity, 13, 140, 183, 188, 190, 191–2, 197, 198, 260n13
Cinaedus, 258n6
Clap, Margaret (Mother Clap), 10, 65–6, 127
Clarissa, 26, 162
Cleland, John, 30, 76, 96, 169, 196, 211, 226

  see also Meibom, Johan Heinrich, *Memoirs of a Woman of Pleasure*
clitorises, 15–16, 80, 208
Clive, Kitty, 79
Cobbett, William, 102
coffeehouse, 24, 63, 65, 163, 184–5
coitus interuptus, 9
Coke, Sir Edward, 88
Colett, Mrs, 103
concubines, concubinage, 3, 4, 32, 70, 184, 220
  see also courtesans; mistresses
Confucianism, 13
Congreve, William, 161, 196, 252
Conquistadors, 6
constructionism, 13, 58–60, 86, 170
contraception, 9, 224n9
convents, 12, 168, 183
  see also nuns and novices
Cook, Captain James, 7, 178
Coote, Eyre, 103
coprophilia, 101, 104
Coram, Thomas, 28
Corkhill, Alan, 180
Corkin, Hannah, 93
corruption, 164, 168, 215–16
Cotton, Charles, 210
counter-Reformation, 190
courtesans, 12, 25–6, 165, 169, 170
  see also concubines, concubinage; mistresses
courtship, 2–4, 8, 20, 25, 40–2, 115–17, 123, 163
Crafty Whore, 29
cross-dressing, 11, 25, 148, 171–7
  female, 11–12, 69, 77–8, 173–4
  male, 25, 65, 68, 70, 73
Crudely, Tommaso, 213
cruising grounds, 64, 73
Cumberland, Duke of, 51
Curll, Edmund, 15, 30, 226n47
"cut sleeve" tradition, 11, 257
Cryle, Peter, 161

Damer, Anne Seymour, 79
Davi, Shakuntali, 187
De Blois, Abraham, 209
Deeds, Pamela, 37
Defoe, Daniel, 26, 128, 162–3, 169
de generatione, see Harvey, William
Denmark, 72, 88
depression (sexual), 145
Desacralization, 217
desire (sexual), 45, 51–6, 70, 74, 116, 140–1, 147, 163, 164, 169, 180, 188, 205, 209, 212, 216, 219
   inflamed, 144
   "unnatural," 76, 85–6, 101–3
     see also lesbians, lesbianism; sexual variations; sodomy
deviant behavior, *see* abnormal, abnormality; sexual variations
diaries, 9, 40, 79–80, 98–9
Diderot, 51, 53–4, 74, 168, 216, 218, 230–1, 264
dissection, 19, 102, 137
   see also anatomy
divorce, 47, 50, 88, 107, 122, 124–8, 132
Dixon, John, 92
Dolgorukov, Ivan, 98, 99
domesticity, 197–8
domestic servants, *see* servants
Dominica, 93
Dowie, Ménie Muriel, 173–4
Dream of a Red Bedchamber, 32
Drummond, William, 98, 241n73
Dryden, John, 161, 163
Dubius-Desaulle, Gaston, 89, 92, 93
Dumay, Abbot, 10
Duncan, Bruce, 169, 254
Dutch erotica, 212–14

Earl of Rochester, 51, 61, 176, 196
Edo, 25, 28, 31, 32, 185
effeminacy, 9, 60, 63, 67, 70, 72, 101, 140, 179, 189, 192–4, 196–7, 219, 220, 221, 260n12

Egan, Anthony, 214
ejaculation, 10, 22, 62, 69, 98, 145, 171, 208, 220
Electrical Eel, 30
electricity, 30, 142
elites, 3, 4, 13, 36, 50, 51, 55, 71, 163, 165–6, 196–7, 216, 297
   see also aristocracy
Encolpius, 197
England, 4, 6, 10, 11, 17–19, 26, 28–30, 38–43, 45, 47–51, 59, 60–1, 67–8, 72–3, 77, 83, 87, 93, 98, 99, 102, 109–14, 118, 120, 123, 124, 146, 152, 162–6, 172, 175, 183–4, 188, 189, 190, 197, 198, 200
epilepsy, 15, 141
Equiano, Olaudah, 179, 256
erection, 14–15, 171
   see also impotence, impotency
erotica, 7, 12, 15, 29–32, 74, 76, 86, 136–222
   erotomania, 144–5
   see also bawdy, poems; pornography
Escole des filles, 30, 99, 203
essentialism, 58–9
Etherage's George, *Man of the Mode*, 25
Evremonde, Charles St., 196
exhibitionism, 104–5
extra-marital affairs, *see* adultery

Fanny Hill, 30, 76, 86, 99, 103, 169–70, 196, 211, 254
fellatio, 196, 208, 235n54
   see also oral sex
female
   friendship, 79, 81
   husbands, 78–9, 236n69, 236n70
   sexuality, 1, 20, 135–8, 150–1, 163, 168, 175, 180, 185, 188, 189, 190–6, 197–202
Fernandez, Andres, 89, 93
fertility, 23, 32, 139–42, 154
fetishism, 85, 86
Fielding, Henry, 27, 79, 169, 175, 236

Fielding, John, 192
flagellation, 14–15, 85, 86, 100, 103–5, 196, 211, 214–15
flagrorum usu in re veneria, 15
flogging, *see* flagellation
Florence, 187
folklore, 23, 151
foot-binding, 18
foot fetishism, obsession, shoes, and stockings, 17
foreplay, 17, 142, 207
fornication, 5–6, 27, 35–6, 40, 41, 43, 45, 77, 101, 107–8, 111–19, 126, 132
Forteguerri, Niccolò, 213
Foucault, Michel, 1, 13, 58–9, 160, 223, 231–2
foundling hospital, 28, 43–4, 46, 113
Fragonard, Jean-Honore, 93, 104
France, 10, 18, 24, 26, 28–30, 41–5, 50, 74, 82, 87, 89, 92, 96, 113, 122, 124, 131, 133, 146, 149, 151, 160, 165, 169, 177, 183, 189–90, 197, 199, 200, 215–16
freak show, 170
Frederick the Great, 71, 87
French Revolution, 82, 102, 169, 192, 196, 199, 217
Fuchs, Rachel, 47
  full-time v. part-time, 199–200
furs, 18

Gavin, Antonio, 214
Gay, John, 25
geishas, 28
genitalia, 30, 136–9, 168, 206, 210
gentry, 4, 9, 49, 106, 114, 230
George IV, 103
German, Germany, German states, 34, 39, 41–2, 46, 47, 49, 54, 56, 71, 87, 89, 94, 99, 101, 111, 118, 133, 151, 160, 165–6
girls, 3–5, 9, 17, 18, 26, 40–1, 55, 99, 111, 113, 128, 131, 193–5, 197, 199, 200, 204, 214, 221

Giton, 197
Glastonbury, 98
Glazer, Thomas, 93
Goadby, Mrs., 198
Goethe, Johann Wolfgang, 71, 166–7
gossip, 6, 20, 107, 109, 110, 111, 132, 172
Gowing, Laura, 34, 224n6
Greece, 11, 165
group sex, 212, 215, 242n106
Gruber, Anne Regine, 99
Guzmán, Felician Enríquez de, 214

Hacketts, William, 92
Hall, Lesley, 207
Halperin, David, 58, 60
Händel, Georg Friedrich, 170
Hapsburg, 27
Hardwicke's Marriage Act, 46–7, 20, 121
harem, 165, 217, 221
Harvard College, 98
Harvey, Karen, 86, 205
Harvey, William, 20, 153
Haustein, Hans, 89
Hayes, Thomas, 195
Haywood, Eliza, 163
Hergomöller, Bernd-Ulrich, 59
hermaphrodites, 58–9, 136–8, 208
Hervey, John, Lord, 67, 136
  heterosexual majority, 183, 189, 193
heterosexuality, 1–9, 12–13, 15, 33–56, 61, 66, 76, 85, 101, 144, 166, 183, 188, 190, 193, 207, 209, 211, 220, 223
hijra, 11, 187
Hill, Aaron, 184
Hill, Susannah, 18
Hindu, Hinduism, 20, 185, 187, 221
Hippocrates, 21
Histoire de Dom Bourge, 31, 99, 215
History of the Frutex Vulvaria, or Flowering Shrub, see *The Natural History of the Frutex Vulvaria, or Flowering Shrub*

Hogarth, William, 115, 171, 195–6, 200–2
Hogg, Thomas, 90
homosexuality, 1, 9–12, 31, 33, 57–83, 89, 127, 211, 221
   homosexual identity, 58, 59, 64, 65, 69–70, 73
   homosexual minority, 183, 189, 193
   homosexual subculture, 57, 63–74, 127
honor, 34–8, 46, 55, 103, 108, 110
households, supervision within, 113–17
Hubbard, Thomas, 59
Hughe, Louis, 218
Hull, Isabel, 56, 96
Humboldt, Alexander von, 71
Hume, David, 88
Huussen, Arend H., 89

Ibne, 185, 258n6
illegitimacy, 36–7, 41–7, 111, 113–14, 117, 122, 147
immodesty, 110, 113, 133, 151, 153
   see also modesty
impotence, impotency, 15, 125, 139, 208
   see also erection
incest, 61, 74, 88, 126, 168, 215
India, Indians, Indian, 6–9, 11, 20, 37–8, 52, 124, 130–1, 178–9, 183, 185, 187, 195, 217–18, 221–2
infanticide, 43, 111, 118–19
interracial sexuality, 73, 130–2
Islam, 35, 183, 184, 185, 188
Israel, Jonathan, 52
Italy, Italians, 4, 11, 12, 23, 27–9, 34, 43, 72, 75, 77, 113, 150, 160, 163, 168, 171, 177, 179, 183–4, 187, 213–14

Jacob, Giles, 87
Jacob, Margaret, 213
James I, King, 87
Japan, Japanese, 4, 8–9, 11–13, 18, 20, 25, 28, 183, 185–7

Jefferson, Thomas, 87
Jews, 35
Johnson, Ben, 188
Johnson, Samuel, 133, 162, 250n64
Jousse, Daniel, 87
Juliette, 19, 31
Justine, 31, 74
Juvenal, 80

Kaempfer, Engelbert, 185
Kangixi Emperor, 185
Kant, Immanuel, 56, 180–1
ken (finger game), 186
Khemka, Anita, 187
King, William, 216
Kleist, Heinrich von, 71
Knight, Richard Payne, 197
Köçek, 185
Koch, Christian Gottlieb, 214
Kotzwara, Frantisek, 18

laborers, laboring poor, 4
   see also working class
Lacan, Jacques, 58, 180, 257n89
Laclos, Choderlos de, 26, 53
   Les Liaisons dangereuses, 26, 53
La Mettrie, 206, 213
Laqueur, Thomas, 21, 56, 58, 96, 208, 225, 228, 231–2, 240
Late Medieval, 190
Latin America, 35, 37, 189
Latouch, Gervase de, 99, 264
laws, 6, 7, 10, 12, 13, 19–20, 23, 26–8, 43, 57, 82–3, 86–9, 92, 94–5, 101, 105, 107–32, 162, 173, 175, 177, 180, 195, 211, 213, 225–7, 230, 235, 237–45
leather, 18, 77, 175
Leda, 93
Leeuwenhoek, 21, 137
Lennox, Charlotte, *The Female Quixote,* 26
Lennox, Lady Sarah, 197
lesbians, lesbianism, 69, 74, 76, 77–81, 175, 211, 220

Lespinasse, Julie, 48
Lettre de Dulis a Son Ami, 102
Lewis, Matthew, 168
libertines, libertinism, 51, 52, 61, 74, 165, 177, 193, 196–7, 212, 216–17
Liliequist, Jonas, 89, 90
Lindo, Francisco de, 188
Link, Catherina, 12
Linnaeus, Carl, 30, 159–60, 205
Lister, Anne, 12, 80–1
literature, 23, 26, 36, 45, 59, 61, 75, 86, 93, 98, 100, 102, 168, 172, 194
  literary genres, 31, 163
  literary market, 162–8, 168
  Lock Asylum, 198
Lock Hospital, 23, 29, 146, 197–8
London, 47, 103, 110, 116, 121, 127–8, 132, 146, 161, 166, 169–70, 179, 198–9
  homosexuals in, 51
  molly houses in, 63–7
  prostitution in, 26, 28–9, 188–95, 198–201
  publisher in, 30
Louis XIV, 71, 86, 216–18
love, romantic, 33–5, 40, 49, 50–6, 197–8
Loving the Fragrant Companion, 31–2
lunatic asylums, 27
Lyndal Roper, 99

McIntosh, Mary, 58
Mackenzie, Sir George, 88
McMahon, Keith, 219–20
  medicalization of homosexuality, 71
  medicals schools, 19
Madan, Rev. Martin, 197
madness, 96, 143–5
Magdalen Hospital, 28–9, 127–8, 198
Magdalen Society (Philadelphia), 128
maids, 28, 164, 175, 186, 194, 213
male sexuality, 25, 64–8, 70–4, 134, 136, 145, 150–1, 170, 176, 185, 187, 188, 189

Malthus, Thomas, 56
Mandeville, Bernard, 27, 100
Manley, Delarivier, 168, 216
mantua makers, 195, 199
Maraichinage vendéean, 40
Maria Theresa, Queen, 27
Marie-Antoinette, Queen of France, 3, 77, 217
markets, 4
Marlborough, Duke of, 197
marriage, 2–5, 6, 8, 9, 13, 20, 24, 25, 29, 33–52, 54–7, 67, 109, 112, 114, 120–6, 130–2, 142, 147–8, 152, 163–4, 168, 175, 185–7, 191, 197, 207, 212, 215, 219, 221, 226–9, 240, 244, 245, 254
  age at time of, 33, 39, 42
  arranged, 3, 8–9, 20, 48, 50–1, 54–5, 131
  companionate, 4
  fraudulent, 9, 12, 77–8, 175
  Hardwicke's Marriage Act, 46–7, 120–1
  "mixed," 6, 37
  "mock," 9, 65
  sexual relations in, 126, 128
Marseilles, 25, 28, 41, 190, 199
Marston, John, 188
Marten, John, 208
masters, 6, 37, 41, 45, 114, 184, 194
masturbation, 14–17, 23, 52, 71, 74, 85–6, 94–101, 143, 147, 152, 176, 180, 194, 207–8, 225, 231, 239, 240
  anti-masturbation treaties, 96–7
  cases of punishment, 100
  female masturbation, 99–100
  and law, 94–5
  male experiences, 98–9
  story of Onan, 94
materialist philosophy, 204, 212–13
Maubray, 209
Maxwell-Stuart, P. G., 87, 93
medicine, 20–3, 86–97, 105, 133–58, 205, 208, 224–5, 240

Medmenham's Abbey, 197
Meibom, Johan Heinrich, 14
　Mémoirs Secrets, 171
　Memoirs of a Woman of Pleasure, 30, 76, 99, 103, 169, 211
memoirs, 30, 31, 99, 161, 165, 168, 172
　Casanova's, 216
　Fanny Hill, 211
memsahibs, 9
menarche, 199
　menstrual blood, 128–30, 139
menstruation, 20, 129, 139, 199
　beliefs about, 128–30
Mercier, Lois, 102
mercury, 23, 134, 141
Mexico, 37, 38, 189
Michelangelo, 93, 149
microscope, 21, 137–8
　Middle Ages, 190
middle class, 4, 32, 49, 55
Middle East, 2, 4
Middleton, Thomas, 172, 188
middling sort, *see* gentry
midwifery, midwives, 23, 41, 45, 98, 108, 112, 114–15, 117, 119, 209
　male midwifes, 150
　Man-Midwife Unmasqu'd, 209
　Mid-wives Book, 23
Mijhardt, Wijnand W., 212
Mikvah, 129
milliners, 193, 199
Ming dynasty, 31
missionaries, 6
missionary position, 5, 33, 56, 148
mistresses, 3, 6, 26, 28, 36, 48–50, 61, 164, 184, 213, 215, 217
　see also concubines, concubinage; courtesans
Mitchell, Juliet, 1
Modest Defence of Public Stews, 27
modesty, 13, 55, 108, 151, 153, 154, 165, 169, 179
　see also immodesty
Mohamet, Dean, 179

Moliere's *School for Husbands, School for Wives*, 34–5
Moll Cutpurse, 172–3
Moll Flanders, 26
molly bodies, 140–1
molly houses, 10, 63–7, 127, 189
monasteries, 29, 168
monks, 31, 33, 185, 197, 213, 215
monogamy 34, 36
monomania, 144–5
Montague, Lady Mary Wortley, 136, 165–6, 221
Montesquiey, 82, 177
Montpellier, 42, 190, 199
Moody, Joseph, 96, 98, 99
More, Hannah, 164–5, 178–9
Morris, Polly, 89
mouches (flies, French police), 10, 71–2
murder, 94, 101
Murrin, John, 92
Muslims, 4, 9, 12, 20, 35, 183, 188, 222
Muyart de Vouglans, P. F., 87
Mysteries of Conjugal Love Reveal'd, 23, 49, 142, 207

nakedness, 6, 105
Nantes, 25
Naples, 27
Native Americans, 11, 124, 130–1, 139
　regulation of sexuality, 130
natives, 6, 7
The Natural History of the Frutex Vulvaria, or Flowering Shrub, 30, 206
Nautch girls, 8–9
necrophilia, 19, 74, 86, 101–3, 242
Neri, St. Philip, 188
nerves, 134
　nervous, 145
　nervous bodies, 136–45
　nervous explanations of sexual processes, 136
　nervous genitalia, 136
　nervous sexual organs, 136

Netherlands, 42–4, 127
　homosexuality in, 67–9, 82, 100, 127
New England, 99, 108–11, 114–17, 126, 130
　courtship in, 41–2, 43
　divorce in, 125
　marriage laws in, 122
　premarital pregnancy rates in, 117
New Haven
　bestiality in, 90
　pregnancy in, 115
　public masturbation in, 95
New Jersey
　buggery in, 93
newspapers, 25, 51, 68, 72, 78, 82, 127, 192
New World, 162
New York, 198
Nodot, François, 196
norms, normal, normality or "natural," 2, 12–14, 17, 59, 85, 91, 101, 105, 136, 141, 147–9, 153, 160, 172, 183, 187, 222
Nougaret, Pierre-Jean-Baptiste, 215
novel, 25–6, 30, 51, 53, 55, 74, 76, 99, 102, 141, 152, 162–4, 167–9, 172, 196, 220
novelists, 51, 54, 175
nuns and novices, 9, 31–3, 74, 180, 213, 215, 216
Nussbaum, Felicity A., 159, 252, 254, 256, 287
nymphomania, 16–17, 144
Nymphomanie, ou Traité de la Fueuer Uterine, 16, 262

obscenity, 52, 196, 205
　of books, 30, 61, 74, 76
　of imagery, 118, 192
　of nature, 2, 179, 213
　of sex and sexuality, 152–6
O'Connell, Lisa, 161
old age, 149–50
Oldham, John, 216
Onania; or the heinous sin of self-pollution, 15, 96, 207–8

onanism, onanists, *see* masturbation
Onanism; or a treatise upon the disorders produced by masturbation, 14–15, 95–6, 99
One Hundred and Twenty Days of Sodom, 31, 74
one-sex theory, 21, 135–7
opera, 24–5, 171, 185
oral sex, 73, 74, 208
　see also fellatio
orgasm, 49, 94, 98, 108, 128, 140
orphans, 5, 45, 131
Ottoman Empire, 27, 184, 221
ovulation, 141

Padgug, Robert, 58
Pamela, Richardson's, 26, 45, 162–3
pamphlets, 11, 18, 25, 70, 72, 77, 79, 82, 102, 175, 214, 216
Paris, 14, 28, 41, 47, 70–2, 79, 94, 100, 102–3, 170, 188, 190, 198–200
　homosexual subculture in, 70–72
parks, 51, 63, 68, 170, 189, 192, 193
Parks, Henry Bamford, 89
Peakman, Julie, 173, 235n60, 235n63, 237n3, 237n4
pederasty, 62, 71, 72, 75, 83, 235n61
pedophilia, 18
penetration, 10, 62, 74, 91, 126, 196
penis, 64, 77, 81, 94, 134, 145, 150, 170, 175, 185, 205–8, 210, 217, 220, 226n43, 235n56
Pennsylvania
　and bestiality, 87–8
　and divorce, 125, 132
　and gossip, 108
　and infanticide, 119
　and prostitution, 127
　and Quakers, 123
　and sodomy, 177
Pepys, Samuel, 15, 105, 142
Persian Letters, 217–18
Petronius, 196–7
philanthropists, philanthropy, 28–9

Philippe d'Orléans, regent of France, 216–17
Philosophical Transactions, 22, 30
philosophy, philosophers, 1, 13, 22, 30, 48, 51–6, 57, 82–3, 113, 161, 165, 177, 180
Philosophy in the Bedroom, 75, 181, 183, 204, 210, 212
physicians, 14, 15, 22, 23, 27, 86, 89, 128, 134–55, 136, 141–2, 145, 147, 150–3, 159, 206, 208–9, 213
  dealing with sexual matters, 133–56
  as pornographers, 142, 152
  professionalism, 152–3
  protocols during birthing, 151
  as romancers, 142–3
  as writers, 152
Picart, Bernard, 104–5
Pilgrim Fathers, *see* Puritans
pimps, 28, 188, 194
Place, Francis, 193, 202
Plane of Guilford, William, 95
Pleasant Spring and Fragrant Character, 31
pleasure, 4, 8, 13, 17, 24, 30, 34, 35, 41, 48–9, 51–3, 72, 75, 76, 79, 94, 99, 101, 117, 140–2, 154, 164, 169–70, 180–1, 196–8, 203–5, 210–12, 215, 221
  see also orgasm
pleasure gardens, 24, 170
  see also Ranelagh Gardens; Vauxhall Gardens
plebian, *see* working class
Plummer, Kenneth, 58
Plymouth, 93
Poland, 89, 165
police, 28, 65, 66, 70, 72, 100, 164, 194, 214
politeness, 32, 55, 197
political erotica, 216–17
polygamy, 37, 197, 219–22
Pompadour, Madame de, 31, 50, 217
Ponsonby, Sarah, 79–80

"poosht," 184
popular culture, 7, 23–6, 40, 45–9, 159–81, 209, 214, 226
  and entertainment, 7, 9, 11, 12, 23–26, 29, 40, 45, 49, 70, 102, 159–81, 209, 214
Pope, Alexander, 67
pornography, 15, 29–32, 53, 74–77, 86, 96, 98–9, 105, 152, 163, 168, 180, 203–22
  see also erotica
Porter, Roy, 134, 170, 207, 210
Portugal, Portuguese, 4, 6, 70, 73, 187–8, 194
Portuguese Inquisition, 188
preformationists, 138
pregnancy, 9, 20, 44–6, 48, 53, 102, 108–9, 114–15, 128, 139–43, 147–8, 150–1, 203
  abnormal cravings during (pica), 141–2
  unmarried women and, 6, 41–3, 49, 108, 109, 113–19, 132, 194
  unwanted, 4, 195
premarital pregnancy rates, 115, 117
premarital sex, *see* fornication
Prescott, Sarah, 163
Prévost, Abbé, 218–19
Priapus, 197
priests, 11, 31, 33–4, 36, 39, 43, 89, 100, 213–15
primitive, primitiveness, 159, 160, 178
Princess Seraphina, 67
print culture, 25, 20, 162, 221
Probert, Rebecca, 47
procreation, 5, 8, 13–14, 20, 23, 32, 34–5, 52–6, 101, 142–4, 147, 149, 247
A Proposal to Render Effectual a Plan to Remove the Nuisance of Common Prostitutes from the Street of This Metropolis, 27
prostitutes, prostitution, 8–9, 13, 18, 23–9, 32, 35, 48, 52,

62, 86, 110, 117, 126–8,
  146, 163, 169–71, 183–202,
  217, 221
 in America, 127–8, 131, 170
 in Asia, 183, 185, 187–8
 boys, 183–90
 in Brazil, 189
 in China, 8, 13, 25–8, 32, 183, 185,
  187
 clients of, 185, 188, 189, 191–6, 198,
  202
 in Costa Rica, 189
 in England, 18, 24–5, 28–9, 48,
  52, 64–73, 103, 127, 146,
  149, 166, 183, 188, 189, 190,
  191–202
 in France, 28–9, 183, 188, 189, 190,
  197–201
 in Germany, 27
 in India, 8–9, 183, 185, 187
 in Italy, 27, 184, 187–8
 in Japan, 8–9, 13, 28, 183, 185
 in Latin America, 189
 in the Mediterranean, 183, 187, 188
 in Mexico, 189–90
 in the Muslim World, 183, 185
 in the Netherlands (Dutch Republic),
  183, 188, 189, 190, 197,
  199–200
 in Peru, 189
 places of
  see bathhouse; bawdy, houses;
  coffeehouse; molly houses;
  teahouse
 in Portugal, 187, 188
 in Spain, 187–8
 in Turkey, 184
Protestantism, 3, 5, 34–5, 38, 49, 55,
  94, 122, 130, 133, 151–2, 177,
  191–2, 198, 214, 222
Prussia, 12, 87, 89, 119
Puritans, 6, 35, 41–3, 95–6, 98,
  108–11, 114–15, 122–3, 126,
  128
Puttana errante, 29

Qing dynasty, 11, 25–6, 31, 219–20
Quakers, 88, 123
queer studies, queer theory, 2, 58, 59, 60
Quillet, Claude, 209

race, 6–7, 37, 70, 130–2, 141, 159,
  160–1, 178, 204, 217, 221–2
Radicati, Alberto, 183–4
Ragionamenti, 29
railways, 162
Raimondi, Marcantonio, 29
Randolph, Thomas, 188
Ranelagh Gardens, 24, 170
rape, 4, 6, 18–19, 26, 34, 45–7, 61,
  101, 108, 119, 130, 132, 185,
  195, 215
*Rare Verities, the Cabinet of Venus
  Unlocked and her Secrets Laid
  Open*, 23, 261
Rave, James, 162
Read, Mary, 12, 173
Reformation, 5, 190
 regulation of, 187, 188, 190, 191–2,
  198, 199
 Palermo, 43
Rembrandt, 105
Renaissance, 59, 135, 145, 150
Rennie, John, 92
reproduction, 75, 133, 137–42, 160,
  206–7
 and Newtonian principles, 139
Restoraton drama, 25, 60–2, 136, 139,
  161
Retorica delle puttane, 29
Richardson, Samuel, 26, 45, 162–3
Richlin, Amy, 59
Roberts, David, 218
Robinson, David, 59
Robinson, Mary, 48
Rocco, Antonio, 75
Rochester, Earl of, 51, 61, 176, 196
romantic love, 33–5, 40, 49, 50–6,
  197–8
rough music, 47
Rousseau, George, 59, 296

Rousseau, Jean-Jacque, 54–5, 59, 96, 98, 99, 149, 162, 213, 231
Rowbottom, Sheila, 1
Rowlandson, Thomas, 40, 102
Roxana, 26, 169
Royal Academy, 205
Royal Society, 30
Russia, 12, 87–9, 92–3, 96–8, 100, 102, 111, 165, 216
Rycaut, Paul, 221
Ryder, Dudley, 194
Rykener, John, 188

Sade, Marquis de, 18–19, 31, 74–5, 102–3, 179–81, 211–12
sadism, 18, 75, 81, 181
sailors, 7, 29, 44, 77, 100, 173, 193–4
salivation, 23, 141
same-sex behavior, *see* homosexuality; lesbians, lesbianism; Sapphic culture
samurai, 11
Sapphic bodies, 147
Sapphic culture, 79, 81, 165–6
  see also lesbians, lesbianism
Scandinavia, 72, 162, 177
scatology, 204, 214
Schellekens, Jona, 47
Schlegal, Friedrich, 71
School of Venus, 203–4
Schurig, Martin, 207
science, 21, 23, 30, 96, 112, 139, 142, 204–6, 208
Scotland, 41–4, 46–7, 92, 98, 118, 121
Secret Memoirs of the Court of Petersburgh toward the Close of the Reign of Catherine II, 216
Secret Memoirs and Manners of Several Persons of Quality, 168
Sedgwick, Eve Kosofsky, 58
Sedley, Sir Charles, 105
seduction, 4, 11, 24, 26, 31, 36, 39, 43, 46, 51, 70–1, 74, 77, 168, 200, 209, 215–16
Sellon, Edward, 221

servants, 4, 30, 32, 39–41, 45, 54, 61, 71, 73, 77–8, 93, 104, 114, 126, 128, 132, 195, 199, 219
sex manuals, 22–3, 48, 141–2, 206–7, 209, 219
sex and medicine, 20–3, 86, 97, 105, 132–58, 205–8
  sex and politics, 168, 169
sexual appetite
  of the elderly, 149
sexual customs, 42–3, 46, 52, 82, 130, 178
  depletion, 145
  difference, 161, 164, 165, 178–9
  experimentation, 86
  excess, 144–6
  mania, "erotomania," 144–7
  see also nymphomania
  stereotyping, 160, 168, 177
  intercourse, 13, 15, 20, 47, 87, 90–2, 108, 111, 130, 139, 141, 144, 153, 196–7, 211
  patients, 151
  perversion, *see* sexual variations
  phylogeny, 136
  predators, 4, 5, 163
  rapaciousness, 6
  see also nymphomania
sexuality
  of the adolescent, 139, 147
  of the aged, 149
sexual variations, 12–19, 85–105, 237
Sharp, Jane, 23
Shiach, Morag, 161
ship's crew, *see* sailors
Simonnet, 100
Singy, Patrick, 96
Sinibaldus, Joannes Benedictus, 206
slander, 6–7, 107, 110
slaves, slavery, 6, 37, 49, 54, 131–2, 179
Smollet, Tobias, 141, 152, 162, 197
Snell, Hannah, 148, 173–5
Snowden, Elinor, 195
social constructionism, 58–59

Societies for the Reformation of Manners, 10, 62, 64, 66, 72, 127, 191–2
Sodom; or, The Quintessence of Debauchery, 61, 176
sodomites, 10, 52, 58–60, 63–73, 73, 83, 101, 147, 184, 188–94, 197, 201
sodomy, 9–10, 13, 17, 19, 26, 30, 32, 35, 52, 57–8, 61–2, 65–71, 74–7, 82–3, 85, 87–9, 94–5, 100–1, 126–7, 147, 149, 160, 168, 175–8, 181, 183, 187–9, 193–7, 201, 208, 211, 212, 215, 221
  see also anal sex
soldiers, 189, 192, 194
Sommer, Matthew, 20
Sonette lussurioso, 29
Sorrows of Young Werther, 166–7
South America, 6, 73, 189
South Carolina, 92, 131–2
South Seas, 7, 23, 178
Spain, Spanish, 4, 6, 10, 35–8, 49, 111, 113, 131, 133, 141, 160, 162, 164, 165, 168, 187–8, 194, 214
Spanish Inquisiton, 10, 36, 188, 214
sperm, 15, 21–2, 131–4, 96, 128, 137–40
  exclusion and retention of, 141–2, 144–5
Spivak, Gyatri, 159
Steen, Jan, 209
stigma, 6
Stone, Lawrence, 96, 103
Stories to Awaken Men, 31
strangling, see auto-asphyxiation
Straub, Kristina, 171–2
Stretzer, Thomas, 168, 210
stripping, 196
Suetonius, 80
Sweden, 17, 41, 43, 45, 46, 88–90, 93, 126, 142

Taiji, 219
Tantric sex, 221
Taoism, 13, 219
taverns, 24, 62–3, 68, 70–1, 191
teahouse, 25, 28, 185
theater, 25, 171–2
Thérèse Philosophe, 31, 53, 213
Thompson, Charles, 184
Thompson, Roger, 205, 207
Three Hours After Marriage, 25
Tianjin, 185
Tissot, Samuel Auguste David, 14–16, 67, 95–7, 99, 143, 152, 208
Torpedo, 30
Tott, François, Baron de, 221
Touchet, Mervyn, Earl of Castlehaven, 61
transvestite, transvestism, 2, 68, 101, 183, 185, 187–9
  see also cross-dressing
travel, 6, 9, 23, 45, 47, 124, 131, 164–5, 170, 178
Treatise of the Use of Flogging in Venereal Affairs, 15
trials, 10, 61, 64, 68, 72–4, 93, 105, 112, 127, 173, 175, 177, 190
Trichtler, Juliane, 99
Trumbach, Randolf, 50, 60, 80, 101

Uffenbach, Baron von, 26
Urophilia, 101, 104

Vanbrugh, John, 60
Vatsyayana, Malanga, 221
Vauxhall Gardens, 24, 65, 170
venereal disease, 23, 27, 73, 107, 119, 125, 141, 145–6, 152, 176, 190–9, 203, 206, 208, 213, 215
  gonorrhea, 23, 146, 208
  syphilis, 23, 27, 86, 146, 190
Venette, Nicholas de, 23, 49, 142, 149, 206–7, 248, 249, 261
Venette's *Tableau de l'amour conjugal,* 23, 207
Venice, 119, 165, 188

Venus, 197
Vénus dans le Coître, 30, 215
Villiaume, Peter, 99–100
Virginia, 41, 43, 87, 110, 132, 228, 230, 237, 243, 245
virgins, virginity, 3–5, 8, 22, 26, 100, 102, 164, 179, 209, 215
    see also celibacy, celibates; chastity
Vizzani, Catherine, 12, 77
Voltaire, 82, 179
Voyeurism, 97, 104–5

Wagner, Peter, 96, 214
Wallace, Robert, 100
weavers, 193–4
Weeks, Jeffrey, 58
Welch, Saunders, 27, 190, 192–3, 260n13
West Jersey, 87
Westminster, 18, 65, 103
White Swan tavern, 66–7
whores, *see* prostitutes
Whore's Rhetorick, 29

widows/widowers, 2–3, 22, 73
wife sales, 48
Wigglesworth, Michael, 98
Wijntjes, Gerrit, 100
Wilkes, John, 52, 197
Winckelmann, Johann, 71
Wintrop, John, 95
witches, witchcraft, 9, 17, 82, 88, 90, 99, 111–12, 118, 150
Wollstonecraft, Mary, 100, 169
Women-Hater's Lamentation, 63
working class, 4, 32, 36, 47–8, 199, 236
    see also laborers, laboring poor
World War II, 187

xenophobia, 177, 179

Yoshiwara, 28
Young, Michael, 59, 61

Ze'evi, Dror, 221
Zeus, 93

www.ingramcontent.com/pod-product-compliance
Lightning Source LLC
Chambersburg PA
CBHW080534300426
44111CB00017B/2721